Look at the Coins!

Look at the Coins!

Essays in Honour of Joe Cribb on his 75th Birthday

Edited by
Helen Wang and Robert Bracey

ARCHAEOPRESS ARCHAEOLOGY

Archaeopress Publishing Ltd
Summertown Pavilion
18-24 Middle Way
Summertown
Oxford OX2 7LG

www.archaeopress.com

ISBN 978-1-80327-610-6
ISBN 978-1-80327-611-3 (e-Pdf)

Cover images:
Front: *Psyche*, Kushan king Vasudeva I, © Stephen Sack, 2002–2003
Back: *Embracing Emptiness*, Early Han period banliang coin, © Stephen Sack, 2015

This book is available direct from Archaeopress or from our website www.archaeopress.com

Contents

Contributors

Susmita BASU MAJUMDAR is Professor and Head in the Department of Ancient Indian History and Culture, University of Calcutta, Kolkata. She specializes in Early Indian Epigraphy and Numismatics. Her publications include *Local Coins of Ancient India: Coins of Malhar* (2000), *Essays on History of Medicine* (with Nayana Sharma Mukherjee, 2013), *Kalighat Hoard: The First Gupta Coin Hoard from India* (2014), *Select Early Historic Inscriptions: Epigraphic Perspectives on the Ancient Past of Chhattisgarh* (with Shivakant Bajpai, 2015), *Barabar and Nagarjuni Hills: A Biography of Twin Sites* (2016), *The Mauryas in Karnataka* (2016), *Money and Money Matters in Pre Modern South Asia* (with S.K. Bose, 2019), *From Hindu Kush to Salt Range: Mauryan, Indo-Greek and Indo-Scythian Coin Hoards* (2020), and *Mahasthan Record Revisited: Querying the Empire from a Regional Perspective* (2023).

Stefan BAUMS teaches Sanskrit, Prakrit, and Pali language and literature and Buddhist Studies at the Institute for Indology and Tibetology of the University of Munich and serves as lead researcher of the Buddhist Manuscripts from Gandhāra project at the Bavarian Academy of Sciences and Humanities. His research areas include Buddhist philology and epigraphy, classical Sanskrit court literature, the development of Buddhist hermeneutics, and the description of Gāndhārī language and literature, and he is currently preparing editions of several recently discovered Buddhist manuscripts and inscriptions. He is editor of the *Dictionary of Gāndhārī* and co-editor of the Gandhāran Buddhist Texts series.

Robert BRACEY is an independent researcher, and historical and numismatic blogger, currently producing the web series *Historical Perspective*. From 2007 to 2019 he worked at the British Museum on the South Asian numismatic collection. His interests include historiography, the Kushan dynasty, and numismatic theory. He is co-author of the first Cambridge Visual Conversations *Images of Mithra* (2017), and author of *Playing with Money* (2019).

DAI Jianbing 戴建兵 is Professor of History at Hebei Normal University, China. He received his PhD at Fudan University. He is Vice President of the Chinese History Society, Vice President of the Chinese Society of Economic History, and editorial board member of many important academic journals in China, Russia and Mongolia. His main research fields are numismatics, Chinese monetary and financial history. His current interests focus on the culture of the ancient city of Tumushuke (Tomuchouq, Tumxuk) along the Silk Road in Xinjiang.

DAI Zhiqiang 戴志强 is the former Director of the China Numismatic Museum, Secretary of the China Numismatic Society, and Editor-in-Chief of the China Numismatics series of publications, having retired in 2004. Since the 1980s he led academic research at the China Numismatic Society, with particular interests in ancient Chinese coins. He led the creation of the China Numismatic Museum, and is the author of 《戴葆庭集拓中国钱币珍品》(Dai Baoting's collection of rubbings of special pieces of Chinese money) and 《戴志强钱币学文选》(Selected works of Dai Zhiqiang on numismatics).

Elizabeth ERRINGTON is former leader of the Masson Project and Curator of pre-Islamic coins of South and Central Asia at the British Museum. She specializes in 19th-century archaeological records of the Buddhist sites of Gandhara and is currently revising her PhD on the subject for publication. Her recent publications include 3 volumes on the Masson Collection in the British Museum: *Charles Masson and the Buddhist Sites of Afghanistan* (2017), *The Charles Masson Archive* (2017) and *Charles Masson: Collections from Begram and Kabul Bazaar, Afghanistan 1833-1838* (2021).

Alex Chengyu FANG FRSA is Professor of Linguistics and Director of the Halliday Centre for Intelligent Applications of Language Studies at City University of Hong Kong. He was Deputy Director of Survey of English Usage at University College London. He founded the Chinese Association for the Study of Numismatic Charms in 2006 and curated the first public exhibition of Chinese charms in Hong Kong in 2008. His publications include *Chinese Charms: Art, Religion and Folk Belief* (2008) and *The Language and Iconography of Chinese Charms: In Search of a Lost Belief System* (with François Thierry, 2016).

Suchandra GHOSH is Professor in the Department of History, University of Hyderabad. Her area of research is Politico-Cultural History of North-West India, Bay of Bengal Buddhist and Trade Networks and the History of Everyday Life. She is the author of *From the Oxus to the Indus: A Political and Cultural Study* (2017) for which she received the Savitri Chandra Shobha Memorial Prize of the Indian History Congress. Her recent co-edited volumes are *Exploring South Asian Urbanity,* (2021) and *The Economic History of India : Historiographical Issues and Perspectives - Essays in Honour of Professor Ranabir Chakravarti* (2023).

Simon GLENN is Lecturer in Ancient History and Numismatics Curatorial Adviser at the University of Leeds. He was previously a Research Fellow in the Heberden Coin Room at the Ashmolean Museum, Oxford and has worked on the coinage of the Graeco-Bactrian and Indo-Greek kingdoms as well as wider Hellenistic monetary history. His publications include *Money and Power in Hellenistic Bactria* (2020), *Alexander the Great. A Linked Open World* (ed. with F. Duyrat and A. Meadows), and a new online numismatic typology: *Coins of the Bactrian and Indo-Greek Rulers* (*BIGR*) with G. Dumke.

Alexandra GREEN is Henry Ginsburg Curator for Southeast Asia at the British Museum. She has a PhD in Southeast Asian Art from the School of Oriental and African Studies, London. Her books include *Buddhist Visual Cultures, Rhetoric, and Narrative in Late Burmese Wall Paintings* (2018), *Burmese Silver from the Colonial Period* (2022), and *Southeast Asia: A History in Objects* (2023). Other projects include *Raffles in Southeast Asia: Revisiting the Scholar and Statesman* for the Asian Civilisations Museum, Singapore in 2019. Currently, she is preparing the exhibition *Burma to Myanmar* for the British Museum in November 2023.

David JONGEWARD is an independent cultural historian and a departmental associate with the Royal Ontario Museum, Department of World Cultures, Toronto, Canada. He was visiting scholar with the Asia Institute, Munk School of Global Affairs, University of Toronto from 2005-2013, and a Research Associate with the Ashmolean Museum, University of Oxford, 2011-2013. His publications include *Buddhist Art of Pakistan and Afghanistan: The Royal Ontario Museum Collection of Gandhara Sculpture* (2003), co-authoring *Gandharan Buddhist Reliquaries* (2012), *Kushan, Kushano-Sasanian, and Kidarite Coins* (2015), *Buddhist Art of Gandhara in the Ashmolean Museum* (2019), and *Kushan Mystique* (2020).

Gul Rahim KHAN is Professor of Archaeology at the University of Peshawar and has been teaching numismatics to the students of Archaeology since 1996. He has successfully conducted excavations at various archaeological sites belonging to Neolithic, Early Bronze Age, Mature Harappan, Early Historic, Buddhist, Medieval and Late Historic periods. For the last four seasons, he has been excavating at the early historic site in Peshawar. He has published a catalogue of sculptures recovered from the well-known Buddhist site 'Butkara III', Swat. He has produced number of articles on South-Asian coins and compiled several field reports.

NAN Fang 南方 is Professor of English-language Literature at Hebei Normal University. She received her PhD at Nankai University.

Aleksandr NAYMARK is Professor of Art History at Hofstra University, Hempstead, New York. He publishes on the art, material culture, and the coinage of the ancient Central Asian country of Soghd (Sogdia), mainly on the Hellenistic and subsequent periods up to the time of the Arab conquests.

Wannaporn RIENJANG is Lecturer in Archaeology, Museum and Heritage Studies at the Faculty of Sociology and Anthropology, Thammasat University. She has been involved in research projects focusing on the art and archaeology of Greater Gandhara and Indian Ocean trade.

Stephen SACK is an American artist residing in Brussels since 1977 (stephensack.com). He uses photography to create an archaeological fantasy of magical images, including 13 coin-based series, photographing worn, destroyed and corroded coins searching to reveal their symbolic mysteries. Exhibitions of coin photography: Center of Fine-Arts, Brussels (1985), British Museum (1999), Gallery Ariel Meyerowitz, New York (2004), Chester Roman Fort Museum (2014), Museum August Kestner, Hanover (2015), Museum of Art and History, Brussels (2015), Rijksmuseum van Oudheden, Leiden (2016), Coin Cabinet, Brussels (2020). Author of *Another Way of Looking at Coins: Numismatic Dreams and Alchemy* (2020), *Rêveries antiques* (2021), *Creatures of the Black Sea* (2022), and *The Alchemy of Money,* seminar Harvard University 2023.

Vesta SARKHOSH CURTIS is Curator of Middle Eastern Coins at the British Museum with responsibility for ancient Iranian coins and coins of the Islamic world. She obtained a PhD from University College London on Parthian Art. She specialises in the art and coinage of the Parthian and Sasanian periods and is particularly interested in royal and religious iconography. Her publications include *Persian Myths* (1993, 2005, 2009), *A Sylloge of Sasanian Coins in the National Museum of Iran* in two volumes (2010, 2012), *Sylloge Nummorum Parthicorum* (*SNP*) *Volume 2: Mithradates II* (2020), *From Persepolis to the Punjab* (2007, 2011) and *Rivalling Rome* (2020, 2022). Together with Michael Alram and Fabrizio Sinisi she is a director and editor of the Sylloge Nummorum Parthicorum Series.

Sutapa SINHA is a Professor in the Department of Islamic History and Culture, at the University of Calcutta. She has been working on the coins and coin hoards of the Bengal Sultans since 1993. She was awarded the Nehru Trust UK visiting fellowship by the V&A Museum in 1998, was Hirayama Trainee Curator in the Department of Coins & Medals at the British Museum in 1999, and attends international seminars and conferences in India, Bangladesh, Europe, UK and Central Asia. Her books include *Coins of Medieval India:*

A Newly Discovered Hoard from West Bengal (co-authored, 1995) and *Coin Hoards of the Bengal Sultans: 1205-1576 AD from West Bengal, Bihar, Jharkhand, Assam and Bangladesh* (2017). She has edited several books of which the latest is *Gold Coins in the Collection of the Asiatic Society, Kolkata* (2010). She has authored several research papers on different aspects of numismatics of the Bengal Sultans, Islamic architecture, and settlement archaeology of Medieval Bengal in national and international journals and books. She initiated the publication of the *Journal of Islamic History and Culture of India* in 2012.

Emilia SMAGUR is Assistant Professor of Archaeology at the Polish Centre of Mediterranean Archaeology, University of Warsaw, where she carries out a project on the value and use of coins in the Indian Ocean ports. Her work focuses on the movement of coins, the Indian Ocean trade, and on the archaeology of port towns. In her recent publications, she has explored diverse aspects of the use of Roman coins in India.

Pankaj TANDON is Associate Professor of Economics at Boston University, where he has been teaching since completing his PhD at Harvard University. He co-authored two books on Privatization of State-Owned Enterprises and is currently working on the second edition of his textbook on Microeconomic Theory. Since the late 1990s, he shifted his research emphasis to Numismatics. He has published some sixty articles on ancient Indian numismatics, developed the educational website coinindia.com, and now serves as Secretary-General of the Oriental Numismatic Society.

François THIERRY is Honorary General Curator of the Département des Monnaies et Médailles of the French National Library (BnF). His work focuses on Chinese, Vietnamese and pre-Islamic Türkic numismatics. He received the Medal of the Royal Numismatic Society in 2006 and the Prix Hirayama of the Académie des Inscriptions et Belles Lettres in 2018. His recent publications include *Les Monnaies de la Chine ancienne* (Paris: Les Belles Lettres, 2017) and *Amulettes et talismans de la Chine ancienne* (Paris: CNRS Éditions, 2021).

TONG Yu 佟昱 is a PhD student at Hebei Normal University. His research focuses on Chinese Qing dynasty coins.

Paula TURNER is an independent scholar and editor of the *Journal of the Oriental Numismatic Society*. After a career in publishing, she has returned to the subject of her book, *Roman Coins from India* (1989), and is now updating it with new finds. She is interested in ancient Indian coins from the first centuries AD and ancient trade in the Indian Ocean.

Wasi ULLAH has an MA in Archaeology from the University of Peshawar, and recently completed his MPhil on a silver hoard of punch-marked coins found a few years back in Peshawar Valley. A businessman, he takes a keen interest in archaeology and coins.

Helen WANG is Curator of East Asian Money at the British Museum, Department of Coins and Medals, British Museum. Her publications include *Money on the Silk Road: The Evidence from Eastern Central Asia to c. AD 800* (2004), *Chairman Mao Badges: Symbols and Slogans of the Cultural Revolution* (2008), and the results of collaborative projects: *Catalogue of the Japanese Coin Collection at the British Museum* (2010), *Textiles as Money on the Silk Road* (2013), *Asia Collections in Museums outside Asia: Questioning Artefacts, Cultures and Identities* (2021), *Chinese Numismatics* (2022) and several books about Sir Aurel Stein and his collections.

WU Danmin 吴旦敏, is a curator of the money collection of the Shanghai Museum. She specializes in Chinese modern monetary history from an economic perspective, and is also engaged in related exhibition planning work. In recent years, her research has focused on the silver monetary system in China. She curated the special exhibition 'Silver in the history of Chinese currency', and is now planning the new Money Galley of the new Shanghai Museum in Pudong.

YAO Shuomin 姚朔民 is the former Deputy Director of the China Numismatic Museum, Editor-in-Chief of *Zhongguo Qianbi/China Numismatics* (the journal of the China Numismatic Society) and the China Numismatics series of publications, having retired in 2007. He has been researching Chinese paper money and the monetary history of China since the 1980s, and was involved in the creation of the China Numismatic Museum, and major publications such as 《中国古钞图辑》 (Illustrated Catalogue of Chinese Paper Money), and the four-volume 《中国货币通史》 (History of Chinese Money).

Figure 1. Dr Joe Cribb holding his honorary degree certificate from Hebei Normal University

Look at the Coins!

This volume represents only a small sample of the people who Joe has worked with, taught, mentored, and supported through his career. The Covid pandemic from 2020 to 2022 limited the number of colleagues who could be invited and the subsequent illness of one of the editors prevented its timely delivery for Joe's 75th birthday. On the occasion of Joe's retirement from the British Museum in 2010,[1] twenty-two colleagues contributed to a volume of papers celebrating his work. Twenty-one colleagues who did not have an opportunity to contribute to that felicitation, some of whom have met Joe since 2010, have been able to show their appreciation of Joe's friendship, academic support, and intellectual encouragement in this volume. The papers are by specialists in their respective fields, and in the spirit of academic friendship, each offers something new and interesting for Joe to enjoy. Our first contributor, Dai Zhiqiang, sets the tone beautifully, presenting a range of good wishes through the ages, in the hope that Joe will continue to guide and inspire us for many years to come, and that we may continue to show our appreciation.

Since 2010 Joe has been extremely active. He has, as the list of publications below shows, continued to write at a prodigious rate. The list includes contributions on North India, Gandhara, Kashmir, Tibet, China, and Cambodia, many of them offering new insights or resolving long-standing problems. He has continued to give talks, and longer lectures, to members of numismatic societies, to the public, and to students.[2] He has also, less visibly, supported a network of colleagues through his regular correspondence on various electronic platforms. In 2021 Joe took up the position of Adjunct Professor of Numismatics in the School of History and Culture at Hebei Normal University. This has revived Joe's longstanding interest in Chinese numismatics, and this volume reflects that in the number of papers from Joe's

old and new friends and colleagues in China. Even more recently, Joe was elected Honorary Vice President of the Royal Numismatic Society in 2022, a welcome voice for Asian numismatics on the Society's council. He is also the Deputy General Secretary, and on the Editorial Board, of the Oriental Numismatic Society. In March 2023 in recognition of his contributions to Chinese numismatics Joe was awarded a honorary doctorate by Hebei Normal University.

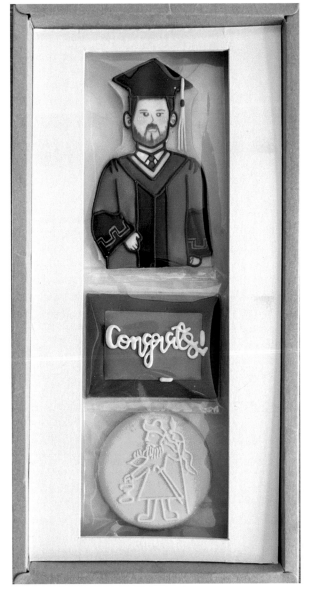

Figure 2. A gift of biscuits from Wannaporn Rienjang to celebrate Joe's honorary doctorate, featuring Joe in graduation gown, congratulations and a Kushan coin showing Kanisha I (made by @theshowroom168)

---

[1] Bhandare, S. and Garg, S. (2011) *Felicitas: Essays in Numismatics, Epigraphy and History in Honour of Joe Cribb*, Reesha Books, Mumbai. The fourth volume of Gandhāran Studies, edited by Nasim Khan, was also dedicated to Joe and featured contributions from eight authors, three of whom have contributed to this volume.

[2] The world changes. Joe has contributed to many changes in scholarly research himself. And since 2010 it has become much more common for talks, once an ephemeral activity, to be recorded. Those who wish to listen to Joe speak now have the opportunity to do so online. For a few examples available at the time of writing see 'Afghanistan: Coinage during the Transition to Arab Rule' *Historical Perspective*, 2019, https://www.youtube.com/watch?v=_A5koUHLKt8; 'Kushan gold coins: using die studies to understand the function of reverse designs', *Oriental Numismatic Society*, 2021 https://www.youtube.com/watch?v=h0HIu3BM5vo&t=29s; 'Coin Collector/ Scholars of Europe', *Coin Stars*, 2022 https://www.youtube.com/watch?v=ZgP99BK-u0k; 'The Origins of Coinage: China and Turkey c. 600 BC' *The Ancient India and Iran Trust*, 2022, https://www.youtube.com/watch?v=ZTSXbyMfcpw&t=1897s

Figure 3. Joe was horrified to discover a Chinese coin in his Indian coin collection

Joe is known for his many aphorisms, the injunction 'Look at the coins!' being one of them, encouraging us always to look closely at the primary material with our own eyes. He is also known for his kindness and support for younger colleagues, often tempered by his self-deprecating sense of humour – as in this modified gift card which he gave to Helen when she took over the East Asian collection.

The card illustrates Joe's firm belief in the importance of fundamental technical numismatics, looking at the coins, and his interest in both Chinese and Indian numismatics – both represented by our contributors. In fact, the card illustrates three different currencies, as it still features its pound sterling price tag. Joe actively encourages the study of modern money, medals, badges, tokens, and paranumismatica, in many cases personally collecting over-looked but fascinating examples of the physical representations of money.[3] Joe's interests and contributions reach far beyond the detailed study of small objects. He has a strong interest in how stories are told through coins, especially in museums, and one

of our contributors, Alexandra Green, picks up that interest in museology, discussing the often contentious problems of displaying colonial collections. He also has a particular interest in art, having written about the sculptor Eric Gill and the earliest depictions of the Buddha. Two of our contributors, Elizabeth Errington and David Jongeward, take up the topic of art history in their contributions. Finally, our last contributor, Stephen Sack, shows the breadth of Joe's interests beyond numismatics by presenting several of Joe's unpublished poems.

A note on the papers. Several contributions were translated for this volume. Where that is the case we have retained the original text after that of the translated paper.

Joe's Bibliography since 2010

2010   *Catalogue of the Japanese Coin Collection (pre-Meiji) at the British Museum*, London, 2010, 218 pp. (with H. Wang, S. Sakuraki, P. Korniki, N. Furuta and T. Screech).

2011   The coins of the Kashmir king Harshadeva (AD 1089–1101) in the light of the 'Gujranwala' hoard,

---

[3] Readers interested in Joe's direct contributions to the British Museum collection can see records of more than a thousand such objects at https://www.britishmuseum.org/collection/term/BIOG106237

Journal of the Oriental Numismatic Society: 28–33 (with M. Ahmed).

2011   *Eric Gill, Lust for Letter and Line*, London, 112 pp. (with R. Cribb).

2012   Coins of Kujula Kadphises from Taxila, *Gandharan Studies* 6: 81–219 (with G.R. Khan).

2012   Late Kushan Copper Hoard(?) from the Collection of the S.R.O. in Directorate of Archaeology and Museums Khyber Pakhtunkhwa, *Ancient Pakistan* 23: 117–43 (with F. Khan and Amanullah).

2012   Editor: R.N.J. Wright, *The Modern Coinage of China 1866-1949*, London: 307 pp. (with H. Wang).

2012   Eastern promise – the Oriental Numismatic Society, *Coin News*, May 2012: 43–44.

2013   Eric Gill's conversion – a key document in Ditchling Museum of Art & Craft, in M.J. Broadley (ed.) *Eric Gill, Work is Sacred*, Manchester: 18–21.

2014   Indian zinc coins, a series from North-western India (Kangra?), *Journal of the Oriental Numismatic Society* 219: 22–26.

2015   Dating and locating Mujatria and the two Kharahostes, *Journal of the Oriental Numismatic Society* 223: 26–48.

2015   *Kushan, Kushano-Sasanian, and Kidarite Coins, a Catalogue of Coins from the American Numismatic Society*, New York, 322 pp., 79 pls. (with D. Jongeward).

2015   Coinage of the Kushans, *American Numismatic Society Magazine* 14.2: 6–17 (with D. Jongeward).

2015   The Soter Megas coins of the first and second Kushan kings, Kujula Kadphises and Wima Takto, *Gandharan Studies* 8: 79–140.

2015   Sources of zinc in early India: the evidence of numismatics, trade and lead isotope analysis, in S. Srinivasan, S. Ranganathan and A. Giumlia-Mair (eds), *Metals and Civilizations*, Bangalore 2015: 174–84 (with P. Craddock, N. Gale and L. Gurjar).

2015   First coin of ancient Khmer kingdom discovered, *Numismatique Asiatique* 6, 2013, pp. 9–16, reprinted in 2015 with afterword in F. Joyaux (ed.), *Monnaies Cambodgiennes*, Paris: 9–16.

2016   Early medieval Kashmir coinage – a new hoard and an anomaly, *Numismatic Digest* 40: 86–112.

2017   Dating the Bimaran Casket – its Conflicted Role in the Chronology of Gandharan Art, *Gandharan Studies* 10: 57–91.

2017   Two curious 'Kidarite' coin types from 5th century Kashmir, *Journal of the Oriental Numismatic Society* 230: 7–12 (with K. Singh).

2017   The Greek contacts of Chandragupta Maurya and Ashoka and their relevance to Mauryan and Buddhist chronology, in K. Sheel, C. Willemen and K. Zysk (eds), *From Local to Global - Papers in Asian History and Culture - Professor A.K. Narain Commemoration Volume*, vol. 1: 3–27.

2017   Cambodia's uniface coins 16th–19th centuries, *Revue Asiatique* 23: 23–52.

2018   The Bimaran casket: the problem of its date and significance', in J. Stargardt and M. Willis (eds), *Relics and Relic Worship in Early Buddhism: India, Afghanistan, Sri Lanka and Burma*, London: 47–65.

2018   Numismatic evidence and the date of Kaniṣka I', in W. Rienjang and P. Stewart (eds), *Problems of Chronology in Gandhāran Art*: 7–34.

2018   Kujula Kadphises and his title Kushan Yabgu, *Sino-Platonic Papers* 280: 1–20.

2019   Fifth century Sasanian coins found in Guangdong Province, southern China, *Journal of the Oriental Numismatic Society* 236: 5–10.

2019   Editor: *Journal of the Oriental Numismatic Society* 238 – In Honour of Stan Goron in his 75th Year, 72 pp. (with K. Singh).

2019   Charles Masson's finds from Begram and identifying the Islamic mint of Farwān, *Journal of the Oriental Numismatic Society* 238: 5–11.

2020   Sino-Kharoshthi coins of Kucha – a new discovery, *Journal of the Oriental Numismatic Society* 239: 2–14. (reprinted in 2022, translated into Chinese, *Zhongguo Qianbi/China Numismatics* 177.4: 10–16.

2020   Foreword, in D. Jongeward, *Kushan Mystique*, London: ix–xii.

2021   The monetary history of Begram, in E. Errington, *Charles Masson: Collections from Begram and Kabul Bazaar, Afghanistan 1833-1838*, London: 81–126.

2021   Greekness after the end of the Bactrian and Indo-Greek kingdoms, in R. Mairs (ed.), *The Graeco-Bactrian and Indo-Greek World*, London: 653–681.

2021   A note on the newly-discovered coin and its context in the Samataṭa gold coin series, *Journal of the Oriental Numismatic Society* 244: 19–22.

2021   Pacifique Chardin's Javanese Magic Coins, *Numismatique Asiatique* 39: 9–18.

2022   Introduction, in H. Wang, F. Thierry and L. Jankowski, *Chinese Numismatics - The World of Chinese Money*, London: 7–14.

2022   Re-reading a Silver Coin of Ancient Arakan and the Chronology of the Chandra Kings, *Journal of the Oriental Numismatic Society* 249: 8–14 (with Md. Shariful Islam).

2022   A not so 'unfortunate' Kushano-Sasanian coins, *Journal of the Oriental Numismatic Society* 249: 4–7 (with H. Loeschner, K. Vondrovec and R. Traum).

2022   Editorial, *Numismatique Asiatique* 40: 5–6.

2023   The Sino-Kharoṣṭhī Coins of Khotan and Their Significance for This Kingdom's Interregional Connections, *Journal of the Economic and Social History of the Orient* 66: 318–93.

2023   *Ch'ing Cash*, le magnum opus de Werner Burger, *Numismatique Asiatique* 44: 9–11.

2023   *Werner Burger's collection of Chinese amulets, The Prestigious Academic Reference Collection of the Late Dr. Werner Burger -part 3 Chinese Charms*: 34–36.

Auspiciousness in Ancient Chinese Coins

Dai Zhiqiang 戴志强

There are two categories of traditional Chinese cast coins: those that were officially made to circulate as currency (*qian* 钱, coins), and those that were not intended for circulation (*yasheng qian* 压胜钱, also written 厌胜钱, 押胜钱, and in English charms or amulets). The latter are similar to modern-day machine-struck commemorative coins or medals.

In terms of economics and finance, coins receive attention because of their role in the circulation of funds, the accumulation of wealth, as the lifeblood of the economy, and the root of people's livelihood. In terms of culture and art, charms receive attention on account of the variety in manufacture, and as a reflection of culture and art, of popular culture and folklore. Charms are a kind of art in the palm of the hand and offer a sort of spiritual nourishment.

There are many categories of charms, and they are used in different ways, including charms with auspicious inscriptions, protect-the-treasury coins, religious charms, pictorial charms, driving-the-horses game pieces, palace coins, burial coins and so on. They are not coins, and do not function as coins, but from a cultural

perspective, their origins lie with traditional currency, and in material, shape, casting technique and other aspects, they share certain commonalities. Indeed, the best-made charms were made in official furnaces, in the same government mints responsible for casting coins.

Charms with auspicious inscriptions are an important branch, and the combination of monetary culture and auspiciousness goes back over 3000 years. From the 8th century BC, during the Warring States period, the Zhou kings issued hollow-handle spades with flat shoulders and arched feet bearing the single-character inscription *ji* 吉 (auspiciousness). This is the earliest example of auspiciousness in monetary culture.

The Han 韩 state issued hollow-handle spades with sloping shoulders and arched feet, many of which bear the single-character inscription *wu* 武, which can also be seen as auspicious (Figure 1). In his study of inscriptions on currency, Ma Ang (1842) writes that *wu* 武 refers to the Seven Virtues (武者，盖取七德之义). The Seven Virtues are defined in the *Zuozhuan* 左传 (12th year of Duke Xuan) as to prohibit violence (禁暴), cease hostilities (戢兵), protect what is great (保大), secure achievements (定功), bring peace to the people (安民), bring harmony to the crowds (和众), and enrich the treasury (丰财). The smaller sized Han spades have similar auspicious inscriptions, such as 武安 and 武采.

Early Warring States period spades with bridge feet usually have plain backs, but among the earliest specimens there are some with inscriptions on the back: for example, *Anyi 2 jin* 安邑二釿 (Anyi, 2 jin) and *Anyi yi jin* 安邑一釿 (Anyi, 1 jin) both have the character *an* 安 on the back, and 梁夸（大）釿百当寽 (Liang kua [great] jin, worth 100 lü) and 梁夸釿二五十當寽 (Liang kua jin, worth 250 lü) both have the character 夸 on the back. The characters *an* and *kua* are both auspicious.

In 378 BC, after regaining independence, the Zhongshan state cast *cheng bo* knives. These knives all have the two-character inscription *cheng bai* 成白, which is pronounced *cheng bo* 成伯（霸） in the Wu language, and is an auspicious wish for the country to be strong and powerful (Figure 2).

Knife-money of the Yan state bore the single character *ming* 明 on the front. This is another auspicious inscription: the sun *ri* 日 and moon *yue* 月 combine to

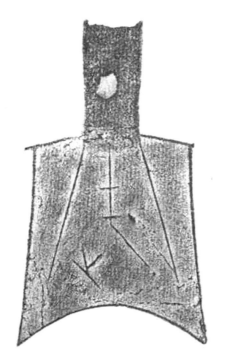

Figure 1. Hollow-handle spade with the character *wu* 武

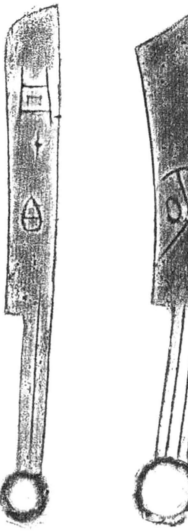

Figure 2. *Chengbo* knife of the Zhongshan state

Figure 3. *Ming* knife of the Yan state

make brightness *ming* 明, which allows one to see far into the distance (Figure 3).

In the Qi state, the knives inscribed齐之大刀 (large knife of Qi) and 節墨之大刀 (large knife of Jimo) have a single- or two-character inscription on the back (安邦, 辟封, 大行, 大昌), which are also auspicious. The Qi knives with a six-character inscription were made when King Xiang restored the state in 279 BC, having defeated the Yan army and recovered lost territory. The inscription 齐返邦长大刀 (Qi recovered land forever, large knife) is auspicious.

In the late Warring States period, some pieces were cast specially for popular use: the charms inscribed Wenxin 文信 and Chang'an 长安 were probably cast by loyal followers of Lü Buwei (Duke Wenxin) and Cheng Jiao (lord of Chang'an). These are the earliest known non-

circulating coins with a square hole. The inscriptions themselves are auspicious: *Wenxin* 文信 (Gentle and faithful) and *Chang'an* 长安 (Eternal peace) (Figures 4–5).

In the early years of the Western Han (206 BC–AD 8) auspicious charms were made by adding an auspicious inscription to small (4-*zhu*) banliang and wuzhu coins, the ordinary coins in circulation:

Chang wu xiang wang – banliang 长毋相忘・半两
(Never forget each other – banliang)

Si jun – banliang 思君・半两
(Thinking of my gentleman – banliang)

Yi zi men sun – wuzhu 宜子门孙・五铢
(Protection of children and grandchildren – wuzhu)

Chang si jun en – wuzhu 长思君恩・五铢
(Forever thinking of my gentleman's kindness – wuzhu)

The same inscriptions are also found on Western Han mirrors and rooftiles (in the category of inscriptions on metal and stone 金石), auspicious inscriptions being very much a part of popular culture at that time.

At first, charms were made by adding auspicious inscriptions to circulating coins and would have circulated alongside them. Later, auspicious coins were made specially, with wishful inscriptions like 寿如西王母、富长安东西市 (the longevity of the Queen Mother of the East, the wealth of the East and West Markets of Chang'an) (Figure 6), 长毋相忘、日入千金 (If we never forget each other, each day will be rich and golden), and 辟兵莫当、去凶除央 (Drive out diseases, drive out evil and misfortune). Charms took on a parallel role, were used in different ways, and became independent of the official currency.

In addition to auspicious inscriptions, charms also often had auspicious images, and the coin-shape was adapted in various ways so that charms could be worn

Figures 4–5. Han dynasty charms. Left: *Wenxin* 文信; Right: *Chang'an* 长安

2

Figure 6. Han dynasty charm. Front: 寿如西王母、富长安东西市 (the longevity of the Queen Mother of the East, the wealth of the East and West Markets of Chang'an)

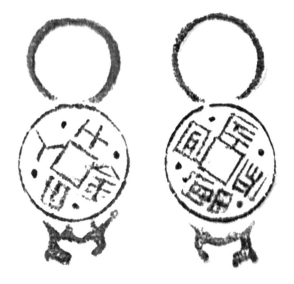

Figure 7. Han dynasty charm. Front: 日入千金 (May 1000 gold come in every day); Back: 佩长宜富 (May your life be long and rich)

on the body, rather like later commemorative badges and medals of honour (Figure 7).

In the Eastern Han (AD 25–220), a particular phenomenon – the coin-tree – appeared in southwestern China, centred in Sichuan. In Chinese these are evocatively called *yaoqianshu* 摇钱树 (trees shaking with coins). They are intimately associated with religious belief – a means to fulfil the wish to ascend to heaven, and a means to communicate with the highest authority. When the tree was shaken, the coins would fall, money would roll, and bring riches and treasures. On the tree branches, in addition to the coins, there were other auspicious things, making it not merely an object of worship, but an object of auspiciousness, an extension of the culture of auspicious coin-shaped charms.

After the Han dynasty, coin-shaped charms moved with the times, and developed both in variety and in content. The auspicious inscriptions were adapted and changed, and reflect popular customs in different periods: for example,

Yong'an wu nan 永安五男
(Eternal peace to five sons) – Northern Wei (Figure 8)

Gui he qi shou 龟鹤齐寿
(Enjoy a long life like the turtle and the crane) – Song/Liao

Jia guo ping an 家国平安
(Peace in the family and the country) – Song/Liao

Qian qiu wan sui 千秋万岁
(For 1000 autumns and 10,000 years) – Song/Liao

Zhuang yuan ji di 状元及第
(First place in the imperial examination) – Ming/Qing

Figure 8. Northern Wei charm. Front: 永安五男 (Eternal peace to five sons); Back: the four animal-spirits of the cardinal directions

Figure 9. Ming/Qing dynasty charm. Front: 五子登科 (Five sons passing the imperial examination); Back: 吉祥 (Auspiciousness)

Wu zi deng ke   五子登科
(Five sons passing the imperial examination) – Ming/Qing (Figure 9)

Wu gu feng deng   五谷丰登
(The five grains all piled up high) – Ming/Qing

These popular culture charms were not only produced at the mints (the official furnaces); anyone was allowed to make them and issue them. As a result, there is a great variation in quality, though of course the finest pieces usually came from the official furnaces. After the Tang and Song dynasties, palace coins (*gongqian* 宫钱) were made specially for use at court, and as the number and variety grew, became another branch of charms. Particular attention was paid to these during the Qing dynasty (1644-1911), especially during the reigns of the Kangxi, Yongzheng and Qianlong emperors, when the Imperial Workshop (造办处) was established and managed, with specialist workshops and technology, a full staff, and detailed division of labour. The palace coins made during those reign periods are clearly different from those made at other mints.

Palace coins were used by the imperial family for amusement. Compared with other charms, they are fewer in number, made in higher quality materials, and with a superior aesthetic – the crème de la crème of charms. A stunning example is the set of twelve gold coins made for the Qianlong Emperor's 25th anniversary in 1760. The edge of each charm is inscribed in high relief in seal script: *Qianlong ershiwu nian Yuanmingyuan Jiuzhou Qingyan*   乾隆二十五年圆明园九洲清晏, Jiuzhou Qingyan being the imperial residence, one of the fourteen beautiful sites of the Yuanmingyuan Palace, to the northwest of the capital in Beijing. The twelve coins were presented in two tiers of six coins,

Figure 10. Palace coin for Cixi's 60th birthday. Front: 万寿无疆 (Ten thousand years, without end); Back: 大雅 (grace)

in a rectangular silver box. Each charm is 45.8 mm in diameter, 4.2 mm thick, with a total weight of 913 g. The inscriptions are in high relief, in Manchu script on one side, and Chinese script on the other, and present twelve different auspicious four-character phrases:

Tian xia tai ping 天下太平
(Peace under heaven)

Jiu an chang zhi 久安长治
(Long-time peace, long-term rule)

Zheng tong ren he 政通人和
(Good government, harmony among the people)

He feng gan yu 和风甘雨
(Gentle winds and sweet rains)

Guo tai min an 国泰民安
(The country calm, the people at peace)

Guang ming zheng da 光明正大
(In full brightness, upright and bold)

Shou tian zhi lu 受天之禄
(Blessed by heaven)

Fu zuo man chang 福祚绵长
(A long run of good fortune)

Shou fu kang ning 寿富康宁
(Long life, wealth, health and peace)

Ji xiang an kang 吉祥安康
(Auspiciousness, peace and health)

Zi qi dong lai 紫气东来
(A purple mist coming from the east)

Wan shou wu jiang 万寿无疆
(For ten thousand years, without end)

In the background, in lower relief, are pictorial attributes of the Eight Immortals, and the outer rims are decorated with an auspicious cloud pattern, all conveying the wish that the seas may be full and the rivers clear, that all under heaven peace may abound, and that the rivers and mountains remain firmly in place.

In the 20th year of the Guangxu Emperor's reign (1894), to celebrate the 60th birthday of Dowager Empress Cixi, a palace coin was made specially. The inscription on the front is a wish for longevity: *chang shou wu jiang* 万寿无疆 (ten thousand years without end), and on the back *Da ya* 大雅 (grace). It had a diameter of 6.33cm, was 1.1cm thick, and weighed 247g. Beautifully made, with a solid heavy flan, it is one of the best palace coins of the Qing dynasty (Figure 10).

With this article I send my sincerest best wishes to Joe Cribb on the occasion of his 75th birthday. May my old friend stay ever youthful and continue to plough the field of Chinese numismatics and reap new results.

References

Ma Ang马昂. 1842. Huobi wenzi kao 货币文字考 [Study of inscriptions on money]. In Sang Xingzhi 桑行之 (ed.) 1993. *Shuoqian*. Shanghai: Shanghai keji jiaoyu chubanshe: 899–962. [On coins]

Translated by Helen Wang
with Alex Chengyu Fang

中国古代钱币中的吉祥钱

戴志强

中国的古钱由两部分组成，一是正式作为货币铸造和行用的"钱"，中国钱币界称之为"行用钱"；一是不作为货币行用的"钱"，中国钱币界称之为"非行用钱"，亦称"压胜钱"，相当于机制币时代所谓的"纪念章"。

从经济、金融的视角来看，无疑十分注重货币，因为它关系到资金的流动，财富的聚集，是经济的命脉，民生的根本。从文化艺术的视角来看，或许会更关注"压胜钱"，因为它更多地注重铸造的工艺技术，更能反映时代的文化艺术、民族的民俗风情，是一种"掌中艺术"，"精神食粮"。

压胜钱（亦称厌胜钱、押胜钱）的品种很多，性质用途各不相同，包括有：吉祥钱、镇库钱、信钱、花钱、打马格钱、宫中行乐钱、瘗钱等等，它们不是货币，不能行使货币职能，但从文化意义上来看，它们和古代的铸币一脉相承，无论从材质、形制、铸造工艺等各个方面，都有共通之处，实际上，铸造精良的压胜钱多是出于"官炉"，即出于政府专门设置的钱监（铸钱局）。

吉祥钱是古代压胜钱中的重要一支，货币文化和吉祥文化相结合在中国已有3000余年的历史。公元前8世纪以后的春秋时期，周王室铸行的平肩弧足空首布中便有"吉"字钱，应该是赋予结样之意的

韩国的斜肩弧足空首布中最常见的"武"字布，"武"便是一个吉语。马昂《货币文字考》卷四曰："武者，盖取七德之义"。《左传》宣公十二年曰：七德，"夫武，禁暴、戢兵、保大、定功、安民、和众、丰财"。此外，小型布中的"武安"、"武采"等，也都是取武德之意。

战国初的桥足布多为素背，但在早期的桥足布中，也有加铸背文的，如"安邑二釿"布、"安邑一釿"布的背面都有加铸"安"字的；"梁夸（大）釿百当寽"、"梁夸釿二五十當寽"布的背面有加铸阴文"夸"字的。背"安"、背"夸"均是吉祥语。

公元前378年中山复国后，铸"成白"刀。刀币正面统一铸上"成白"二字，"成白"在吴语中读为"成伯（霸）"，取国家强盛，成就霸业之意，也是吉语词。

战国燕的刀币正面都铸有一个"明"字，"明"亦是吉祥之词，日月相推而明生，光明而能视远。

齐国的"齐之大刀"、"節墨之大刀"的背文，有一个字的，也有两个字的，凡两个字的几乎都是吉语，如"安邦"、"辟封"、"大行"、"大昌"

等。齐六字刀是齐襄王复国时的铸币，即公元前279年齐将田单击败燕军，收复失地后的铸币。面文当释读为"齐返邦长大刀"，"返邦长"是吉祥之语，含收复失地天长地久之意。在齐刀中六字刀的铸量较少，故有人称它具有纪念意义，是当时的一种"纪念币"。

战国末期，有了专门铸造的古代民俗钱：文信侯吕不韦铸的"文信"钱，和长安君成蛟铸的"长安"钱，它们应该是吕不韦、成蛟氏族内部的一种信物，是目前所见到的最早的不作货币行用的方孔圆钱，"文信"和"长安"也都含有吉祥之意。

西汉（公元前206—公元8年）早期的吉语钱仍是在普通行用的四铢"半两"钱和"五铢"钱的基础上添加吉语文字，如"长毋相忘·半两"、"思君·半两"、"宜子门孙·五铢"、"长思君恩·五铢"等等，其用词，在西汉铜镜、瓦当等金石器中也经常可以见到，是当时的一种民俗文化，多取吉祥之意。

在钱币上加铸吉祥之语，开始时也和普通货币一样可以流通使用，但随后便有了"寿如西王母、富长安东西市"、"长毋相忘、日入千金"、"辟兵莫当、去凶除央"等专门铸造的吉语钱，于是便逐步形成了相对独立的非行用钱系列，在性质用途上，从正式的通货中剥离出来。

除加铸吉语外，钱身也往往会加铸吉祥图纹，器形也不再是单纯的圆钱，有了佩饰，挂件等多种形式，犹如后来的纪念章、勋章。

东汉时期（公元25—220年），在以四川为中心的中国西南地区，出现了青铜铸造的"摇钱树"的特殊物件，"摇钱树"和宗教信仰有密切关系，可以通过它实现"升天"的愿望；也可以和上蒼对话；摇晃树身，树上的金钱便会散落下来，财源滚滚，招财进宝。树上除了铸有钱币外，还铸有其它吉祥物，所以它不仅仅是一种信物，也是吉祥之物，是吉祥钱文化的延伸。

汉以后，随着时代的推移，民俗钱的门类和内容又大大丰富，吉语钱所用的吉祥词汇，随着时代的推移，多有变化，反映了不同时代不同的民俗风情，如北魏时的永安五男，宋辽时的龟鹤齐寿、家国平安、千秋万岁，明清时期的状元及第、五子登科、五谷丰登等等。

民俗钱除了铸钱局（官炉）铸造外，也允许民间铸造和发行。所以民俗钱良莠差别很大，其中的精品当然主要出自官炉。唐宋以后，专供内廷使用的"宫钱"，数量和品种逐渐增加，在民俗钱中形成一

支独立的体系。尤其是清朝康熙、雍正、乾隆时期，内廷重视对"造办处"的建

设和管理，造办处设有专门的作坊，采用专门的工艺技术，人员充实，分工精细，不少宫钱便由造办处制造，它们和铸钱局的大生产有明显的区别。

宫钱是皇家的用物，更是皇家的玩物，数量少，用料精，讲究艺术性，成为民俗钱中的佼

佼者。宫钱中也有不少吉祥钱，诸如乾隆御制祈福金钱，钱轮侧边钤有阳文篆书"乾隆二十五年（1760年）圆明园九洲清晏"字样，全套12枚金质方孔圆钱，分上下两层装在长方形银盒内。每枚钱的直径4.58厘米，厚0.42厘米，总重913克。钱的

正背面分别錾刻高浮雕的满、汉文四字吉语："天下太平"、"长治久安"、"政通人和"、"和风甘雨"、"国泰民安"、"光明正大"、"受天之禄"、"福祚绵长"、"寿富康宁"、"吉祥安康"、"紫气东来"、"万寿无疆"。並有暗八仙吉祥图案点缀其间，钱币边郭也有祥云纹整齐排列为饰，寓意海晏河清，天下升平，江山永固。

清光绪二十年（1894年），为贺慈禧太后六十岁大寿，专门制作了祝寿钱"万寿无疆"背"大雅"的宫钱，直径6.33厘米，厚1.1厘米，重247克，钱体厚重，铸造精良，堪称清代宫钱中的大珍之品。

谨以此文祝贺乔·克力勃先生75岁寿。愿老朋友青春常在，继续为钱币研究事业耕耘，再结硕果。

Han Dynasty Gold Currency Unearthed in the Tomb of the Marquis of Haihun, Jiangxi

Yao Shuomin 姚朔民

Introduction

In 2011, Chinese archaeologists discovered an ancient aristocratic cemetery about 60 kilometres north of Nanchang, the provincial capital of Jiangxi province. After survey and preliminary excavation, it is believed to be the family cemetery of the Haihun Marquisdom during the Western Han dynasty. The cemetery contains several generations of the Marquis of Haihun, their family members and close retainers. The cemetery once had ceremonial and momumental buildings and walls. In 2014 the excavation of the largest tomb (M1) was completed. This was a large 甲-shaped tomb, typical of aristocratic tombs. The tomb chamber was slightly rectangular, over 17 metres wide and the tomb passage was 16 metres long. At the centre of the tomb chamber was the coffin chamber made from solid planks of wood and numerous funerary goods (Figure 1) (Jiangxi 2016).

Archaeologists believe that a major earthquake occurred in this area 300 years after the burial took place, which caused the coffin chamber to collapse and be filled with earth and sand. As a result of the earthquake, the water table rose and the tomb was submerged in water, which made it difficult for tomb-raiders to gain access. In recent years, the water level has dropped, revealing tomb-raiders' holes in the top and sides of the tomb chamber. But as the tomb chamber was covered with mud and sand, further access was difficult. Very few burial goods were stolen, and the tomb remained as an almost intact Han dynasty burial. It is extremely rare.

Owing to the above, the burial goods unearthed in tomb MI are exceptionally rich, numbering over 10,000 items (sets), and in diverse categories: bronzes, iron ware, jades, gold, textiles, lacquer ware, bamboo etc. They can be classified as ritual objects, objects associated with eating, weapons, horse and carriage equipment, objects for entertainment, grain, documents, coins, etc. Objects of different categories and classification had been placed in different parts of the coffin chamber.

Liu He

Two coffins were found inside the coffin chamber, and the body of the tomb occupant had been laid to rest in the innermost coffin. Only his teeth had survived, and a jade seal, apparently placed by his waist. The inscription on the seal identified him as Liu He 刘贺 (fig. 2). This was a very rare find indeed.

Records of Liu He can be found in the *Han Shu - Biography of Liu Bo* 汉书·刘髆传. Born in 91 BC, Liu He was the grandson of the great Emperor Wudi 武帝 (Liu Che 刘彻). In the Western Han dynasty there were only two aristocratic titles: vassal prince (*zhuhouwang* 诸侯王) and marquis (*liehou* 列侯). In 97 BC, Liu He's father, being Wudi's son, was enfeoffed as the Prince of Changyi 昌邑 (today's Heze City, in Shandong province). He died in 88 BC, and the following year Wudi himself collapsed and died. The emperor's eight-year old son took the throne, with the affairs of state managed by the Grand General Huo Guang 霍光. It was probably around the time of

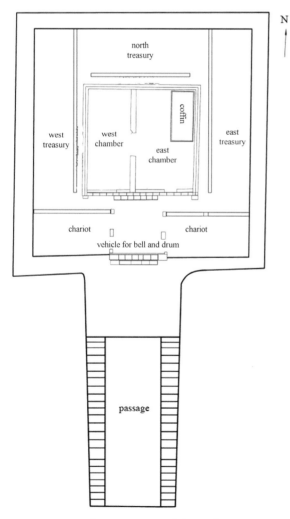

Figure 1. Layout of the tomb

[Diagram labels: N; north treasury; coffin; west treasury; west chamber; east chamber; east treasury; chariot; chariot; vehicle for bell and drum; passage]

Figure 2. Liu He's seal

this grand occasion that the five-year old Liu He was made the Prince of Changyi.

The new emperor grew up under the charge of the Grand General. A delicate child, he died, aged 21, without issue. The Great General decided to look for a successor among Wudi's grandsons, and finally chose the 16-year old Liu He, Prince of Changyi.

Liu He, a minor prince with a feoffdom far from the court, was completely ignorant of political life in the capital. He was moved immediately to the capital to be emperor, but his ways were completely at odds with existing political rules. He thought he could do as he pleased, which infuriated the Grand General. After only 27 days on the throne, he was deposed by the Grand General on the grounds of poor moral character, and went back to Changyi without any title.

The Grand General installed a new emperor, who was the same age as Liu He, but a generation behind him in the imperial line, and easier for the Grand General to control. In 68 BC, the Grand General died of an illness, and the 23-year-old emperor finally broke free from his control. To show his political leniency, he examined Liu

He's performance in his home area, and believing that Liu He did not pose a threat to his imperial position, made him Marquis of Haihun county, in Yuzhang prefecture (modern day Jiangxi) – a minor title, far away from the capital at Xi'an.

Liu He was obliged to live in his new marquisdom. He moved his family, servants and possessions all the way to a place near Haihun county, in the northern part of Nanchang city, in Jiangxi province (the site itself is in modern-day Yongxiu county in Jiujiang city, very close to Nanchang), and re-established himself with his new title. After only four years as Marquis of Haihun, Liu He died in 57 BC, aged 46. In his short life, he had been Prince of Changyi, emperor, and Marquis of Haihun. He had a lot of property, much of which he took to his grave.

The currency found in the tomb

The relics unearthed from the Marquis of Haihun's tomb (M1) are many and diverse, but what really stands out is the astonishing amount and complete range of currency. Nothing like this had ever been seen before. In addition to the enormous amount of bronze coins, a large quantity of gold was unearthed, including gold plates, round ingots, and gold hoof-shapes – a total of 478 pieces in gold, weighing 115 kg. These forms of currency will be discussed below. The decorative pieces in gold will not be discussed here.

Bronze coins

The coins unearthed in tomb MI are basically all wuzhu 五铢 coins. The quantity is enormous, over 2 million coins, weighing almost 10 tonnes (Figure 3).

The coins were strung together on hemp strings, 1000 coins to a string, and were all new coins that had never been circulated. This tomb contained more coins than any other aristocratic tomb of the Han dynasty known to date. For comparison, in the tomb of Prince Jing of

Figure 3. Strings of bronze coins as found in the tomb (L), most of which were wuzhu coins (R)

Zhongshan 中山靖王 (Liu Sheng 刘胜) and his wife, in a huge cave dug out of the mountain, in Hebei province, more than 2000 newly minted coins were found stacked up in the antechamber. The Han dynasty tombs at Beidongshan 北洞山 and Shizishan 狮子山 in Xuzhou 徐州 contained over 100,000 coins, but these were a mix of coins that had been in circulation, and were of poor quality and low weight. The coins from the tomb of the Marquis of Haihun were found in concentration in the western part of the northern treasury. The eastern half contained musical instruments, the central part contained grain, and the western part was specifically used for coins.

Gold plates

Twenty gold plates 金版 were unearthed in the Marquis of Haihun's tomb (Figure 4).

The gold plates are rectangular in shape, of varying size and weight. Most are about 23 cm in length, 15 cm in width, about 0.3 to 0.5 cm thick, and weigh between 800 and 1200 grammes (Figure 5).

This was the first time that gold plates had been unearthed in a tomb of the Han dynasty. During the Han dynasty, gold circulated in round cakes (*jinbing* 金饼), and a large quantity of these were found in the Marquis of Haihun's tomb. However, judging from the inconsistent size and weight of the rectangular gold plates, it is likely that these were treasury pieces, kept in the stores as raw gold.

Small round gold ingots (gold cakes)

When small round gold ingots were unearthed in the Tang and Song dynasties, they were referred to as "persimmon gold" (*shizi jin* 柿子金) because they resembled dried persimmons (which are still known as "persimmon cakes" [*shibing* 柿饼] today). Since 1949, archaeologists have found gold cakes at sites across China, and scholars have confirmed they were already in use by the late Warring States period, when they were circulating pieces of the Chu state (Yang Jun 2018). In the Western Han dynasty gold cakes became the main form of gold currency.

The shape of gold cakes changed slightly from the Warring States to the Western Han, following the production technology available at the time. Most had a diameter of 5.5–6.5 cm, and weighed 250±5 g. One side of the cake is slightly concave, and often has cracks, the

Figure 4. Gold plates as found in the tomb 《新华网》 2015-12-26

Figure 5. Gold plates after excavation

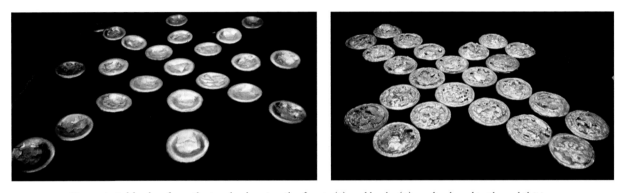

Figure 6. Gold cakes from the tomb, showing the fronts (L) and backs (R), as displayed in the exhibition

Figure 7. Gold cakes laid out in rows on the floor of the coffin

other side is slightly convex, and quite wrinkled. The weight, 250 g, was roughly equivalent to 1 Han-dynasty *jin* 斤 (Qiu Guangming et al 2001). In Han times, gold cakes were usually counted by weight, measured in units of *jin* and *liang* (1 *jin* = 16 *liang*). A Han-dynasty woodslip unearthed in the Han tomb at Zhangjiashan 张家山, in Jiangling 江陵 (Hubei), titled "Year 2 Regulations" 二年律令, records laws announced in 186 BC. One states that the monetary alternative to the death penalty is 2 *jin* 8 *liang* of gold (赎死金二斤八两). As each gold cake weighed 1 *jin*, it would have been necessary to cut a cake in order to have 8 *liang*. Indeed, in archaeological finds, there are many gold cakes that have been cut into smaller pieces.

A total of 385 intact gold cakes were found in the Marquis of Haihun's tomb. Most had a diameter of 6.1–6.5 cm (a few were slightly larger or smaller) and weighed 250±5g (Zhang and Li 2020) (Figure 6).

A hundred gold cakes were laid out in rows of five on the floor of the innermost coffin (Figure 7); and the rest were found inside three lacquered wooden boxes.

They were basically the same as other Han dynasty gold cakes found previously across China, but close examination showed that the gold cakes from this tomb had inscriptions carved into them with crude tools, giving personal names, place names, numbers, cardinal directions or weights.

Niao-hoof gold ingot 裹蹏金

These pieces of gold have a very particular shape: they are cylindrical and slightly oval horse-hoof shaped pieces, hollow inside, with one end sloping and one end flat. The flat ends were originally fitted with a piece of jade or thin glass, but because the tomb collapsed, most of these jade and glass pieces shattered long ago and no longer exist. The sloping ends are slightly heart-shaped, like the bottom of a horse's hoof, slightly concave, and bearing one of three characters: 上 (top), 中 (middle), 下 (bottom). Around the body of each cylinder is a wavy line, and around the top is a very fine gold filigree band (Figure 8).

A total of 48 niao-hoof gold ingots were found in the Marquis of Haihun's tomb. The larger ones, 17 in number, are about 3.6 cm in height, and weigh 250±5 g. In other words, each piece weighed about 1 *jin*, the standard weight of gold in the Han dynasty.

The smaller niao-hoof gold pieces, 31 in number, were only about 1.7 cm high, with a diameter of 2.3±0.5cm (a few were longer) and weighing 29–38 g. They were basically the same shape as the larger ones. It has been suggested that they came in 3 sizes: 3.5 liang, 2.5 liang, and 2 liang, However, this is a recent and subjective view, and not necessarily the intention of the people who made them.

Linzhi gold (Lin-foot gold) 麟趾金

Linzhi "qilin's foot" refers to the mythical animal qilin, sometimes compared with the West's unicorn. Linzhi gold is similar in form to the niao-hoof gold, but has an oval cross-section, a sharper angled shaft and a pointed end. It had a jade or glass piece inlaid at one end (now mostly shattered and lost), and fine filigree decoration. The shaft usually bears one of three characters: 上, 中 and 下. It imitates the hoof-shape of the deer family. The qilin is a mythical Chinese animal, described as having

Figure 8. Niao-hoof gold, as displayed in the exhibition

Figure 9. Linzhi gold (the central one complete with jade inset), as displayed in the exhibition

Figure 10. Horse-hoof gold from the hoard of gold discovered at Xiang-xian (Henan), in 1978
(Source: Yang Jun 2018)

a lion's head, an elk's body, an ox's tail, and a deer's foot. The deer is an even-toed ungulate, of the mammalian order *Artiodactyla*, and these gold pieces were modelled on deers' feet, hence the use of foot rather than hoof in the name.

A total of 25 pieces of linzhi gold were unearthed in the Marquis of Haihun's tomb. They are about 3.5±0.2 cm tall (a few are higher or lower), the slanting part 5.5±0.2cm（或有更长或更短） and weigh 75-84g (a few are heavier or lighter). Yang Jun (2018), in his 《A study of gold wares form the Marquis of Haihun's tomb》 also proposed that these pieces represent three weights: 6 liang, 5.5 liang and 5 liang.

Horse-hoof gold

There is another form of Han dynasty gold currency, the horse-hoof gold (*mati jin* 马蹄金) . These are often unearthed during archaeological work, sometimes in tombs, sometimes in hoards. In hoards they are frequently found with gold squares (*yingyuan* 郢爰) of the Chu state in the late Warring States period. For this reason, many scholars believe that gold cakes and horse-hoof gold first circulated as gold money in the late Warring States period, and that in the Han dynasty, gold cakes and horse-hoof gold were probably used together in society. As to why a horse-hoof shape was chosen, perhaps the main reason was to show the purity of the gold – once the makers had mastered control of the melting temperature of gold, and the liquidity of molten gold, they could pour layer by layer on gold cakes to make horse-hoof shapes, thereby demonstrating the purity of the gold.

In fact, according to research by Zhang Yeliang and Li Wenhuan (2020), the purity of the linzhi gold, horse-hoof gold and gold cakes unearthed in the Marquis of Haihun's tomb is at least 98% or more, with most pieces at 99% or more pure gold. From the gold found in this tomb, we can see that linzhi gold and horse-hoof gold had different forms from the horse-hoof gold used in society in the late Warring States period. The differences are closely connected with royal sacrifices.

Ritual sacrifice was very important in ancient China: "the main affairs of a country are sacrifice and weapons" to quote the *Zuozhuan* 左传. The Western Han dynasty had many sacrificial events: sacrifices to the spirits and gods, to the mountains and rivers, on important occasions, on the emperor's and empress's birthdays, and the birthday of Liu Bang 刘邦, founding emperor of the Han, in particular. When the fourth Han emperor, Jingdi, came to the throne, he set rules for sacrifices on the birthdays of Liu Bang and his son Wendi (Jingdi's father). The sacrifices were to be performed in the temple next to the tombs of the deceased emperor, the ritual was very elaborate, and was to be repeated throughout the year. The rituals involved domestic animals – cattle, sheep and pigs – and a large quantity of alcohol. The ritual supplies were to be presented by the lords, and each lord was to send an envoy to be stationed close to the temple by the tomb, and to represent him in the rituals.

A particular kind of alcohol was used, known as *zhou* 酎. It was made of specially selected grain that was fermented, then filtered three times to make the alcohol clear and pure. To ensure the rituals were carried out, the tombs of the founding emperor of the Han dynasty, and his successors, Emperors Huidi, Wendi, and Jingdi were guarded year round by a force of more than 40,000 people. Another 10,000 were needed to perform the sacrifices and play music. On top of that were the people who raised the cattle, sheep and pigs for sacrifice. The lords were expected to supply gold to pay for these expenses. This was known as *zhou jin* 酎金 (sacrificial-wine gold). The amount of gold to be contributed was determined by the population in each lord's territory. This was done every year from 156 BC onwards.

Frustrated by these annual expenses, the lords often quietly reduced the quality of their contributions: for example, by adulterating the gold with copper. When Wudi came to the throne in 112 BC, the office responsible receiving gold for the sacrificial rituals noticed the debasement, adulteration and poor quality of the gold contributed by the lords. Wudi was outraged, and ordered a thorough inspection. A total of 106 lords (including relatives and nobles) were stripped of their titles. The prime minister lost his job, was sent to jail, and killed himself. This sent a warning to all the aristocracy, that the gold sent for sacrificial rituals must be up to standard. This famous event in Han history is known as *Jiu jin shi hou* 酎金失侯 (When the sacrificial wine gold stripped the lords of their titles).

In 95 BC, Wudi took the decision to make a batch of very special gold samples. He had three reasons: first, when he climbed the mountain to make a sacrifice to the supreme Shangdi, he caught a white *qilin* (probably some kind of small deer). Second, farming-soldiers stationed in Dunhuang had caught several wild horses when they came to drink from the lake, including some tall, strong horses, which the military had presented to the emperor. Wudi had always loved horses, and called these fine specimens "heavenly horses" (*tianma* 天马). Third, someone reported finding gold on the sacred mountain of Taishan. With these three things in mind, Wudi commissioned two special gold pieces.

The first was a Heavenly Horse's hoof – actually, this was a refinement of the horse-hoof shape gold, used in society, which showed the quality of the gold. The wavy pattern on the outside imitated the ripples of the liquid gold as it set, and symbolised the lines on the cuticle of the heavenly horse's hooves. A piece of jade was set at one end with fine filigree work in gold (Figure 11). Wudi called this item a niao-hoof 裛蹏 (where 蹏 *ti* was an ancient way of writing 蹄 *ti*, meaning hoof). 裛 *niao* originally referring to the Zhou emperor's horse which had a bridle made of silk, and was used here to convey the high status of this gold piece.

The second was the hoof of the "qilin" he had caught on the mountain, which takes the form of one its feet, hence the name "lin-foot".

These two gold pieces were made in the imperial workshops in batches of very pure gold, in order to reward the princes, and to provide a standard example of the sacrificial wine gold they were to contribute. Such pieces were only given to the princes who were related to the emperor. They were not given to other lords (who were much greater in number), and this explains why they are seldom seen today. That is also why later generations have had such difficulty determining the shape of the lin-foot gold and horse-hoof gold pieces, despite their being clearly recorded in the *Han Shu* 汉书. The excavation of the tomb of the Marquis of Haihun has finally solved the mystery.

Figure. 11 Golden hoof with jade inset and fine filigree work

Conclusion

Liu He's father was the son of Emperor Wudi, born to one of his favourite women, Lady Li. In 97 BC, two years before Wudi commissioned the lin-foot gold and niao-hoof gold, Liu He's father was enfeoffed with the title Prince of Changyi, thereby qualifying to receive the two new gold pieces. As the son of one of the Emperor's favourite women, he received not just one or two pieces, but 48 pieces of niao-hoof gold and 25 pieces of lin-foot gold. Prior to the excavation of the Marquis of Haihun's tomb, only one example of niao-hoof or lin-foot gold had been found, in the Han dynasty tomb (M40) in Dingxian (Hebei), excavated in 1970 (Hebei 1981). The archaeologists excavating tomb M40 identified it as belonging to Liu Xun, the sixth Prince of Zhongshan, who died in 54 BC.[1] Liu He, Marquis of Haihun, died five years earlier, in 59 BC, so they can be considered as being of the same generation.

Emperor Wudi died twenty-eight years before Liu He. There are no records of any subsequent emperors making gifts of lin-foot gold and niao-hoof gold. So the pieces found in the tombs of the Marquis of Haihun and Prince Huai of Zhongshan must have been gifts to their ancestors, which were handed down to them. For Prince Huai of Zhongshan, the only ancestor likely to have received such a gift is his great-grandfather Prince Kang, and perhaps his son and grandson took some of

that gift to their graves, leaving only 4 pieces of niao-hoof good and 1 piece of lin-foot gold for Liu Xun, a very small amount compared with that of Liu He, son of the Marquis of Changyi.

As mentioned above, Liu He inherited the title of Prince of Changyi in 87 BC, became emperor in 74 BC, lasted 27 days on the throne, and in 63 BC (Yuankang 3) he was given the title Marquis of Haihun, and moved to his own territory in Yuzhang. At the time he received the title, he was living in his homeland of Changyi (in Shandong), and holding on to his dream of rising

Figure 12. Gold cake with ink inscription

---

[1] In the *Hanshu - Biography of the Prince of Zhongshan* 汉书.中山王传, the prince of Zhongshan 中山王 is named as Liu Xun 刘循. In the list of princes in the *Hanshu*, he is named as Liu Xiu 刘脩. In the excavation report, his name was also given as Liu Xun. His posthumous name is Prince Huai of Zhongshan 中山怀王.

Figure 13. The author with Joe Cribb, at the International Numismatic Congress, in Madrid, 1999

again. Among the gold cakes unearthed in his tomb are five pieces with identical inscriptions written in ink. After two thousand years of being submerged in earth and water, the inscriptions are barely legible, but by examining all five pieces, it is possible to reconstruction the inscription: "1 *jin* of sacrificial-wine gold presented by the Marquis of Haihun, in Nanhai, in the 3rd year of the Yuankang reign period" (南海海昏侯臣贺所奉元康三年酎黄金一斤) (Figure 12). Liu He was excited to receive the new title, and believed it gave him the right to pay the sacrificial-wine gold, and to make a trip to the capital at Xi'an, to take part in the sacrificial ritual in honour of Liu Bei, founder of the dynasty. He had even prepared the gold cakes to take with him.

Not long after the emperor notified Liu He of his new title, some officials raised an objection. They claimed he was not of good moral character, had been deposed, and did not qualify to participate in sacrificial rituals to the ancestors. The emperor agreed, and Liu He, with some resentment, had to forego the sacrifices and head south to Haihun by himself. The newly prepared gold and the *niao*-hoof and *lin*-foot gold he had inherited, in order to participate in the country's politics again, went with him to his grave.

*

I have known Mr Cribb since 1986, when he invited us to his office, showed us all the Sino-Kharosthi coins in the British Museum, and gave us a copy of his articles on those coins. I translated them into Chinese and published them in *Zhongguo Qianbi*. Two years ago, a collector in Xinjiang told me they still use that article! Mr Cribb and I were born in the same year, and we will both be 75 this year. I wish Joe good health and happiness!

Translated by Helen Wang

References

Cribb Joe, tr. Yao Shuomin 姚朔民译. 1987. Han Qu erti qian (Hetian maqian) yanjiu gaikuang 汉佉二体钱（和田马钱）研究概况. *Zhongguo Qianbi* 1987.2: 31–40 and 41–47. [On the Sino-Kharoshthi coins of Khotan]

Hebei. 1981. Hebei sheng wenwu yanjiusuo 河北省文物研究所. Hebei Dingxian 40 hao Han mu fajue bagao 河北定县40号汉墓发掘简报, *Wenwu* 1981.8: 1–10. [Report on the excavation of the Han dynasty tomb M40 at Dingxian, Heibei]

Jiangxi. 2016. Jiangxi wenwu kaogu yanjiusuo 江西文物考古研究所. Nanchang shi bowuguan 南昌市博物馆and Nanchang shi xinjianqu bowuguan 南

昌市新建区博物馆: Nanchang shi Xi Han Haihun hou mu 南昌市西汉海昏侯墓, *Kaogu* 2016.7: 45–62. [The Marquis of Haihun's tomb, Western Han, in Nanchang City]

Qiu Guangming 丘光明, Qiu Long 邱隆 and Yang Ping 楊平. 2001. *Zhongguo kexue jishushi: Duliangheng juan* 中國科學技術史.度量衡卷. Beijing: Kexue chubanshe. [The history of science and technology in China, metrology volume]

Yang Jun 杨君. 2018. Zhanguo Qin Han dai jinbing huobi lei yanjiu 战国秦汉金饼货币类型略, *Zhongguo guojia bowuguan guankan*, 2018.11: 46–61. [A study on the types of cake-shaped gold ingots from the Warring States, Qin and Han dynasty]

Zhang Yeliang 张烨亮 and Li Wenhuan 李文欢. 2020. Haihun hou mu chutu bufen jinqi chubu yanjiu 海昏墓出土部分金器初步研究. *Nanfang Wenwu*, 2020.6: 189–207. [Preliminary study of some of the gold pieces unearthed in the tomb of the Marquis of Haihun]

Shoudu bowuguan 首都博物馆: *Haihun mu chutu wenwu zhanlan* 海昏侯墓出土文物展览 [Exhibition of Cultural Relics unearthed in the tomb of the Marquis of Haihun] – exhibition from the Jiangxi Province Institute of Archaeology and Cultural Relics displayed at the Capital Museum, Beijing, 2016

Han Shu 汉书
Zuozhuan 左传

江西海昏侯墓出土的汉代黄金

姚朔民

2011年，中国的考古学家在江西省的省会南昌市以北约60千米的地方，发现了一处古代的贵族墓园。经过勘察和初步发掘，它被认为是西汉时代海昏侯国（the Haihun Marquisdom）的家族墓园。墓园中埋葬着几代海昏侯爵、侯爵的家眷和他们的亲信扈从。墓园曾经建有祭祀和纪念性建筑和围墙。2014年，完成了其中最大的一座墓M1的发掘。这是一座甲字形（甲-shaped plan）大墓。甲字形墓是高等级贵族的埋葬形式，M1墓的主墓室略呈正方形，长、宽都超过17M，墓道长达16M，墓室中用整根的大木围建成主椁室（main funeral charmber）和多间随葬库（图1[1]）。

据一些考古学家认为，这座贵族墓在入葬300年后，此地发生了一次大地震，致使墓椁室坍塌，椁室的空间被泥沙掩埋。由于地震，地下水位上升，墓室又被水掩没，致使古代盗墓贼难于施盗。近代水位下降，墓室上方和旁边也发现有盗洞，但由于墓室掩没在泥沙中，也难于施工，所以这是一座被盗器物很少，保存较为完整的汉代墓葬。这是极为难得的。

也由于这个原因，M1出土的随葬品极其丰富。随葬总数超过10 000件（套），品种很多，有青铜器、铁器、玉器、金器、纺织品、漆器、竹木器，等等。若以品种区分，则有礼器、餐食器、兵器、车马具、娱乐用品、粮食、文书、货币，等等，分门别类地存放在椁室的不同区域。

二

椁室中的主棺有两重木棺，墓主遗骸躺在内棺中，仅存牙齿。在清理椁室内棺时，发现墓主尸身虽然不存，但随葬的器物都大体完整，其中在尸身腰部存放有一枚玉印，印面文字是墓主的姓名"刘贺"（图2）。这是一条非常珍贵的信息。

根据印文查找历史文献，在《汉书》中可以看到关于刘贺的记载[2]。刘贺出生于公元前91年，是汉代的伟大帝王武帝刘彻的孙子。父亲因为是武帝之子，公元前97年被封为昌邑王（the Prince of Changyi Kingdom）[3]。昌邑在今天中国山东省的菏泽市境内。公元前88年，刘贺的父亲薨逝，第二年，武帝也崩逝了，年仅8岁的幼子登基做了皇帝，国家政事由大将军（the Grand General）霍光掌握。大约是作为新皇帝登基的庆典，5岁的刘贺便被命继位为昌邑王。

新皇帝年幼体弱，在大将军的庇护下成长到21岁就也崩逝，却没有留下子嗣。大将军霍光决定在武帝的孙子中寻找继位人，最后决定由16岁的昌邑王刘贺继位做皇帝。

刘贺本来只是一个分封在外地的小诸侯，完全不懂京城的政治生活，忽然被送到京城做了皇帝，行为完全不符合原有政治的规则。他自以为可以随心所欲，却惹恼了掌握实际政权的大将军。刘贺仅仅做了27天皇帝，就被大将军以个人品德不佳为理由而废黜，仍回到昌邑家中，却没有了任何爵位。

大将军另外扶立了一位新的皇帝。新的皇帝与刘贺同岁，但在皇帝的家族中却比刘贺还低一辈，较易为大将军控制。公元前68年，大将军霍光病逝，23岁的皇帝终于摆脱了大将军的控制。为了表现自己政治的宽松，在考察了刘贺在家乡的表现后，认为他不会再威胁自己的皇位，于是重新把刘贺加封为贵族。但是没有把他封为"王"，而只是把他封为侯爵。但是皇帝也没有让刘贺在家乡继续做侯爵，而是把他封到了偏远的豫章郡（今江西省一带），那里有一个海昏县，皇帝就把刘贺封为远离首都长安的海昏侯。

作为一个侯国的君主，刘贺必须住在自己的侯国。于是刘贺带着自己的家人、奴仆和自己的财产，千里迢迢，来到了今天江西省南昌市北部的海昏县（县址在今九江市永修县，与南昌紧邻）附近，重新建立起自己小小的海昏侯国。公元前59年，刘贺实际上只做了4年侯爵就去世了，年仅46岁。但是他毕竟曾经是昌邑王，又做过皇帝，身后留下的财产不少，很多都被带进了他的坟墓。

三

海昏侯墓M1出土的文物数量大，品种多，其中非常引人注目的是货币。这些货币的数量之大、品种之完全，是前所未见的。除有数量巨大的青铜钱币外，还出土了大量黄金。其中的金版、金饼、裹蹄、麟趾黄金等金器有478件，重达115kg。本文所述，不涉及用黄金作为装饰的器具，主要介绍货币类黄金。

（一）青铜货币（bronze coin）

---

[1] According to Institute of Cultural Relics and Archaeology of Jiangxi,etc.《The tomb of Marquis of Haihun of West Han Dynasty in Nanchang City》, Kao Gu，2016,7。

[2] 《汉书·刘髆传》

[3] there ware only two kind of the title of nobility for the aristocracy in West Han Dynasty：the Prince and the Marquis（诸侯王和列侯）。

海昏侯墓出土的钱币基本上全部是五铢钱，数量极其巨大，共有约200万枚，重量近10吨（图3）。

这些青铜钱币用麻绳穿连成串，每1000枚成为一串，钱币都是没有经过流通磨损的新钱。特别值得注意的是，这是在已发现的汉代贵族墓葬中随葬钱币最多的一例。譬如河北中山靖王（the Jing Prince of Zhongshan Kingdom）刘胜夫妇墓是建在山上挖出巨大的山洞中的，洞中前厅堆放了2000多枚新铸的五铢钱币。徐州的北洞山、狮子山等汉墓中随葬的钱币比较多，数量达到10万枚以上，但都是市场流通的杂币，质量差而重量低。而海昏侯墓中的钱币是集中保存在墓椁室的北藏室的西部，北藏室的东半部是乐器库，中部是粮食库，西部就是专门保藏钱币的钱库。

（二）金版（plate-shaped gold）

海昏侯墓中出土有板形黄金20块（图4）。

这些金版都呈矩形，大小不一，厚度也略有出入。金版长度多在23cm左右，宽度约15cm，厚度仅约0.3到0.5cm，重量在800到1200g之间（图5）。

汉代这类金版此前尚没有发现过，这是第一次在汉墓中发现。

汉代在市场中流通和应用的黄金是一种圆饼形的金块，中国钱币学界和历史学界通常称之为金饼。这在海昏侯墓中也有不少。而从这些金版的大小不一、重量不一而形状相近来看，它们应该是作为黄金原料而储存的。

（三）金饼（cake-shaped gold ingot）

金饼（abbr. gold cake）是一种类似食品面饼形状的扁圆形金块。在中国的唐宋时代就有出土发现，因为形似干制后的柿子（今民间称为柿饼），古代被称为"柿子金"。1949年以后，这种金饼在各地的考古中也常有发现，通称为金饼。据学者考证，这种金饼在战国晚期已经出现，主要是楚国的流通工具[4]。到西汉时代，成为社会黄金货币的主流形式。

这种金饼在战国到西汉的历史进程中，形式略有变化，限于当时的生产技术条件，主流大体保持在直径5.5—6.5cm左右，重量约为250±5g。圆饼的一面略向内凹陷，往往有很多裂纹，另一面向上凸起，充满褶皱。250g的重量大致相当汉代的一斤[5]。但是在社会上的实际流通中，它往往并不以枚计数，而是以重量计价的。在湖北省江陵张家山汉墓中出土的汉简《二年律令》是汉代早期公元前186年发布的法律。其中就有"赎死金二斤八两"的规定，即用黄金赎买死罪，以求免死。二斤八两的八两，就必须将一整块金饼切割成小块才能做到。实际上，在考古发现中，就有很多被切割成小块的金饼。

在海昏侯墓中，共整理出完整的金饼385枚，直径多在6.1—6.5cm之间（少数略高或略低），重量多为250±5g（图6）[6]。

其中有100枚以5枚一排的方式，平铺在内棺底部（图7），其余分别放置在3个漆木盒里。

这些金饼与此前在全国各地出土的汉代金饼形制基本一致。不过据学者研究，这些金饼上有一些工匠用简陋工具刻划的文字，或是人物姓名，或是地名，或是数字或方位字，或是表示重量轻重的加减，等等。

（四）褭蹏金（Niaoti-shaped gold ingot）[7]

这是一种外形非常独特的金块，圆柱形略呈马蹄状椭圆，中空，一端为一个斜面，另一端则是平面。平面端镶嵌着玉石或是玻璃薄片，因为墓穴的坍塌，多数镶嵌的玉石或玻璃都已粉碎不见。斜面的一端略呈心形，像马蹄的底面，微向内凹，有一个"上"或"中"、"下"字。圆柱形的外面是水波形线条，顶端边缘还有非常精美的金丝花饰（图8）。

海昏侯墓中的褭蹏金（abbr. Niaoti Gold）总数有48枚。这48枚褭蹏金大小不一。大的有17枚，通高约3.6cm（个别更高或更低些），横径约5.8±0.2cm，重约250±5g。实际上即汉代标准的金块一斤。

墓中的小褭蹏金有31枚，这种褭蹏金比较小，通高只有约1.7cm（或有更高或更低者），横径约2.3±0.5cm（个别更多），重量在29—38g不等，但形制与大褭蹏金基本一样。《A study of gold wares form the Marquis of Haihun's tomb》的作者将这些小褭蹏金分为3.5两、2.5两、2两三个等级（1斤=16两，即1 jin = 16 liang）。但实际上可能这些褭蹏金的制造者主观上并没有把它们分为这么多等级，这只是当时工艺制造水平和出土后内部所含杂物的误差。

（五）麟趾金（Linzhi-shaped gold ingot）

所谓麟趾，指的是一种神兽"麒麟"（Qí Lín）的蹄趾。这种神兽或可以比附为西方的Unicorn。所以这种黄金也可以简称Unicorn toe gold。麟趾金与褭蹏金的形状类似，只是它的剖面成扁椭圆形，斜面角度更大，前端呈尖状。它的平面端同样镶嵌有玉石或玻璃（大多粉碎不存），周边镶嵌着精美的金丝花饰。斜面端往往有"上""中""

---

[4] Yang Jun《A Study on the Types of Cake-shaped Gold Ingots from the Warring States Period to the Han Dynasty》，JOURNAL OF NATIONAL MUSEUM OF CHINA，2018，11。

[5] Qiu Guangming, Qiu Long, Yang Ping《A History of Science and Technology of China·length, capacity and weight》，Science Publishing，2001。

[6] Zhang Yeliang and Li Wenhuan：《A study of gold wares form the Marquis of Haihun's tomb》，NAN FANG WEN WU，2020，06。Data of next gold wares are the same.

[7] 褭蹏，汉语拼音的读法是niǎo tí，读如"鸟蹄"。

下"字样。它模仿的是鹿科动物的蹄趾形状。中国的神兽麒麟在古代神话故事的描绘中有狮头、麋身、龙麟、牛尾、鹿蹄等等的说法。鹿是哺乳纲偶蹄目（Mammalia Artiodactyla）动物，蹄子分成两瓣，Unicorn toe gold模仿的是其中一瓣，所以不称麟蹯而称麟趾。

海昏侯墓出土有麟趾金25枚，通高约3.5±0.2cm（少数更高或更低），斜长5.5±0.2cm（或有更长或更短），重约75—84g（或有更重或更轻）。《A study of gold wares form the Marquis of Haihun's tomb》的作者更把这些麟趾金比照汉代衡制细分为6两、5.5两、5两三个等级。

四

在汉代的黄金货币中，还有一个很奇特的品种，称"马蹄金"（horse's hoof-shaped gold ingot, abbr. Horse's hoof gold），在考古工作中常常被发现，有时在墓葬中，有时在窖藏中。窖藏马蹄金往往和战国末年楚国的金币"郢爰"同出，所以有不少学者认为，饼形金币和马蹄金是战国末年开始流通的黄金货币。进入汉朝，饼形金币和马蹄形金币大约同时在社会上使用。之所以把金币铸成看上去像马蹄的形状，可能主要是由于控制了黄金的熔化温度后，黄金熔液的流动性会发生变化，可以把金液一层层浇上金饼，形成马蹄形状，显示出黄金的纯度。

事实上，海昏侯墓中出土的麟趾金、褭蹄金和金饼，根据Zhang Yeliang and Li Wenhuan的研究，黄金含量都在98%以上，而且大部分都超过99%。从海昏侯墓出土黄金可以看出，这些褭蹄金、麟趾金和原来从战国末期就存在于社会的马蹄金有着形制上的变化渊源。而且这个变化是和皇家的祭祀活动有着密切的关系。

中国古代，一向重视祭祀，有"the most affairs of state are Sacrifice and Military"（国之大事，在祀与戎）的说法[8]。西汉国家，有很多祭祀活动：对待神灵要祭祀，对山川自然要祭祀，重大节日要祭祀，皇帝或太后的生日要祭祀，等等，特别是对大汉的开国皇帝刘邦的生日，更要大规模祭祀。汉朝第四位皇帝景帝一登基，就规定了对开国皇帝刘邦和他的儿子文帝（即景帝的父亲）的祭祀方式。祭祀在已故皇帝的陵墓旁边所建的庙宇进行，仪式极其繁复，而且一年间要反复举行。祭祀需要用牛、羊、猪等牲畜，还要用大量的酒。这些祭祀用品都需要由诸侯奉献，而且每位诸侯还要派出使者常驻于陵墓的庙旁，代表诸侯参与祭祀。

特别是祭祀用酒，是一种特殊的酒，要用特别选择的粟酿造，而且要重复发酵、重复过滤三次，使酒液清冽，酒香纯净。这种酒叫做"酎（Zhòu）"。为陵墓用酎酒祭祀，汉朝的开国皇帝、后续的惠帝、文帝、景帝的陵墓都长年驻有警卫部队，人数

---
[8] 《左传》

多达4万多。为祭祀，还长年备有礼仪人员、乐队人员。也多达万人以上。还有饲养祭祀用的牛羊猪等牲畜的人员。所有这些人员的费用，都要求诸侯们用黄金资助，这叫做"酎金"。贡献酎金的数量，依贵族领地占有的人口多少来决定。从公元前156年开始，年年如此。

然而诸侯们对年年贡献，颇不耐烦。常常偷减贡献的质量。诸侯们在贡献的黄金中想方设法地掺加杂质，通常是铜，致使成色降低。武帝继位后的公元前112年，举行祭祀典礼的时候，负责接受黄金的机关发现诸侯贡献的金饼大量地存在重量减轻、掺杂铜料而使成色降低的现象。武帝大怒，命令彻查。结果是查出做假的诸侯（包括亲王和侯爵）达106人，全部被削去爵位。甚至丞相也因为失职而入狱自杀。这就对所有的贵族发出一个警告：祭祀献金一事绝不允许轻视玩忽。这就是汉朝著名的"酎金失侯"（Remove the title of nobility as gold for Sacrificial Wine）事件。

公元前95年，汉武帝做了一个决定，制造一批特殊的黄金样品。理由有三条：一，皇帝登山祭祀上帝的时候，捉到了一只白色的麒麟（可能是一种小型的鹿科动物）；二，驻守敦煌的屯田士兵捉到了几匹来湖边饮水的野马，其中有的马身高体壮。于是部队把马献给了皇帝。武帝一生爱马，看到这样好马，就命名为天马"Tiān mǎ"（heavenly horse）；三，在被看作神山的泰山，有人报告发现了黄金。以这三个事件为理由，武帝制作了两种特殊的金器。

一种以"天马"的马蹄为原形，实际上是把社会上为表达金饼的成色而制成马蹄形的金器精缬化，在马蹄外表面做成水波纹，既模仿了马蹄金表面黄金熔液堆积的纹路，又象征"天马"蹄壁的角质层生成时形成的纹路。金器表面的平面端镶嵌了玉石，还在四周用金丝花纹围绕（图11）。武帝为这种金器起名"褭蹄"。其中的"蹄"（tí）字就是蹄字的古代（当时的"古代"）写法。"褭"字的原意是周天子的佩带用蚕丝制成缰绳的高贵的马。这里用以表示这种金器的高贵身份。

另一种以登山捉获的"麒麟"的蹄趾，即蹄子两瓣中的一瓣为原型，所以称为"麟趾"。

这两种金器，由皇家的工场用纯度很高的黄金成批制做，用来赏赐给诸侯王。实际上是向诸侯们提供一种贡献酎金的黄金标准。这次赏赐只涉及诸侯王们，也就是皇帝家族的王（Princes），而不涉及数量更大的侯爵们，所以现在很少见到。因此，尽管在《汉书》中，麟趾金和褭蹄金都有明确的记述，后代却难以了解它们的实物形象，成为千年来困扰学者们的问题。海昏侯墓的发掘，终于最终解开了麟趾、褭蹄的谜团。

五

海昏侯墓的墓主刘贺的父亲，是汉武帝的儿子，由武帝最宠爱的一个女人李夫人所生。正是在武帝制造麟趾、褭蹏的前两年，公元前97年，他被封为昌邑国王（the Prince of Changyi），所以他正好获得了被赐麟趾褭蹏的资格。也因为他是武帝最宠爱的女人所生，所以获得的赏赐不是一件两件，而是有褭蹏48枚、麟趾25枚之多。在此之前，在诸侯王墓中发现褭蹏麟趾的只有一例，是1970年在河北省定县发掘的40号汉墓[9]。发掘者认定墓主是汉朝第六代中山王刘循[10]，死于公元前54年。海昏侯刘贺死于公元前59年，早于刘循5年，可以说他们是同代人。

早在海昏侯刘贺死前28年，武帝已经崩逝。后世皇帝也没有再赐褭蹏麟趾的记载。可见海昏侯墓和中山怀王墓中的褭蹏金和麟趾金都是祖上受赐流传下来的。中山怀王的祖上只有他的曾祖父糠王赶上了受赐，很可能糠王的儿子、孙子都将部分受赐黄金带进了坟墓，轮到刘循，墓中只有4枚褭蹏金、1枚麟趾金，远逊于昌邑王的儿子刘贺。

前面第一节我们曾经介绍，刘贺的父亲死于公元前87年，刘贺继为昌邑王。公元前74年，当时的汉昭帝去世，刘贺被立为皇帝。他在皇帝位子上只做了27天，就被废黜。公元前63年（这一年汉朝的纪年是“元康三年”），刘贺被封为海昏侯，搬到豫章郡自己的封国中去住。当他被封为海昏侯的时候，他还抱着“东山再起”的幻想。在海昏侯墓出土的

金饼中，有5枚饼面上有墨写的文字。5枚墨写的文字内容都一样，但是由于2000多年的土埋水淹，文字都已难于保全。把5枚金饼的文字相互补充拼凑，可以基本复原文字内容：“南海海昏侯臣贺所奉元康三年酎黄金一斤”（图12）。可见，刘贺被废黜后，在家乡昌邑居住期间接到了被封为侯爵的诏书后，曾经兴奋激动，以为获得了缴纳“酎金”的资格，准备到首都长安去，参加祭祀开国皇帝刘邦饮“酎酒”的祭礼，连缴纳的金饼都准备好了。

但是皇帝封侯的诏书发出后，有官员举报，说刘贺其人品德不佳，又曾经被废黜，没有参与祭祀祖先的资格。皇帝同意了这个意见，刘贺只得悻悻地自己到南方的海昏国去了。那些准备重新参与国家政治的黄金和祖上留下的褭蹏、麟趾，也只能带进坟墓了。

附记：

Joe Cribb 与我相识于1986年。那时，Mr. Cribb 兴致勃勃地请我们到他的工作室，给我们看了大英博物馆收藏的全部Sino-Kharosthi Coins，并且把他的研究论文送给我。我把他的论文翻译后发表在《中国钱币》上，直到前两年，新疆的钱币收藏家还告诉我，他们一直在参考我翻译的 Cribb 的论文。

我和Mr. Cribb是同年，2022年都是75岁。我祝Joe 幸福，健康！

---

[9] The institute of cultural relics of Hebei Province:《A report of excavated tomb M40 of Han Dynasty》, WEN WU, 1981, 08。

[10] 《汉书》“中山王传”记载王名是刘循，同书“王表”中记为“刘修”。《发掘简报》作者写作刘修，此处依本传作刘循。他死后的谥号是“怀”，所以也称“中山怀王”。

A Thousand Glistening Years —
Silver in the History of Chinese Currency

Wu Danmin

In 2013, I had the privilege of visiting the British Museum for three months on the British Museum and Shanghai Museum Exchange Programme, hosted by Helen Wang in the Department of Coins and Medals. It was during that very fruitful research visit that I met Joe Cribb, the former head of the department. I was young and a bit nervous about meeting this senior scholar, but he turned out to be very easy to talk to. When I asked him about the process of machine-printing banknotes, he didn't mind at all, and took the trouble to answer my questions, sometimes demonstrating with his hands to help me understand, which immediately put me at ease. I was touched by his thoughtfulness. Although I met Joe only once when I was in the UK, he left a very deep impression on me.

Joe is a leading expert in the history of money around the world and has made a great contribution to the history of money in East Asia. His *Catalogue of Sycee in the British Museum. Chinese Silver Currency Ingots c.1750–1933* has been particularly important for me and was my introduction to silver currency. Joe recorded 1,300 silver ingots, almost all with inscriptions, covering a period of 183 years from the reign of the Qianlong Emperor (1736–1795) to the currency reforms of 1933. He arranged them in a new way, according to how they were made and used, the aim being to reveal through their manufacture and usage how the monetary system worked. He looked at the shape of each ingot, its manufacture, size, and the content and arrangement of its inscription. It is clear from the catalogue that Joe's approach to classification is to look at the historical artefacts as objectively as possible, and the results reflect his own philosophical thinking. His presentation of the evidence is also very clear – including key terms in Chinese, and an introduction in Chinese – which enables readers to grasp quickly the various forms and main functions of silver ingots, which were not objects in general circulation. Joe's method of classification inspired me to do further research on silver ingots.

The Shanghai Museum's first exhibition on silver as currency

In 2019 I had the honour of curating the Shanghai Museum's special exhibition 'A Thousand Glistening Years – Silver in the History of Chinese Currency' (Figures 1, 2, 3). This was the first exhibition in China to focus on silver as currency and brought together different forms of silver and related currency. It presented the development and evolution of silver in monetary history, and showed how its role(s) changed over time, reflecting changes in the monetary system. The exhibition was arranged in three parts: traditional silver, the eastward movement of silver, and silver and paper money. The three sections explained the important role of traditional silver ingots in the national finances; the impact of foreign silver on the Chinese silver system; the gradual emergence and development of Chinese silver dollars, which became the national silver dollar system in the late Qing and early Republic; and the development of paper money in the modern period and its relationship with silver currency. The exhibition also included several silver ingots excavated from two recent important archaeological discoveries: the Nanhai No.1 shipwreck site[1] (Figure 4) and the Jiangkou battlefield site[2] (Figure 5). The large quantities of silver found underwater at these sites provide scientific evidence of the important role of silver in long distance maritime trade and taxes.

The exhibition raised an important point: that although silver had a monetary function in China from as early as the Tang dynasty (618–907), it took another thousand years for the first regulations relating to silver as a legal currency to be put into effect. The forms, fineness and weight of silver currency were officially standardized for the first time in 1910 (*Bizhi zeli*). I will give a brief outline of that journey below; fuller details and illustrations can be found in the book that accompanied the exhibition (Shanghai Museum 2019).

Chinese silver ingots are a unique form of silver currency in Chinese monetary and financial history. The origins of the shape of the earliest ingots remain unclear, however, we know from surviving examples

---

[1] The Nanhai No. 1 shipwreck (literally, the 'South Sea No. 1' wreck) was found in the sea between Taishan and Yangjiang (Guangdong). Archaeological excavation began in 2014, and since then more than 100,000 pieces of cargo and items of everyday use have been recovered or surveyed underwater. The main finds are porcelain, ironware, bronzeware and coins, and about 190 kg of silver ingots.

[2] The Jiangkou Shenyin site (literally, the 'sunken silver at the mouth of the river' site), located in Jiangkou Town, in Pengshan District, Meishan City (Sichuan), is the remains of an old battlefield buried in the riverbed of the Minjiang River. Since 2016 there have been two seasons of archaeological excavation. Over 40,000 objects have been retrieved from the water: mostly gold, silver, bronze and iron pieces, including golden books, gold and silver coins inscribed 'Awarded by the Western king for service' (Xi wang shang gong 西王賞功), Dashun copper coins, and a large number of silver ingots and chunks of silver.

Figure 1. Entrance to the exhibition 'Silver in the History of Chinese Currency' at the Shanghai Museum
(© Shanghai Museum)

Figure 2. Ingots displayed in the exhibition 'Silver in the History of Chinese Currency' at the Shanghai Museum
(© Shanghai Museum)

Figure 3. Banknotes displayed in the exhibition 'Silver in the History of Chinese Currency' at the Shanghai Museum
(© Shanghai Museum)

Figure 4. Silver ingot, Southern Song dynasty, from the Nanhai No. 1 shipwreck (Shanghai Museum 2019, original photograph by Shanghai Museum)

Figure 5. 50-ounce silver ingot, Liao dynasty, from Shimen county, found at the Jiangkou Shenyin battlefield site (Shanghai Museum 2019)

that silver ingots were already playing a significant role as currency by the Tang dynasty.[3]

In the early- to mid-Tang there were two forms of silver ingot: the long bar ingot (*ting* 铤), and the round cake ingot (*bing* 饼). There have only been a few finds of Tang dynasty ingots, the most significant site being Hejiacun 何家村 (Figure 6), which yielded a total of 90 silver bars (*ting* 铤), plaques (*ban* 板) and cakes (*bing* 饼) (Figure 8).

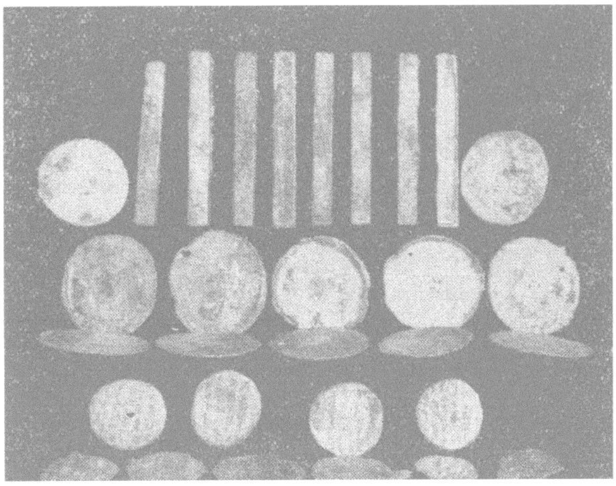

Figure 6. Silver cakes and silver bars from the Hejiacun hoard, Xi'an (from Qin Bo 1972)

Some Tang dynasty ingots from the Hejiacun deposit had inscriptions. For example, the inscription on one bar-shaped ingot records that it was a 50-liang ingot of *heshi*-silver 和市银 ('agreed transaction silver') presented by Chancellor Yang Guozhong 杨国忠 (d.756) to Emperor Xuanzong 玄宗in 753 (Li 1957) (Figure 7).[4] In the Tang and Song dynasties officials purchased goods from the people at fixed prices. In reality, there was forced acquisition of goods, taking advantage of the people.[5] The full inscription records that officials of Xuancheng county acquired goods through the fixed price system and converted their acquisitions into silver. In the middle ages, silver was a precious metal used only by the ruling class and was offered by officials to the rulers of the country.

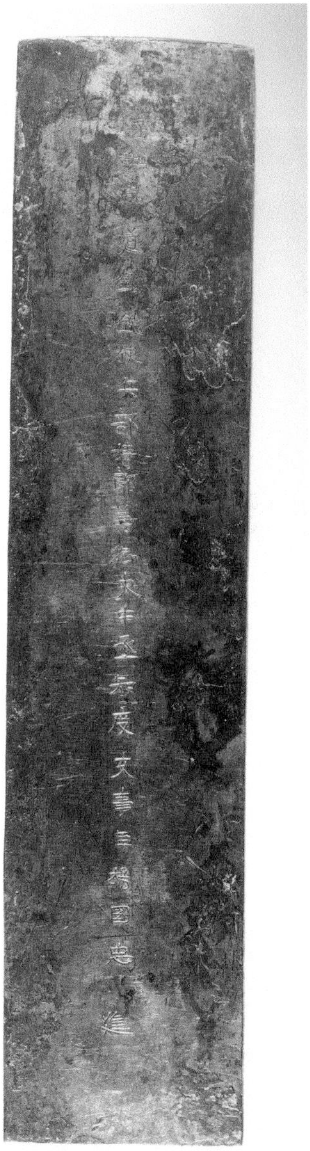

Figure 7. Silver ingot with inscription naming Yang Guozhong (from Wang Chunfa 2022)

An inscription on another ingot records that it was *hedong*-silver 贺冬银 ('celebrate winter silver'), presented to the emperor on the occasion of the winter solstice.[6]

Four round ingots found at Hejiacun came from Jian'an 溶安 (Qin Bo 1972) and Huaiji 怀集 and have *yongdiao* 庸调 incised in them (Figures 9.1-2). This refers to the *zuyongdiao* 租庸调 tax system, in which the *yong* tax, reckoned and payable in textiles, was actually paid in silver. These round silver ingots represent *yongdiao*, tax payments in place of silver. As the earliest silver pieces that clearly reflect this aspect of the tax system, they are important objects in economic history.

These inscribed bar and round ingots from the early- and mid-Tang show that silver reached the court in different ways, including presentation and taxation. The more commonly seen boat-shaped silver bars

---

[3] In traditional economics money has four functions: as a measure of value, a means of exchange, a method of payment, and a store of wealth. The historian Shigeshi Katō 加藤繁 (1880-1946) believed that in the Tang dynasty silver was already functioning as a store of wealth and a method of payment.

[4] The full inscription reads: 专知诸道铸钱使兵部侍郎兼御史中丞知度支事臣杨国忠进　宣城郡和市银一铤五十两专知官太中大夫使持节宣城郡诸军事守宣城郡太守上国柱臣苗奉倩　天宝十载四月廿日.

[5] *Xin Tang Shu*《新唐书》卷一百二十五："今和市颛刻剥，名为和而实夺之。"《新唐书》卷一二七：裴耀卿……，累迁长安令。旧有配户和市法，人厌苦，耀卿一切责豪门坐贾，豫给以直，绝僦欺之敝。

[6] The full inscription reads: 容管经略使进奉广明元年贺冬银壹铤重贰拾两 容管经略招讨处置等使臣崔焯进.

Metal	Item (quantity)	Dimensions / Weight
Gold	Kaiyuan tongbao coin (30)	2.3 cm
	Gold leaf	4388 g
	Gold dust	126 g
Silver	Kaiyuan tongbao coin (421)	2.5 cm
	Bar ingot (8)	27-28 cm x 3.5 cm
	Eastern Market Treasury silver cake (12)	14.5-15.5 cm
	Jian'an cake ingot (3)	9.8-10.8 cm
	Huaiji cake ingot (1)	9.8 cm
	Small cake ingot (6)	9-12 cm
	Taibei 10-ounce weight silver plaque (1)	24 x 7.2 cm (shoulders) / 6.0 cm (waist)
	Taibei 5-ounce weight silver plaque (2)	16.5 x 6.4 cm (shoulders) / 5.1 cm (waist)
	5-ounce Chao-zi silver plaque (55)	20.8 x 3.7 cm
	San-bao (?) silver plaque (1)	13.8 x 4.5 cm
	Silver plaque without inscription (1)	17.2 x 4.3 cm

Figure 8: Gold and silver currency items found at Hejiacun (Shaanxi 1972: 33)

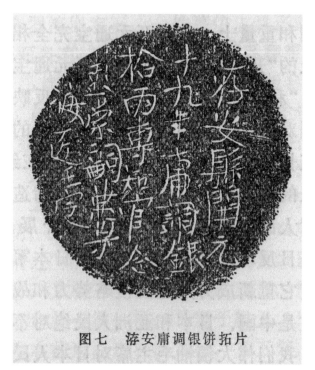

图七　溢安庸调银饼拓片

Figure 9.1. Silver yongdiao cake from Jian'an, Hejiacun hoard, Xi'an (Shaanxi Provincial Museum 1972)

图四　西安何家村出土的唐代庸调银饼

Figure 9.2. Silver yongdiao cake from Huaiji, Hejiacun hoard, Xi'an (Qin Bo 1972)

appeared in the late Tang, but rarely have inscriptions. The origins of the boat-shape remain unknown.

There was a noticeable increase in the use of silver in the Song dynasty, mainly in the collection of over a dozen different types of taxes (Figures 10.1-2).[7] After the Southern Song established the capital at Lin'an, the population there increased rapidly as did the need for all kinds of consumer goods. This not only drove the commercial economy, but also the diversification of monetary forms: in addition to paper money, bronze and iron coins, which were the main forms of currency, gold and silver became increasingly important as a government store of wealth, and in nationwide taxation, monopolies, foreign trade, local government tributes to court and large-scale commerce.

The form, content and size of ingots were adapted to suit the needs of the Song dynasty. For example,

---

[7] For example: 宋铤既有上供银、经总银、钞库银，又有关税银、商税银.

Song dynasty ingots (*ting*) were smaller in size and weight, had a flatter surface, and were made in graded weights. In tax payments, we see a greater variety of ingots, terms for silver purity and standardization. Inscriptions included terms referring to the purity of the silver,[8] indicating that silver received by the Song government was expected to indicate the quality of the silver. The size and shape of ingots also indicates that they were made to a more consistent standard. There were also graded weights of ingots: 50-liang, 25-liang, 12-liang, weighing 1895–2000g, 918–1000g and 434–490g, respectively (Zhejiang Provincial Museum 2015: 11). Most inscriptions give the weight of the ingot, with the 12-liang ingot being the most common. In the Southern Song, shops specializing in the trade and exchange of gold and silver appeared. Known as gold-, silver-, salt-, and paper money exchange-shops, they were concentrated in the imperial street of Lin'an. These shops were also allowed to make gold and silver currency, vessels and jewelry. The silver ingots made by these shops usually have the stamped impression *Jing xiao (ting) yin* 京销（铤）银 ('capital melt/sell [ingot] silver'), giving the location of the shop. The term *jingxiaoyin* 京销银also functioned as an indicator of quality. For example, it appears on ingots from the Nanhai No.1 Shipwreck (Figure 11). Its appearance on ingots for official purposes (eg presentation and tax payments) suggests that there was official approval of the products from these shops. Specialist agencies like these would have been able to respond to the needs of the developing social economy. In short, greater attention began to be paid to silver in the Song dynasty, in tax and trade, in the state treasuries, in state income and expenditure, and silver became an important source of income for state finances.

The era of the great seafaring voyages opened up maritime trade routes between Europe, Africa and Asia, and connected Chinese markets with the world. At that time, the Americas and Japan were the main places producing and exporting silver. From the mid-sixteenth century onwards, silver flowed into China in exchange for tea, silk and porcelain. The huge inflow of silver into the interior filled a gap in Ming dynasty currency, but also brought subversive changes to the currency system. The early Ming dynasty (1368–1644) had continued the Yuan dynasty currency system, using a combination of paper money and copper coins, and prohibiting the use of silver. However, even in the Hongwu period (1368–1398) paper money was starting to lose its value—in Hongwu 23 (1390) a note for 1 string in the two Zhe-provinces was only worth 200 cash (Peng Xinwei 2007: 491). In Zhengtong 1 (1436), the government removed the prohibition of tax payment in silver and allowed rice and grain to be commuted into

Figure 10.1. Silver 12-ounce half bar-ingot, relating to shipping, Guangnan, Southern Song (from Zhejiang Provincial Museum 2015)

Figure 10.2. Guangdong *chaoku* silver (from Zhejiang Provincial Museum 2015)

---

[8] For example: 真花银, 肥花银, 煎销花银, 京销细渗, 京销正渗.

Figure 11. Rubbing of a silver bar-ingot stamped *Jing xiao yin*, from Nanhai No.1 shipwreck (rubbing by Shanghai Museum)

silver (*Ming Shi*: Shihuozhi 5),[9] thereby reducing the use of paper money. After this, silver could be legally used in payments, and the number of places using silver increased. From Jingtai 3 (1452), salaries for civil and military officials in Beijing (previously paid in *baochao* 宝钞 notes) could be paid in silver, which advanced the use of silver even more (Peng Xinwei 2007: 484). In Wanli 9 (1581), the Single Whip Reform commuted all kinds of tax payments into silver, thereby completing the transition of payments to the government from goods in kind to silver. At the same time, corvée duty was also payable in silver, which consolidated the conversion of labour to silver. Previously, silver was sometimes paid to the government as a substitute for physical goods and labour. After this point, tax payments were specified in silver, an important stage in the development of silver to a standard form of currency. The Single Whip Reform also led to a more widespread use of silver among the people.

From the mid-Ming onwards, there are quite detailed records, especially regarding the use of silver in tax payments. From Zhengtong 1 (1436) *jinhuayin* 金花银

was used specifically for field taxes commuted into silver, and thereafter for all payments in silver rather than grain (*Ming Shi*: Shihuo 2).[10] In Jiajing 9 (1530) laws concerning corvée labour paid in silver were issued (*Da Ming huidian*),[11] and after the Single Whip Reform in Wanli 9 (1581) all payments of labour duty were made in silver. These records show that the Ming government measures concerning the collection of silver underwent a process of constant revision and improvement.

The Ming dynasty marks a watershed in the collection of tax in silver. In previous dynasties taxes were mostly paid in kind, which the local government then converted into silver, casting ingots according to a particular standard and appearance for the state treasury. But in the Ming dynasty tax payments in kind gradually shifted to payments entirely in silver, even down to the individual level. This is reflected in the varieties and names of silver tax ingots which exceeded those of the Song dynasty. The main types of silver ingots – field-tax silver, corvée silver, salt and tea silver, military payments, various kinds of commercial silver, imperial household silver – had many sub-types (Li Xiaoping 2013).

Most of the surviving examples of Ming dynasty ingots are from the late Ming (Figure 12). These are a different shape from Southern Song dynasty ingots, and there is also a difference in the inscriptions. The information in the late Ming inscriptions is basically the same as that seen on Tang dynasty ingots: the time, place, use, weight and the name and rank of the officials involved in its production. However, the Ming dynasty inscriptions follow a more standardized arrangement, and sometimes omit the official's rank and name. The key details in the late Ming inscriptions are place, metal, purpose and weight. Metal and use were the most important, and related to government taxation and service, and fiscal revenue and expenditure.

During the Qing dynasty silver ingots became more complicated. Although world trade and domestic trade both developed during this period, silver ingots did not become simpler and more convenient for trade and circulation, but became more complex in name and shape. There is a greater variety of shapes and weights. The exchange value of the *liang* ('tael') varied, and

Figure 12. 50-ounce silver bar-ingot, Ming dynasty, dated Zhengde 8 (1513) (Shanghai Museum collection)

different places had different weights/scales. According to a record in the *Qing Wenxian tongkao*, in Qianlong 10 (1745), there were about 100 different names for currency-silver (*baoyin* 宝银), the majority being types of 50-, 10- or 5-*liang*. Different types of currency-silver could be bought and sold at coin shops, but they were not directly exchangeable: for example, Beijing's Songjiang-yin 松江银could not be exchanged directly for Shanghai er-qi-bao 上海二七宝. The actual silver could not circulate at parity owing to the difference in fineness of the silver in different regions. The root cause was because there was no standard or uniformity in the casting. Weighed silver played important roles in national finances and collection of taxes, and exchange among the people. The weighed silver system lasted the whole of the Qing dynasty.

When we consider that silver was initially intended to facilitate the payment of taxes for the state finances and for storage of wealth in the national treasury, it seems hard to understand why there was no standard in production, and why the government did not engage in this. The reason why the physical shapes and appearance did not change is that the nature and usage of silver did not fundamentally change. Thus, the complex situation continued until the end of the Qing dynasty.

To sum up, silver ingots were basically used in the nationwide management of finances, a system that saw a very gradual development and improvement. Silver ingots with inscriptions always followed an upwards trajectory: from officials to the emperor, from local government officials to central government organs. The final destination was the state and imperial treasuries. Silver was therefore considered as an important stream of revenue for the state finances. After the fall of the Song dynasty, there was an ever-increasing use of silver in the payment of various taxes (for convenience, taxes paid in kind were converted to silver for the upward trajectory), but it was only with the Single Whip Reform in Wanli 9 (1581), when silver could be used for payment of all taxes, that silver officially became a legal form in the tax payment system – after about 600 years!

Figure 13. Changping yinyuan, Jilin (Shanghai Museum collection)

Figure 14.1. Old Man dollar (Shanghai Museum collection)

Figure 14.2. Zhangzhou military silver
(Shanghai Museum collection)

The first official silver dollar coins were the Guangxu yuanbao 光绪元宝 made in 1890 at the Canton Mint established by Zhang Zhidong 張之洞. However, they were not China's first machine-struck silver dollars – that title goes to the Changping yinyuan 厂平银元 made by the Jilin Machinery Office 吉林机器局 in Guangxu 10 (1884) (Figure 13). The design of the Changping yinyuan harks back to the "old man dollars" (*shouxing yinbing* 寿星银饼) of Taiwan and the Zhangzhou military silver (*Zhangzhou junxiang* 漳州军饷) (Figures 14.1-2). There does not appear to be a link between these two types of silver cake-ingots and traditional silver bar-ingots – that question is directly related to the inflow of silver from the West, and beyond the scope of this paper.

To conclude, there were two main forms of silver in Chinese monetary history. The cast silver ingots were an important object of value in the financial system of the state – they were a store of wealth and were used in high value transfers and payments, but did not enter circulation. The machine-struck silver dollar was the first silver currency issued directly for circulation – it was officially established as a national form of currency in 1910, and was not officially promoted until the Republic. China caught the last train of the silver dollar system and entered the era of non-exchangeable credit currency.

Translated by Helen Wang

References

Chen Yang 陈阳. 2019. Baiyin huobi beihou de caizheng tuishou – Tangdai zhi Mingdai yinding zhong suojian baiyin yu caizheng de guanxi 白银货币背后的财政推手 - 唐代至明代银锭中所见白银与财政的关系 / Pushing Hands Behind: The Relationship between the Silver Ingots and the Finance from the Tang to the Ming Dynasties. Pages 20–27 in Shanghai Museum 2019.

Cribb, J. 1993. *A Catalogue of Sycee in the British Museum. Chinese Silver Currency Ingots c. 1750-1933.* London: British Museum Press.

Li Wenqu 李问渠. 1957. Mizu zhenguo de Tianbao zaowu – Xi'an shi jiao fajue Yang Guozhong jingong yinting 弥足珍贵的天宝造物——西安市郊发掘杨国忠进贡银铤, *Wenwu cankao ziliao* 文物参考资料1957.4. [Precious treasure made in the Tianbao period: Yang Guozhong's tribute ingot(s) excavated in the suburbs of Xi'an]

Li Xiaoping 李小萍. 2013. *Mingdai fushui yinding kao* 明代赋税银锭考. Beijing: Wenwu chubanshe. [Research on Ming dynasty silver tax ingots]

Liu Zhiyan 刘志岩. 2019. Zheji chensha yin wei xiao: Jiangkou chen yin yizhi fajue ji 折戟沉沙银未销：江口沉银遗址发掘记 / The Underwater Archaeological Finding of Silver from the Jiangkou Site. Pages 28–32 in Shanghai Museum 2019.

Peng Xinwei 彭信威. 1965 (2007 edition), *Zhongguo huobi shi* 中国货币史. Beijing: Renmin chubanshe. [A Monetary History of China]

Qin Bo 秦波. 1972. Xi'an jinnian lai chutu de Tangdai yinting, yinban he yinbing de chubu yanjiu 西安近年来出土的唐代银铤、银板和银饼的初步研究, *Wenwu* 文物 1972.7: 54–58. [Preliminary research on Tang dynasty silver ingots, plaques and cakes unearthed in Xi'an in recent years]

Shaanxi Provincial Museum 陕西省博物馆1972. Xi'an nanjiao Hejiacun faxian Tangdai jiaocang 西安南郊何家村发现唐代窖藏文物, *Wenwu* 1972.1: 30–42.

Shanghai Museum 上海博物馆 (ed.). 2019. *Yiyi qiannian - Zhongguo huobi shi Zhong de baiyin* 熠熠千年: 中国货币史中的白银 / Silver in the History of Chinese Currency. Shanghai: Shanghai Museum. [This book included four forewords by Yang Zhigang, Xu Xiang, Tang Fei and Sun Jian; four essays by Wu Danmin, Chen Yang, Liu Zhiyan and Ye Daoyang; illustrations and captions relating to the three sections of the exhibition; and an index]

Wang Chunfa 王春法 (ed.). 2022. *Zhongguo guojia bowuguancang jingcui*中国国家博物馆馆藏精粹. Beijing: Beijing Shidai Huawen shuju北京时代华文书局.

Wu Danmin 吴旦敏. 2019. *Zhongguo huobi shi zhong de baiyin* 中国货币史中的白银 / Silver in the History of Chinese Currency. Pages 14–20 in Shanghai Museum 2019.

Ye Daoyang 叶道阳. 2019. 'Nanhai yihao' chutu de yi pi jinshu huobi '南海一号'出土的一批金属货币 / Metal Coins Excavated from the *Nanhai I* Shipwreck. Pages 33–35 in Shanghai Museum 2019.

Zhejiang Provincial Museum 浙江省博物馆 (ed.). 2015. *Yin de licheng* 银的历程. Beijing: Wenwuju chubanshe. [The Course of Silver]

Bizhi Zeli 币制则例 [Currency Regulations]

Da Ming Huidian 大明会典 [Collected Statues of the Great Ming]

Ming Shi 明史 [Ming History]

Qing Wenxian Tongkao 清文献通考 [Qing Comprehensive Investigations Based on Literary and Documentary Sources]

Xin Tang Shu 新唐书 [New Tang History]

略论中国的银锭

吴旦敏

2013年，我有幸通过大英博物馆和上海博物馆学术交流计划前往大英博物馆币章部展开三个月的访问考察和学习交流，Helen Wang（汪海岚）女士是币章部亚洲钱币专家，那段时间她给予我不少帮助令我此行收获满满。在这段十分有意思的学习时期，我通过Helen的引见，见到了币章部原主任Joe Cribb。Joe是一位非常平易近人的老者，但那时还年轻的我在见到他的一刻仍然有些紧张，我向他请教了机器印制纸币有关的工艺流程，他不但丝毫不介意，并十分用心地为我解答，配上手势让我理解。这让我马上心情轻松下来，我有一些感动。这是我在英期间唯一一次见到Joe，却使我印象深刻。

Joe是国际上货币史领域的权威专家，在远东货币史研究上成果卓著。其中《A Catalogue Of Sysee In The British Museum——Chinese Silver Currency Ingots c.1750-1933》这本书对我来讲尤其重要。它是我涉及到白银通货研究的入门书籍。Joe 的这部著作中，共收录了中国银锭1300件，它们基本都有铭文，时间范围从清乾隆朝至1933年币制改革共183年。书中对所见银锭，Joe开创了一种新的分类方法，根据元宝的制作和使用作为分类标准，这种分类的目的，是想根据银锭的铸造和使用来揭示这种货币制度。分类的依据主要是银锭的形制、铸造技术、大小和铭文的内容与安排。" "通过这份目录，我们可以看到在全国范围内，银匠钱庄和其他跟货币有打交道的行家是如何控制这种民间非官方货币的。他们按当地的习惯来定每个地方铸造和使用的银锭，包括银锭的形制大小、成色和重量衡制。" 这些话很平实，从中了解到Joe对历史实物尽量以客观角度去看待，也反映了他的治学理念。根据他的分类法，能够使读者很快抓到银锭这种并不利于流通便利的外形以及它所担负的主要功能倾向。这一分类法显然对于我在白银研究上成长有了启蒙。

2019年上海博物馆举办了一次《熠熠千年——中国货币史中的白银》特展（图1、2、3），以白银为线索，将不同形式的白银及相关货币糅合在一起，展现货币史上白银的发展和演变，承担的角色的变化，也反映出货币制度的变革和前进。展览分为三个部分：传统银两、白银东渐、银与纸钞。三部分逐次说明了中国传统银锭在国家财政上的重要作用，外来白银对中国传统白银造成的制度冲击，以及中国银元为什么逐渐产生和发展起来、在清末民初终于形成国家银元制度，中国近代纸钞发展与白银货币的相互关系。在展览中，同时展示了南海一号沉船遗址和江口古战场遗址所发掘出的银锭（图4、图5），这两地是近年来的重要考古发现，两处出水了大量白银，科学有力地证明了白银在在历史上远洋贸易和赋税方面发挥的重要作用。

作为这个展览的策划，我很荣幸能够有机会做一个专门展示白银货币的特别展，这也是国内呈现货币白银的首次展。展览提出了一个重要的点，白银虽然在唐代就已经具有了一些货币功能，然而中国国家法定的白银货币制度是颁行于宣统二年的《币制则例》，白银货币的形制、成色和重量才被正式确定，中间却已经相差了一千年左右。这是一个值得思考的问题。

中国银锭是中国货币史和金融史上独特的一种白银通货形式，其外形的由来至今仍然是一个无法说清的问题。从现有实物看，唐朝的白银已较显著地表现出具有一部分货币功能。

唐朝早中期白银具有两种形式，一种是长条形，一种近似圆形。这些遗存存世并不多，目前所发现的实物以何家村出土最为集中（图6），此窖藏出土了银铤、银板和银饼共90件（详见图8）。唐朝长条形银铤以杨国忠上贡银铤最为典型（图7），其中的一件上面铭文"专知诸道铸钱使兵部侍郎兼御史中丞度支事臣杨国忠 宣城郡和市银一铤五十两 青 专知官太中大夫使持节宣城郡诸军事守宣城郡太守上国柱臣苗奉倩 天宝十载四月廿日"，得知这是杨国忠以五十两的白银进献给唐玄宗的礼物。"和市"的本义是交易买卖价格与数量需经交易双方同意，而在唐宋时期官府按价格向民间购买实物，但实际是强行摊派，掠夺民间财物。和市银是在市场中得到的财物折变成的白银，这银锭即是宣城郡的官方从民间搜刮获得的财物折成白银所铸而成。中古时代贵金属白银只有统治阶层的人才有权使用，它其实是官员向国家统治者进奉示好的一种财物。同样作为上贡或进奉的还有"贺冬"银，铭文为"容管经略使进奉广明元年贺冬银壹铤重贰拾两 容管经略招讨处置等使臣崔焯进"，"贺冬"即官员为庆贺冬至这个重要的节日进奉给皇帝物品。何家村出土了刻有"庸调"字样的洊安、怀集银饼4枚（图9），"庸调"指用布帛缴纳赋税，是唐代租庸调制的重要内容之一，"庸调"银饼和这一赋税制度有直接关联，即用白银来代替布帛缴纳赋税，这是目前最早明确反映赋税制度的白银实物，也是经济史上的重要实物。唐早中期带有铭文的实物较明确地表示了白银在皇室收入和赋税上的用途。较常见的船型银铤出现于唐晚期，它的外形源于何处尚未可知，但这类银铤有铭文者尚很少见。

宋代已降，白银的使用程度较唐代有明显的提升，其使用主要在国家各种税务上，宋铤既有上供银、经总银、钞库银，又有关税银、商税银等，各种名目不下十几种，如图示（图10）。南宋定都临安后，城区人口的迅速增加，各种消费品的需求扩大，不仅促使商业经济繁荣，还促进了货币形式的多样化，除纸币与铜铁钱等重要通货外，贵金属黄金白银也作为政府的基本财富，在国家税收、专卖制度、海外贸易、地方政府的上供、大宗商业贸易等方面都发挥重要的作用。

宋代银铤在外观、内容、大小上都朝着更适应于使用需要而改变，比如宋铤的体积、大小都较唐铤缩小，铤面较平，重量分等级。作为赋税的银品类发生多样化，银的成色、重量都产生了等级要求。铤面上"真花银"、"肥花银"，"煎销花银"、"京销细渗"、"京销正渗"等都是指白银的成色，表明了南宋政府对所收白银需要标识上成色予以辨识地需要。 宋铤的制造有一定的标准，这可能也是现存宋铤形态和大小趋同之故。宋铤呈现十分规整的重量等级，常规有伍十两，二十五两，十二两半三种，实际重量分别在1895-2000克，918-1100克，434-490克。多数铭文中显示有重量，以十二两半为多，体现了此重量级别的相对广泛性。南宋出现专门经营买卖、兑换金银的商铺，名为金银盐钞交引铺，密集分布于南宋临安御街。它们还被允许铸造金银财物和金银器饰。由金银交引铺制造的银铤多会打上"京销（铤）银"的记号，并伴随有铺位的具体方位，这就是京销银的由来。"京销银"类似一个符号，而使用于各种需要白银的场合。南海一号沉船中银铤有"京销银"戳记（·图11），不少上供银、运司银、关税银上也有此戳记，它们都来自于金银交引铺。似乎这些店铺制造金银器饰财货经得官方许可，并可在那里进行金银兑换。这类专营机构的出现，是适应社会经济发展需要而产生的。白银在赋税和贸易中被重视，国家财富充盈，白银被计入国家财政收支是从宋朝开始的，上述提到的各类名目成为国家财政收入的重要来源。

大航海时代的到来，开辟了欧洲与非洲、与亚洲的海上贸易线路，贸易路线把中国同世界市场连接起来。当时美洲和日本是主要的白银生产和出口地，16世纪中期开始，白银源源不断地流入中国，换取中国的茶叶、丝绸、瓷器等。巨额白银源源不断地流入内地，不仅弥补了明朝货币材料不足，还给明朝货币体系带来了颠覆性的变化。明朝初期虽然沿袭了元的货币制度，使纸钞和铜钱平行使用，禁止使用白银。但是纸钞在洪武年间就已经开始贬值了，洪武二十三年宝钞一贯在两浙只能值钱二百文。到正统元年，政府收赋税取消银的禁令，米麦可以折成银两 ，减少钞的使用。此后白银可以合法使用，使用的地方也多了。景泰三年后对北京文武群臣的折俸钞（官员的俸禄用宝钞支付），可以用白银来支付，这将白银的使用又向前推进了一步。万历九年推行一条鞭法，各类赋税都可以用白银缴纳，自此完成了中国政府财政上由实物税向白银的完全转变。同时，差役完全可以用银来代替，实现了劳力与银的转换。如果说在这之前，白银是作为实物或者劳力的替代品上缴至政府的，在此以后，白银成为税项合法的进项物品，这是白银向货币形式发展的重要标志。同时也不难否认一条鞭法的使用促进了白银向民间普及化的程度。

明中期以后，尤其在赋税中用银，典籍已经有较为详细的记录。金花银自正统元年（1436）后，专用于田赋折银，并在之后推广至所有折粮银的总称。嘉靖九年推出了规范徭役银的具体实施办法，至万历九年一条鞭法的实施使得力差全部实现银差征收。这些记录说明了明朝政府对于重要财政征银的措施经过了不断修订和完善的过程。

明朝赋税白银与前几朝的赋税白银性质上截然不同。前朝所课征的主要为实物税，由地方政府收征以后折换成白银，按照规定的标准和样式铸造上缴国家库藏。而明朝由实物税逐渐过渡到可以完全由白银来交付，民间上缴税银也逐渐个体化。体现在上缴的税银的品类和名称在广度和深度上都超越了宋朝，往往同一品类能细分出不同的小类和名称。明朝银锭的实物品类主要是田赋折银、徭役银、盐茶税银、军饷银、各种商业税银、皇室内库银等，不仅如此，如田赋折银这一类中，又可以细分出各种名目，折粮银，如秋粮银、仓米银、谷价银、南粮改折银等，还有田赋折银派生而出的草价银、马草银和绢丝折银，以及运粮过程中产生耗米折银轻赍银，和藩王俸禄折银等等都归于田赋折银这一类。

现存实物较多的是明朝中晚期银锭（如图12），外形已然完全不同于南宋银锭。银锭上的铭文已经有了规范形式。唐代银铤已有少数凿刻有铭文，记述时间、性质、用途、重量、从铸造至成品中的各级有关官员职位姓名等，如贺冬进奉银铤共有73字。铭文的作用是记录该银铤制造的性质用途、所涉及到的各层级官员以及制造工匠，以备分类查需。明代银锭依然保持了这一传统习惯。铭文的内容基本不变，但格式似乎趋于统一化，通常的格式是：地区／（年份）／性质或用途／重量／官职和姓名／匠名，到晚明时期有些银锭铭文中的官职或者官员姓名也被省去，其中最基本的要素是地区、性质用途、重量，而性质和用途是基本中的核心。从总体上来看，这些银锭的性质和用途都与政府赋役和财政收支有关。

清朝银锭取形于明，却比明更为复杂化。尽管全球贸易和国内贸易同时发展，但银锭并没有向使交易和流通更为简易的方向转化，其名称和形式反而更加繁复。不但外形和重量较以往更为丰富多样，尤其清代的银两兑换更为复杂，各地银两都有不同的秤砝，根据《清文献通考》中乾隆十年的记录，全国的宝银名称有100种左右，主要有五十两、十两、五两三等称重。不同的宝银在钱铺里可以买进卖出，但不可以互相替代，也就是比如，北京的松江银不能直接换成上海的二七宝，说明了实银之间欠缺等质流通性，这种不能等质流通的实质是各地白银成色的差异性，追其根本仍然是铸造没有标准和统一性。银两同时在国家财政赋税和民间交易上发挥重要作用。这样的银两制度横跨了整个清朝。

当再回首中国白银最初是为简易国家财政的税赋而折换，最终作为财物进入国库贮藏，似乎就不难理解为什么银锭的铸造没有标准、政府不过于干涉，而其外形完全没有向有利于流通而改变，其根本原因很大程度上因其性质和用途没有根本性的改变，这种情况一直延续到清末。

综合上述，中国传统银锭基本都使用于国家财政体系中，它本身有一个逐渐发展和制度完善的过程。从有铭银铤（锭）来看，白银基本是由下而上的传送途径，有臣子传递给皇帝、有地方政府官员传递至中央政府机构，最终的目的地都是国家和皇室库藏，因此它是国家财政收入的重要部分。从宋朝已降，虽然越来越多地使用白银来用于各种税赋的折变（即使用白银等价于相等价值的实物税，以方便上缴），但一直到明朝万历九年颁行了一条鞭法，以法令的形式规定白银可以缴纳各种赋役，白银才正式成为赋税制度中的合法形式，这中间历经了600年左右。

中国银元的官方正式铸造是在1890年，由张之洞令广东造币厂铸造光绪元宝，而在此之前光绪十年吉林机器局铸造了厂平银元，这是中国使用机器铸造银元的开始（图13）。就外形而言，它最早可以追溯到的是台湾"寿星"银饼和漳州军饷银饼（图14）。这两种银饼的产生和传统银锭之间似乎不存在关联。这一问题和西方流入的白银有直接关系，此不赘言。所以，中国货币史中的白银应有两种形式，前述的银锭（铤）是使用于国家财政体系中的重要有价物，一直是作为财富储藏或者大额的价值转移和支付，并非进入流通市场。银元才是直接参与市场流通的货币，但它正式被中国政府确立下来并作为国家货币使用已经晚至清末（1910年），正式推广已经到民国了。所幸的是，中国终于赶上了银元制度的末班车，在此之后踏入了不兑换信用货币的时代。

A New Interpretation of the *Jiaxiqian* (Coins Containing Tin) of the Song Dynasty

Dai Jianbing 戴建兵 Tong Yu 佟昱 Nan Fang 南方

The *jiaxiqian*[1] of the Song dynasty (960–1279) have been a subject of research in numismatics and monetary history since the 1980s. Some scholars believe that the *jiaxiqian* mentioned in historical records were coins made of iron and that they were issued during the reign of Emperor Huizong, from the Chongning period (1102–1106) to the Zhenghe reign period (1111–1118) (Zhao Kuanghua, Hua Jueming 1986; Ye Shichang 1996). They take as evidence two records in the *Comprehensive Textual Research of Historical Documents: Coins, Part 2* 《文献通考·钱币二》 (Ma Duanlin 1317).

The first states that in the second year of the Chongning period (1103), Hong Zhongfu 洪中孚 sought the Emperor's approval to cast *jiaxiqian*:

> 二虏（金、西夏）以中国钱铁为兵器，若杂以铅锡则脆不可用，请改铸夹锡当三、当十铁钱，从之。

The two defeated enemies (the Jin and the Xixia) use Chinese iron coins to make weapons. If lead and tin were to be mixed in, their weapons would be too brittle and unusable. He asked for the Emperor's approval to cast *jiaxi* iron coins worth 3 [standard cash] and worth 10 [standard cash]. Approval was given.

The second states that:

> 崇宁四年（1105）二月甲申，置陕西、河东、河北、京西监，铸当二夹锡铁钱。

On the jiashen day of the second month of the Chongning period (the 16th day of the second lunar month in 1105), an order was issued to set up Coin-casting Inspection Offices in Shaanxi, Hedong, Hebei and Jingxi to cast *jiaxi* iron coins worth 2 [standard cash].

However, the *History of the Song Dynasty* 《宋史》, vol. 180, states:

> 初，蔡京主行夹锡钱，诏铸于陕西，亦命转运副使许天启推行。其法以夹锡钱一折铜钱二，每緡用铜八斤，黑锡半之，白锡又半之

At the beginning, it was [minister] Cai Jing [1047–1126] who initiated the circulation of tin-bearing coins. An order was issued to cast them in Shaanxi, and Xu Tianqi, Inspector General of Finance and Tax was ordered to carry it out. The rule was that 1 *jiaxi* coin was to exchange for 2 bronze coins, and that for each string [of coins] 8 *jin* [weight] of bronze should be used, half black-tin [lead], half white-tin [tin].

It is clear that *jiaxiqian* here refers to coins made of a copper alloy.

For our investigation, we started with the claim that *jiaxiqian* were made in order to render weapons unusable. First, we asked metal specialists if it was possible to make iron coins alloyed with tin. They said that the melting points of the two metals were different, which meant it was basically impossible. Then, we asked if iron containing tin could, after high temperature reheating, be converted back to iron. They said yes. This confirmed that the so-called *jiaxi* iron coins could not have been made into weapons unless they had been reheated, and that the claim that coins were cast in *jiaxi* iron in order to render weapons unusable cannot be sustained.

Then we turned to other historical accounts. The term *jiaxi xinqian* (*jiaxi* new coins) appeared during the reign of Taizong (976–997) in the Northern Song dynasty.

Information on Systems in Past Dynasties 《历代制度详说》, vol. 7, records that in the 7th year of the Taiping Xingguo Period (982):

> 部内钱多是江南私铸夹锡新钱。诏禁之，私铸人弃市。

Within [Luzhou], coins were mostly *jiaxi* new coins privately cast in Jiangnan. An order was issued to ban them, and those who privately cast [them] were publicly executed in the market.

---

[1] *Jiaxiqian* 夹锡钱 translates directly as "coin containing tin" (*jia* – contain, *xi* – tin, *qian* – coin).

The History of the Song Dynasty 《宋史》, vol. 180:

> 熙宁初，诏秦凤等路即凤翔府斜谷置监，已而所铸钱青铜夹锡，脆恶易毁，罢之。

At the beginning of the Xining reign period [1068–1077], an imperial edict was issued to set up Coin-casting Inspection Offices in Qinfeng-lu and other places, mainly Fengxiang-fu in Xiegu, but after a short time the casting was stopped because when tin was put into bronze it resulted in brittle and easily broken *jiaxi* coins.

The *General Annals of Shaanxi* 《陕西通志》:

> 熙宁时已而所铸钱青铜夹锡，脆恶易毁，罢之。

During the Xining period, coins were made from *jiaxi* bronze [bronze with tin in it] and became brittle and easily broken, therefore, the casting was soon ended.

A Continuation of Zi Zhi Tong Jian 《续资治通鉴长编》, vol. 41, records that in the 7th year of the Xining reign period (1074):

> 凤翔府眉县兼锡、铜铸折二钱，皆脆恶

Mei-xian [county] in Fengxiang-fu used tin and copper to cast worth-2 coins, and they were all brittle.

Similarly, *The Veritable Record* 《实录》 states:

> 熙宁七年，诏罢凤翔府眉县铸夹锡青铜折二钱

In the 7th year of Xining [1074], it was ordered that *jiaxi* bronze coins worth 2 standard coins cast in Mei-xian [county] in Fengxiang-fu be stopped.

Before the Ming dynasty, Chinese coins were mainly made of bronze, that is, copper coins bearing lead (black tin) and tin (white tin). Metallurgical analysis of iron coins of the Song dynasty shows that most samples contain no tin at all, and only a small number contain trace amounts of tin. In 1991, the China Numismatic Society used a Scanning Electron Microscope-Energy Dispersive X-ray Detector (SEM-EDX) to make a systematic composition analysis of more than 300 large iron coins unearthed in Shaanxi, Henan, Guangxi, Gansu, Ningxia and other places. Most contained no tin, with only 2 Zhenghe tongbao coins containing about 3% tin, and 3 Daguan tongbao coins containing about 1% tin (Dai Zhiqiang and Zhou Weirong 1999). In 2005, Huang Wei used SEM-EDX to test the composition of 124 iron coins of the Northern Song dynasty, and the average tin content was less than 1% (Huang Wei 2005). However, when X-ray Diffractometer (XRD) was used to analyze a part of the microstructure of these samples with a tin content of 1%–3%, it was found that there was indeed a high tin phase in the alloy, and the proportion reached Fe 65% and Sn 35% (Dai Zhiqiang and Zhou Weirong 1999). Metallurgical research has given a reasonable explanation for this phenomenon. Tin ore is mostly found together with iron ore, which causes tin to exist in cast iron. For example, modern ferrosilicon contains 1%–3% of tin (Sn), sometimes even as high as 4%, which should be categorized as impurities (Shevryukov 1959). Therefore, the high tin content in a small number of iron coins simply reflects natural tin deposits, but does not mean that tin was added intentionally when making the coins.

From a financial point of view, given Cai Jing's sporadic promotion of *jiaxiqian* in several places across the country, and the stipulation that 1 *jiaxiqian* was equivalent to 2 bronze coins, if *jiaxiqian* were iron coins, that would mean making people pay 2 bronze coins for 1 iron coin. It would be such an obvious deception (in Chinese we say "pointing to a deer and calling it a horse") that no official of any intelligence would implement it, and ordinary people would not accept it. But if a particular coin looking dazzlingly bright would exchange for 2 old bronze coins with a lower tin content, then that coin could be forced into circulation, and it could also cause the market turmoil due to the inflated value of the coins, as recorded in the histories.

To test this hypothesis, we compared the alloy composition of *jiaxiqian* with the characteristics of ordinary bronze coins of the Northern Song dynasty. The Northern Song Bronze Coin Alloy Database records the composition of 849 ordinary bronze coins from Songyuan tongbao (960) to Xuanhe coins (1119–1125).[2] The mean, and standard deviations, are copper 66.38±5.67%, lead 23.87±5.84%, tin 8.78±2.97%. The modest deviations

---

[2] The information source of the Northern Song Dynasty Bronze Coin Database is detailed in the bibliography. Coin samples include standard cash and worth-2 Daguan and Chongning bronze coins.

are testament to the superb minting technology and management of the Northern Song. For the *jiaxiqian* the alloy is consistently copper 57.14%, lead 28.56%, tin 14.28%. Table 1 shows the difference between the *jiaxiqian* and the bronze coins. Even if the alloy is relaxed by ±3% (copper 57.14±3%, lead 28.56±3%, tin 14.28±3%) (*Foundry Nonferrous Metals Manual* 1978), there is not a single bronze coin in the database that compares. This

result shows that very different alloy compositions were used for ordinary bronze coins and for *jiaxiqian*, and that this was deliberate. It also answers our question.

For our test, we selected 58 Northern Song dynasty coins (from the Zhidao to Zhenghe reign periods), and after removing corrosion we tested the alloy composition. The results for four coins fell within

Table 1. Composition data of jiaxiqian

Coin inscription	Figure	Alloy composition (wt. %)		
		Copper (Cu)	Lead (Pb)	Tin (Sn)
Zhiping Yuanbao (regular script)	Fig. 1	57.37	26.06	15.44
Shengsong Yuanbao (running script)	Fig. 2	57.76	28.09	12.64
Huangsong Tongbao (seal script)	Fig. 3	56.53	28.18	13.06
Yuanfeng Tongbao (running script)	Fig. 4	56.73	28.59	13.19
Mean values		57.10	27.73	13.58

All coins above are in the collection of the Numismatics Laboratory
of New Liberal Arts at Hebei Normal University

Test environment: Bruker S1 TITAN-800 XRF, rhodium target, 50kV, copper alloy mode; Different test parts cause slight deviations in composition data; Tested area smooth, corrosion removed.

Figure 1. Zhiping yuanbao (regular script) – jiaxiqian. File No. 21-0413-22

Figure 3. Huangsong tongbao (seal script) – jiaxiqian. File No. 21-0514-1

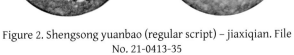

Figure 2. Shengsong yuanbao (regular script) – jiaxiqian. File No. 21-0413-35

Figure 4. Yuanfeng tongbao (running script) – jiaxiqian. File No. 21-0606-5

Table 2a. XRF Metal Composition Test of Coins in Northern Song Dynasty

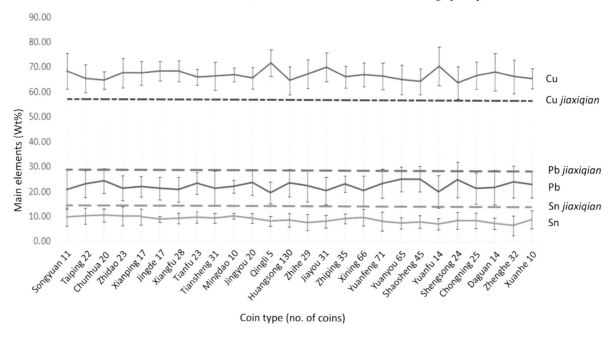

Coin type (no. of coins)

Table 2b. XRF Metal Composition Test of Coins in Northern Song Dynasty

Test Serial Number	Coin Number	Coin Inscription	Main Metal	Cu	Sn	Pb	Fe	Sb	Ag	Bi	Zn	Ti钛
Average of 8	0611-02 to 09	Tianxi tongbao-Regular Script	Cu,Sn,Pb	42.01	29.63	26.49	0.77	0.01	0.15	0.60	0.08	0.13
Average of 7	0612-02 to 08	Yuanyou tongbao-Running Script	Cu,Pb,Sn	42.19	25.52	30.25	1.15	0.28	0.15	0.10	0.12	0.10
Average of 6	0612-09 to 14	Yuanyou tongbao-Seal Script	Cu,Pb,Sn	37.45	29.06	29.98	2.00	0.79	0.11	0.20	0.12	0.17
Average of 13	0612-17 to 29	Yuanfeng tongbao-Seal Script	Cu,Sn,Pb	40.76	32.11	25.47	0.99	0.05	0.03	0.22	0.08	0.12
Average of 2	0613-01 to 02	Tianyuan shengbao-Regular Script	Cu,Sn,Pb	40.43	32.96	24.61	0.38	0.35	0.25	0.67	0.03	0.00
Average of 10	0613-03 to 12	Tianyuan shengbao-Seal Script	Cu,Sn,Pb	44.23	28.57	25.34	0.95	0.01	0.32	0.26	0.07	0.13
Average of 8	0615-01 to 08	Xiangfu tongbao-Regular Script	Cu,Sn,Pb	40.72	30.04	27.75	0.70	0.02	0.22	0.25	0.06	0.12
Average of 10	0618-02 to 11	Zhiping tongbao-Seal Script	Cu,Sn,Pb	41.03	27.63	28.35	1.72	0.20	0.27	0.39	0.10	0.12
Average of 3	0621-01 to 03	Shengsong yuanbao-Seal Script	Cu,Sn,Pb	41.24	31.17	26.03	0.43	0.13	0.19	0.42	0.08	0.11
Average of 2	0622-01 to 02	Huangsong tongbao-Regular Script 1	Cu,Sn,Pb	47.29	30.77	20.25	0.72	0.04	0.23	0.31	0.08	0.14
Average of 3	0622-04 to 06	Huangsong tongbao-Regular Script 3	Pb,Cu,Sn	31.84	30.83	33.77	1.02	1.61	0.00	0.55	0.05	0.00
Average of 11	0622-07 to 17	Huangsong tongbao-Seal Script	Cu,Sn,Pb	42.74	29.69	25.67	1.11	0.04	0.10	0.22	0.12	0.09

the range for *jiaxiqian* suggested above (Figures 1-4). These are *jiaxiqian*. The chain of evidence is now complete. The discovery of *jiaxiqian* provides a physical foundation and route for further research on these coins.

In fact, when examined from a financial perspective, the coins clearly show that the governments of the Northern Song dynasty cast *jiaxiqian*, deliberately reducing the proportion of copper and increasing the

Figure 5a. Chinese charm with the character长生保命 (long life)

Figure 5b. the Big Dipper and fairies making the elixir of immortality with Yutu (Jade Hare) on the moon

tin and lead content in bronze coins to achieve actual devaluation of currency and expansion of finance.

Following this, metal composition analysis was done on a number of coins in Song dynasty in the collection of the Numismatics Laboratory of New Liberal Arts at Hebei Normal University. Therefore, *jiaxiqian* were copper alloy coins issued by the Northern Song dynasty to solve financial difficulties caused by long periods of war. The alloy composition was adjusted by the addition of more tin (which was cheaper), and increasing the value of the coins, thereby putting into effect an inflationary policy, which would help resolve the financial situation. As for the historical sources relating to *jiaxiqian*, one is incorrect, and the others refer to a collective term for the various new coins cast in the Chongning reign period.

Our findings also throw light on other historical references to *jiaxiqian*: for example, the expression 染 为铜色 "to dye a bronze colour":

A Continuation of Zi Zhi Tong Jian 《续资治通鉴长编》, vol. 27, records that in the first year of the Daguan reign period (1107), there was an imperial edict:

河北昨铸夹锡当五钱，其样制大小类当十铜钱，奸民趋利，染为铜色，私作当十

Hebei cast worth-5 *jiaxiqian*, which resemble in manufacture and size the worth-10 bronze coins. Cheats seeking to make a profit, dye them a bronze colour, and pass them off as worth-10 coins.

Outlines of the Reign of Ten Emperors of the Song Dynasty 《皇宋十朝纲要》, vol. 17, also records that in the second year of the Daguan reign period:

河北昨铸夹锡当五钱，其样制大小类当十铜钱，奸民趋利，染为铜色，私作当十

Hebei cast worth-5 *jiaxiqian* which resemble in manufacture and size the worth-10 bronze coins. Cheats seeking to make a profit dye them a bronze colour and pass them off as worth-10 coins.

So we can see that *jiaxiqian* were a kind of bronze coin with a very bright white colour owing to its abnormally high tin content.

*

My heartfelt thanks to you, Mr Cribb, for the guidance you give to the doctoral students here at Hebei Normal University. For this birthday volume, I present here a *Changsheng baoming* coin which has strong Chinese cultural characteristics. On one side, the inscription 长生保命 means 'long life'; on the other side is the Big Dipper and moon fairies making the elixir of immortality with Yutu (Jade Hare)(Figures 5a-b). I originally thought of writing about Chinese charms that wish for a long life, then I decided to write a more academic article. But I will still wish you a happy birthday in the Chinese way! 愿克里布先生长命百岁，生命长青!

Translated by Li Lihui 李丽辉, edited by Helen Wang

References

Dai Zhiqiang 戴志强, Zhou Weirong 周卫荣, Li Yanxiang 李延祥, Liu Wei 刘伟. 1999. 'Jiaxiqian' wenti zai yanjiu "夹锡钱" 问题再研究, *Zhongguo Qianbi* 1999.1: 9-14. [Further study on jiaxi coins]

Editorial Team铸造有色金属手册编写组. 1978. *Zhuzao youse jinshu shouce* 铸造有色金属手册. Jixie gongye chubanshe机械工业出版社. [Foundry Nonferrous Metals Manual. China Machine Press, 1978]

Hua Jueming 华觉明 and Zhao Kuanghua 赵匡华. 1986. Jiaxi qian shi tie qian, bu shi tong qian 夹锡钱是铁钱, 不是铜钱, *Zhongguo Qianbi* 1986: 21-22+20. [Tin-bearing coins are iron coins, and not copper coins]

Huang Wei黄维. 2005. 'Jiaxi qian' yi an heshi jie? "夹锡钱" 疑案何时解?, *Jinshu shijie* 金属世界, 2005.2: 58-59. [When will the mystery of 'jiaxi coins' be solved?, in Metal World]

Pereira, M.J. 2013. Chinese coins in copper based alloys: elemental and microstructural characterization, *Materials Science*.

Shevryukov, H.H. 谢夫留可夫. 1959. *Xi yejin xue* 锡冶金学Beijing: Yejin gongye chubanshe 冶金工业出版. [Tin Metallurgy, translated by Kunming gongxueyuan youse zhongjinshu yelian jiaoyanshi 昆明工学院有色重金属冶炼教研室, Metallurgical Industry Press]

Takeda, M., Mabychi, H. and Tominaga, T. 1977. A Tin-119 Mössbauer Study of Chinese Bronze Coins. *Radiochemical and Radioanalytical Letters* 29: 191-197.

Wang, H., Cowell, M., Cribb, J., and Bowman, S. 2005. *Metallurgical Analysis of Chinese Coins at the British Museum*. London: British Museum Research Publication 152.

Wang Jin and Yang Guoliang. 1959. The Trend in the Changes of Coin Alloy Chemistry. *Hangzhou University Journal* 1959.5: 43-50.

Ye Shichang 叶世昌. 1996. Jiaxi qian shi tie qian er fei tong qian 夹锡钱是铁钱而非铜钱, *Zhongguo Qianbi* 1996.3: 31-32+82. [Tin-bearing coins are iron coins not copper coins]

Zhou Weirong 周卫荣. 2004. Zhongguo gudai qianbi hejin chengfen yanjiu 中国古代钱币合金成分研究. Beijing: Zhong Hua Book Company. [A Study on the Alloy Composition of Ancient Chinese Coins]

Huang Song shi chao gangyao 17 皇宋十朝纲要17 [Outlines of the Reigns of Ten Emperors of the Song Dynasties, vol. 17]

Lidai zhidu xiangshuo 7 历代制度详说 7 [Information on Systems in Past Dynasties, 7]

Shaanxi tongkao 陕西通志 [General Annals of Shaanxi]

*Shilu*实录 [The Veritable Record]

Song shi 180 宋史 180 [The History of the Song Dynasty, vol. 180]

Song shi. Shi huo zhi. Xia er. Qianbi 宋史·食货志·下二·钱币 [History of the Song Dynasty: Food and Money Part 2, Section 2. Coins]

Wenxian tongkao. Qianbi er 文献通考·钱币二 [Comprehensive Textual Research of Historical Documents: Coins, Part 2]

Xu zi zhi tong jian chang bian, vols 27 and 41 续资治通鉴长编 [A Continuation of the Zi Zhi Tong Jian, vols 27 and 41]

中国宋代的"夹锡钱"新解

戴建兵，佟昱，南方

"夹锡钱"这种中国宋代钱币，从上世纪80年代兴起讨论迄今，是为钱币学和货币史的共同焦点已近30年。

有一种观点认为文献中所提及的"夹锡钱"是铁钱。（赵匡华、华觉明，1986）（叶世昌，1996），其考察的时间范围集中于徽宗崇宁至政和时期。

"铁钱说"的主要证据如下：《文献通考·钱币二》载：崇宁二年（1103），洪中孚请旨："二虏（金、西夏）以中国钱铁为兵器，若杂以铅锡则脆不可用，请改铸夹锡当三、当十铁钱，从之。"这是"夹锡铁钱"这一词汇最早的出处。《文献通考·钱币二》又载："崇宁四年（1105）二月甲申，置陕西、河东、河北、京西监，铸当二夹锡铁钱。"

而《宋史·食货志·下二 ·钱币》记载："初，蔡京主行夹锡钱，诏铸于陕西，亦命转运副使许天启推行。其法以夹锡钱一折铜钱二，每缗用铜八斤，黑锡半之，白锡又半之"。明确地说夹锡钱是铜合金钱币。

首先我们看一下铸造夹锡钱的目的是"以中国铁钱为兵器，若杂以铅、锡，则脆不可用。"为此我们请教金属专家，首先，铁中夹锡铸钱是否可以合金。专家说因为两种金属熔点的问题基本上不可能。其次，铁中夹锡后高温回炉可否转换回铁。回答是当然可以。鉴于得到所谓"夹锡钱"不可能不回炉才能再制造成兵器。因此如果以铁夹锡铸钱，根本达不到上面史料所追求的目的。

再回到史料，北宋太宗时期出现"夹锡新钱"。《历代制度详说》卷7载：太平兴国七年（982）"部内钱多是江南私铸夹锡新钱。诏禁之，私铸人弃市。"这是迄今发现最早关于夹锡钱的记载。《宋史》卷180载："熙宁初，诏秦凤等路即凤翔府斜谷置监，已而所铸钱青铜夹锡，脆恶易毁，罢之。"《陕西通志》载："熙宁时已而所铸钱青铜夹锡，脆恶易毁，罢之。"《续资治通鉴长编》卷41载：熙宁七年（1074）"凤翔府眉县兼锡、铜铸折二钱，皆脆恶"。同样《实录》载："熙宁七年，诏罢凤翔府眉县铸夹锡青铜折二钱"。

中国古代铸币明代以前主要是青铜钱，也就是铜、铅、锡钱，铅和锡古称为黑锡、白锡。对宋代铁钱的合金成分测试的结果表明，绝大多数样品不含锡，少数含有微量的锡（Sn）。1991年，中国钱币学会使用扫描电镜—能谱仪（SEM-EDX）对陕西、河南、广西、甘肃、宁夏等地出土的300余枚

大铁钱作了系统的成分分析，其中绝大多数不含锡（Sn）。只有2枚政和通宝含锡（Sn）在3%左右，3枚大观通宝含锡（Sn）为1%左右（戴志强、周卫荣，1999）。2005年，黄维用扫描电镜能谱（SEM-EDX）对124枚北宋铁钱进行微区成分测试，平均锡（Sn）含量均不到1%（黄维，2005）。但是，当用使用X 射线衍射仪（XRD）对这些含锡量在1%-3%样品进行局部微观结构分析时，发现合金中确有高锡相的存在，局部比例可以达到Fe65％、Sn35％（戴志强、周卫荣，1999）。冶金学研究对这一现象给出了合理的解释。锡矿多与铁矿伴生，会使得铸成的铁器中有锡存在。例如：现代硅铁中，锡（Sn）含量在1%-3%，少数高的可达4%，应属于杂质范畴。（H.H.谢夫留可夫，《锡冶金学》，1959）。所以，少数锡（Sn）含量略高的铁钱局部具有高锡特征，并不能证明为铸币时有意添加的结果。

从金融学的角度分析，当年蔡京断断续续主持全国多处铸行的"夹锡钱"，同时规定一枚夹锡钱等于二枚铜钱，如果夹锡钱是铁钱，让百姓以二枚铜钱换一枚铁钱，这种大白天指鹿为马的事，再笨的官员也不会施行，老百姓更不会接受。而只用一枚含锡较多，外表较白亮的钱折合二枚两枚过去含锡较低的旧铜钱，才会强制流通，并引发史书记载的由于币值虚高产生市场动荡。

我们将"夹锡钱"的配方与北宋普通铜钱的实际合金特征进行对比。北宋铜钱合金数据库收录了从宋元至宣和的849枚普通铜钱合金成分[1]。其中铜、铅、锡总平均值和标准差分别为：66.38±5.67%、23.87±5.84%、8.78±2.97%，数据离散度低较为稳定，足见北宋高超的铸币工艺与管理水平。"夹锡钱"的配方换算成百分比为：铜57.14%，铅28.56%、锡14.28%。图1曲线直观地反应了二者的差异。从误差线可以看出，各数据散布范围基本游离于"夹锡钱"线之外，没有交集。即便充分考虑铸造误差的因素，将"夹锡钱"的合金配比放宽至：铜57.14±3%，铅28.56±3%、锡14.28±3%（±3%参考《铸造有色金属手册》，1978），整个数据库中仍然没有一枚钱币的合金数据能够与之匹配。这一结果说明古人有意将夹锡钱与普通制钱配方进行了清晰划分，同时也合理解释了上述问题。

根据记载中对夹锡铜钱的特征描述，我们将收集到的58枚北宋钱币（年号涵盖至道～政和）在除锈后分别进行了成分检测。结果显示，合金比例分布于铜57.14±3%、铅28.56±3%、锡14.28±3%区间的有4枚。这就是"夹锡钱"。实物的发现，使得证据

---

[1] 北宋铜钱数据库信息来源详见参考文献4-17。钱币样品包括小平、折二、折十（大观、崇宁）铜钱。

链形成闭环。同时，也为未来对"夹锡钱"的深入研究提供了实物基础和搜寻路径。

总之这样吧是铜合金钱，是宋朝为了解决因为长时间的战争而引发的财政困境，力图以钱币铸造过程中加入较铜更贱的锡，并扩大其价值，所施行一种通货膨胀政策，以此来解决政府的财政困难。至于史料中一些夹锡钱钱的记载，一是误记，另外就是人们对崇宁时期新铸各种钱币的统称。

这样你就可以理解下面的这些史料记载了。夹锡钱"染为铜色"。《续资治通鉴长编拾补》卷27大观元年四月壬戌：大观元年（1107）诏"河北昨铸夹锡当五钱，其样制大小类当十铜钱，奸民趋利，染为铜色，私作当十"。《皇宋十朝纲要》卷17又载：大观二年河北西路"本路小民以药染擦夹锡钱，如铜色，与当十钱混淆"。由此可知。夹锡钱是由于含锡过多而发白亮的一种铜钱。

非常感谢克里布指导河北师范大学的博士生。恰逢他的生日之际，本来想写一篇关于中国历代厌胜钱中有关祝寿钱币的文章。后来还是想用一个更有学术品位的文章来庆贺老先生的生日吧，附上一枚中国的厌胜钱。上面是用各种书法文体书写的汉字寿字，按照中国传统，愿克里布先生长命百岁，生命长青。

Cast Iron Furnaces of Modern Diplomacy in China: The Department of Iron Coins at Dongtangzi Hutong in Beijing[1]

Alex Chengyu Fang

Introduction

Since the late twentieth century, digitization of archives and collections, and commercial sales of antiquities, have opened up unprecedented opportunities for research. The inspiration for this paper was the discovery of a hand-drawn floor plan of the Department of Iron Coins in Dongtangzi Hutong, Beijing, produced in the early 1850s (Figure 1). This unique document, Article No: SHU0003590 in the collection of the Palace Museum, Beijing is captioned *Dongtangzi hutong qianju huayang xidi* 东堂子胡同錢局畫樣细底 or *A Drawn Floorplan of the Department of Iron Coins at Dongtangzi Hutong with Detailed Annotations*. It was first discussed in 2014 by Zhang Zhaoping, librarian at the Library of the Palace Museum, Beijing, in a journal devoted to discussions of Ming and Qing history. Indexed in the category of architectural science and engineering, Zhang's article has so far received no citation nor made any impact on the numismatic world. In this paper, I will discuss the floorplan in detail, making it accessible to English readers for the first time. I will also discuss the history of the property at Dongtangzi Hutong, and its conversion from a private residence to the Department of Iron Coins. I will expand upon the work by Zhang Zhaoping by bringing in more archival evidence relating to the property, and discuss in greater detail the practical workings of a Qing dynasty mint.

The site on Dongtangzi Hutong is not a neutral location. Initially built as a luxurious private residence, the property was confiscated in 1851, converted into a mint in 1854, suspended as a mint in 1859, then converted again in 1861, this time into the Zongli Yamen, China's first Ministry of Foreign Affairs. The site remains today at the heart of the diplomatic area in Jianguomen, Beijing. Dongtangzi Hutong runs from Dongdan North Street east to Chaoyangmen South Street. The history of the site and the choice of this location for China's first modern ministry of foreign affairs was deliberate, and must be seen in the context of China's urgent need to address relations with foreign countries in the second half of the 19th century, following the Taiping Rebellion

(1850–1860), the Second Opium War (1856–1860), and ahead of the Boxer Rebellion (1900–1901). It was a very significant site. As Henry Kissinger summed it up,

> Only under the pressure of Western incursions in the nineteenth century did China establish something analogous to a foreign ministry to manage diplomacy as an independent function of government, in 1861 after the defeat in two wars with the Western powers. It was considered a temporary necessity, to be abolished once the immediate crisis subsided. The new ministry was deliberately located in an old and undistinguished building previously used by the Department of Iron Coins, to convey, in the words of the leading Qing Dynasty statesman, Prince Gong, 'the hidden meaning that it cannot have a standing equal to that of other traditional government offices, thus preserving the distinction between China and foreign countries.' (Kissinger 2011: 17)

Part 1: The creation of the Department of Iron Coins in Dongtangzi Hutong

The Department of Iron Coins in Dongtangzi Hutong was the first mint to cast iron cash coins in Beijing, and was established in 1854 during a period of turmoil shortly before the Second Opium War (1856–1860). The year 1850 marked the start of the Xianfeng reign and also saw the Taiping Heavenly Kingdom rising in the south. Saishangga 賽尚阿 (1794–1874), a Mongolian Plain Blue Bannerman, who rose to Minister of Works (1841–1845) and Minister of Revenue (1845–1850), was entrusted by Emperor Xianfeng as Imperial Envoy to crush the rebellion. He failed to do so and was condemned to death in 1851. Although he was shortly released from prison and dispatched to an army barrack in Chili Province, Saishangga's family members were stripped of their official status and privileges, and his family properties in Beijing were confiscated. In the meantime, the Taiping troops had advanced from the south and occupied the eastern regions of China, cutting off copper supplies from Yunnan in the southwest, which resulted in severe fiscal problems with regard to military expenditure and administrative expenses. The Qing Court resorted to paper money (*Da-Qing baochao* 大清寶鈔) and issued large denomination cash coins (*daqian* 大錢), which caused a severe shortage of small change in the market. Iron cash coins were proposed as a solution.

[1] This work would not have been possible without the worldwide effort to digitize holdings of historic archives and objects. I was honoured to be part of this effort at the British Museum ten years ago in 2012 supported by the Robinson Fellowship in the Department of Coins and Medals. It is only appropriate for me to acknowledge here the generosity and advice that I have received over the years from Joe Cribb, Helen Wang and Philip Attwood.

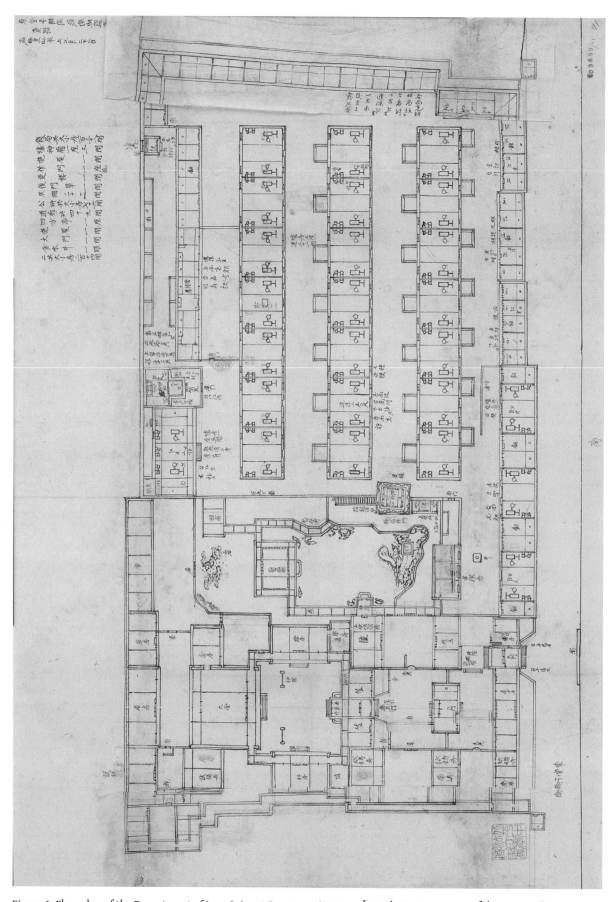

Figure 1. Floorplan of the Department of Iron Coins at Dongtangzi Hutong [Article No: SHU0003590] (*Dongtangzi hutong qianju huayang xidi* 东堂子胡同钱局畫樣細底 [书0003950]). 748 × 520 mm. Image provided by the Palace Museum.

Prince Hui, uncle of Emperor Xianfeng, was an ardent advocate of iron coins and instrumental in the establishment of departments of iron coins (*tieqianju*鐵錢局). In a memorial to the throne dated 7 May 1854, he proposed the repurposing of a confiscated property as the first iron coin department in Beijing:[2]

> *Prince Hui et al. humbly report to your Majesty that, upon your imperial approval of our proposal on 20th of March to open furnaces for the minting of iron coins, ... we have decided that the Imperial Household Department should register the vacant confiscated property, consisting of 226 rooms and located at Dongtangzi Hutong near the Dongdan Archway, for such an imminent use.*

The vacant property at Dongtangzi Hutong was none other than Saishangga's family seat in Beijing. It would be the first of the five iron coin departments in the capital city, with a total of 100 furnaces. It is remarkable that the floorplan for the conversion of this residential property to a mint survives in the Yangshi Lei 樣式雷 Archives, now in the Palace Museum, Beijing.

Date of the floor plan

The floorplan, in black and red ink on paper, measures 748 mm by 520 mm. It contains inscriptions, annotations and stamped marks that provide useful information. Handwritten inscriptions on the back note that the property record for the mint in Dongtangzi Hutong was retrieved on the 21st day of the 7th month of the 4th year of the Xianfeng reign (1854), just over two months after Prince Hui first proposed the property be used as a mint.

Provenance of the floor plan

A red seal impression stamped in the lower left of the floorplan indicates that it was once held in the library of the School of Arts of the Sino-French University in Beijing, inaugurated in 1920. The floor plan had been produced by the Yangshi Lei Studio, architects to the imperial court. Following the collapse of the Qing dynasty in 1911 the descendants of the Lei family had been obliged to sell their extensive archive of design drawings of imperial construction works in order to make a living. The Sino-French University, assisted by the Society for the Study of Chinese Architecture (*Zhongguo yingzao xueshe*中國營造學社), purchased

some 1,000 drawings from the Lei family in 1930 alone for a total of 4,500 silver dollars. When the Sino-French University was dissolved in 1950, its collection of over 2,000 drawings from the Yangshi Lei Archive, including the floorplan, were integrated into the Palace Museum, Beijing, where they now constitute the largest portion of the Museum's collection of the Lei family's designs (Project Yangshifang of the Palace Museum 2001).

Significance of the floor plan

Although the Qing dynasty left an extensive collection of historical records about its fiscal policies, decisions and laws regarding the issuance of cash coins, these tend to focus on administrative and financial issues. Very little is known about the technological aspects relating to the production of cash coins. In fact, the only specific Chinese documentation of the coin-making process is Song Yingxing's 宋應星seminal *Tiangong Kaiwu*天工開物, published with illustrations in 1637. The floorplan for the Department of Iron Coins in Dongtangzi Hutong is therefore the only officially certified pictorial description of a coin mint in China. Although the mint was closed in 1861 and the property was subsequently repurposed, the floorplan is of supreme value. Supplemented with other archival material and historical relics, it offers unprecedented insight into how a Qing dynasty mint operated.

Navigating the floorplan of the Dongtangzi Department of Iron Coins

The floorplan shows a site more or less rectangular in shape, averaging 60 m north to south and 80 m west to east, and occupying an estimated 4,800 m². The site is in two parts: the left half showing the office section (*gongsuo* 公所), and the right half showing the workshop section (*qianju*錢局). The office section shows an aerial view of an elaborate version of a *siheyuan* 四合院, the courtyard residence typical of Beijing. Saishangga's property at Dongtangzi Hutong was significantly larger than the standard *siheyuan*, and also had a garden with a pond to the right. The garden appears to be of a style specific to Suzhou in Jiangsu, suggesting that the property may date back to the Ming dynasty, when Beijing was abundant with high officials from Jiangsu.

A: The office section

The rooms are annotated on the floorplan to show their respective functions. For convenience, the annotations found in the office section are listed in Table 1 with their frequencies and translations. The frequencies are only approximate, as not all the rooms are labelled or annotated on the floorplan.

---

[2] Unless otherwise stated, the memorials by Prince Hui referred to in this paper are from The First Historic Archives of China (2018), a compilation of memorials to the throne archived at The Grand Council (*Junjichu*軍機處) and The Ministry of Foreign Affairs (*Waiwubu*外務部) on matters relating to the issuance of iron coins in the capital city of Beijing.

Table 1. The named locations in the office section

No	Chinese	Transliteration	Translation	Frequency
1	大使所	da shi suo	Director's office	1
2	大使值宿房	da shi zhi xiu fang	Director's night duty room	1
3	試鑄房	shi zhu fang	Trial casting room	5
4	庫房	ku fang	Store room	3
5	科房	ke fang	Clerical room	1
6	檔房	dang fang	Archive room	1
7	值房	kan shou zhi fang	Duty/guard's room	6
8	看守房	kan shou fang	Guard's room	2
9	更樓	geng lou	Watchtower	1
10	南房	nan fang	Southern room	2
11	抱廈	bao sha	Veranda in front of a house	1
12	大堂	da tang	Big hall	1
13	套房	tao fang	Suite room	1
14	敞廳	chang ting	Open hall	1
15	歇山敞廳	xie shan chang ting	Hip roofed open hall	1
16	四方亭	si fang ting	Four-sided pavilion	1
17	東堂子衚衕	dong tang zi hu tong	Dongtangzi Hutong	1
18	大門	da men	Main gate	1
19	二門	er men	Second gate	1
20	三門	san men	Third gate	1
21	垂花門	chui hua men	Canopied floral gate	2
22	錢局作門	qian ju zuo men	Gate to coin workshops	1
23	角門	jiao men	Side door	6
24	元光	yuan guang	Moon door	2
25	屏	Ping	See-through door	2
26	影	Ying	Screen wall	2
27	遊廊	you lang	Gallery	1
28	扒山遊廊	pa shan you lang	Sloping gallery	1
29	花瓦大牆	hua wa da qiang	High wall with floral tiles	1
30	踏跺	ta duo	Banquette slope	1
31	秤架	cheng jia	Stilyard	2
32	山石	shan shi	Stone hill	1
33	水池	shui chi	Water pond	1
34	上馬石	shang ma shi	Mounting stone	2
35	丹陛	dan bi	Decorated stepping stone	1
36	一出水硬山	Yi chu shui ying shan	Single-sloped saddle roof	1

To familiarize and understand the floorplan, I will guide readers through the two sections. Visitors to the Department of Iron Coins would come along Dongtangzi Hutong, the road running east and west along the bottom of the floorplan. They would see the main gate flanked by two mounting stones with a screen wall (No 26) immediately opposite on the other side of the road. They would go up the steps into a covered entrance. On either side of the entrance are guards' rooms (No 7). From the entrance they would see another screen wall and, turning left, go down a set of elaborately carved stone steps (No 35) into the first courtyard, with the second gate (No 19) at the centre of the courtyard. Below the courtyard is at least one guard's room and to the left is a moon door (No 24) leading to an enclosed area containing trial casting rooms (No 3) and a southern room (No 10). The second gate opens into a second courtyard with a see-through door (No 25) on the left, and another moon gate on the right. At the top of the second courtyard are two side doors (No 23) and the third, most elaborate, gate (No 20), flanked by guards' rooms. The guard's room on the right leads to the director's night duty room (No 2), and a verandah (No 11) looking out over a garden. From the third gate, visitors would pass through the canopied floral gate (No 21) into the third courtyard, where they would see two stilyards (No 31) on either side of the courtyard for weighing materials and coins. A gallery (No 27) runs around the third courtyard, leading to more guards' rooms, store rooms (No 4), clerical rooms (No 5) and archive rooms (No 6). At the top of the courtyard is a big hall (No 12), flanked by a trial casting room and a suite room (No 13). Above the big hall is a fourth courtyard with two side doors (No 23), and store rooms (No 4). The side door on the left gives access to more trial casting rooms and a gallery. The side door on the right gives access to more store rooms and more open space. Another see-through door (No 25) allows the viewer to see into a second, smaller garden with a stone hill (No 32), an open hall (No 14) and a hip-roofed open hall (No 15). On the other side of the hip-roofed open hall is the first, larger garden surrounded by a gallery. To the right of the garden is a high wall with painted tiles (No 29), a curving gallery (No 28), and below that a banquette slope (No 30), a watch-tower (No 9) and gate to the coin workshop (No 22) and the directors' office (No 1) with a single-sloped saddle roof (No 36). Immediately below the garden are three coin-stringing rooms (workshop section, No 5).

B: The workshop section

The annotations of the workshop section are listed in Table 2, again with their frequencies and translations. The floorplan shows that the workshop section is also more or less rectangular, and measures about 60 m north to south, and 55 m west to east.

Table 2. Annotated locations in the workshop section.

No	Chinese	Transliteration	Translation	Frequency
1	爐房一座五間	lu fang yi zuo wu jian	A furnace workshop with five rooms	1
2	爐房一座三間	lu fang yi zuo san jian	A furnace workshop with three rooms	1
3	爐房七座一連二十一間	lu fang qi zuo yi lian er shi yi jian	A stretch of seven furnace workshop with twenty-one rooms	1
4	磨錢房	mo qian fang	Coin polishing workshop	1
5	串錢房	chuan qian fang	Coin stringing workshop	1
6	爐神廟	lu shen miao	Temple of the Furnace God	1
7	飯	Fan	Canteen	6
8	灰棚	hui peng	Shed	1
9	中廁	zhong ce	Middle toilet	1
10	屏門	ping men	See-through door	1
11	角門	jiao men	Side door	3
12	後門	hou men	Back door	1
13	井	Jing	Well	1
14	眉子坐凳	mei zi zuo deng	Friezed stool	1
15	板瓦	ban wa	Pan tile	1
16	筒瓦	tong wa	Convex tile	1
17	清水脊原有	qing shui ji yuan you	Original tilted roof ridge	1
18	灰梗	hui geng	Putty powder	1
19	七棟	qi dong	Seven houses	1
20	八尺	ba chi	2.4 metres	1
21	進深二丈二尺	jin shen er zhang er chi	6.6 metres deep	1
22	更樓	geng lou	Watchtower	1

The floorplan for the workshop section shows two entrances/exits: the main entrance under the watchtower to the right of the garden in the office section and the backdoor (12, Table 2) in the northeast corner of the floorplan. At the centre of the workshop section are three long rows of rooms (No 3), each row consisting of seven furnace workshops, and each workshop consisting of three rooms. Below the main entrance is a side door (No 11) leading into an enclosed area of the coin-stringing workshop (No 5), again consisting of three rooms. The southern wall of the workshop section is lined up with another three furnace workshops and a total of seven canteens (No 7). Along the northern wall at the top of the workshop section of the plan is a furnace workshop with five rooms (1), pan-tiles (15) and an original tiled roof ridge (15). Between this area and the outer wall is an ash shed (No 8), presumably for storage of charcoal ashes from the furnace. To the right of this furnace workshop is a larger building that juts out: it has a see-through door (No 10), leading into a hall covered under convex tiles (No 16) with frieze-stools (No 14) and some steps leading up to the Temple of the Furnace God (No 6). To

the right of the temple is a narrow passage leading to the toilets (No 9) and the back door in the northeast corner. Also to the right of the Temple building is a side door opening into a walled section containing the coin-polishing rooms (No 4). On the other side of the coin-polishing rooms are six more canteens. Along the eastern wall on the right is a series of rooms or cubicles of unspecified uses. They likely function as ash sheds to temporarily store charcoal ashes from the furnaces.

Part 2: Discussions of the floorplan of the Department of Iron Coins at Dongtangzi Hutong

An inscription in the top right margin of the floor plan lists the officially verified number of rooms: 76 rooms in the office section and 138 rooms in the workshop section, thus a total number of 214 rooms. Zhang (2014) suggests that the workshop section was newly constructed for the mint. However, there is evidence that suggests otherwise. The inscription in the top right margin of the floorplan notes a total of 214 rooms on this site for rooms in both the office and workshop sections. This almost matches the 226 rooms mentioned in Prince Hui's memorial to Emperor Xianfeng, dated 7 May 1854, in the first proposal to adapt the confiscated property to an iron coin mint. This suggests that the workshop section already existed at that time and remained largely unchanged in the floorplan, at least as far as the number of rooms is concerned. The difference of twelve rooms (a 5–6% discrepancy) is probably due to how a room was defined. It is possible that the workshop section had previously been used as a compound for the family's servants and bodyguards, or that such dwellings were rented out to generate extra income for Saishangga's family, a practice observed in other mints, or that the workshop section was originally used as stables.

The director's office

According to the floorplan, the director's office is surprisingly small. Located in the southeastern corner of the garden,[3] on the right of the entrance to the workshop section under the watchtower, it comprises three rooms. If the floorplan is to scale, the director's office measured only 4.2 × 1.6 m. In other words, it was only half the size of a proper room, with a single-sloped saddle roof according to its annotation while most buildings have a double-sloped roof). The so-called "director's office" was not a magnificent place at all, but probably more of a duty room in which to monitor the comings and goings of the department personnel, and any goods they were carrying. In addition to the director's office, there was a director's night-duty room, behind the veranda looking over the main garden. We know more about the administration of the Department

---

[3] Zhang (2014) mistakenly refers to the north-eastern corner.

of Iron Coins from Prince Hui's report to the Emperor, dated 25 December 1855, and I will discuss this in Part 3.

Security and safekeeping in the office section

The office area is dotted by a significant number of guards' rooms and duty rooms. The guards' rooms are located around the first and second courtyards, with none beyond the third, floral gate opening to the central courtyard. In effect, there was a forbidden area from the central courtyard to the back wall of the office section. The stretch of twelve storerooms found in the backyard at the top of the plan were used to store raw materials such as cast iron and charcoal as well as finished strings of coins. For comparison, the Guilin Mint (*Baoguiju* 寶桂局) with twenty furnace workshops was facilitated with four storerooms for copper, three for lead and tin, ten for charcoal, and four for cash coins (Xie [1800] 1988). In his memorial to the Emperor dated 20 March 1854, Prince Hui stated that each furnace would use 374 kg of iron and 220 kg of charcoal per day. If we apply those figures to the 25 furnace workshops at Dongtangzi Hutong, that would give us a daily consumption of 9.35 tons of raw iron and 5.5 tons of charcoal. We can also infer that no material of value was left in the workshop section over night; workmen would check out the raw material, cast the coins and return the finished products to the office section. The two stilyards standing in the central courtyard would be used for weighing and checking out the raw material and the submission of completed products, all transacted on the same day. The Grand Council (*junjichu* 軍機處) would come to fetch finished coins on a regular basis to supply the army and civilian market with urgently needed cash coins.

The trial casting rooms

The next significant revelation from the floor plan is the number of trial casting rooms found in the office section. Five rooms are marked as trial casting rooms, all located down the left hand side of the floorplan. It is possible that adjacent unlabelled rooms were also trial casting rooms. If so, there may have been as many as twelve trial casting rooms, matching the number of store rooms. Logically, we can suggest two scenarios for trial casting. In the first, trial casting would be needed only when a new type of cash coin was introduced. The pattern coin officially issued from the Board of Revenue and the Board of Works would be used in such rooms to test the weight and quality before rolling out production on a larger scale. For example, according to a document issued by the Board of Revenue to the Imperial Household Department, dated 3 March 1854, the Board of Revenue experimented and succeeded in trial casting iron coins at another location prior to the mint at Dongtangzi. Upon receiving a report about the trial casting experiment, the Ministry of Military

Affairs instructed the Board of Revenue to submit three pattern iron coins, including two 5-cash and one 1-cash, which were to be used as pattern coins for the Board of Revenue to start producing coins of the same weight and type. Secondly, for the previous two hundred years, the Qing dynasty had been minting brass coins and from long experience had created an ideal formula of metal composition for perfect casting results. Changing from brass to iron created technical challenges: a new metal composition had to be identified and possibly also new sand-molding techniques. This change may have required extensive trials and, as acknowledged in one of Prince Hui's memorials, met with fairly open resistance from workmen at the copper mints of the Board of Revenue and Board of Works. The imperial archive provides further documentation about the trials conducted by officials of the iron coin project. On 20 March 1854, Prince Hui submitted the following memorial to Emperor Xianfeng about the trial casting of iron coins:

> Your servant Mianyu et al. humbly report that the trial casting of iron coins has been successfully performed and await your Majesty's edict. On 2nd February of the 4th Year of Xianfeng, Zaiquan orally conveyed your imperial edict that Prince Hui, Prince Gong and Prince Zaiquan should delegate Wencai (Deputy Minister of Court of Censors), Chonglun (Deputy Treasurer), and Xiling (Minister of Board of Revenue) to trial cast one furnace of iron coins. If successful within one month, we should report and await instructions. Your imperial edict was obeyed. We started the furnace on 7th of February and began casting. However, not all the casting materials were available and the iron workmen were yet inexperienced. We continued for three days and, largely failing, stopped the furnace and investigated better casting methods. We identified and employed three sand casting specialists and started trying again on the 10th. The coins turned out fine with complete inner and outer rims, mostly ready for public issuance. On 15 February, we presented coin trees together with their sand molds for your imperial inspection.

> Nevertheless, we only used ladles to melt iron and the weight was small. The coins that we managed to cast with a whole day's energy were not enough to compensate for the cost of the raw materials including iron and coal plus the cost of labour. For this reason, your servant Zaiquan would like to request the minting of 10-cash big coins instead.

Prince Hui's report is a firsthand account of the initial difficulties incurred during the process of trial casting iron coins and is a rare technical description of the trials. His report hinted at extra raw materials and enhanced sand molds as the key to success in the minting of iron coins. The report's suggestion of shifting to 10-cash coins instead of the 5-cash and 1-cash coins requested by the Ministry of Military Affairs was clearly based on the technical difficulties of working with iron and increased costs. It is likely that extensive trials would have been needed. However, it is unimaginable that the trial process would have required twelve individual rooms. Thus, the need for twelve trial casting rooms is intriguing and further attention is needed to ascertain the true and full functions of the trial casting rooms. It is also interesting to note that, as indicated by the floor plan, the trial casting of new coins was performed on the premises of the office section away from the area of production workshops, perhaps by a different group of workmen, who were presumably more experienced and skilled.

The clerical rooms and archive rooms

On the office floorplan, we see that the central courtyard is flanked by clerical rooms and archive rooms, as would be expected of any such place serving administrative functions. The clerks working in this restricted area would weigh the raw material coming into the coin mint before distributing it to the furnaces in the workshop section. They would also measure and record the finished coins submitted from the workshop section. They would also deliver finished coins to, for example, the Grand Council and duly record the numbers. Each transaction would be meticulously recorded and archived. According to a publicly auctioned specimen of a monthly receipt and delivery account of brass and iron coins, by the end of 8th month of the 8th year of Xianfeng (1858), there was a balance brought forward of 20,280.620 strings of 10-cash coins, a new receipt of 5,619,348 strings of 10-cash coins, and a delivery of 585,144 strings of 10-cash coins, with a balance carried forward of 25,312,824 strings of 10-cash coins. Such records would be the source of data on which the total production was calculated, documented and then reported.

The furnace workshops

On the floorplan, the central part of the workshop section was occupied by three rows of seven furnace workshops, with each furnace workshop comprising three rooms and having two furnaces and two sets of bellows. Each workshop measures 7.5 × 8 m wide. In the northwest corner of the workshop section is a furnace workshop consisting of five rooms, and there are a further three standard furnace workshops in the southwest corner. Thus, there are 25 furnace workshops on the floorplan, which agrees with Prince Hui's proposal to establish 100 furnace workshops, i.e. 25 at each of the four mints.[4] Indeed, the workshops on

the floorplan match the descriptions in Prince Hui's memorial to the Emperor:

> We thoroughly discussed the matter (of producing iron coins) and have tentatively decided the following: One hundred furnace workshops are to be established, gradually, one by one; Each workshop should cast coins for twenty-five days per month; on each day, every workshop, assisted by two bellows, should cast 44 batches of coins; thirty such batches should be given to 1-cash coins and, discounting those with minting flaws, twenty chuan of coins should be delivered…; the remaining fourteen batches should be allocated to 10-cash big coins and four chuan of them, including those with casting holes, should be delivered. Once established, thus, each furnace workshop should deliver iron coins worth one hundred and twenty diao of bronze coins. Each workshop will use twenty-five workmen paid a total of twenty-five diao[5] of bronze coins for each workday.

The recommendation of two bellows per furnace was an important finding arising from the trials that Prince Hui conducted, and due to the melting point of iron at 1,538°C, almost 50% higher than the melting point of copper at 1,083.4±0.2°C. The same memorial also mentioned a standard assignment of 25 workmen per furnace workshop. According to A General Examination of Qing Dynasty Documents (Qingchao wenxian tongkao 清朝文獻通攷), the major personnel in the workshop would include the headman (lutou 爐頭), the superintendent, the fire watcher (kanhuojiang 看火匠) who controlled the fire temperature, the sand caster (fanshajiang 翻砂匠) who imprinted sand molds with mother coins, and the powder painter (shuahuijiang 刷灰匠) who applied specially mixed powder onto the sand mold to facilitate the smooth flow of molten iron and easy removal of the coin-tree from the mold.

The coin polishing workshop

The coin polishing workshop is located in an enclosed courtyard above the three rows of furnace workshops. It was accessible by a side door next to the Furnace God Temple. The floor plan indicates a total of eight rooms for this process. The iron coins cast in the furnace workshops would be transported here to be cold processed. According to A General Examination of Qing Dynasty Documents, coin polishing required the following specialized processes: cuobian 銼邊: filing away flashings from the outer rim, gunbian 滾邊: mill-finishing the outer rim, moqian 磨錢: polishing the surface of the coin, and xiyan 洗眼: cleaning the inner

---

[4] Zhang's (2014) count of 50 furnace workshops appears to be

incorrect.

[5] Like chuan 串, diao 吊 is a measurement of coin quantities. While the actual number differed according to location and period of time, one diao on average would have 800 cash coins.

Figure 2. A *Xianfeng tongbao* brass coin, Board of Revenue, 41mm x 3mm, showing filing marks on its surface and milling marks on its outer rim, a clean square hole, and traces of dark grey powder on the flan. The powder was painted on to the sand mold to ensure the smooth flow of the molten metal and to facilitate easy removal of the coin (Fang 2008: 144-145, No. 103). The obverse of the coin has the inscription of the reign title and the inscription on the reverse reads *Tianxia taiping* 天下太平 (Peace under heaven). Such pieces were conventionally produced to commemorate the enthronement of a new emperor.

Table 3. A brief summary of documented events, 1854–1859, regarding the formation of the iron coin departments in Beijing and their eventual abolishment

Date	From	About
2 February 1854	Zaiquan	Trial casting of one furnace of iron coins proposed
7 February 1854	Prince Hui	Trial casting performed but failed
12 February 1854	Prince Hui	Trial casting succeeded
15 February 1854	Prince Hui	Coin trees and sand moulds presented to the throne
1 March 1854	Board of Revenue	Trial production in a temporary location. 1-cash and 5-cash pattern coins requested by Office of Military Affairs
3 March 1854	Board of Revenue	Properties for iron coin departments requested
20 March 1854	Prince Hui	100 furnaces, 4 departments and 1 commission proposed
7 May 1854	Prince Hui	Property at Dongtangzi Hutong approved as Eastern Department
18 July 1854	Prince Hui	Property at south of Dong Changan proposed as Southern Department. Property at Jinyu Hutong proposed as Western Department and approved. Property of the Sixth Princess near Jinyu Hutong proposed as Northern Department.
21 July 1854	Yangshi Lei	Floor plan of property at Dongtangzi Hutong drawn up
3 December 1855	Prince Hui	100 furnaces, 4 departments and 1 commission established
3 December 1855	Prince Hui	Property at Binzhan Hutong proposed as warehouse of iron coins
25 December 1855	Prince Hui	Administrative appointments proposed for supervisors and directors of iron coin departments
12 August 1857	Prince Hui	Property at Binzhan Hutong proposed as Middle Department
19 April 1859	Board of Revenue	5 departments and 125 furnaces reported and confirmed. Abolishment of the Middle Department and 25 furnaces proposed
28 July 1859	Prince Hui, Board of Revenue	Abolishment of the iron coin commission and iron coin furnaces at Revenue and Works.

rim of the square hole. Filing traces can be observed on well preserved specimens such as the one in Figure 2 below.

The coin stringing workshop

After the coins had been finished, they were taken to the coin stringing workshop to be counted, threaded onto strings, and transported from the workshop section to the office section. On the floorplan, the coin stringing workshop is located away from the other workshops, in three rooms just below the garden of the office section. Strictly speaking, thus, the coin stringing workshop is in the office section, accessed through a side door from the workshop section and exiting directly into the office section. Once the coins had been placed on strings, they would be carried through the gallery, then through the moon door into the second courtyard, then into the central courtyard, where they would be weighed at the stilyards, counted, recorded and then taken to the stores in the backyard.

The Temple of the Furnace God

At the top left of the workshop section of the floorplan is the Temple of the Furnace God, measuring 10 m by 6 m. It is the largest construction in the workshop section, highlighting its importance in the fire and metal industries. We do not know which idol was worshipped in the temple – perhaps Laozi, who was the central figure in a Ming dynasty Temple of the Furnace God at another site in Beijing (Li 1980: 40). There were probably rituals at the temple when the furnaces were started. Major ceremonies would take place when

there were new coin types and at the start of the New Year, and regular minor ceremonies on the first and fifteenth days of the month (Zhang 2012: 27). Next to the Temple of the Furnace God was an area fitted with stools, which suggests that the temple may have been used as a regular meeting place for discussions by those in the workshop section. A parallel for this can be seen in the trade guilds for those working in iron foundries, who met four times a year on 15 February, 14 June, 15 October, and 23 January (Qiao 1978: 35).

Other rooms

Many of the rooms in the workshop section lining along the southern wall on the floor plan were eating areas. At the upper right of the plan is another eating area. A total of 25 eating rooms or canteens can be counted on the plan, which suggests that each furnace workshop had its own eating area. The back door in the northeast corner was most likely used by foundry workers when they came in the morning and went home in the evening. The narrow passage along the northern wall between the Temple to the Furnace God and the toilets and back door would have allowed for tight security checks when people entered and exited the mint. Against the eastern wall of the premises is a stretch of twenty rooms not annotated on the plan and, together with the one annotated ash shed in the northwest corner, they would represent a perfect match with the 21 ash sheds stated on the floor plan, for the temporary storage of charcoal ashes from the 25 furnaces.

Thus, the floorplan for the workshop section reveals three important and relatively independent stages,

Figure 3. Approximate locations of the five iron coin departments in Beijing, all located to the east of the Forbidden City.

as well as areas, in iron coin production: casting, polishing, and stringing. It is by no means coincidental that coin polishing and coin stringing are located in enclosed areas. The same would apply to the forbidden area found in the central court of the office section. It is therefore evident at this point that access to and exit from these areas were restricted, involving possibly some form of body search.

Part 3: The other departments of iron coins in Beijing

As mentioned earlier, the Department of Iron Coins in Dongtangzi Hutong was the first of the five iron coin mints in Beijng. All five were established on repurposed premises of different properties. The specific architectural features would have varied from department to department, yet the primary functions and arrangements would be common to them all. They would produce iron coins on the same scale, and according to the same protocols and regulations laid out by Prince Hui. The iron coin mints ceased operating in 1859.

Figure 3 shows the approximate locations of the five iron coin departments in Beijing. The Middle Mint, also with 25 furnaces, was added in 1857, but was the first to be abolished in 1859. It is worth noting that Peng Xinwei correctly recorded a total of five iron coin mints in Beijing in his masterful work on Chinese monetary history and mentioned a total of 225 furnace workshops

(Peng [1965] 2007: 617), apparently quoting from a memorial from the Board of Revenue to the throne, dated 19th April 1859 (The First Historic Archives of China 2018). However, there is good reason to suggest that the Board of Revenue may have made a mistake and that the intended number was 125 (not 225), because in the same memorial the Board of Revenue proposed to abolish the Middle Mint in order to reduce the number of furnaces by 25. The association of 25 furnaces per iron coin department is so entrenched in the records that it is difficult to believe the figure of 225. The issue needs to be investigated further.

The directors of the iron coin mints in Beijing

By the time Prince Hui submitted his report to the Emperor on 25 December 1855, he had already set up 100 iron coin furnaces and drafted 54 regulations governing the manufacturing process. In the 25 December 1855 report, he proposed that the administrative structure for the iron coin mints should have four supervisors (*jiandu*監督), two Manchu and two Han, and nominated Sanshou三壽 from the Ministry of Revenue and Detai 德泰 from the Ministry of Justice as the two Manchu supervisors. The four supervisors would be in charge of a total of twenty directors for the five iron coin departments, thus four directors per department, as usual, two Manchu and two Han. This information is vitally important to resolve questions regarding the status of the iron coin department. Zhang (2021) is of the view that the five iron coin departments were

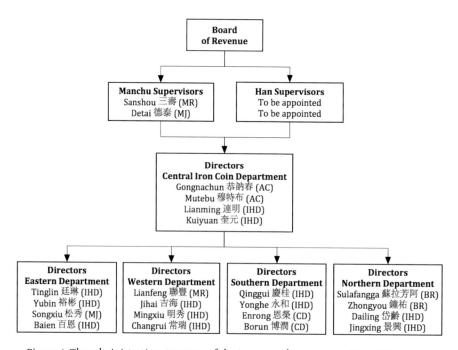

Figure 4. The administrative structure of the iron coin departments. Keys: *AC*: Appeals Commission; *BR*: Board of Revenue; *CD*: Court of Dependencies; *IHD*: Imperial Household Department; *MJ*: Ministry of Justice; *MR*: Ministry of Rites.

administered separately, parallel to the Board of Revenue and Board of Works. However, Prince Hui's report suggests that the administration was handled directly under the Board of Revenue. Prince Hui's report also proposed that in addition to the four coin departments being named according to the cardinal directions, there should be a General Iron Coin Department to coordinate matters relating to iron coins. Like the other departments, the General Department had four directors, but seems to have had more of a liaison role than to have been directly involved in the manufacturing of coins. Further attention is needed to understand the full functions and responsibilities of the general department and its relation to the four supervisors. Prince Hui's proposed appointments are summarized in Figure 4.

The Dongtangzi iron coin department was commonly referred to at the time as the Eastern Department (*Dongju* 東局). The four directors were Tinglin 廷琳, Yubin 裕彬, Baien 百恩, all from the Imperial Household Department (*Neiwufu* 內務府) and Songxiu 松秀 from the Ministry of Justice (*Xingbu* 刑部). The First Director Tinglin, whose full name was Liu Tinglin 劉廷琳, was also known as Accountant Liu (*suanfang Liu* 算房劉). He came from a family of accountants serving in the Imperial Household Department, and worked closely with Yangshi Lei on imperial construction projects. Architect Lei would produce the architectural plans for construction work and Accountant Liu would calculate the construction cost and budget. He was said to have been capable of producing an accurate budget to within ten bricks. According to the Veritable Record of the Qing (*Qingshilu* 清實錄), in 1868, during the Tongzhi reign, Tinglin was still serving in the accounting office of the Fengchenyuan 奉宸院, one of the three commissions in the Imperial Household Department overseeing the maintenance of imperial properties such as palaces, gardens and villas. The appointment of an accounting expert such as Tinglin was probably representative of the calibre of the other appointments, showing the resolution of Prince Hui to execute the iron coin project in a most professional manner to ensure its cost-effective completion.

Part 4: The Zongli Yamen

The production of iron coins was called off completely in 1859 as a result of the acute social and economic problems that the enormous quantities of iron coins had caused. The mint in Dongtangzi Hutong fell into disuse until 1861, when it was repurposed into the Zongli Yamen 總理衙門, literally meaning 'Office in Charge of Affairs Concerning All Nations'. A new gate was added to the left of the main gate seen on the floor plan at the instruction of Prince Gong, younger brother of Emperor Xianfeng, in order to enhance the official appearance of

the property. A plaque above the gate read 'Prosperity for both China and foreign countries (*Zhongwai tifu* 中外提福). Following the Boxer Rebellion in 1901, the Zongli Yamen was replaced with the *Waiwubu* 外務部, or the Ministry of Foreign Affairs, which was ranked above the other six boards in the government, i.e., Ministries of Personnel, Rites, War, Justice, Works, and Revenue. The central court area, according to some sources, was used mainly as the residence of Chinese ambassadors training in preparation for outposts overseas. In 1862, the first year of Emperor Tongzhi's reign, the workshop section of the iron coin department was repurposed as the Tong Wen Guan 同文館. Known in English as the School of Combined Learning, or Imperial College, it was intended to be a training school for interpreters, translators and diplomats of China, where English, French, Russian, German and Japanese were taught. Other courses included mathematics, chemistry, physics, law, history and astrology. The school was suspended in 1900 and, after 1902, became an important founding component of the Imperial University of Peking (now Peking University). According to Chen Wei (2014), the Tong Wen Guan consisted of seven enclosed areas, with the side rooms used as dormitories for students and the main rooms used as classrooms and offices. This account fits well with the findings in this chapter that the workshop section contained several restricted areas. The Tong Wen Guan also housed the earliest museum in China, established in 1874 as a science museum for teaching purposes (Chen 2014).

We are fortunate to have photographic evidence of the property after its repurposing in 1861, taken by, most notably, John Thomson (1837–1921), who was living and working in Beijing. His photographs (Figures 5–9) confirm that the garden area of the former iron coin department was used as the major administrative and reception area of the Zongli Yamen. Figure 9 is a rare photograph showing a professor of mathematics with his students in the Tong Wen Guan converted from the workshop section.

Conclusion

The floorplan of the Department of Iron Coins in Dongtangzi Hutong is a unique document, being the only officially certified floorplan of a mint in Chinese dynastic history. A close study of the floorplan, supplemented with archival records and material objects, now available online, allows us to bring together a variety of evidence to throw light on a unique site in Beijing. This paper has laid open the administrative structure and the workshop arrangement of the mint, revealing previously unknown numismatic features – such as the prominent central position of the stilyards, the restricted area at the back of the office section for storing finished coins and raw materials, and restricted

Figure 5. Prince Gong 奕訢 sitting in the gallery in front of the open hall facing the garden of the Zongli Yamen, formerly the office section. Credit: Peking, Pechili province, China: Yi Xin (Prince Gong). Photograph, 1981, from a negative by John Thomson, 1869. Wellcome Collection [Ref. 19631i]. Public Domain Mark.

Figure 6. Officials Chenglin 成林, Wenxiang 文祥 and Baojun 寶鋆 sitting next to the open hall in front of the curving gallery. The wall of floral tiles can be seen in the background, beyond which is the Tong Wen Guan, the former workshop section of the department of iron coins. Credit: Peking, Pechili province, China. Photograph, 1981, from a negative by John Thomson, 1869. Wellcome Collection [Ref. 19635i]. Public Domain Mark.

Figure 7. Shen Guifen沈桂芬, Dong Xun董恂 and Mao Changxi毛昶熙, high officials of the Zongli Yamen, sitting in front of the open hall next to the curving gallery on the right. The windows of the second, smaller open hall can be seen behind the pillars in the background. Credit: Peking, Pechili province, China. Photograph by John Thomson, 1869. Wellcome Collection [Ref. 19637i]. Public Domain Mark.

Figure 8. Chinese official sitting in what is believed to be the watchtower overlooking the workshop section from the office section of the Dongtangzi Hutong Iron Coin Department. Credit: China. Photograph, 1981, from a negative by John Thomson, 1869. Wellcome Collection [Ref. 19550i]. Public Domain Mark.

Figure 9. Li Shan-lan李善兰 (1810–1882), professor of mathematics, and his pupils in Tong Wen Guan, possibly in front of the coin polishing workshop. Credit: Wellcome Collection. Public Domain Mark.

areas within the workshop section for separate and yet related coin minting tasks. For the first time, we know who served as directors in this important new enterprise, where they worked in the mint and how they monitored the daily running of coin-production, observing from the director's office located by the side gate linking the two halves of the property, watching the furnace area from the top of the watch tower, and sleeping in the duty room, if necessary. The floorplan also revealed the size of each furnace workshop, the separated areas of coin polishing and coin stringing, and location of the Temple of the Furnace God, temple rituals being a regular practice at foundries.

Equally importantly, we have seen how the personal property of Saishangga at Dongtangzi Hutong in Beijing witnessed a series of changes, social, economic and ideological, that fundamentally shook the power base of the Qing dynasty. Its confiscation during the Taiping uprising, its conversion to an iron coin department as a means of monetary reform to solve fiscal problems facing the empire, the re-conversion of the office area into the Zongli Yamen as a pre-cursory ministry of

foreign affairs and the re-conversion of the workshop area into an imperial college to train personnel in contemporary knowledge and the art of diplomacy – these are all reminiscent of the inevitable process that eventually saw the downfall of the empire and the foundation of the republic. Akin to the monetary reforms conducted by Wang Mang王莽 in the Xin Dynasty (*Xinchao*新朝; CE 9–23) and Huizong 徽宗 in the Song Dynasty (*Songchao*宋朝; CE 960–1127), both followed by the downfall of the emperors, the issuance of iron coins during the Xianfeng reign (CE 1850–1861) in the mid-nineteenth century is a fitting symbolic representation of the turbulent changes that subsequently took place in China. Amongst these, it is remarkable to think that the emergence of modern diplomacy of China, as a direct consequence of the Second Opium War, started on the grounds of a disused iron coin mint in Beijing.

A small section of this interesting historical relic still stands on Dongtangzi Hutong, closely surrounded by a bustling, busy, fast developing cosmopolitan city, where even the relatively recent past is soon forgotten.

Acknowledgement

I would like to thank Dr Helen Wang, curator of East Asian Coins of the British Museum and first editor of this volume, for reading an earlier draft of this chapter and for her insightful comments.

Bibliography

Chen Wei 陈为. 2014. Beishi Tong Wen Guan bowuguan kaolue 京师同文馆博物馆考略, in *Zhongguo bowuguan* 中国博物馆, 2014.3: 84–89. [A cursory story of the museum of the Tong Wen Guan of the imperial capital, in Museums of China]

Fang, Alex Chengyu 方稱宇. 2008. 中國花錢與傳統文化 / *Chinese Charms: Art, Religion, and Folk Belief*. Beijing: The Commercial Press.

Kissinger, H.A. 2011. *On China*. New York: Penguin Press.

Li Hua 李华. 1980. *Ming Qing yilai Beijing gongshang huiguan beike xuanbian* 明清以来北京工商会馆碑刻选编. Beijing: Wenwu chubanshe. [A selection of inscriptions on stone tablets in industrial and commercial guild halls in Beijing since the Ming and Qing dynasties]

Peng Xinwei 彭信威. 1965 (2007 edition). *Zhongguo huobi shi* 中國貨幣史. Shanghai Renmin chubanshe. [A Monetary History of China]

Project Yangshifang of the Palace Museum = Gugong bowuyuan Yangshifang ketizu 故宫博物院样式房课题组. 2001. Gugong bowuyuan cang Qingdai Yangshifang tuwen dang'an shulue 故宫博物院藏清代样式房图文档案述略, *Gugong bowuyuan yuankan* 故宫博物院院刊2001.2(94):60–66. [A brief description of the Yangshi Lei architectural designs of the Qing Dynasty in the collection of the Palace Museum, in Journal of the Palace Museum]

Qiao Zhiqiang 乔志强. 1978. *Shanxi zhitie shi* 山西制铁史. Taiyuan: Shanxi renmin chubanshe. [A history of iron foundries in Shanxi]

The First Historic Archives of China = Zhongguo diyi lishi dang'anguan 中国第一历史档案馆. 2018. Xianfeng nianjian Beijing tieqianju xing zhu tieqian dang'an 咸丰年间北京铁钱局行铸铁钱档案, *Lishi dang'an* 历史档案 2018.1:43–67. [Archival documentations of the department of iron coins in Beijing during the Xianfeng reign]

Xie Qikun谢启昆. 1800 (1988 edition). Fiscal Administration经政略. Volume 178 in *General Gazetteer of Guangxi*广西通志 compiled by Xie Qikun in ca. 1800. Guangxi People's Press广西人民出版社.

Zhang Anhao 张安昊. 2021. Qing chao bao quan ju jigou yange kao 清朝宝泉局机构沿革新考, *Gugong bowuyuan kan* 故宫博物院院刊 2021.3 (227):67–79. [A new investigation about the administrative structure of the Board of Revenue of the Qing dynasty, in Journal of the Palace Museum]

Zhang Huoding 张或定 and Zhang Shaofeng 张哨峰. 2002. Tianjin chutu daliang tieqian yu Xianfen jiunian jidiao Baofuju tieqian fu Jin youguan天津出土大量铁钱与咸丰九年急调宝福局铁钱赴津有关, Xian jinrong西安金融2002.7:61–62. [The large quantities of iron coins unearthed in Tianjin are related to the Fujian Mint iron coins urgently summoned to Tianjin in the Nineth Year of Xianfeng, in Xian Finance]

Zhang Lihui 张礼惠. 2012.Qingdai Zezhou gongshangye jingji yanjiu 清代泽州府工商业经济研究. MA thesis, Normal University of Shaanxi. [Research on the economics of the manufacturing and commercial industries of Zezhou prefecture in the Qing dynasty]

Zhang Zhaoping 张兆平. 2014. Yangshi Lei 'Dongtangzi Hutong tieqianju dipan xidi' de wenxian jiazhi 样式雷《东堂子胡同钱局地盘画样细底》的文献价值, *Ming Qing luncong* 2014.13:297–303. [The documentary value of the floorplan of the Department of Iron Coins in Dongtangzi Hutong', Ming Qing Discussions]

The Canton Ransom –
What Happened to the Six Million Dollars of Silver?

Helen Wang

During the First Anglo-Chinese War, also known as the First Opium War (1839–1842), two major events resulted in significant quantities of silver being demanded by the British from China. The first was the Canton Ransom in May 1841, when, in response to Lin Zexu's burning of opium in 1839, British troops attacked Canton (Guangdong) and Charles Elliot (1801–1875), Superintendent of Trade at Canton, demanded six million dollars of silver as one of the conditions for ending hostilities. The second was the Treaty of Nanjing, in May 1842, when China agreed to pay Britain 21 million dollars of silver. Known as the Canton ransom and Chinese indemnity, respectively, these terms are sometimes used interchangeably. The events are well-known and have been discussed by historians elsewhere (eg Platt 2018). In this paper, I will focus on the physical aspects of the Canton Ransom (1841), and attempt to trace how the silver was paid, in which forms it was paid (sycee [bullion/ingots/specie], coin, remittance notes), how it was transported, what the British did with it, and what, if anything, survives. Although this is still work in progress, the overall narrative presents for the first time the material culture of the Canton Ransom and its journey to the west.

According to the terms of the agreement set forth by Elliot in May 1841, six million dollars in silver were to be paid within the week: one million to be paid before sunset on 27 May 1841, the entirety to be paid within seven days. Non-payment would raise that amount to seven million after seven days, eight million after 14 days and nine million after 20 days (Elliot 1841: 345–346).

Six million dollars were paid within the week. Four million in sycee were paid by the authorities in Canton on 29 March, and the remaining two million was paid by the hong merchants [who were licensed by the Chinese government to trade with foreigners] (Table 1) (Bingham 1843: 168).

In addition to this, Bingham (1843:168) notes an indemnity to British merchants and government for property destroyed (628,372 dollars) and an indemnity to foreigners, including the value of the Bilbaino, a Spanish vessel (41,243 dollars), which raised the total to 6,669,615 dollars.

Four million dollars were loaded on to HMS Modeste, a British Royal Navy corvette,[1] on 29 May (*Chinese Repository* X, 346–347). As Elliot estimated that 6 million dollars in silver could weigh about 150 tons, we can reckon on those 4 million dollars weighing about 100 tons. It is probably also reasonable to suppose that the silver was already packed in boxes for convenience of storage and transport. In the British Museum collection there are parts of a box (or boxes) that were used to transport silver from China to England in 1843 (and thus part of the Chinese Indemnity, not the Canton Ransom). Sir James Everard Home, 2nd Baronet (1798–1853), an officer in the British Royal Navy, who captained the HMS North Star at Canton in 1841–1842, donated several pieces from China to the British Museum, which were displayed to the public in the Ethnographical Room from 1848 (perhaps earlier), including on Shelf 2 'A wooden trunk, in which the Sycee silver of the Chinese ransom money was transported to England' (Synopsis 53, 1848: 7). The trunk remained on display for at least nine years (Synopsis 63, 1856: 268), and possibly longer. Two parts have survived, possibly from different boxes, and both measure 106 × 18 × 5 cm (length × width × depth) (Figures1-2).

The painted inscription on one piece reads 'One of the wooden trunks which contained the ransom silver paid by the Chinese 1843. Pres[ented] by Sir Everard Home. Bar. R. N.' Roughly in the middle of the other piece is 'Sir E. Home' written in black, with a letter H (or possibly the Chinese character *gong* 工) above it above. Incised at the top on the left we can read *xin san shi* 心三十 [Xin 30] and on the right *xin shi* 心十 [Xin 10], probably a serial number, which would indicate that the boxes of sycee were labelled. There are also some numerals written in black at the bottom of the piece on the left: perhaps 354/ 46?

Cribb published three photographs showing 50-ounce (50-tael) sycee packed in boxes at the Shanghai

Acknowledgements: I am indebted to Joe Cribb, Sushma Jansari and Jessica Harrison-Hall at the British Museum, to Graham Dyer and Sarah Tyley at the Royal Mint, and Clare Baxter and Lisa Little at Alnwick Castle for their help and suggestions.
[1] There is a plan of the Modeste, 1838, in the collection of the National Maritime Museum, Greenwich [ZAZ4189] https://www.rmg.co.uk/collections/objects/rmgc-object-83980 (accessed 10 Oct 2022)

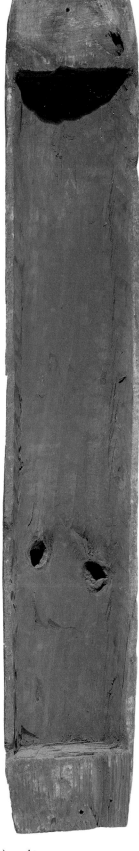

Figure 1. Box parts (outsides) used to carry sycee.
BM As 1847,0827.23.a-b, presented by James Everard Home.
© Trustees of the British Museum.

Figure 2. Box parts (insides) used to carry sycee.
BM As 1847,0827.23.a-b, presented by James Everard Home.
© Trustees of the British Museum.

Table 1.

Source	Payment (dollars)
Howqua	820,000
Pwankequa	260,000
Samqua, Saoqua, Footae and Gowqua, each 70,000 dollars	280,000
Mowqua, Kingqua, Mingqua and Punhoyqua, each 15,000 dollars	60,000
Cash in the consoo [公所] treasury, being taxes upon the foreign trade, and intended to pay the debt of bankrupt hong merchants	380,000
Samqua, Saoqua, Footse and Gowqua, each gave obligations for 50,000 dollars, to be reimbursed from the first surplus in the consoo funds, or offset against any duties they may owe to the consoo	200,000
TOTAL	2,000,000

Branch of the Chartered Bank of India, Australia and China (Cribb 1992: 30, fig. 4, and 32, fig. 6, after White [1920], opposite 266 and 274, respectively); and at the Hongkong and Shanghai Banking Corporation, 1936 (37, fig. 11). Although decades later than the Canton Ransom, the photos show sixty 50-ounce ingots per box (approximately 110 kg per box). This seems to be a norm, at least in the 1920s and 1930s, as Young (1931: 683) also describes 50-tael ingots packed 60 to the box, thus 3000 per box, and Sigler (1943: 25) describes 50-tael ingots packed 50-60 to the box, noting that there was little risk of theft as the boxes were heavy and easily identifiable.

The intention was that 2½ million dollars in sycee would be taken to Calcutta in HMS Calliope, and 1½ million to England in HMS Conway (*Bombay Gazette*, 21 Sept 1841: 2). The decision to ship the silver away from China was met with consternation, if not derision. The *Bombay Gazette* (21 Sept 1841: 2) highlighted three areas of concern. First, the financial cost – 'sycee in the London mint will not give more than 4s. 1d. per dollar, while sycee in China is usually at a premium, ranging from 2 to 7 per cent: on the remittance to England, freight and charges must be added; we have been told the sycee per Conway could now be exchanged here for dollars at a premium of 5 per cent.' Second, the decision to send ships, men and money from China to Calcutta made no sense when Britain would need to call on Calcutta for assistance and supplies in the Eastern Expedition (the Calliope's 32-pounder armament made her one of the most efficient ships in the squadron [*The Evening Chronicle*, 5 Nov 1841: 2]). Third, sending silver to London made even less sense: the sycee in the Calliope would pass through the Calcutta mint and be coined into rupees within two months, while the sycee in the Conway would take five months to reach London.

The tone of the reporter is palpable:

Should this money be carted from Portsmouth to the bank [Bank of England] as in the days of galleons – the people will not fail to be *moved* to enquire, whence is it, how obtained, and at what *cost* of money, loss of commerce, and sacrifice of the lives of their countrymen on the shores of China; and if they go into a calculation, they will find that it will cost them more to supply the loss of the gallant men who have miserably perished in this miserable war; and the procession, then, of the Canton ransom on the *railroads* of England will scarcely be regarded by the people of the 19th as similar processions on the *highways* were by those of the 18th century; what, then, except sheer nepotism, can be the motive of sending this bullion to London, and further weakening the expeditionary force of the Calliope to Calcutta; in the name of common sense, of finance, of the rule of three, of the rule of thumb, – what does the crown of England want of 1½ million of dollars wrung from the hong merchants and others of Canton? – for they have been assessed by the local government for the sum – it has not been supplied from either the imperial or local coffers. (*Bombay Gazette*, 21 Sept 1841: 2)

There is some confusion in contemporary newspaper accounts as to which ships actually carried the silver. One source, originating on 20 July and published in newspapers across the UK and Ireland in early October, stated that HMS Nimrod had been expected to carry 5 million dollars to Calcutta, leaving China on 15 June (eg *London Evening Standard*, 7 Oct 1841; *Dublin Morning Register*, 9 Oct 1841: 2). Others correctly state that the silver was shipped in the Calliope to Calcutta and in the Conway to London in July (eg *Morning Post*, 5 Nov 1841: 3).

Criticism of the whole situation extended to the silver itself: 'Of the sum actually paid to the Superintendent, it was the general impression at Macao that a large quantity of the sycee was so mixed with alloy as to be of little value' (*The Sun*, London, 8 Oct 1841: 6).

Figure 3. Medal made from gold extracted from Chinese sycee from the Canton Ransom. BM M.6467. © Trustees of the British Museum.

Figure 4. Medal made from gold extracted from Chinese sycee from the Canton Ransom, made into a pendant. BM 1940,0602.1, presented by Mrs Hedley Calvert. © Trustees of the British Museum

HMS Calliope, captained by Augustus Leopold Kuper (1809–1885), set sail on 6 July, carrying between 2 and 2½ million dollars,[2] and arrived in Calcutta on 5 August (*Evening Chronicle*, 5 Nov 1841: 2) or 5 September (*Morning Chronicle*, 5 Nov 1841: 2). There was a theft in

Calcutta: some silver sycee was reported missing, and two European seamen were seen trying to sell it at 10 pm on 24 September (*Star*, 25 Sept 1841, quoted in *Bombay Gazette*, 8 Oct 1841: 2).

HMS Conway, captained by Charles Ramsay Drinkwater Bethune (1802–1884) set sail for England on 17 July, with 1½ million Spanish dollars in sycee, and 500,000 Spanish dollars in coin, the remainder having been

---

[2] *The Chinese Repository* XI: 582-583, says 2 million. *The Bombay Gazette*, 20 Sept 1841says (2.5 million). *The Bombay Gazette* also says The Calliope left China on the 9th ultimo.

invested in Navy and Treasury Bills (*Chinese Repository* XI: 582–583; *Bombay Gazetteer*, 20 Sept 1841). The cost of transmitting the silver to England in specie, instead of the usual remittance, besides the value of the vessel's services, was said to amount to £40,000 (*The Evening Chronicle*, 5 Nov 1841: 2).

The Conway, carrying 2 million dollars, arrived in Portsmouth on 1 January 1842 (*The Times*, 5 Jan 1843: 5), and its cargo of 60 tons of silver, approximately valued at £550,000 sterling, was delivered to the Royal Mint, London on 10 January 1842 (*The Illustrated London News*, 31 Dec 1842). 'There is no precedent for such a large amount of sycee silver being received into this country' reported the *Morning Advertiser* (10 Jan 1842: 3), adding that it would reach the Bank of England the following week, and that 'the value of this, the favourite and much-cherished metal of the Celestial government, is intrinsically greater than that of British silver.'

In fact, it was known that Chinese silver often contained small amounts of gold. John Robert Morrison (1814–1843) wrote in his *A Commercial Guide to China*: 'When assayed at London, the sycee is frequently found to contain a small admixture of gold' (Morrison 1834: 95). Charles Toogood Downing (1811-1873), a surgeon working in China in the 1830s, also mentioned this: 'The exportation of sycee silver is also considered a serious misfortune by the government. This bullion consists of battered dollars and some portion of native metal, melted together and cast into ingots of a convenient size. These are usually found, upon examination in England, to contain a portion of gold of which the Chinese are not aware' (Downing 1838, vol. 3: 183, cited in *Witness* [Edinburgh] 25 Mar 1840).

Some gold was indeed extracted from the Chinese silver, and a small number of gold medals were made at the Mint in March 1842 to commemorate the event (Bowker 1964; Brown 1987: 75, no. 2070; British Museum M.6467; CNG Sale 103, lot 1252; Baldwins 36, lot 159; Münzgalerie München auction, 26 Feb 1983, lot 624).

The medals measure 16–16.5 mm in diameter, weigh 1.55 g, and have the inscription: 'This gold/discovered in/sycee silver/the prize of British/arms in China/was extracted/at H.M. Mint/March/ 1842' and on the reverse, 'The Rt. Hon/W. Gladstone/master/by a process first/applied to the public/service and to the/benefit of British/commerce under/the Rt. Hon./J.C. Herries/1829.' The inscription names William Ewart Gladstone (1809–1898), Master of the Mint from 1841–1845,[3] and John Charles Herries (1778–1855), Master of the Mint from 1828 to 1830.

The process of extracting gold from silver ('the sulphuric acid process') had been established in France in 1802. Gilbert Mathieson (1803–1854),[4] formerly a clerk in the Colonial Audit office, had become Melter (in charge of the Refinery) at the Mint in 1828, and the following year had been allowed by Herries, then Master of the Mint, 'to experiment in a private capacity whilst reserving an option for the government should the experiments be successful' (Brown 1987: no. 2070; Hansard 1843: Sycee Silver). The process was effective, but not commercial, and the gold medals were presumably made as mementoes by Mathieson, who was still working at the Mint when the Chinese silver arrived in 1842.

Questions continued to be asked about the silver. Joseph Hume (1777–1855), MP for Montrose District of Burghs requested details of the silver imported in HMS Conway, 'to ascertain whether any losses resulted to the country from the forwarding of the same to the Mint' (*Morning Advertiser*, 4 Feb 1843). 'It was important to have the result of this first operation; because the whole 20,000,000 dollars might be subjected to the same operation' (Hansard 3 Feb 1843, vol. 66: 189–190).

Hume received a full response:

> Sycee Silver. A parliamentary paper delivered this morning, shows that the quantity of silver imported from China in her Majesty's ship Conway in January, 1842, amounted to 2,001,200 dollars, weighing 143,639 lb. 2 oz. 5 dwt. gross, the standard weight of which was 148,526 lb. 4 oz. 2 dwt. This, sold from the Mint, realised 440,729 l. 10s. 6d., at the respective prices of 59½ d., 59⅜ d., and 59¼ d. per ounce. There was no charge for melting the silver, Mr Mathison [sic], the Mint refiner, under the sanction of the Treasury, having undertaken to defray all expenses, in consideration of being allowed 3½ grains of gold (less 10 per cent.) on every pound weight gross of silver. The gross weight of gold extracted therefrom was 2530 oz. 1 dwt. 17 gr.; allowance to Mr Mathison [sic], after deducting 10 per cent., 940 oz. 13 dwt. 9 gr., leaving 1589 oz. 8 dwt. 8 gr., gross, which produced in standard weight 1729 oz. 7 dwt. 21 gr. The expense of transporting the treasure from Portsmouth to the Mint, was 200 l. 15 s. 8 d. Gratuities to Mint officers, clerks, porters, &c., for extra exertions, 466 l. 15 s. 8d. The amount which the gold produced, at 3 l. 17 s.9 d. per oz., was 6723 l. 0 s.

---

[3] Gladstone strongly opposed the Opium Wars with China; see his speech, 8 April 1840, to Parliament https://api.parliament.uk/historic-hansard/commons/1840/apr/08/war-with-china-adjourned-debate

[4] Gilbert Farquhar Graeme Mathieson had left Oxford without a degree, and after working for a while in the opium trade, which he abandoned on moral grounds, went on to become private secretary to the Chancellor of the Exchequer and finally Secretary to the Mint (Blair 2004: 27).

Figure 5 & 6. The silver ingot at Alnwick Castle. Collection of the Duke of Northumberland. Reproduced with permission.

4d. By sending the silver to the Mint, instead of selling it in the market, at the estimated price of 59¾ d. per oz., the Mint obtained a profit of 654 l. 12 s. 9d (*London Evening Standard*, 7 March 1843).

Today, no silver survives from the Canton Ransom in either the Royal Mint or Bank of England collections.[5] However, there is one ingot, now in the collection of the Duke of Northumberland at Alnwick Castle [object no. DNC 42194], which may have arrived in England on the HMS Conway in January 1842.

The ingot sits on a custom-made wooden mount, with a metal plaque on the side inscribed *Canton Ransom*. This in itself is not sufficient to prove its provenance, and there are no archival materials associated with this piece, so we must examine the evidence carefully.

The shape of the ingot and the arrangement of the inscription identify it as a Guangdong Province Square Trough Ingot (*Guangdong fang caoding* 廣東方槽錠) (Cribb 1992: 213–216). The inscription is in three parts, arranged as Cribb Type LVIIIB: *Weng yuan* 翁源 at the top, *Dao guang er shi nian* 道光二十年 [Daoguang 20th year] in the right hand column, *er yue Jun yu* 二月均裕 [2nd month, Junyu] in the left hand column, which would suggest it was cast in March–April 1840 by the Junyu Bank for the Wengyuan Bank. However, it differs

from Cribb Type LVIIIB in that Wengyuan is the name of a county (*xian* 縣) in Guangdong province.

The object record notes the weight as 10 ounces, and the dimensions as 70 × 70 × 32 mm (length × width × height). These measurements are for the ingot and wooden mount combined. The weight refers to the Chinese ounce (or *tael*, in Chinese: *liang* 兩) on the Guangdong Customs Scale, where the ounce was about 37.7 g. The weight of the ingot itself is 387 g, and the measurements of the ingot without the stand are 58 × 47 × 27 mm, which matches the LXVIIIB specimens recorded by Cribb (1992: 216).

A 10-ounce ingot made for use in Guangdong and dated March–April 1840 could certainly have been among the sycee silver from the Canton Ransom.

The only person known to have examined and recorded inscriptions on silver ingots from the Canton Ransom is Samuel Birch (1813–1885), curator at the British Museum, who presented a paper on 'Sycee Silver' to the Royal Numismatic Society on 23 January 1845 (Birch 1845: 173–179). In the Proceedings of the same volume (1845: 5) his presentation was recorded as 'a description of the Sycee silver received from the Chinese government, in payment of the indemnity due to this country,' however, in the published account, Birch writes (173–174) about 'an examination [of several ingots] which I made some time since, on the occasion of the transfer of part of the Chinese ransom to Her Majesty's Mint,' (173–174). Birch is better known as an Egyptologist, but also knew Chinese: one of his

---

[5] Cribb (1992: #550) records a round silver ingot from Zhejiang, with an English inscription 'Sycee silver from China, 1842', from a collection from the USA, sold at Glendining's, London, 30 June 1965. Its current location is unknown.

first tasks on joining the British Museum was to put the Chinese coins in order, and he continued to translate from Chinese until at least the 1870s (Budge 1901). As Birch refers to the 'Chinese ransom' and examined the ingots 'some time since', perhaps we can assume that he was referring to the Canton Ransom of 1841.

In the early 1840s there were probably no Chinese silver ingots in the British Museum (the Eduard Kann Collection was acquired in 1978, during Joe Cribb's curatorship, and the first catalogue of sycee in English, by Cribb, was published in 1992. Birch writes that his references for studying the ingots were 'Robert Morrison's publication' (actually John Robert Morrison's *A Commercial Guide to China* [1834]) and a communication (letter?) from Mr Reeves (probably John Reeves, 1774–1856, tea inspector in Canton, who was in China from 1812 to 1831).

In a very brief description of sycee, Morrison (1834: 94–95) wrote that they were stamped with the issuer's mark, and date, came in various forms and weights, the most common weight being 10 taels each. He described the five most current kinds of sycee in Guangdong province as follows:

1. 関餉 *Kwan-heäng* [pinyin: *guanxiang*] the hoppo's duties, or the silver which is forwarded to the Imperial treasury at Peking. This is always of 97 to 99 touch. On all the imperial duties, a certain percentage is levied, for the purpose of turning them into sycee of this high standard,

and of conveying them to Peking, without any loss in the full amount. This percentage is, however, increased by the hoppo to an amount far exceeding what is requisite, that he may be enabled to retain the remainder for himself and his dependents.

2. 藩庫 Fan koo or fan foo [pinyin: *fanku*], – the treasurer's receipts, or that in which the land-tax is paid. This is also of a high standard, but inferior to that of the hoppo's duties, and being intended for use in the province, not for conveyance to Peking, no percentage is levied on the taxes which are paid in it.

3. 元寶 *Yuen paou* or *une po* [pinyin: *yuanbao*], literally, chief in value. This kind is usually imported from Soochow in large pieces of fifty taels each. It does not appear to belong to any particular government tax.

4. 鹽餉 *Yen*, or *eem, heang* [pinyin; *yanxiang*], salt duties. It is difficult to account for these being of so low a standard, the salt trade being entirely a government monopoly. This class is inferior only, to –

5. 勿汰 *Wuh-tae* or *mut-tae* [pinyin: *wutai*], the name of which, signifying 'uncleansed' or 'unpurified', designates it as the worst of all.

Birch recorded that 'the Chinese Canton ransom contained a large proportion of pieces of the second kind, or land-tax, many of them of a period long past. The following list will, however, exhibit the actual state of the ransom' (Birch 1845: 176). Birch must

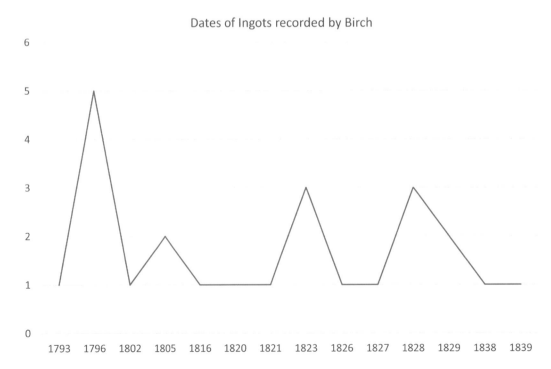

Figure 7. Dates of Ingots recorded by Birch

SYCEE SILVER.

Figure 8. Illustration from *The Illustrated London News* on 8 March 1845 © Illustrated London News/Mary Evans Picture Library

have taken notes during his visit to the Mint as he recorded the inscriptions he was able to read, and published a transliteration and translation of them. Birch paraphrased Morrison, not entirely accurately: '2. Fan hoo, land-tax. High standard but less than the Hoppoo. These two are government duties, and are probably issued by the local governments for salaries' – and quotes Reeves: '[he] states, in illustration of a particular ingot, that the duties are all paid at Canton in pieces of this exact weight (ten taels); and the families of the payers, etc., are always held responsible for its purity. The marks are put on by the refiner (not the government), who is employed by the payer of the duties. They are paid into the treasury in the present state. Probably again re-issued in part for the payment of salaries... Every piece must be made to the *exact* weight of ten taels; hence you will see on the under side of it, whence particles have been drilled out.' (Birch 1845: 176)

Birch noted the inscriptions of 40 ingots in total. His list is not easy to follow but can be reconstructed to some extent (see Appendix). It is clear that the Alnwick Castle ingot is not on the list, although the place name Wengyuan is seen on one ingot (G.5).

However, even from this small sample of 40 ingots (plus some smaller pieces, for which details are not given), we can draw some useful conclusions. First, the ingots are grouped A to R (B is missing), so it is probably safe to assume that the ingots were selected and grouped visually, by size and shape, and by the arrangement and clarity of the inscription. Although Birch implies the majority were 10-ounce ingots, there are three 50-ounce ingots (groups C and D), and some smaller

pieces at the end, which may not have been 10 ounces. Birch appears to have made no attempt to weigh or measure the ingots he saw.

Second, Birch was able to read the date on 25 pieces. The 1430 date (E.1) seems unlikely, and the format of the inscription suggests a place name (順德Shunde) rather than a reign period. The other dated pieces range from 1793 to 1839, a period of 47 years (see Figure 7). This confirms that sycee in China remained in use or storage for several decades.

Third, for the most part, Birch's identifications seem sound, although some aspects of his report are surprisingly careless given that he was at the time of the article's publication on the staff of the British Museum, a Member of Council of the Royal Numismatic Society, and a Fellow of the Society of Antiquaries. For example, he appears to have confused a place name with a reign period (E.1), did not mention the weights and dimensions of the ingots he saw, and paraphrased John Robert Morrison's *A Guide to Commercial China* (1834) referring to his father Robert Morrison and omitting the title of the book. In the same printed volume as Birch's list, is a record of the Society's meeting on 28 December 1843, at which Birch showed a Chinese silver award shangpai 賞牌 (Birch 1880a: 15). The record includes a written description and a drawing of the medal. If only Birch had included some illustrations of the silver ingots he saw at the Mint!

There is an intriguing link between Birch and the Alnwick Castle ingot, namely that Birch produced the *Catalogue of the Egyptian Antiquities* at Alnwick Castle in 1880. Is it possible that Birch was given the silver ingot on his visit to the Mint that day? Or that someone at the Mint had kept it as a memento?

Or was the ingot from another source, perhaps an instalment of the Chinese indemnity specified in the Treaty of Nanjing (1842)? This seems unlikely, as *The Military Annual for 1844* (370) tells us that when the first consignment of that indemnity was brought to England by the Modeste, forwarded by the Southampton Railway to the Vauxhall terminus in London, transferred to Messrs Chaplin and Horne's (horse-drawn) wagons and taken to the Mint, the silver was 'in a very dirty condition and will be melted down in the crucibles prepared for the purpose, and sold without delay. The last consignment of Sycee silver from China, the ransom for Canton, was refined; but the process was so expensive to the Government that it will not be repeated, and the silver will be simply melted and sold to the refiners.'

While we cannot be sure how this ingot arrived in England, we do know that it arrived before March 1845, as an illustration of it was published in *The Illustrated London News* on 8 March 1845 (148). [A slightly shorter version of this article with the same illustrations was published in *The People's Illustrated Journal of Arts, Manufacturers, Practical Science, Literature, and Social Economy* XIII, 24 July 1852: 193–196).]

The illustration appears in a two-page article titled 'Bullion Office – Bank of England'. The ingot was drawn accurately at the Bank of England, as the author acknowledges 'the very liberal assistance we have received of W.[illiam] Cotton, Esq., the Governor of the Bank of England, by whose permission we were enabled to make the sketches for our illustrations from life.'

Neither the illustrator nor the author are named. On the second page there is a paragraph on sycee silver, which appears to have been copied from a general reference as it contains inaccuracies that suggest that neither the author nor the people at the Bank of England who hosted this visit could read Chinese and used a generic source, or sources, or confused their notes.

The paragraph reads 'Sycee Silver. With this, as in the specie used by his Celestial Majesty in the payment of the Chinese ransom, the public have become, in name, at least, familiar. Sycee is the colloquial pronunciation of the phrase Se-sze [pinyin: *xisi* 細絲], which strictly means "fine silk", but which is also used to mean "pure silver", intimating that it may be drawn out as fine as silk. The proper Chinese term for it is Wan-yin [pinyin: *wenyin* 紋銀], and the average quality of this silver is "98 touch, 980 fine" or a little above 13 dwts., better than British standard. It contains gold amounting, on an average, to about 12 or 13 grains in the pound

Troy. The ingots or shoes of this silver, are stamped, as shown in the engraving, with the name (top line) of the assayer, "Ung-un" [pinyin: Wengyuan] ; the name and reign of the Emperor (right col.) "Taou Kwang [pinyin: Daoguang], 20th year, 2nd month"; and the words (left col.) "assayed and cast" – the latter term signifying that in quality the silver cast was of the legal fineness.' This interpretation does not match the inscription in the illustration.

Conclusion

Very little remains of the material culture of the Canton Ransom of 1841. There are some small gold medals made at (but not by) the Mint, and probably issued to individuals as mementoes. And there is the silver ingot in the Duke of Northumberland's collection, which is possibly the only silver ingot that remains of the Canton Ransom. There are gaps in my account, and if we can fill those gaps, perhaps we will be able to confirm this.

References

Bingham, J.E. 1843. *Narrative of the Expedition to China from the Commencement of the War to its Termination in 1842 with sketches of the manners and customs of that singular and hitherto almost unknown country*, 2 vols. London. [2nd edition, with additions]

Birch, S. 1845. Sycee Silver, *The Numismatic Chronicle and Journal of the Numismatic Society*, vol. 7: 173–179. http://www.jstor.org/stable/42686139. Accessed 10 Oct. 2022.

Birch, S. 1880 *Catalogue of Egyptian Antiquities at Alnwick Castle*. London.

Blair, K. 2004. *John Keble in Context*. London. [She cites James Pereiro, 'Tractarian and National Education (1838–1845)' in S. Gilley and V.A. McClelland (eds), *Victorian Churches and Churchmen. Essays presented to Vincent Alan McClelland* (Boydell Press (for) The Catholic Record Society, 2005)]

Bowker, H.F. 1964. The William Ewart Gladstone Medalet. *Museum Notes 11 (American Numismatic Society)*: 311–312. http://www.jstor.org/stable/43573747

Brown, L. 1987. *A Catalogue of British Historical Medals 1837-1901. The Reign of Queen Victoria*. London.

Budge, E.A.W. 1901. Samuel Birch (1813–1885), *Oxford Dictionary of Biography*. Oxford. https://doi.org/10.1093/odnb/9780192683120.013.2435

Cribb, J. 1992. *A Catalogue of Sycee in the British Museum: Chinese Currency Ingots, c.1750-1933* (London).

Downing, C.T. 1838. *The Fan-qui in China, in 1836-37*, 3 vols. London.

Elliot 1841. Attack on Canton. *The Chinese Repository* X: 345–346.

Hansard 1843 = Sycee Silver. HC Deb 03 Feb 1843, vol. 66: 189–190. https://api.parliament.uk/historic-hansard/commons/1843/feb/03/sycee-silver)

Military Annual. 1844. Anecdotes. *The Military Annual for 1844*. London.

Morrison, J.R. 1834. *A Chinese Commercial Guide, consisting of a collection of details respecting foreign trade in China*. Canton, China. https://catalog.hathitrust.org/Record/100620973

Platt, S. 2018. *Imperial Twilight. The Opium and the End of China's Last Golden Age*. London.

Proceedings 1845 = Proceedings of the Numismatic Society, Session 1844–5, *The Numismatic Chronicle and Journal of the Numismatic Society*, vol. 8 (1845): 1–20. *JSTOR*, http://www.jstor.org/stable/42682431. Accessed 10 Oct. 2022.

Sigler, P.O. 1943. Sycee Silver. *Numismatic Notes and Monographs 99*: 1–37. New York. http://www.jstor.org/stable/43607287

White, B. 1920. *Silver, Its History and Romance*. London.

Young, J.P. 1931. The Shangai Tael. *The American Economic Review*, 21(4), 682–684. http://www.jstor.org/stable/498

Journals/Newspapers

Bombay Gazette
China Repository
Dublin Morning Register
Evening Chronicle
Illustrated London News
London Evening Standard
Morning Advertiser
Morning Chronicle
Morning Post
People's Illustrated Journal of Arts, Manufacturers, Practical Science, Literature, and Social Economy
The Star
The Sun
Synopsis = Synopsis of the Contents of the British Museum
The Times
Witness

Appendix . The silver ingots examined by Birch, with reconstructed Chinese inscriptions

Birch No.	Birch's description	Reconstructed Chinese	Date
A.1	*Keen lung woo shih pa neen shih yih yue* 11th month of 58th year of Keen lung, AD 1793 R. *Chang ying heen tseang Wangfow* The Chang ying heen; refiner Wangfow	乾隆五十八年十一月 x x 縣匠 x x	1793
A.2	*Kea jing yuen neen sze yue* 4th moon of first year of Kea King, AD 1796 R. *... heen tseang Foo wan* The ... heen; refiner, Foo wan	嘉慶元年四月 ... 縣匠 x x	1796
[A.3]	L. Same. R. *Seang shan heen tseang Wangkae* The Seang shan heen; refiner, Wangkae	嘉慶元年四月 x x縣匠 x x	1796
[A.4]	L. Same. No month. R. *Hwang gan heen tseang Wang jin* The Hwang gan heen; refiner Wang jin	嘉慶元年 x x 縣匠 x x	1796
[A.5]	L. Do. R. *Yang kang heen tseang Wang jin*	嘉慶元年 x x 縣匠x x	1796
[A.6]	L. Do. R. *Seaou shan heen tseang Kang tseu* The Seaou shan heen; refiner, Kang tseu	嘉慶元年 x x 縣匠 x x	1796
C.1	*Fung ching heen* The Fung ching heen L. *Kea king urh shih sze neen woo yue* 5th moon, 24th year of Kea king, AD 1820 R. *Woo shih leang tseang Hwang jin* 50 ounces; refiner Hwang kin	x x 縣 嘉慶二十四年五月 五十兩匠 x x	1820
D.1	*Ta yin heen* The Ta yin heen L. *Taou Kwang tseih neen sze yue* 7th year of Taou Kwang, 4th moon, AD 1827 R. *Woo shih leang tseang Leu mow* 50 ounces, refiner, Leu mow	x x 縣 道光七年四月 五十兩匠 x x	1827

Birch No.	Birch's description	Reconstructed Chinese	Date
D.2	*Taou Kwang yuen neen* 1st year of Taou Kwang, AD 1821 R. Same as No.1, impressed *yu* 'excessive', 'over'	道光元年 五十兩匠 x x 餘	1821
E.1	*Luh neen shih urh yue. Seuen tih Chin hang foo Sin yang heen* 6th year, 12th month of Seuen tih, AD 1430 Ching hang foo, refiner; the Soo yang heen	六年十二月宣德 x x 府 x x 縣 x x 府	1430
F.1	*Hoo foo* city of Hoo foo R. *Kea king yuen neen* 1st year of Kea king, AD 1802 *Kew yue Kwang yuen* 9th moon; refiner, Kwang yuen	x 府 嘉慶元年 九月 x x	1802
F.2	Above. *Paou chang* R. *Kea king tseih neen* 7th year of Kea king L. *San yue, Kwang yuen* 3rd moon; refiner, Kwang yuen	x x 嘉慶七年 三月 x x	1805
F.3	*Ying tih* R. Do. L. *Sze yue Yuen chang ke* 4th moon; refiner, Yuen chang	英德 四月 x x x	1805
F.4	Above, *Sze hwuy* R. Do. L. Do.	四會	1816
F.5	Above. *Lo kwei* R. *Kea king urh shih neen* 20th year of Kea king, AD 1816 L. *San yue Kwang ching* 3rd moon; Kwang ching, refiner	x x 嘉慶二十年 三月 x x	1816
G.1	*Sin hwuy heen* town of Sin hwuy R. *Taou kwang san nian* 3rd moon [sic] of Taou kwang, AD 1823 L. *Shih yue yin tseang Kwang yuen* 10th moon; refiner, Kwang yuen	新會縣 道光三年 十月銀匠 x x	1823
G.2	*Tih too chow* city of Tih too R. *Taou Kwang san neen* 3rd year of Taou kwang, AD 1823 L. *Shih yue yin tseang Hwang tsung mow* 10th moon; silver refiner, Hwang tsung mow	地都州 道光三年 十月銀匠 x x x	1823
G.3	*Chaou king foo* city of Chaou king. R. As preceding. L. *Shih yue yin tseang ... Yuen chang* 10th moon; refiner ... Yuen chang	潮境府 道光三年 十月銀匠 ⋯ x x	1823
G.4	*Tae ke* R. *Taou kwang luh neen* 6th year of Taou kwang, AD 1826 L. *Shih yih yue... ke* 11th moon; refiner...ke	x x 道光六年 十一月 x x	1826
G.5	*Ung yuen heen* Town of Ung yuen R. *Taou kwang pa neen* 8th year of Taou kwang, AD 1828 L. *Ching yue yin tseang kwang yuen* 1st moon; refiner, Kwang yuen	翁源縣 道光八年 正月銀匠 x x	1828
G.6	*King chow fu* City of King chow R. *Taou kwang pa neen* 8th year of Taou kwang, AD 1828 L. *Woo yue yin tseang Keang Kwang yuen* 5th moon; silver refiner, Keang Kwang yuen	x x 府 道光八年 五月銀匠	1828

Birch No.	Birch's description	Reconstructed Chinese	Date
G.7	*Sin hing heen* Town of Sin hing R. *Taou kwang pa neen* 8th year of Taou kwang, AD 1828	新興县 道光八年	1828
G.8	*Tae ke* Tae ke R. *Taou kwang kew neen* 9th year of Taou kwang, 1829 L. *Woo yue Ping tsoo ke* 5th moon; Ping tsoo ke, refiner	x x 道光九年 五月 x x x	1829
G.9	*Ho ping heen* Town of Hoping R. As before L. *Urh yue yin tseang Ping le chin* 2nd moon; silver refiner, Ping le chin	和平縣 道光九年 二月銀匠 x x x	1829
G.10	*Ta poo heen* Town of Ta poo R. *Taou kwang shih pa neen* 18th year of Taou kwang, AD 1838 L. *Sze yue yin tseang Keang kwang yuen* 4th moon; silver refiner, Kwang yuen, or Keang kwang yuen	大埔縣 道光十八年 四月銀匠 [x] x x	1838
G.11	*Tae ping kwan* The Tae ping barrier R. *Taou kwang shih kew neen* 19th year of Taou kwang, AD 1839 L. *Ta shun hao uke* Ta shun (refiners') firm	太平関 道光十九年 大順號 x	1839
H.1	*Chang shing*, refiner, or firm's name		
H.2	*Chang shing*, refiner, or firm's name		
H.3	*Chang shing* refiner, or firm's name		
I	*Ta shun,* Ta shun (name of a firm)	大順	
K	*Hoo yun, Nan mow,* (name of a firm)		
L	*Kwang ... chen ke,* Kwang ... chen, refiner		
M	Above, *Tae ho* San sin, impressed Fan (foreign)	x x x x / 番	
N	*Sin gan* probably town of Sin gan, near Canton R. Below *Tong fow*	新岗 x x	
O	*Fuh tsing heen* Town of Fuh tsing R. *Shih neen shih yue Lin yung* 10th year, 10th moon (name of a firm)	x x 縣 十年十月 x x	
P	Above, *Kaou* *Shih urh yue* 12th moon *Wan ho* Name of a firm	x 十二月 x x	
Q	*Sze kwan heen* Town of Sze kwan R. L. *Kew neen* 9th year	x x 縣 九年	
R.1	*Wan ho haou* Firm of Wan ho	x x 號	
R.2	Sin ting	x x	
R.3	Wan tsuh	x x	
R.4	Yuen paou, tseang pe yuen Refiner, Pe yuen	元寶 匠 x x	
Also	Along with these were some smaller pieces		

A Hoard of Chinese Coins Found in Turkey

François Thierry

For many years Joe Cribb has published, in *Coin Hoards* and elsewhere, data about Chinese coins unearthed outside of China, mainly in Malaysia, Indonesia, Thailand, Sri Lanka, India, Tanzania, and some rare finds in the Middle East (Cribb 1977–1985; Cribb and Potts (1996); Cribb and K.K. Rao (1999–2000). I can now add to his file a small, previously unpublished, hoard that was discovered in Turkey. In the spring of 1986, during agricultural work, a farmer discovered a small deposit of Chinese cash near the village of Ortahisar, in Ürgüp canton, Nevşehir. These soon found their way to the stall of a second-hand dealer at the tourist site of Göreme. The group comprised six copper coins of the Dezong Emperor, Guang Xu 光緒 era (1875–1908).[1]

Five coins were of the same type (figures 1 to 5) with a Chinese inscription on the obverse, and an inscription in Chinese and Manchu script on the reverse. The obverse inscription read *Guang Xu tongbao* 光緒通寶 (Circulating coin of [the] Guangxu [era]). The reverse inscription read top-bottom in Chinese *Xin shi* 新十 (Xin[jiang], [worth] 10), and left-right in Manchu script *boo sin*, transcribing the Chinese *bao Xin* (Mint of Xin[jiang]) (Zhu and Zhu 1991: 159–160; Mu Yuan 1994: 127, no. 35). Xinjiang 新疆 (New Territory) is the name given by the Chinese to Eastern Turkestan and Chinese Turkestan. The number 10 gives the exchange value of this coin, expressed in the legal currency (*zhiqian* 制錢) in brass coins.

The sixth coin is of a different type (figure 6). It has the same obverse inscription, but a different reverse: top-bottom in Chinese *Ku shi* 庫十 (Ku[ça], [value] 10), and left-right in Manchu script *boo iuwan*, a transcription of the Chinese *bao yuan*, "Mint [of] the Ministry of Works" (compare Zhu and Zhu 1991: 159–160; Mu Yuan 1994: 127, no. 35).

According to the *Xinjiang tuzhi* 新疆圖志, following the reforms of Liu Jintang 劉錦棠, coins with the inscription *Ku shi* 庫十 on the reverse were cast from the 8th month of the 11th year of the Guang Xu era (September 1885) in the Kuça (Kucha) workshop, which closed in the winter of 1886 (Zhu and Zhu 1991: 43–44, 156, 159). The deposit did not contain a single coin of the type *Xin shi boo chiowan* (*bao quan* 寶泉, the workshop

under the Ministry of Finance) that were cast as soon as the provincial workshop opened in Urumçi (Dihua), in the 7th month of the 12th year of the Guang Xu era (August 1886). What is interesting about this hoard is, on the one hand, the very low value of the coins, and on the other hand, the fact that these coins do not belong to the circulating currency of the late Ottoman Empire.

It should be noted that the composition of this deposit, as far as the date of the coins is concerned, is very similar to one discovered at Tarsus-Gözlükule (Esenbel 2005: 173–175), at least as far as we know, because the identifications of those coins need to be checked. The author says 'the 31 bronze coins were minted between the years 1875–1908 during the reign of the Qing Emperor Guangxu whose name is inscribed on one side of the coin'. However, of the five coins illustrated, three are not in the name of Guang Xu: two are in the name of Qian Long, and one is in the name of Tong Zhi. It would be necessary to correct the identifications of the five coins in the plate (p.175) :

Figure 1 Obverse: *Tong Zhi tongbao* 同治通寶 (circulating coin of [the] Tong Zhi [reign period]). Rev: at the top is the Chinese character *Ku* 庫, for Kuça, to the right is *Kuça* کوحا in Uyghur, and to the left is *Kuça* in Manchu. Although this coin has the reign period Tong Zhi of the Emperor Muzong (1862–1874), it was a supplementary issue cast at the workshop in Kuça in 1885. (Zhu and Zhu 1991: no. 482).

Figure 2 Obverse: *Guang Xu tongbao* 光緒通寶 (circulating coin of [the] Guang Xu [reign period]). Rev: top-bottom in Chinese, *Xin shi* 新十 (Xin[jiang], [value] 10), and left-right in Manchu script, *boo chiowan*, a transcription of the Chinese *bao quan* (Mint [of the] Board of Revenue). This coin was cast in 1886, in the Kuça workshop for the Board of Revenue office in Urumçi (Zhu and Zhu 1991: no. 597).

Figure 3 Obverse: *Qian Long tongbao* 乾隆通寶 (circulating coin of [the] Qian Long [reign period]). Rev: *Aksu* اقسو in Uyghur on the right and Manchu on the left. Although this coin is in the name of the Qian Long Emperor (1736–1795), it was a supplementary issue cast in the Aksu workshop in 1878 (Zhu and Zhu 1991: no. 26)

Figure 4 Obverse: *Guang Xu ding-wei* 光緒丁末, (*ding-wei* [year] of [the] Guang Xu [reign period]), i.e. 1907.

---

[1] I am grateful to the people who kindly told me about these coins and provided information in 1987. According to that information, there were only six coins in the deposit.

Figure 1. *Guang Xu tongbao, Guang* written in the form of the character *qi* 七 (7).
Rev: *Xin shi, boo sin*, thicker at 11 o'clock. AE, Ø 26.6mm, 3.96g.

Figure 2. *Guang Xu tongbao, Guang* in the form of the character *qi*. Rev: *Xin shi, boo sin*.
AE, Ø 26.8mm, 5.04g.

Figure 3. *Guang Xu tongbao, Guang* in the form of the character *qi*. Rev: *Xin shi, boo sin*.
AE, Ø 25.5mm, 3.1g, with damage at 5 o'clock, where the coin was separated from the
casting channel.

Figure 4. *Guang Xu tongbao*, small characters. Rev: *Xin shi, boo sin*. AE, Ø 25.9mm, 2.99g.

Figure 5. *Guang Xu tongbao*, *Guang* in the form of the character *qi*. Rev: *Xin shi, boo sin*, with casting flaws. AE, Ø 25.5mm, 5.4g.

Figure 6. *Guang Xu tongbao*, long *tong*. Rev : *Ku shi, boo iuwan*. AE, Ø 25.5mm, 3.48g.

Rev: as Fig. 2. This coin was cast in the Kuça workshop for the Board of Revenue office in Urumçi (Zhu and Zhu 1991: no. 588).

Figure 5 Obverse: *Qian Long tongbao*. Rev: at the top, in Chinese, *A* 阿, for Aksu, and *shi* 十, ([value] 10), Aksu, in Uyghur to the right, and in Manchu to the left. This coin was also a supplementary issue cast in the Aksu workshop in 1886 (Zhu and Zhu 1991: no. 59).

Coin hoards are usually classified in one of three ways: emergency, savings or loss. However, none of these apply to the small hoard from Ortahisar, which is in no way emergency safekeeping, the savings of an individual or an institution, or the chance loss of a sum of money. There is no trace of Chinese coins having circulated in the Ottoman Empire, let alone under Abdülhamid II (1876–1909), whose reign began after the important monetary reforms of 1843–1844 initiated by Abdülmecid (1839–1861). These coins could not have been in circulation, even clandestinely, or as small change. It should also be noted that these six copper cash are of very poor quality. The only conclusion that we can draw is that this hoard was not a monetary hoard, in the strictest sense.

If the hoard was not monetary, then what was it? It seems likely that this deposit is linked to the troubled history of Xinjiang in the last third of the nineteenth century, a history in which Turkey played a reluctant, but significant role, if only symbolically. Since the end of the reign of Wenzong (Xian Feng咸豐 reign period, 1851–1861), Chinese Muslims (*Hui*) in Gansu and Shaanxi provinces had been taking advantage of the Taiping Rebellion in southern and central China, and of the Nian Rebellion in Henan to secede from the Chinese Empire. Their rebellion rapidly spread to all Turkic populations (Uzbeks, Uyghurs, Kirghiz) in Xinjiang province (Eastern Turkestan) (Saray 2003: 230–240). The first of the great Turkic revolts was that of Seyyid Cahangir Sultan (1824–1828). A descendant of the khans of Kaşghar, Cahangir wanted to restore the khanate of the Hodja of Kaşghar. He put himself in charge of Kashgar, Yangisar, Yarkand and Khotan, and then threatened Aksu. He was defeated in 1828 and executed in Beijing. His son Buzurg Khan sought refuge with the khan of Khokand. The main uprisings after that were those of Vali Khan and Yusuf Hodja (Iklil 1995: 76–82).

While China's attention and military effort was focussed on the Taipings, these other rebellions were able to gain momentum. In some cases, they worked together and acted in concert (Chu Wen-djang 1966: 23–87). Following the Gansu revolt, the uprising of Ghazi Raşidin of Kuça inflamed Xinjiang from 1864 to 1867 (Thierry 2001: 39–43). along with that of Habibbüllah, who proclaimed himself pasha of Khotan (1864–1866), and that of Sadik Khan, a Kyrgyz leader who seized Kaşghar (1864–1865). It was then that Atalik Ghazi Mehmed Yakub Beg (1864–1877) entered the scene, initially as commander-in-chief of Buzurg Khan's troops, who wanted to restore the Kaşghar Khanate. After rallying, subduing or destroying the other rebels, Yakub Beg gradually made himself leader of East Turkestan. He sent Buzurg Khan into exile and seized supreme power. He founded the Khanate of Yedişehir (the Seven Cities) and placed his state under the protection of the Ottoman Empire, becoming a theoretical vassal. This connection was not only affirmed and officially proclaimed by a firman from the sultan, dated 10 recep 1292 (12 August 1875) (Saray 2003: 328), but also by the issue of coins: gold *tilla*, silver *tenga* and copper *pul* (Nuri 1968: no.915); that were struck at Kashgar in the name of Sultan Abdülaziz (1861–1876).

Some rare gold *tilla* struck in the name of the Ottoman sultan Abdülhamid II are known (Cüneyt 1987: 93; Baldwin 2007: no. 621). Yakub Beg paid homage to the new sultan, sending his nephew Seyyid Yakub Khan Töre on a special mission to Istanbul to congratulate Abdülhamid II on his accession to the throne (Saray 2003: 233).

While the Ottoman Empire faced Russian and Austrian aggression in the Balkans and the Caucasus, and was considered "the sick man of Europe", in China it was perceived as another imperialist power intent on carving up the Qing Empire.

It is true that the Khanate of Yakub Beg maintained quasi-subsidiary relations vis-a-vis Ottoman Turkey that went beyond being the only link uniting the Sunni Muslims of Central Asia to the Sultan-Caliph. The British secret agent Robert Shaw's 1871 account of his journey from Ladakh to Kashgar shows how Russian aggression in the Ottoman Moldavian provinces (1853), the Crimean War (1854–1856) and the victory of the Franco-British allies in favour of Sultan Abdülmecid (1839–1861) had repercussions in Turkestan, where Russia was the most bitter adversary. Shaw met Yakub Beg and many officials of the khanate, who were perfectly aware of the alliances and conflicts that were agitating Eurasia, and who gauged perfectly their interest in establishing solid relations with the British in India. (Shaw 1871/1984: 163, 179, 190, 197, 261). More specifically, many of the people Shaw met were *haci*, that is, Muslims who had made the pilgrimage to Mecca, which at the time was in Ottoman territory. Between Kargalik and Yarkent, he travelled with a tea merchant from Bukhara who had been to Istanbul and Turkey; and he was received by the *beg* (prefect) of Kokhrobat (between Yarkent and Yengishar) who told him about his journey to Istanbul via Bukhara, Persia and Trebizond (Shaw 1871/1984: 167, 378). Finally, he reported how some Ottoman prisoners, captured by the Russians in Wallachia or during the Crimean War, had managed to escape from camps in Siberia and had reached the Khanate of Yakub Beg where they were received by the Atalik Ghazi himself; the latter had treated them with great consideration and had given them the means to return to their country.

Thus, far from being a small, isolated rebel government, the Yedişehir Khanate was a state that was well versed in international relations and maintained diverse and quite intense relations with the Ottoman Empire. In this light, we can better understand the fears of Li Hongzhang 李鴻章, the powerful governor of Zhili, who in a memorandum to Emperor Muzong (Tong Zhi) in 1784 said, 'This territory [Xinjiang] borders Russia to the north, various Muslim countries such as Turkey, Arabia and Persia to the west, and is close to British India in the south. These neighbours have become stronger as we have grown weaker, a situation that is quite different from the past. [...] I have read in the newspapers and received other information from the West that the Muslim leader of Kaşghar has recently received protection from Turkey and has also concluded trade treaties with Britain and Russia' (Chu 1966: 166–167).

Having dealt with the Taiping rebels, thanks to the decisive intervention of Western troops, China could now, in 1874, turn against Yakub Beg. There were opposing factions who had different approaches to dealing with Turkestan. Li Hongzhang considered that Xinjiang province, should be abandoned, as it was too expensive for what it brought in, and that it should be turned into a semi-independent vassal state; Zuo Zongtang, on the other hand, considered that Xinjiang was an essential link in national security and that it should be held with an iron fist. In 1875, after the death of Emperor Muzong, the war party, led by the empress dowager, Minister Wen Xiang 文祥, Wang Wenshao 王文詔 and Zuo Zongtang 左宗棠, secretly entrusted Zuo with recovering Xinjiang (Chu 1966: 166–167). Yakub Beg died suddenly in Korla on 22 May 1877, and his khanate disintegrated rapidly, Kaşghar was taken on 18 December, Yarkent on the 21st and Khotan on 2 January 1878. Beg Kulu, Yakub Beg's son, and the leaders who had escaped death or capture fled to Russia. There are witness accounts from Muhammed Yusuf Efendi, Yakub Beg's officer, who accompanied Beg Kulu in the last days of the emirate, and from Captain Ali Kazim, head of the Ottoman military mission in Kashgar, and from Seyyid Yakub Khan Töre, as well as the letter from Beg Kulu to the sultan, on 13 November 1881 (Saray 2003: 235–236, 335–336, 366, 371–374; Chu Wen-djang 1966: 177, n. 34).

Having regained control of Xinjiang, China passed the civil government to the Manchu Nayancheng, governor of Gansu-Shaanxi, but the real power was entrusted to the military. From 1878 to 1884, the Chinese authorities hesitated about which status to give to Xinjiang. Eventually, in 1884, Xinjiang became a province with special status, with Liu Jintang as governor (Chu 1966: 191–196). In the years 1885–1886, he delivered a monetary reform that had three key points: minting and circulation of silver *tenga* was prohibited, minting of *hongqian* 紅錢, (red [copper] coins) was revived, and paper money was issued by the workshop in the provincial capital at Urumçi (Dihua). The six coins found at Ortahisar were cast at the beginning of this period and taken to Turkey. Who took them there? Perhaps they were taken to Anatolia by a Turk who remained in Xinjiang after the defeat of Yakub Beg? Or by someone from Kashgar fleeing the new Chinese province? Or

by a Turkish or Andicani[2] merchant trading between Xinjiang and the Ottoman Empire... Who's to know?

Translated by Helen Wang

References

Baldwin. 2007. *Coins of Islamic World* XIII, 30 October Sale.

Chu Wen-djang. 1966. *The Moslem Rebellion in Northwest China 1862-1878*. Taipei: Rainbow Bridge Book Co.

Cribb, J. 1977–1985. *Coin Hoards* III, IV, V, VI, VII. London: Royal Numismatic Society.

Cribb, J. 1996. Chinese coin finds from South India and Sri Lanka, in K.K. Maheshwari and B. Rath (eds), *Numismatic Panorama, Essays in Memory of late Shri S.M. Shukla*: 253–269. New Delhi: Harman Publishing House.

Cribb, J. and Rao, P.K. 1999–2000. Chinese coin found at Kottapatnam, Nellore District, Andhra Pradesh, *Numismatic Digest (Nasik)*, vols 23–24: 133–158.

Cribb, J. and Potts, D. 1996. Chinese coin finds from Arabia and the Arabian Gulf, *Arabian Archaeology and Epigraphy* 7: 108–118.

Dong Qingxuan 董慶煊. 1986. Xinjiang Tiangang yinbi kao 新疆天罡銀幣考, *Zhongguo Qianbi* 1986.11: 15–32. [On the silver coins of Tiangang, Xinjiang]

Esenbel, S. 2005. Comment on the Chinese coins from Tarsus-Gözlükule, in *Field Seasons 2001–2003 of the Tarsus-Gözlükule interdisciplinary Research Project*: 173-175. Istanbul: Ege Yayınları.

Jiang Qixiang and Dong Qingxuan. 1991. *Xinjiang qianbi/ Xinjiang Numismatics*. Hong Kong: Xinjiang Art and Photo Press, and Hongkong Educational and Cultural Press.

Kurban, I. 1995. *Doğu Türkistan için savaş*. Ankara: Türk Tarih Kurumu.

Lin Gwo-Ming and Ma Tak-Wo. 1990. *Xinjiang jin yin bi tushuo – Illustrated catalogue of Sinkiang gold and silver coins*. Taipei: Quantan zazhi.

Mu Yuan 穆淵. 1994. *Qingdai Xinjiang huobi shi* 清代新疆貨幣史. Urumqi: Xinjiang daxue chubanshe. [A monetary history of Xinjiang in the Qing dynasty]

Ölçer, C. 1987. *Sultan Murad V ve Sultan Abdülhamid II dönemi Osmanlı paraları*. Istanbul : Yenilik Basımevi.

Pere, N. 1968. *Osmanlılarda madenî paralar*. Istanbul: Yapı ve Kredi Bankası.

Saray, M. 2003. *The Russian, British, Chinese and Ottoman rivalry in Turkestan*. Ankara: Türk Tarih Kurumu.

Shaw, R. 1871. *Visits to High Tartary, Yarkand and Kashgar*. Reprint: Hong Kong: Oxford University Press, 1984.

---

[2] The town of Andican (Andijan), situated in Ferghana (east of the khanate of Bukhara) was very active in international trade. The traders of Andican, in particular, took themselves to Xinjiang, which is why the people of the Bukhara khanate were often called "Andicanis" in Xinjiang.

Thierry, F. 2001. Le monnayage de Ghazi Rashidin Khan (1864–1867), *Cahiers Numismatiques* 149: 37–46.

Wang Yongsheng 王永生. 2007. *Xinjiang lishi huobi* 新疆历史货币. Beijing: Zhonghua shuju. [Historical money of Xinjiang].

Zhu Zhuopeng 朱桌鹏and Zhu Shengtao 朱圣弢. 1991. *Xinjiang hongqian* 新疆红钱. Shanghai: Xuelin chubanshe. [The red coins of Xinjiang]

Un dépôt monétaire chinois trouvé en Turquie

François Thierry

Durant plusieurs années, pour *Coins Hoard*, puis pour le *Numismatic Chronicle* et dans d'autres publications, Joe Cribb a recensé les trésors de monnaies chinoises exhumés hors de la Chine, principalement en Malaisie, en Indonésie, en Thaïlande, au Srilanka, en Inde, en Tanzanie, ainsi que les rares découvertes faites au Moyen-Orient.[1] Je verse au dossier un petit trésor monétaire chinois inédit découvert en Turquie. Au printemps de l'année 1986, au cours de travaux agricoles, un paysan fit la découverte, dans les environs du village d'Ortahisar (canton d'Ürgüp, vilayet de Nevşehir, Turquie), d'un petit dépôt de sapèques chinoises de cuivre rondes à trou carré. Ces monnaies se sont rapidement retrouvées sur l'étal d'un brocanteur du site touristique de Göreme. L'ensemble était composé de six monnaies de cuivre de l'empereur Dezong, ère Guang Xu 光緒 (1875-1908).[2]

Il y avait cinq pièces du même type : le droit porte l'inscription chinoise *Guang Xu tongbao* 光緒通寶, « monnaie courante de [l'ère] Guang Xu » ; le revers porte, verticalement en chinois, *Xin shi* 新十, « Xin[jiang], [valeur] 10 », et de gauche à droite, en écriture mandchoue, *boo sin*, transcription du chinois *bao Xin*, « [Hôtel des] monnaies du Xin[jiang] ».[3] La valeur 10 indique le taux de change de cette pièce de cuivre exprimé en monnaie légale (*zhiqian* 制錢) en laiton.

La sixième monnaie est d'un type différent : le droit porte l'inscription chinoise *Guang Xu tongbao*, mais au revers on a, verticalement en chinois, *Ku shi* 庫十, « Ku[ça], [valeur] 10 », et de gauche à droite, en mandchou, *boo iuwan*, transcription du chinois *bao yuan*, « [Hôtel des] monnaies du ministère des Travaux».[4]

Selon le *Xinjiang tuzhi* 新疆圖志, suite aux réformes de Liu Jintang 劉錦棠, la fonte des monnaies au revers *Ku shi* commence à la 8e lune de la 11e année de l'ère Guang Xu (septembre 1885) dans l'atelier de Kuça qui est fermé à l'hiver 1886 ; pour ce qui est des monnaies au revers *Xin shi*, *bao Xin*, les émissions ont commencé à être lancées dès l'ouverture de l'atelier provincial installé à Urumçi (Dihua), à la 7e lune de la 12e année de l'ère Guang Xu (août 1886).[5] Le dépôt ne comprend aucune monnaie au type *Xin shi boo chiowan* (*bao quan* 寶泉, atelier dépendant du Ministère des Finances), fondues en 1886, après les *Xin shi*, *bao Xin*. Ce qui est intéressant dans ce dépôt, c'est d'une part, la piètre valeur des monnaies qui le constituent, et d'autre part, le fait que ces monnaies ne peuvent pas s'insérer dans la circulation monétaire de la fin de l'empire ottoman.

On notera que la composition de ce dépôt – en ce qui concerne la date des monnaies – est très similaire à celui qui fut découvert à Tarsus-Gözlükule, du moins pour ce que nous en connaissons.[6] À ce propos, il convient de corriger certaines identifications. L'auteur dit en effet : « The 31 bronze coins were minted between the years 1875-1908 during the reign of the Qing Emperor Guangxu whose name is inscribed on one side of the coin ». Or parmi les cinq monnaies de la planche de cet article,[7] trois ne portent pas le nom d'ère de Guang Xu, deux sont au nom de Qian Long et une au nom de Tong Zhi.

Figure 1 : *Tong Zhi tongbao* 同治通寶, « monnaie courante de [l'ère] Tong Zhi » ; au revers, en haut *Ku* 庫, pour *Kuça*, à droite *Kuça* كوﭼ en ouighour et à gauche *Kuça* en mandchou ; bien que portant le nom de règne de l'empereur Muzong (1862-1874), cette pièce est une « monnaie supplémentaire » fondue dans l'atelier de Kuça en 1885.[8]

---

[1] - Voir, par exemple, *Coins Hoard* 1977 III, 1978 IV, 1979 V, 1981 VI, 1985 VII, et aussi « Chinese coin finds from Arabia and the Arabian Gulf », *Arabian Archaeology and Epigraphy* 7, 1996, p. 108-118. (avec D. Potts) ; « Chinese coin finds from South India and Sri Lanka », in K.K. Maheshwari and B. Rath (éd.), *Numismatic Panorama, Essays in Memory of late Shri S.M. Shukla*, New Delhi, Harman Publishing House, 1996, p. 253-269 ; « Chinese coin found at Kottapatnam, Nellore District, Andhra Pradesh », *Numismatic Digest (Nasik)*, vol. 23–24 (1999–2000), p. 133-158 (avec K.P. Rao).

[2] - Je tiens à remercier ici les personnes qui ont eu la gentillesse de me communiquer ces monnaies et ces informations en 1987. Selon ces informations, ce dépôt ne comprenaient que six pièces.

[3] Pour ce type, voir Zhu Zhu Zhuopeng 朱桌鵬 et Zhu Shengtao 朱聖弢, *Xinjiang hongqian* 新疆红钱, Shanghaï, Xuelin chubanshe, 1991, p. 159-160, Mu Yuan 穆淵, *Qing dai Xinjiang huobi shi* 清代新疆貨幣史, Urumçi, Xinjiang daxue éd., 1994, p. 127, n° 35. Xinjiang 新疆, « Nouveau territoire », est le nom que les Chinois donnèrent au Turkestan oriental ou Turkestan chinois.

[4] - Pour ce type, voir Zhu Zhu Zhuopeng 朱桌鵬 et Zhu Shengtao 朱

圣弢, *Xinjiang hongqian* 新疆红钱, Shanghaï, Xuelin chubanshe, 1991, p. 159-160, Mu Yuan 穆淵, *Qing dai Xinjiang huobi shi* 清代新疆貨幣史, Urumçi, Xinjiang daxue éd., 1994, p. 127, n° 35. Xinjiang 新疆, « Nouveau territoire », est le nom que les Chinois donnèrent au Turkestan oriental ou Turkestan chinois.

[5] - Pour ce type, voir Zhu Zhuopeng et Zhu Shengtao, *op. cit.*, p. 44 et 157, n° 550.

[6] - Zhu Zhuopeng et Zhu Shentao, *op. cit.*, p. 43, 44, 156, 159.

[7] - Esenbel Selçuk, « Comment on the Chinese coins from Tarsus-Gözlükule », in *Field Seasons 2001-2003 of the Tarsus-Gözlükule interdisciplinary Research Project*, Istanbul, Ege Yayinlari, 2005, p. 173-175. Il serait bon en effet d'avoir des photographies de toutes les monnaies pour les identifier correctement car la lecture semble avoir été pour le moins superficielle : l'auteur dit que les pièces portent toutes le nom de Guang Xu, alors que sur les cinq monnaies illustrées, seules deux portent effectivement le nom de Guang Xu.

[8] - Esenbel Selçuk, *op. cit.*, p. 175.

Figure 2 : *Guang Xu tongbao* 光緒通寶, « monnaie courante de [l'ère] Guang Xu » ; au revers, verticalement en chinois, *Xin shi* 新十, « Xin[jiang], [valeur] 10 », et de gauche à droite, en écriture mandchoue, *boo chiowan*, transcription du chinois *bao quan*, « [Hôtel des] monnaies du ministère des Finances » ; cette monnaie a été fondue en 1886 dans l'atelier de Kuça pour le compte du bureau du ministère des Finances d'Urumçi.[9]

Figure 3 : au droit, *Qian Long tongbao* 乾隆通寶, « monnaie courante de [l'ère] Qian Long » ; au revers, *Aksu* اقسو en ouighour à droite et en mandchou à gauche ; bien que portant le nom de règne de l'empereur Gaozong (1736-1795), cette pièce est une « monnaie supplémentaire » fondue dans l'atelier d'Aksu en 1878.[10]

Figure 4 : au droit, *Guang Xu ding-wei* 光緒通寶, « [année] *ding-wei* de [l'ère] Guang Xu », soit 1907 ; même revers que la figure 2 ; cette monnaie a été fondue dans l'atelier de Kuça pour le compte du bureau du ministère des Finances d'Urumçi.[11]

Figure 5 : *Qian Long tongbao* ; au revers, en chinois, en haut, *A* 阿, pour *Akesu*, et *shi* 十, « [valeur] 10 », à droite *Aksu* en ouighour et à gauche en mandchou ; cette pièce est aussi une « monnaie supplémentaire » fondue dans l'atelier d'Aksu en 1886.[12]

On a généralement l'habitude de classer les trouvailles monétaires en trois types principaux, les trésors d'urgence, les trésors d'épargne et les trésors perdus, mais aucun d'eux ne peut s'appliquer au petit dépôt d'Ortahisar, qui ne constitue en rien la sauvegarde dans l'urgence d'une valeur menacée, le résultat de l'épargne d'un particulier ou d'une institution, ou la perte fortuite d'une somme plus ou moins importante. Il n'est pas de trace que les sapèques chinoises aient eu cours dans l'empire ottoman, à plus forte raison sous Abdülhamid II (1876-1909), dont le règne vient après les importantes réformes monétaires de 1843-1844 initiées par Abdülmecid (1839-1861). Ces monnaies ne pouvaient pas s'intégrer, même clandestinement, même comme menue monnaie, dans la circulation monétaire ; il faut bien constater, de surcroît, que ces six sapèques de cuivre sont de bien mauvaise qualité. La conclusion que nous devons tirer de la constitution de ce dépôt monétaire, c'est qu'il n'a pas de caractère monétaire *stricto sensu*.

Si donc ce dépôt n'est pas à proprement parler un trésor monétaire, de quoi s'agit-il ? Il nous semble qu'il faille rattacher ce dépôt à l'histoire troublée du Xinjiang dans le denier tiers du XIXe siècle, histoire

au cours de laquelle la Turquie joua, à son corps défendant, un rôle non négligeable, ne serait-ce qu'au niveau symbolique. Depuis la fin du règne de Wenzong (ère Xian Feng 咸豐, 1851-1861), les Chinois musulmans (*Hui*) des provinces du Gansu et du Shaanxi avaient profité de l'insurrection du Céleste Empire de la Grande Paix (*Taiping Tianguo*) en Chine méridionale et centrale et de celle des Nian au Henan pour entrer en sécession ; leur rébellion s'était étendue rapidement à toutes les populations turques (Ouzbeks, Ouïghours, Kirghizes) de la province du Xinjiang (Turkestan oriental).[13] Comme toute l'attention et tout l'effort militaire de la Chine étaient tournés contre les Taiping, les autres soulèvements bénéficiaient d'une situation particulièrement favorable pour se développer ; et dans certains cas, ils agissaient de concert.[14] À la suite de la révolte du Gansu, le soulèvement de Ghazi Raşidin de Kuça enflamme le Xinjiang de 1864 à 1867 ;[15] d'autres soulèvements accompagnent celui de Raşidin, celui de Habibbüllah qui se proclame Pacha de Khotan (1864-1866), et celui de Sadik Khan, un chef kirghize qui s'est emparé de Kaşghar (1864-1865). C'est alors que l'Atalik Ghazi Mehmed Yabub Beg (1864-1877) entre en scène ; au début, il opère en tant que commandant en chef des troupes de Buzurg Khan qui veut restaurer le khanat de Kaşghar. Après avoir rallié, soumis ou liquidé les autres rebelles, Yakub Beg se rend maître du Turkestan oriental. Il envoie Buzurg Khan en exil et s'empare du pouvoir suprême. Il fonde le khanat de Yedişehir (« les Sept Cités »), et il place son État sous la protection de l'Empire ottoman, dont il devient un vassal théorique. Ce lien est non seulement affirmé et officiellement proclamé par un *firman* du sultan daté du 10 *recep* 1292 (12 août 1875),[16] mais aussi par des émissions monétaires de *tilla* d'or, de *tenga* d'argent et des *pul* en cuivre[17] frappés à Kaşghar au nom du sultan Abdülaziz (1861-1876).[18] Alors que dans les Balkans et au Caucase, l'Empire ottoman est en butte aux agressions russe et

[13] La première des grandes révoltes turques est celle de Seyyid Cahangir Sultan (1824-1828). Descendant des khans de Kaşghar, Cahangir entend restaurer le khanat des Hodja de Kaşghar ; il se rend maître de cette ville, de Yangişar, Yarkent et Khotan, puis menace Aksu. Vaincu en 1828, il est exécuté à Pékin. Son fils Buzurg Khan se réfugie auprès du khan de Khokand. Les principaux soulèvements sont ensuite ceux de Vali Khan et de Yusuf Hodja. Voir Kurban Iklil, *Doğu Türkistan için savaş*, Ankara, Türk Tarih Kurumu, 1995, p. 76-82, Saray Mehmet, The Russian, British, Chinese and Ottoman rivalry in Turkestan, Ankara, Türk Tarih Kurumu, 2003, p. 230-240.

[14] - Zhu Zhuopeng et Zhu Shentao, *op. cit.*, n° 26.

[15] - Thierry François, « Le monnayage de Ghazi Rashidin Khan (1864-1867) », *Cahiers Numismatiques* 149, 2001, 37-46, p. 39-43.

[16] - Zhu Zhuopeng et Zhu Shentao, *op. cit.*, n° 588.

[17] - Zhu Zhuopeng et Zhu Shentao, *op. cit.*, n° 59.

[18] - La première des grandes révoltes turques est celle de Seyyid Cahangir Sultan (1824-1828). Descendant des khans de Kaşghar, Cahangir entend restaurer le khanat des Hodja de Kaşghar ; il se rend maître de cette ville, de Yangişar, Yarkent et Khotan, puis menace Aksu. Vaincu en 1828, il est exécuté à Pékin. Son fils Buzurg Khan se réfugie auprès du khan de Khokand. Les principaux soulèvements sont ensuite ceux de Vali Khan et de Yusuf Hodja. Voir Kurban Iklil, *Doğu Türkistan için savaş*, Ankara, Türk Tarih Kurumu, 1995, p. 76-82, Saray Mehmet, *The Russian, British, Chinese and Ottoman rivalry in Turkestan*, Ankara, Türk Tarih Kurumu, 2003, p. 230-240.

[9] - Zhu Zhuopeng et Zhu Shentao, *op. cit.*, n° 597.

[10] - Zhu Zhuopeng et Zhu Shentao, *op. cit.*, n° 482.

[11] - Zhu Zhuopeng et Zhu Shentao, *op. cit.*, n° 588.

[12] - Zhu Zhuopeng et Zhu Shentao, *op. cit.*, n° 597.

autrichienne, et qu'il est considéré comme « l'homme malade de l'Europe », en Chine, il est perçu comme l'une des puissances impérialistes qui s'acharnent à dépecer l'empire des Qing.

Il est vrai que le khanat de Yakub Beg entretenait vis à vis de la Turquie ottomane des relations quasi filiales qui dépassaient le seul lien qui unissait les musulmans sunnites d'Asie centrale au sultan-calife. Le récit du voyage de Robert Shaw, agent secret britannique qui fit le route du Ladakh jusqu'à Kaşghar, montre combien l'agression russe dans les provinces moldo-valaques ottomanes (1853), puis la guerre de Crimée (1854-1856) et la victoire des alliés franco-anglais au bénéfice du sultan Abdülmecid (1839-1861) avaient eu de répercussion au Turkestan où la Russie était l'adversaire le plus acharné. Robert Shaw rencontra Yakub Beg ainsi que de nombreux officiels du khanat qui étaient parfaitement au courant des alliances et des conflits qui agitaient l'Eurasie, et qui mesuraient parfaitement l'intérêt d'établir des relations solides avec les Anglais des Indes.[19] Plus précisément, plusieurs personnages rencontrés par Shaw étaient des *haci*, c'est-à-dire des musulmans ayant fait le pèlerinage à La Mecque qui, à l'époque, se trouvait en territoire ottoman. Entre Kargalik et Yarkent, il fit route avec un marchand de thé de Boukhara qui avait été à Istamboul et en Turquie ; il fut reçu par le *beg* (préfet) de Kokhrobât (entre Yarkent et Yengishar) qui lui raconta son voyage à Istamboul par Boukhara, la Perse et Trébizonde.[20] Enfin, il rapporte comment quelques prisonniers ottomans, capturés par les Russes en Valachie ou durant la guerre de Crimée, avaient réussi à s'échapper des camps de Sibérie et à rejoindre le khanat de Yabub Beg où ils avaient été reçus par l'Atalik Ghazi en personne ; celui-ci les avait traités avec beaucoup d'égard et leur avait donné les moyens de retourner dans leur pays.

On voit donc que loin d'être un petit gouvernement rebelle isolé, le khanat de Yedişehir était un État très au fait des relations internationales qui entretenait avec l'Empire ottoman des relations diverses et assez intenses. On comprend mieux, alors les craintes de Li Hongzhang 李鴻章, le puissant gouverneur du Zhili, qui dans un mémoire à l'empereur Muzong (Tong Zhi) disait en 1874 : « Ce territoire [le Xinjiang] est frontalier de la Russie au nord, de divers pays musulmans comme la Turquie, l'Arabie et la Perse à l'ouest, et est proche de l'Inde britannique au sud. Ces voisins sont devenus de plus en plus forts alors que nous sommes devenus de plus en plus faibles, une situation bien différente de celle des temps anciens. [...] J'ai lu dans les journaux et j'ai reçu d'autres informations de l'Ouest de ce que

le chef musulman de Kaşghar a récemment reçu la protection de la Turquie et a également conclu des traités commerciaux avec la Grande Bretagne et la Russie ».[21]

Débarrassée des Taiping grâce à l'intervention décisive des troupes occidentales, la Chine peut, en 1874, se tourner contre Yakub Beg. Deux factions s'opposent au sujet du Turkestan. Li Hongzhang considère qu'il faut abandonner cette province qui coûte bien trop chère pour ce qu'elle rapporte et en faire un État vassal semi indépendant ; Zuo Zongtang, en revanche, estime que le Xinjiang est un maillon essentiel de la sécurité nationale et qu'il faut le tenir avec une poigne de fer. En 1875, après la mort de l'empereur Muzong, le parti de la guerre, dirigé par l'impératrice douairière, le ministre Wen Xiang 文祥, Wang Wenshao 王文韶 et Zuo Zongtang 左宗棠, charge secrètement ce dernier de la reconquête.[22] Yakub Beg meurt soudainement à Korla le 22 mai 1877, son khanat se délite rapidement, Kaşghar est prise le 18 décembre, Yarkent le 21 et Khotan le 2 janvier 1878. Beg Kulu, le fils de Yakub Beg, et les chefs qui avaient échappé à la mort ou à la capture s'enfuirent en Russie.[23]

La Chine, à nouveau maîtresse du Xinjiang, en donne le gouvernement civil au mandchou Nayancheng, gouverneur du Gansu-Shaanxi, mais la réalité du pouvoir est confiée aux militaires. De 1878 à 1884, les autorités chinoises hésitent sur le statut à donner au Xinjiang. Ce n'est qu'en 1884 qu'on le transforme en province à statut spécial, avec pour gouverneur Liu Jintang.[24] Dans les années 1885-1886, celui-ci met au point une réforme monétaire qui s'articule en trois points, interdiction de la frappe et de la circulation des *tenga* d'argent, reprise de la fonte des *hongqian* 紅錢, « monnaies rouges » (monnaies de cuivre), et émission de monnaie de papier par l'atelier de la capitale provinciale, Urumçi (Dihua). Les six monnaies trouvées à Ortahisar ont été fondues au début de cette période et transportées en Turquie. On peut avancer plusieurs hypothèses : elles ont pu être

19 - Chu Wen-djang, *The Moslem Rebellion in Northwest China 1862-1878*, Taibei, Rainbow Bridge Book Co., 1966, p. 23-87.
20 - Thierry François, « Le monnayage de Ghazi Rashidin Khan (1864-1867) », *Cahiers Numismatiques* 149, 2001, 37-46, p. 39-43.
21 - Saray, *op. cit.*, p. 328.
22 - Nuri Pere, *Osmanlilarda madenî paralar*, Istamboul, Yapı ve Kredi Bankası, 1968, n° 915 ; Lin Gwo-Ming et Ma Tak-Wo, *Xinjiang jin yin bi tushuo - Illustrated catalogue of Sinkiang gold and silver coins*, Taibei, Quantan zazhi, 1990, p. 1-2, 12-16 ; Wang Yongsheng 王永生, *Xinjiang lishi huobi* 新疆历史货币, Pékin, Zhonghua shuju, 2007, p. 207-210 ; Jiang Qixiang et Dong Qingxuan, *Xinjiang qianbi*, Hong-kong, Xinjiang Art and Photo Press et Hongkong Educational and Cultural Press, 1991, p. 70-72 ; Dong Qingxuan 董慶煊, « Xinjiang tiangang yinbi kao » 新疆天罡銀幣考, *ZGQB* 1986-II, p. 15-32.
23 - On connaît aussi quelques rares *tilla* frappées au nom d'Abdülhamid II (Cüneyt Ölçer, *Sultan Murad V ve Sultan Abdülhamid II dönemi Osmanlı paraları*, Istamboul, Yenilik Basımevi, 1987, p. 93 ; vente Baldwin *Coins of Islamic World* XIII du 30 octobre 2007, n° 621). Yakub Beg avait rendu hommage au nouveau sultan, en envoyant son neveu Seyyid Yakub Khan Töre en mission spéciale à Stamboul pour féliciter Abdülhamid II pour son accession au trône (Saray, *op. cit.*, p. 233).
24 - Shaw Robert, *Visits to High Tartary, Yarkand and Kashgar* (1871), reprint Hogkong, Oxford University Press, 1984, p. 163, 179, 190, 197, 261.

apportées en Anatolie par un Turc resté au Xinjiang après la défaite de Yakub Beg, ou par un Kaşghari fuyant la nouvelle province chinoise, ou par un marchand turc ou andicani[25] commerçant entre le Xinjiang et l'Empire ottoman...

25 - Shaw Robert, *op. cit.*, p. 167 et 378.

Coins of Kesh with the Legend ΦΣΕΙΓΑ ΧΑΡΙΣ
(South Soghd, Second Half of the 1st to the End of the 2nd Centuries AD)[1]

Aleksandr Naymark

Survey of scholarly literature

As far as I can judge, coins of Phseighacharis first appeared on the pages of a scholarly publication in 1886: two specimens along with the coins of Sapadbizes constituted the section entitled "Kings of uncertain name" in the British Museum catalogue of "Greek and Scythic Kings of Bactria and India" (Gardner 1886: 19). Despite the claimed 'uncertainty' the legend was reproduced absolutely correctly as ΦΣΕΙΓΑ ΧΑΡΙΣ. Percy Gardner, however, abstained from any comments on other aspects of the coins. Yet the very fact that this section immediately followed the one with the coins of Heraios and Hyrcodes implies that Percy Gardner attributed these three coinages to the same epoch.

A few publications of separate specimens and some brief mentions of the coins with the legend ΦΣΕΙΓΑ ΧΑΡΙΣ in general discussion that appeared in print prior to the beginning of the 1970s (see for example, Cunningham 1889: pl. I, no. 14; Whitehead 1914: 166, pl. XVI, no. 29; Rosenfield 1967: 17), brought to light more coins and made even clearer the affinity of the royal image on these coins with the group of very specific portraits constituted by the monetary effigies of Hyrcodes, Heraios, and Ashtat.

At the beginning of the 1970s coins with the legend ΦΣΕΙΓΑ ΧΑΡΙΣ caught the eye of a well-known English numismatist Michael Mitchiner. The most important result of his work was the publication of the specimens held in British public collections: all six coins of the British Museum and one belonging to the Heberden Coin Room at the Ashmolean Museum (Mitchiner 1973: 55–57, Pl. XI, no. 94; Mitchiner 1975: 304, type 513; Mitchiner 1978: 387, no. 2833; Mitchiner 2004: 568, nos. 1687–1690). Less successful was his attribution of

Phseighacharis coinage to the Yuezhi principality 'Hi-Sum', which he located in Bamiyan (Mitchiner 1973: 55–57; Mitchiner 1975: 285; Mitchiner 1978: 387). It should be noted, that in his latest grand compendium Mitchiner turned Phseighacharis into 'a Yuezhi chief who moved south with his followers and conquered ... an unspecified city-state in Bactria', where 'Pabes, a native Bactrian chief, ruled' previously (Mitchiner 2004: 567). Unfortunately, this new interpretation, as we shall see below, also proved to be mistaken.

About the same time, coins with the legend ΦΣΕΙΓΑ ΧΑΡΙΣ attracted the attention of Eugene V. Zeymal, who discussed them in his article devoted to South Sogdian coinage with images of Hercules and Zeus. The Leningrad scholar thought that the figures of Hercules on the coins of these two series were 'geographically' and 'chronologically' very close to each other (Zeymal 1973: 71).

He also wrote that coins of Phseighacharis were 'typologically adjacent' to Hyrcodes coinage. On the other hand, Zeymal noted a similarity between the portrait on the coins of Phseighacharis and some of the portraits on the coins of the Western Kshatrapas, who ruled in Gujarat (Zeymal 1975: 14, 17, fig. 7). Partially because of the drastically diverging directions of the stylistic and iconographic connections with Sogdian and Indian coins that Zeymal postulated, and partially because of the lack of information regarding the find spots of the coins with the legend ΦΣΕΙΓΑ ΧΑΡΙΣ he refrained from any precise conclusions about the locus of this coinage.

In general, the notion that Phseighacharis was a ruler of some Bactrian principality completely dominated in the scholarly literature. Robert Göbl placed the coins of Phseighacharis in the Bactrian sections of his *Antike Numismatik* (Göbl 1978, Table 113, no. 2319]. In the monumental survey of *Nomina Propria Iranica in Nummis* Michael Alram called Phseighacharis 'Clanchef zur Zeit der frühen Kušan' (Alram 1986: 293–4, Table 40, no. 1262). Robert Senior included the coins of Phseighacharis in the same section as the coins of Pages, Arsilis, Pulages and Sapadbiz (Senior 2001: vol. II, 214, A7.1). Joe Cribb qualified them as 'silver reduced-weight drachms of Bactria' (Cribb 2007: 251, #73).

[1] I am indebted to Yekaterina Gracheva for the design of the map and of all coin plates. I also would like to express my gratitude to the curators of different museum, who have allowed me access to the coins in their collections and provided all kinds of help during my research: Joe Cribb and Robert Bracey (British Museum), Shailendra Bhandare and Luke Treadwell (Ashmolean Museum, Oxford), Konstantin Kravtsov (State Hermitage, St Petersburg), and Anvar Atakhodzhaev (Coin Room of the Samarqand Institute of Archaeology). I am also grateful to Vladimir Belyaev for the opportunity to use materials in the magnificent resource that is Zeno.ru. Last but not least, I would like to thank all the collectors and dealers, whose coins I was able to take into consideration during my work and especially those whose coins are included in the plates supplied to this article.

Figure 1. Map of ancient Soghd (Sogdia, Sogdiana) with the places of finds of Phseigha Charis coins (the numbers on the map correspond to the numbers in Plates 1-5).

E.V. Rtveladze followed the same tradition when he published a specimen of the Tashkent Museum in a popular book (Rtveladze 1987: 95–96), and five years later devoted a special article to the coins of Phseighacharis (Rtveladze 1992). In the latter publication Rtveladze summarized and significantly broadened the argumentation of his predecessors. He touched upon the question of the square script, discussed the format of the royal portrait and the physical type of the ruler, examined the iconography of Hercules and debated its probable origin. With regard to the first major question of attribution, Rtveladze suggested that the realm of Phseighacharis could be situated in the center of Southern Bactria, i.e. in the province of Samangan in Northern Afghanistan. As to the date, based on various properties, he proposed a period between the 1st century BC and the middle of the 1st century CE (Rtveladze 1992: 154). These conclusions, however, did not reflect another important observation made in his article: the manner in which the eye is rendered and the prominent eyebrow were quite similar to those of the ruler depicted on some imitations of South Sogdian coins of Alexander the Great (Rtveladze 1992: 151-152).

Finally, in 1999, Rtveladze printed a note devoted to a single coin of Phseighacharis, which preserved a legend behind the ruler's head on the obverse (Rtveladze 1999: 82; Rtveladze 2002: 183–184). In this publication the scholar wrote that 'three (?) or four (?) letters can be discerned in this inscription, written,

most likely, in the Sogdian script of Aramaic origin. Transcription of these letters is rather problematic: δ/enp/w.' Although this combination of characters escaped sensible interpretation, the very fact of the use of a writing system derived from Aramaic allowed Rtveladze to suggest, that 'the coins of Phseighacharis could be minted not only in Bactria, where inscriptions of Aramaic origin were absent from the coins, but also in Soghd, where, on the contrary, such legends were constantly present, probably, from the 1st century BC – 1st century AD, in all Sogdian realms: Bukhara, Maraqanda, South Soghd.'

In 2001, I summarized the argumentation put forward by Zeymal and Rtveladze, and on the basis of mostly typological criteria offered the following sequence of early coin series in the Kashka-darya basin: (1) imitations of Seleucid coins with the types of Alexander → coins with ΦΣΕΙΓΑ ΧΑΡΙΣ inscription → coins with the images of Hercules and Zeus (Naymark 2001: 56; see also Naymark 2008: 57–58). At that moment, however, there were no materials that would allow one to determine which of the main two South Sogdian principalities was responsible for this sequence of three series: Kesh or Nakhshab?

Fifteen years later it became clear that the principality of Nakhshab was responsible for another sequence of four coin series that were minted from the second half of the 1st century AD and up to the end of the 3rd century: (1) it started with three silver denominations of Ashtat coins (largest one with archer on the reverse and smaller ones with a horse protome); (2) by the end of the 2nd century a new type of archer coins was introduced, now struck in both silver and copper; (3) the "sword bearer" type replaced it in the first quarter of the 3rd century AD and then (3) in the second half of the 3rd century Nakhshab mint returned to the archer type, but struck only in copper (Naymark 2016; Naymark 2020). Since this sequence of issues has been firmly attributed to the mint of Nakhshab, I suggested that the second South Sogdian sequence of three coinages (Alexander imitations → coins with ΦΣΕΙΓΑ ΧΑΡΙΣ inscription → coins with the images of Hercules and Zeus) should, by elimination, be placed in Kesh (Naymark 2016: 65).

Recorded finds

The south Sogdian attribution of ΦΣΕΙΓΑ ΧΑΡΙΣ coins rests mainly on typological arguments, i.e. mostly on indirect considerations. In order to become a firmly established fact this localization still needs documentary proof. Fortunately, in the last two decades a significant amount of reliable information about the find spots of ancient Sogdian coins has come to light. As of today, we have records of nine finds of coins with ΦΣΕΙΓΑ ΧΑΡΙΣ legend. Seven of them (pl. 1-5, coins 6, 8, 9, 10, 12, 14, 18) came from one compact region – the eroded banks of the Chim-kurgan reservoir in the middle of the Kashka-darya valley (Belyaev and Naymark 2022). Two more specimens (pl. 5, coins 19 and 20) were found on the surface near the archaeological site conventionally called a 'castle' some 50 km SWW of Samarqand, in the immediate vicinity of Sarykul. No single coin with ΦΣΕΙΓΑ ΧΑΡΙΣ legend has been registered outside of the core lands of Sogdiana—no provenance information is attached to the remaining 13 specimens in our plates (including the lost prototype of three Hermitage cast copies). In other words, the known findspots prove the Sogdian origin of the ΦΣΕΙΓΑ ΧΑΡΙΣ coins beyond any doubt.

Of the two areas of Soghd, where the ΦΣΕΙΓΑ ΧΑΡΙΣ coins have been recorded, the Kashka-darya Valley is much more likely to be their place of origin. It is not only the number of finds (seven out of nine), but more importantly, the weight of these seven specimens in the general statistics of finds in these two areas. The group of seven 'drachms' from the shores of the Chim-kurgan reservoir constitutes a very noticeable share of the still very limited pool of recorded finds of ancient coins in South Soghd. And vice versa, the two specimens recorded in the area of Sarykul appear to be an insignificant admix to rather numerous finds of ancient coins belonging to the various series that were minted at that time by four different principalities situated in the central part of the Zarafshan Valley. As to the status of the two South Sogdian coins in the area of Sarykul, their appearance in this area could be explained by the following considerations: (1) these were silver coins with high intrinsic value and thus they were capable of long-distance travel; (2) Sarykul lies on the major route connecting South Soghd to Samarqand. In fact, the area around Sarykul is remarkably rich in early South Sogdian coins: it yielded at least one specimen from every single series minted in the basin of the Kashka-darya. For these reasons, the coins with the legend ΦΣΕΙΓΑ ΧΑΡΙΣ can be securely attributed to South Soghd/the Kashka-darya basin.

Unfortunately, seven recorded Chim-kurgan finds of ΦΣΕΙΓΑ ΧΑΡΙΣ coins provide little help when it comes to the exact identification of the mint responsible for this coinage. The problem is in the composition of the finds on the banks of the Chim-kurgan reservoir: this area yields both Kesh and Nakhshab coins. All major varieties and denominations of Nakhshab archer and sword bearer coins have been found at the same sites as Kesh imitations of Alexander drachms and Kesh coins with the images of Hercules and Zeus (Naymark 2016; Belyaev and Naymark 2022 forthcoming). The causes of this phenomenon are quite obvious—this was the borderland between the principalities of Kesh and Nakhshab.

Placing the sequence of three related series (Ashtat → "reformed archer" → sword bearer's coins) in Nakhshab in my earlier publication, I suggested that the method of elimination by itself can be sufficient for the attribution of other contemporary South Sogdian coinages to the principality of Kesh (Naymark 2016: 65). Since then, however, it has become clear that at least one more coin series was minted in South Soghd in antiquity – the coinage developing the type of the Bactrian imitations of the obols of Eucratides, but supplied with new Greek inscriptions (Belyaev and Naymark 2015). In other words, that there could be other ancient polities within the Kashka-darya basin. It is all the more possible, as there were three principal irrigation zones in South Soghd: in addition to the lands of Kesh and Nakhshab that were based on the waters of the Kashka-darya, there was a separate oasis in the delta of the Ghuzar-darya, the major tributary of the Kashka-darya. In fact, during the Arab conquest, i.e. the only moment in the pre-Islamic history of the area when the local political geography features prominently in narrative sources, there was a separate principality of Ghuzar with it own ruler who resided in the stronghold of Subah (Tabari/ De Goje 1893: 1448; Tabari/Powers 1989: 179).

Keeping this in mind, we should concentrate our attention here on the connection between ΦΣΕΙΓΑ ΧΑΡΙΣ coins and other South Sogdian series. Zeymal and Rtveladze already wrote about the connections between ΦΣΕΙΓΑ ΧΑΡΙΣ coins and South Sogdian series of Alexander imitations. Unfortunately, the poor state of preservation of the earliest known ΦΣΕΙΓΑ ΧΑΡΙΣ coins [pl. 1, nos 1–5] does not allow us to base any conclusions on them and our comparison has to start with somewhat later specimens [pl. 2, nos 6–8].

The most noticeable feature that links the two coinages is the manner of rendering the eye in the ruler's portrait (compare pl. 1, no. 0022, pl. 2, nos 6–8, and pl. 3 nos 9–14 to pl. 2, nos 23–24). First of all, this is a classic case of the composite view—the eye is shown *en face* on a face turned in profile. Secondly, in both cases the slightly curving lines of eyelids frame the apple of the eye from above and beneath, but do not meet at the corners of the eyes. Finally, the eye is shown with a significant tilt to the left. This peculiar and unusual combination of features does not appear in any other Sogdian monetary portrait.

Less noticeable, but also important, is the manner in which the mouth is depicted: lips are shown with two dots set on the external contour of the face and two slightly curving slanting lines decsending from these dots (pl. 2, compare 23–24 with 7). This is a simplified version of the mouth rendering commonly found on Hellenistic coins. It survived on some early Sogdian imitations, but for a long time it remained in use only in the Kesh line of Alexander imitations.

The large aquiline nose—apparently the only common feature in the early versions of the portrait on ΦΣΕΙΓΑ ΧΑΡΙΣ coins—is also derived from Alexander imitations (pl. 2, compare 23-24 with 7 and 8). There are no other noses of 'such scale' in coin portraits of early Soghd, which makes the connection between these two series highly probable. It is worth mentioning that this 'proud decoration' disappears from the royal effigy almost immediately.

The least obvious, but undoubtedly very important coincidence, is that the ruler's hair is shown with the same short curved strokes with sharp 'needle-like' ends, that survived on Alexander's effigy as the rudiment of a lion's mane. This reflects a rather individual manner of using cutting tools in the process of the die manufacturing.

The commonality in such elements demonstrates at minimum a continuity of craft tradition amongst the mint workers. I believe that the sum of these observations is sufficient to consider the coins with the legend ΦΣΕΙΓΑ ΧΑΡΙΣ the next stage in the work of the mint that originally produced Alexander imitations. In order to strengthen this argumentation, I can offer here an explanation for the logic behind the alterations undertaken by the die sinker(s) responsible for the ΦΣΕΙΓΑ ΧΑΡΙΣ coins. The task of the die sinker(s) responsible for the early coins with the legend ΦΣΕΙΓΑ ΧΑΡΙΣ was to remove the individual attributes of Alexander's portrait: essentially, his exceeedingly rich hair, the divine horns, and the lion's skin. The removal of these features significantly simplified, and thereby clarified the image, as it eliminated intricate minor details which by that time were mostly incomprehensible to the general public. Following this new stylistic trend the die sinker(s) also simplified the general contour of the face by 'sraightening' some of the lines, such as the nose.

Another connection with ΦΣΕΙΓΑ ΧΑΡΙΣ coins was noticed by Zeymal who suggested that the reverse image of Hercules was closest to that on the Hercules and Zeus coins (Zeymal 1973: 71). With a number of new specimens at our disposal this suggestion acquires a firmer footing: on early ΦΣΕΙΓΑ ΧΑΡΙΣ coins the hero placed most of his body weight on his straight left leg, while his right leg was slightly bent at the knee and relaxed. On the terminal issues of the ΦΣΕΙΓΑ ΧΑΡΙΣ series, the weight shifted to the right leg, while the left was shown bent (pl. 5, nos 17–8). It is this 'left-turned' version of the image that was adopted by the earliest coins with Hercules and Zeus (pl. 5, no. 0025).

There were, however, some changes in iconography that require explanation. The image on the latest ΦΣΕΙΓΑ ΧΑΡΙΣ coins (pl. 5, nos 17–18) was severely distorted such that the lion skin, which was not quite readable from the very beginning, blended with the remnants of the completely blundered legend, forming a chaotic combination of lines. The die sinker(s) of the earliest Hercules and Zeus coins transformed this mess into a wreath with ribbons. This, however, created a logical problem as there was already a wreath on the head of the hero. In order to remove the contradiction, the Kesh die sinker 'took the wreath off' the head of Hercules (compare pl. 5, nos 18 and 0025). The image of the hero holding a wreath in the left hand is otherwise not known in the standard Hercules iconography (already noted in Yakunchikov 1911).

Close connections of the ΦΣΕΙΓΑ ΧΑΡΙΣ coins to the earlier (Alexander imitations) and later (Hercules and Zeus coins) series suggest that these were three stages in the work of a South Sogdian mint (cf. Naymark 2001: 56; see also Naymark 2008: 57-58; Naymark 2016: 63). No doubt, this was a major mint as it kept working for over 450 years. It is very likely that this was the mint of Kesh. The general picture of South Sogdian coinages now includes three series of Kesh coins (Alexander imitations → ΦΣΕΙΓΑ ΧΑΡΙΣ coins → coins with Hercules and Zeus), three series of Nakhshab coins (three denominational coinage of Ashtat(w) → 'reformed' archer coinage in silver and copper → Nakhshab sword bearer coins) (Naymark 2016: 68–74; Naymark 2020b: 223–229), the series of coins developing from the type of Tokharistanian imitations of Eukratides (only four specimens are known) (Rapson 1904: 321, Table XXVII, 26; Zeimal 1983b: 100; Zeimal 1984: 185; Rtveladze and Nefedov 1995: 60–62; Rtveladze 2002: 114–116; Belyaev and Naymark 2015: 53–55) and, possibly, one more series of so far unpublished obols.

The recognition of the fact that Alexander imitations and Hercules and Zeus coins were issued by the same mint provides us with additional evidence for the mint localisation: we can now take into consideration findspots of Alexander imitations and of Hercules and Zeus coins. The majority of recorded finds of these series also come from the banks of the Chim-kurgan reservoir (Kabanov 1965: 84–85, fig. 6; Kabanov 1981: 77, fig. 40, 6, 7, 10; Belyaev and Naymark 2022 forthcoming), one specimen of each series was recorded in the Sarykul area of the Samarqand region (Atakhodzhaev and Naymark 2022). There is no need to repeat the explanation why these finds cannot provide a solution to our problem.

More important are the finds in the mountain areas of Kesh. An early specimen of the Alexander imitation series was lifted from the surface of a small hillock situated near Jar-tepa in the area of kishlak Bugazhil in the Ayakchi-darya Valley (Omel'chenko 2001: 14). One Hercules and Zeus coin came from the excavations of Turtkul-tepa in Yakkabag region (Abdullaev 1997: 9–16; Abdullaev 2000: 147–152). Two more Hercules and Zeus coins were found in areas of North-West Tokharistan adjacent to Kesh: in the temple of Dalverzin-tepe (Gorin 2012: 188) and in the upper stratum of Jandavlat-tepe (Abdullaev 2011: 178, no. 83,182). However slim, this data has a significant value, especially since no coin of any of the three series in question has ever been found in the Ghuzar and Nakhshab oases.

The legend

One line of inscription runs from top to bottom to the right of the figure of Hercules and reads: ΦΣΕΙΓΑ. To the left of the hero is another vertical line that also reads from top to bottom: ΧΑΡΙΣ. The position of the letters leaves no doubt that the line placed to the right of the image was supposed be read first. As reverse legends on the Hellenistic coins of Central Asia commonly contained royal names, scholars assumed that Phseighacharis was a local name rendered in Greek script.

We now know, however, that the ΦΣΕΙΓΑ ΧΑΡΙΣ coins were struck in the Sogdian principality of Kesh. Besides the series in question, there were eight separate coinages in Soghd during the 1st century AD (Naymark

2020b: 207, fig. 2). Two of them are non-epigraphic: (1) the Samarqand line of Antiochus imitations, a previously unpublished type with a blank obverse and a horse head dissolving into a combination of large dots on the reverse (Naymark 2020b: 206, 207, fig. 2. # 1); and (2) the East Sogdian imitations of the Bactrian imitations of the obols of Eucratides (Atakhodzhaev and Naymark 2020). On four of the six remaining coinages the name of the ruler is placed behind his head on the obverse: (3) on a series minted in the Zarafshan valley west of Samarqand (Naymark 2020b, 210–212, figs 3–6); (4) on the coins of Hyrcodes (*Zeymal* 1978: 203, Table III, nos 13–25) most likely minted in Kharqana (Naymark 2020b, 205–210); (5) on the coins of Nakhshab ruler Ashtat (Naymark 2016: 68–71; Naymark 2020b: 222–228); and (6) on a South Sogdian coinage developing from the type of the Bactrian imitations of the obols of Eucratides (Belyaev and Naymark 2015). A royal name was placed in front of the royal head on the obverse on (7) the coins of a series developing the Antiochus type, but with the portrait turned left (Zeymal 1983a: 72–73, 78, # 96–103, 162. Table XX, # 97–103) that was minted in an un-identified centre in the Zarafshan Valley west of Samarqand (Naymark 2020b, 207, fig. 1 and, fig. 2. no. 1). Only the coins of (8) Bukharan Soghd preserved the traditional Hellenistic format: the Sogdian legend with the title and name of a ruler replaced distorted Greek on the reverse of silver denomination reproducing the types of Euthydemus' tetradrachms (Naymark 2022), while the reverse of a single known copper specimen preserved the heterogram *MR'Y* above the image of a prancing horse (Naymark 2021). In other words, the most common position for the royal name on Sogdian coins of the 1st century AD would be behind ruler's head on the obverse, but other variants also existed.

The principal layout of the reverse of the ΦΣΕΙΓΑ ΧΑΡΙΣ coins is the same as that of the large denomination in the coinages of Hyrcodes and Ashtat: a human figure standing between the two vertical lines of the inscription. In full accordance with the legend ΒΑΣΙΛΕΟΣ ΑΝΤΙΟΧΟΥ, the reverse of Ashtat's coins have the image of Seleucid King Antiochus I, apparently in the capacity of the progenitor of the local dynasty (Naymark 2020b: 235-6). As to the drachms of Hyrcodes, there is a fiery creature on the reverse, most likely the Zoroastrian deity Sraosha/Srosh. The legend by the sides of the image of Sraosha, though rendered in Greek letters, is in fact bilingual: ΟΡΔΗΘΡΟΥ on the left is an Iranian compound, mostly likely meaning 'the protector of the fire' with Greek genitive ending. On the right is the Greek epithet ΜΑΚΑΡΟΣ 'happy, fortunate, blessed', also in the genitive form ΜΑΚΑΡΟΥ.

I sent a letter to Nicholas Sims-Williams asking for help with the legend ΦΣΕΙΓΑ ΧΑΡΙΣ. He immediately suggested that ΧΑΡΙΣ was a Greek word with meaning 'grace', and wrote the following note about ΦΣΕΙΓΑ:

> An initial *fs-* is quite unlikely in any Iranian language, but since the standard Greek alphabet has no letter š it is possible that φσ- stands for **fš-*. This sequence appears in initial position in a very few Iranian words, all or virtually all of which are derivatives of **pasu-/*fšu-* 'sheep', e.g. **fšu-pāna-* 'shepherd', **fšuyant-* 'farmer, gentleman, master, lord' (Sogdian *fšy'ws*, Bactrian φινδο, Choresmian *fynd*). I would therefore take seriously the suggestion of Humbach (1966: 41, n. 1) that **fšuya-ka-*, a plausible side-form of **fšuyant-*, might have resulted in φσειγα in some unknown East Iranian language. The language in question, which would seem to have some features in common with Sogdian (*fš-*) and others in common with Bactrian (**k > g*), could conceivably be the dialect of Kesh, though other conjectures would be equally possible.

In other words, ΦΣΕΙΓΑ ΧΑΡΙΣ is not a personal name, but a phrase meaning something like 'lord's grace'. The coin design by itself does not allow us to identify whom this epithet describes: a ruler depicted on the obverse or the god of the reverse. There is a purely Sogdian word combination in the repertory of much later Sogdian coin legends that comes to mind as a comparanda -- *prn bgy,* which O.I. Smirnova considered to be the invocation of the name of a Sogdian deity (Smirnova 1981: 314, 336, 348), and which V.A. Livshits persuasively interpreted as a title.

Unfortunately, there is no illustration in Rtveladze's article devoted to the ΦΣΕΙΓΑ ΧΑΡΙΣ coin with the Sogdian inscription behind the head of the ruler on the obverse. Current whereabouts of this specimen are not known (at the end of the 1990s it was in a private collection in Tashkent). Luckily, the same element can also be seen on a rather well-preserved specimen in the Panjab Museum in Lahore (Whitehead 1914: 166, pl. XVI, no. 29; Mitchiner 2004: 568, # 1689; see also pl. 2, no. 4), on two obols recently found near Sarykul (pl. 5 and 6, nos 19 and 20), and on a silver cast reproduction of a lost original drachm that are held in State Hermitage Museum (pl. 2, no. 0022). It was undoubtedly present on the dies used to strike specimens 2, 5 (Table 2) and 9, 10, 14 (Table 4). Most probably, the inscription did not fit on the blanks of the early coins 1, 3 (Table 2), and it appears that it was not a part of the original design of a typologically compact group of coins represented by specimens 6–8 (Table 3). It also disappeared from the latest issues (pl. 5, 33 15–18).

The position this element occupies on the coin—behind the ruler's head on the obverse—is exactly 'right' for a

ruler's name on a Sogdian coin of the first century AD. And yet among the better-preserved specimens this element could pass for an inscription only on coins 4 and 22. Theoretically, it could be a combination of two letters: *n/z* on the right and *x/γ* on the left, which could be read as Zagh, Nagh, or Zah, Nah. One may add to this that the name ζαγο has been recorded on a Bactrian seal (Lerner and Sims-Williams 2011: 122–123, AB 6). Nevertheless, this element of the design cannot by any means be an inscription. In order to make sense, it would need to be read as a well-developed cursive and there was no cursive in Sogdian paleography until at least the 5th century AD. Indeed, nothing of this nature appears on coins until the 6th century.

In fact, an attentive look at the early coins 2 and 19 reveals an elegantly curved line that could represent a small plume or tassel. Similar decorations are seen on the helmets of warriors on contemporary (no later than the first half of the 2nd century AD) Orlat bone carvings: on the buckle with the depiction of the battle and on the belt decoration with the scene of single combat (Ilyasov and Rusanov 1997/98: 146, pl. IV, 1; 147, pl. V, 1).

The reverse legend provides us with important clues for the date of the ΦΣΕΙΓΑ ΧΑΡΙΣ coins. First of all, there were no new 'conscious' (as opposed to those which were simply copied) Greek legends in Sogdian coins prior to the launching of Hyrcodes coinage at the very beginning of the common era. On the other hand, we are not aware of any Greek legends after the first century AD. In other words, the language employed in the legends limits the date of our coins to the 1st century AD.

More can be derived from the paleography of the inscriptions. The most characteristic features of the script: *phi, sigma,* and *epsilon* have square shapes; *alpha* is triangular, its left cathetus/leg being absolutely vertical, while the 'tail' stretching from the right corner of the triangle is rendered practically horizontally; *rho* has an open loop. Characteristic elements of this paleography started forming in the 1st century BC, but the closest parallels to the ΦΣΕΙΓΑ ΧΑΡΙΣ legend are found in Greek inscriptions on the casting molds for large cauldrons discovered at Takht-i Sangin (Drujinina 2008; Ivanchik 2011; further discussion with the summary of the literature: Balakhvantsev 2014; the date of the cauldrons of this type as the second half of the 1st century: Demidenko 2014), among the Greek legends of the coins of Kujula Kadphises and Vima Taktu (Cribb and Bracey forthcoming), and in the Greek section in the inscription of Vima Taktu at Dasht-i Nawur (Sims-Williams and Cribb 1995/6: 95–6. Fig. 9). These are all Greek inscriptions belonging to the early Kushan epoch. In other words, the aforementioned paleographic parallels suggest a date in the second half of the 1st century or the very beginning of the 2nd century CE (Ivanchik 2011: 67).

Weights and dates

There is a significant difference in weight between the latest Alexander imitations and the very first coins with the ΦΣΕΙΓΑ ΧΑΡΙΣ legend. The three latest Alexander imitations weigh 1.02 g (Tashkent Museum 13/7), 1.15 g (Hermitage 37079), and 0.88g (British Museum 1894,0506.1803) with an average weight of 102.5 g. The earliest ΦΣΕΙΓΑ ΧΑΡΙΣ coins (the first eight in a sequence built with 18 currently known 'drachms') have an average weight of 2.34 g. The heaviest weighs 2.59 g, while the lightest is 1.9 g. These figures make it absolutely clear that the metrology of ΦΣΕΙΓΑ ΧΑΡΙΣ coins was not dictated by the internal development of Kesh coinage.

Observations on the weights of Sogdian silver coins of the beginning of the common era suggest that: (1) there were several principal denominations (tetradrachm, drachm, hemidrachm, and obolus); (2) that coins in each of these denominations were gradually losing weight; and that (3) the existence of the common market to some extent regulated this process of weight reduction in these coinages so that mints in different principalities had to respond to the general trend. If this is the case, we have good reason to think, that the weights of the early ΦΣΕΙΓΑ ΧΑΡΙΣ coins were dictated by the metrological characteristics of some other popular coins, i.e. coins with which Kesh issues were supposed to compete on Sogdian markets.

The most probable 'competitor' for the coins of Kesh were the coins of the neighboring Nakhshab principality: 'drachms' and 'hemidrachms' with the name of Ashtat. As the weight of the majority of early ΦΣΕΙΓΑ ΧΑΡΙΣ coins significantly exceeds 2 g, we can safely exclude Nakhshab 'hemidrachm' from our consideration. As to the 'drachm' (i.e. Nakhshab silver coins with the archer image on the reverse), following the original issue of rather heavy coins weighing over 4 g, there was a sharp reduction to approximately 3.3 g , and only then do we see a relatively smooth curve leading to 2.5 g (Naymark 2016: figs 1 and 2). With this dynamic, weight would reach 2.5 g after some time (Naymark 2016: 70–71, nos 9–10, and p. 68, no. 7; Göbl 1978, no. 2304 = Alram 1985, no. 1249), possibly a decade or two.

Unfortunately, we cannot yet translate this 'typological' date into a precise absolute one. The date of the beginning of Ashtat coinage itself rests mainly on the stylistic comparison with Heraios coins and the 'typological distance' from the earliest Hyrcodes issues (Naymark 2016: 62; Naymark 2020b, figs 3–7). The dates of Heraios coinage are now given a broad chronological bracket 'between 50 and 90 CE' (Cribb 1993: 107–134; Falk and Bennet 2009; Falk 2012) and Ashtat coins can be placed within the same chronological span. This means that ΦΣΕΙΓΑ ΧΑΡΙΣ coins can be attributed to the second half of the 1st century, most likely, closer to its end.

Iconographic and stylistic traits as testimony for the date

The obverse image on ΦΣΕΙΓΑ ΧΑΡΙΣ coins belongs to the group of Sogdian monetary portraits executed in the Hellenistic die sinking techniques, but depicting local rulers with their ethnic traits: long faces with equally long or prominent aquiline noses; clearly visible cranial deformation; very specific hair style such as long locks at the back of the head, moustache, and goatee beard. Another clearly 'non-Hellenic' feature of this portrait is the torque on the neck. There were three monetary portraits of this type in 1st century Sogdiana: (1) the earliest was on the coins of Hyrcodes, which most likely were minted by a Kharaqana principality in Zarafshan Valley (near modern Karmana) (Naymark 2020b: 205–210); issues of the Nakhshab ruler Ashtat (Naymark 2016: 68–71; Naymark 2020b: 215–235), and, finally, a series of obols with the image initially derived from the Bactrian imitations of Eucratides that can be localized in South Soghd, albeit without more precise attribution (Rapson 1904: 321, Table XXVII, 26; Zeymal 1983b: 100; Zeimal 1984: 185; Rtveladze and Nefedov 1995: 60–62; Belyaev and Naymark 2015: 53–55). The affinity of the image on ΦΣΕΙΓΑ ΧΑΡΙΣ coins with this group of portraits suggests a 1st century AD date.

The principal iconographic features of the Hercules image on the reverse are the figure of the hero *en face* in contrapposto stance; in his left hand he holds the club which almost reaches the ground; the lion skin, sometimes with two dots for paws and a long line representing the tail, hangs over his bent left hand; a 'check mark' on the chest of Hercules might represent a cloak, although no traces of this garment are visible behind the figure; dots around the head apparently meant to show a wreath; and two lines stretching to the right and left parallel to the outline of the shoulders that are definitely depicting the ribbons of a diadem. While images of Hercules are quite common in the early coinages of the Central Asian/Gandharan region, there is only one instance when ***all*** the listed major features are present—the coins of the Indo-Greek ruler Theophilos [Bopearachchi 1991, pl. 48, K and L]. Yet these rather rare coins are quite distant from the image on ΦΣΕΙΓΑ ΧΑΡΙΣ coins geographically, chronologically (ca. AD 130), and stylistically, which means that they could hardly serve as the immediate prototype for their reverse image. Other known monetary representations of Hercules in this iconography usually lack at least one of the aforementioned major features. For example, very similar images on the early coins of Pabes (Mitchiner 2004: 567, no. 1683) and on the coppers minted by Kujula Kadphises in Taxila (centers A, phase 2, and B, phase 1) (Cribb and Bracey forthcoming) lack the wreath on the hero's head. This, however, should not be considered a principal obstacle for establishing a possible connection, after all, the die sinker of the Kesh mint was not under an obligation to reproduce one particular prototype. More telling for us in this case would be the style which actually most of all resembles coins of Kujula Kadphises minted in Taxila, particularly those struck in centre B during the first phase (Cribb and Bracey forthcoming). It is important to note, that Kujula's coppers of the Taxila mint were known in Soghd (Atakhodzhaev and Naymark 2021: 44–45, 56–58).

Yet the search for the prototype of the Hercules' figure should not be limited solely to numismatic materials. The image of the hero with a club in his right hand and the lion skin hanging over his bent left arm was well known in the sculpture of the Bactro-Gandharan region. It was also widespread in the artistic media which by their technical nature were always closely connected to the monetary tradition: for example, there are more than enough comparanda in glyptics (Borell 2017). In fact, a bulla with an imprint of a seal bearing an image of Hercules with this particular version of the iconography was discovered during the excavations of the countryside residence of Samarqand Ikhsids at Riwdad, the site of Kafir-Kala near Samarqand (Begmatov 2017: 208, 8c). This particular bulla was attached to a document that was kept in the archive burned during the Arab conquest of Samarqand. In the meantime, the iconographic type of Hercules employed on the original seal is best known from the Taxila coins of Kujula Kadphises, while the carving technique and the style of the image would fit an even earlier Hellenistic period. In other words, this find is not very helpful in dating our coins, although it suggests that seals with images of Hercules in this particular iconography were known at some point in Soghd.

Incipient date of the ΦΣΕΙΓΑ ΧΑΡΙΣ coinage

Let us sum up all the evidence for dating discussed so far. First of all, the use of Greek script in the inscriptions suggests the 1st first century AD and does not really allow us to extend the date to the 2nd century. The paleography of the inscription testifies to the second half or even the end of the 1st century AD at the earliest. All the typical features of the portrait are consistent with the 1st century date: the cranial deformation, long hair at the back of the head, moustache and goatee beard appear in Sogdian monetary portraits during that time. The closest stylistic parallel for the Hercules

figure is provided by the coins of Kujula Kadphises minted in Taxila in the 50–90s AD. The weight of the earliest specimens seems to correspond to that of the Nakhshab drachms datable to the 60s–80s AD. In other words, the most likely date for the beginning of the ΦΣΕΙΓΑ ΧΑΡΙΣ coinage lies within the last third of the 1st century AD.

Terminal date of the ΦΣΕΙΓΑ ΧΑΡΙΣ coinage

It is clear that the process of decomposition of the images as well as the complete distortion of the legend on the immobilized ΦΣΕΙΓΑ ΧΑΡΙΣ type would have taken significant time. The same can be said about the falling weight of the coins, which in the latest specimens constitutes only about two fifths of the orignal. Unfortunately, analysis of such changes in immobilized types cannot provide us with precise dates.

In order to establish absolute dates for the terminal stage of ΦΣΕΙΓΑ ΧΑΡΙΣ coinage we would need to digress from our immediate theme and discuss the general situation in Sogdian coinages from the second half of the 2nd to the middle of the 3rd century AD. The only 'firm' chronological anchor that we currently have within this time span is the date of the Sasanian invasion of Soghd which resulted in the annexation of the Bukharan oasis and the consequent incorporation of it into the Kushano-Sasanian monetary circulation zone.

The Sasanian occupation of Bukhara was established on the basis of coin finds: as of now over 160 post-Kushan, Kushano-Sasanian, and early Sasanian coppers are recorded as having been found at sites of Bukharan Soghd (Kum-Sovtan, Paykand, Varakhsha, and various sites in the vicinity of the latter) (Naymark 1987: 51; Naymark 1995: 36–37; Naymark 2001: 68–70; Gorin 2015: 53–62; Omelchenko and Gorin 2019). This very specific monetary assemblage is characteristic of Kushano-Sasanian circulation. The quantity of the finds excludes the possibility that this was just a spill over the border. Indeed, for the previous two centuries only seven Kushan (Atakhodzhaev and Naymark 2021) and two Parthian coins (Atakhodzhaev and Naymark forthcoming A) have been recorded as found in the Bukharan oasis, and an even smaller number of coppers from Sasanian Marw and Tokharistan has been recorded for the 5th and 6th centuries. Most importantly, excavations on Paykand citadel revealed significant archaeological strata where only coins characteristic of Kushano-Sasanian circulation were recorded (Omel'chenko 2016: 83–84; Omelchenko and Gorin 2019, 129–130, 134).

The North-Eastern border of Iranshahr as described in the inscription of Shapur I on Kaab-i Zardusht (Huyse 1999: 23–24) includes the Bukharan oasis (Naymark

2001: 69) and we can safely assume that these events took place prior to AD 262. The further narrowing of this date is not yet possible. The annexation of Bukhara likely happened during one of the large military campaigns conducted by the Sasanians in the east. The earliest of these was the Eastern campaign of Ardashir I, which some scholars date to 226/7, others later up to 233 (Alram 2007: 232–240). Furthermore, there is an opinion that there were two different campaigns, one in 226/7 and another in 233 (Olbrycht 2014: 29). Another distinct possibility for the Sasanian conquest of Bukhara is the eastern campaign of Shapur I that took place in 241–242. Less probable would be 250–251, when Shapur I was once more engaged in Khurasan.

Coin finds on sites of the Bukharan oasis include imitations of Huvishka, Kanishka II, early types of Vasudeva imitations, and a few early Sasanian coppers minted in Marw: a specimen of the so-called Marw horsemen (Nikitin 1986: 244; cf. Schindel 2010) and a coin of Shapur I from Paykand (Omel'chenko 2016, p. 107, fig. 25, no. 1), one Shapur I copper from the Varakhsha area (private collection, Bukhara). These could testify for the relatively early date, but in order to arrive at any firm conclusions in regard to this matter one would need either a bulk of unambiguous hoard evidence, similar to that assembled by Zeimal in Tokharistan (Zeymal 1983b: 231–268) or a significant amount of numismatic material from well-recorded archaeological contexts. In absentia of such supporting data, we have to put up with a 25-year long spread in dates.

The Sasanian conquest of Bukhara in the second qarter of the 3rd century had a profound effect on Sogdian coinage. It caused a termination of all five Sogdian coinages that had continued into the second quarter of the 3rd century: Hercules and Zeus (*MR"Y aywnwn*) series of Kesh; swordbearer series Nakhshab; Bukhara *MR'Y wnwk* coins (the last stage in the coinage with the type of the tetradrachms of Euthydemus); Hyrcodes coinage (minted in Kharqana?); and the run of Antiochus imitations minted in Samarqand.

During the next 100 to 125 years there were three very different zones of monetary circulation in Sogdiana: (1) the Bukharan oasis remained within the zone of Kushano-Sasanian monetary circulation; (2) South Soghd also adopted copper as the main coin metal and there seems to have been only one coinage: the copper imitations of 'reformed archer' coins, which in the middle of the 4th century were replaced by leontomachia coins that continued to the middle of the 6th century (Naymark 2016: 68–76); (3) Samarqand Soghd launched a three denomination silver archer coinage which also continued into the 6th century (Naymark 2020a: 181–183).

Between this major turning point in Sogdian numismatic history and the terminal issues of the ΦΣΕΙΓΑ ΧΑΡΙΣ series lies the Hercules and Zeus coinage. While scholarly opinion concerning the dates of the latter varies greatly, the archaeological context of the finds is unambiguous: two specimens received during the excavations in Tokharistan come from an early Kushano-Sasanian context (Gorin 2012: 188; Abdullaev 2011: 178, # 83: 182), and the ceramic complex of Smaller Kyz-bibi in South Soghd where the third one was found has been reasonably dated to the 3rd–4th century (Kabanov 1965: 79, fig. 4, 81, fig. 5; Kabanov 1981: 80–85).

On the other hand, there is a dramatic drop in weight between the early Hercules and Zeus coins, which weigh up to 0.85 g (Zeymal 1973, fig. 1, no. 1) and the terminal issues where it falls to below 0.3 g. There are also significant distortions in imagery. Finally, there is a clear change in the paleography of the legend: the cruciform *aleph* of earlier legends is replaced by an *aleph* similar to the one known from the Sogdian Ancient Letters. While these observations do not allow us to define the duration of this coinage and thus to suggest 'precise' dates, it is clear that these changes took several decades. In other words, the transition from ΦΣΕΙΓΑ ΧΑΡΙΣ type to Hercules and Zeus type at the Kesh mint took place either at the end of the 2nd century AD or at the very beginning of the 3rd century.

The ΦΣΕΙΓΑ ΧΑΡΙΣ coinage of Kesh and general tendencies in the development of Sogdian coinage

With the beginning of the ΦΣΕΙΓΑ ΧΑΡΙΣ coinage attributed to the last third of the 1st century AD and its termination dated to the end of the 2nd century, the story of this Kesh series starts resonating with general tendencies in the development of Sogdian coinage. The second half of the 1st century AD was a 'creative' moment in the history of Sogdian numismatics which saw the introduction of mutiple new types. By the beginning of the 2nd century AD, however, Sogdian mints switched to the imitation mode: new designs stopped being introduced and they kept dwelling on immobilized types. We also see a drastic reduction in weight and quality of metal in each and every Sogdian coinage. This stagnation process continues throughout the entire 2nd century. Only by the very end of the 2nd or possibly even at the beginning of the 3rd century do we see improvements. At that time, mints of Bukhara and Nakhshab started reworking old types in an attempt to improve and standardize the quality of their coins. In the Kesh coinage this process was manifested by the transition from the completely denegrated ΦΣΕΙΓΑ ΧΑΡΙΣ type to the new Hercules and Zeus type.

References

Abdullaev, K. 1997. Монета с изображением Зевса и Геракла из Кашкадарьи [A coin with images of Hercules and Zeus from Kashka-darya]. Нумизматика Центральной Азии, вып. II: 9–16. Tashkent.

Abdullaev, K. 2000. A Coin from the Kashkadarya Valley with Representation of Zeus and Hercules. *Parthica* 2: 147–152.

Abdullaev, K. 2012. Numismatic Finds (2002–2006). *Dzhandavlat-tepe. The Excavation Report for Seasons 2002–2006.* Vol. 1: 172–183. Prague: Karolinum Press.

Alram, M. 1986. *Nomina Propria Iranica in Nummis. Iranisches Personenamenbuch,* Band IV. Vienna: Verlag der Österreichischen Akademie der Wissenschaften.

Alram, M. 2007. Ardashir's Eastern Campaign and the Numismatic Evidence, in J. Cribb and G. Herrmann (eds), *After Alexander: Central Asia before Islam.* London: British Academy: 228-242.

Atakhodzhaev and Naymark 2020 = Атаходжаев, А.Х. Наймарк, А.И. 2020. *Самаркандские подражания тохаристанским подражаниям оболам Евкратида* [Samarqand imitations of Tokharistan imitations of obols of Eucratides]. Узбекистан и Центральная Азия в системе мировой цивилизации. Материалы международной научной онлайн конференции, посвященной 50-летию Самаркандского института археологии Национального центра археологии Академии наук Республики Узбекистан и 85-летию академика А.А. Аскарова. Самарканд: 184–186.

Atakhodzhaev and Naymark 2021 = Атаходжаев, А.Х. Наймарк, А.И. 2021. *Неопубликованные находки кушанских монет в Согде* [Unpublished finds of Kushan coins in Sogdiana]. *Археология Узбекистана,* вып. 1: 42–62.

Atakhodzhaev and Naymark forthcoming A = Атаходжаев, А.Х. Наймарк, А.И. forthcoming A. Три медные парфянские монеты из Согдианы [Three Parthian coppers from Sogdiana]. *Ellinistic sharq: an'ana va inovatsiya.*

Atakhodzhaev and Naymark forthcoming B = Атаходжаев, А.Х. Наймарк, А.И. forthcoming B. Монетные находки из района Сарыкуля в Сазаганской степи к западу от Самарканда [Coin finds from Sarykul area in Sazagan Steppe, west of Samarqand].

Balakhvantsev 2014 = Балахванцев. А.С. 2014. Новая надпись из Тахти-Сангина и некоторые проблемы восточного эллинизма [New inscription from Takht-I Sangin and some problems of eastern Hellenism]. Российская Археология 4: 89–96.

Begmatov, A. 2017. Divine and human figures on the sealings unearthed from Kafir-kala. *Japan Society for Hellenistic-Islam Archaeological Studies* 24: 203–212.

Belyaev and Naymark 2015 = Беляев, В.А. Наймарк, А.И. 2015 Чекан Нахшеба второй половины I века н.э.? [Coinage of Nakhshab in the second half of the 1st century AD?]. Восемнадцатая Всероссийская Нумизматическая Конференция, Москва, Коломна, 20-25 апреля 2015. Тезисы докладов и сообщений. Москва: Государственный исторический Музей: 53–55.

Belyaev, V.A. and Naymark, A.I. forthcoming. Ancient coins from Southern Soghd.

Bopearachchi, O. 1991. *Monnaies gréco-bactriennes et indogrecques: catalogue raisonné. Paris: Bibliothèque Nationale.*

Borell, B. 2017. Herakles on an Intaglio Seal Found at Phu Khao Thong in the Upper Thai-Malay Peninsula. *Zeitschrift für Archäologie Außereuropäischer Kulturen.* Band 7: 59–82.

Cribb, J. 1993. The Heraus Coins: Their Attribution to the Kushan King Kujula Kadphises, c. AD 30–80, in M. Price, A. Burnett and R. Bland (eds) *Essays in Honour of Robert Carson and Kenneth Jenkins.* London: Spink: 116-140.

Cribb, J. 2007. Money as a Marker of Cultural Continuity and Change in Central Asia, in J. Cribb and G. Hermann (eds.) *After Alexander. Central Asia before Islam, Proceedings of the British Academy* 133. Oxford University Press: 334–375.

Cribb J. and Bracey R. forthcoming. *Kushan Coins: A Catalogue based on the Kushan, Kushano-Sasanian and Kidarite Hun Coins in the British Museum, 1st-5th centuries AD.* London: British Museum Publications.

Cunningham, A. 1889. Coins of Tokhari, Kushans and Yue-ti. *Numismatic Chronicle,* 3rd ser., 9: 268–311.

Demidenko 2014 = Демиденко, С.В. 2014. Котлы типа 'Тахти-Сангин–Бармашино': к проблеме взаимопроникновения традиций металлообработки в Центральной Азии [Cauldrons of the type "Takht-I Sangin – Bormashino": towards the problem of mutual infiltration of the metal-working tradition in Central Asia].- Российская археология 4: 75–88.

Drujinina, A. 2008. Gussform mit griechischer lnschrift aus dem Oxos-Tempel. *Archäologische Mitteilungen aus Iran und Turan* 40: 121–135.

Falk, H. 2012. Ancient Indian Eras: An Overview. *Bulletin of the Asia Institute* 21 (2007): 131–45.

Falk, H. and Bennett, C. 2009. Macedonian Intercalary Months and the Era of Azes. *Acta Orientalia* 70: 197–216.

Gardner, P. 1886. *The Coins of the Greek and Scythic Kings of Bactria and India in the British Museum.* London.

Göbl, R. 1978. *Antike Numismatik (Einführung-Münzkunde-Münzgeschichte Geld-geschichte-Methodenlehre-Praktischer Teil),* 2 vols, Munich.

Gorin 2012 = Горин, А.Н. 2012. Монеты из раскопок второго буддийского храма Дальверзинтепа (По материалам археологических исследований

2006–2007 гг.) [Coins from the excavations of the second Buddhist temple of Dalverzintepa (Materials of the archaeological research of 2006-2007)]. Дальверзинтепа. Итоги раскопок на втором буддийском храме: 173–222. Tokyo: Soka University.

Gorin 2015 = Горин, А.Н. 2015. Кушанские монеты из Бухарского оазиса [Kushan coins from the Bukharan oasis]. *Бухарский оазис и его соседи в древности и Средневековье: на основе материалов научных конфнренций 2010 и 2011 гг. Труды Государственного Эрмитажа, Т. LXXV*. Санкт-Петербург: Государственный Эрмитаж: 53–62.

Huyse, P. 1999. *Die dreisprachige Inschrift Šābuhrs I. an der Kaʿba-i Zardušt (ŠKZ) [Corpus Inscriptionum Iranicarum, III. - Pahlavi Texts, I]*. London.

Humbach, H. 1966. *Baktrische Sprachdenkmäler* I. Wiesbaden, 1966.

Ilyasov, J.Y. and Rusanov, D.V. 1997/98. A Study on the Bone Plates from Orlat. *Silk Road Art and Archaeology* 5: 107–159.

Ivanchik, A.I. 2011. New Greek Inscriptions from Takht-i Sangin and the Question as to the Emergence of the Bactrian Written Language. *Bulletin of Miho Museum*, 11: 39–77.

Kabanov 1965 = Кабанов, С.К. 1965. Руины поселения III–IV вв. в долине Кашка-дарьи [Ruins of a settlement of the 3rd–4th centuries in the valley of Kashka-darya]. *История материальной культуры Узбекистана [Istoriya materialnoy kultury Uzbekistana]*, vyp. 6: 71–86.

Kabanov 1981 = Кабанов, С.К. 1981. Культура сельских поселений южного Согда III-VI вв. По материалам исследований в зоне Чим-Курганского водохранилища *[The culture of the rural settlements of South Soghd in the 3rd-6th centuries. Materials of the exploration in the zone of Chim-Kurgan reservoir]*. Ташкент: Фан.

Lerner, J. and Sims-Williams, N. 2011. *Seals, Sealings and Tokens from Bactria to Gandhara (4th to 8th century CE)*. Wien, ÖAW.

Mitchiner, M. 1973. *The Early Coinage of Central Asia*. London: Hawkins Publications.

Mitchiner, M. 1975. *Indo-Greek and Indo-Scythian Coinage*, 5 vols. London: Hawkins Publications.

Mitchiner, M. 1978. *Oriental Coins and Their Values. The Ancient and Classical World*. London: Hawkins Publications.

Mitchiner, M. 2004. *Ancient Trade and Early Coinage*, 2 vols. London: Hawkins Publications.

Musakaeva 1990 = Мусакаева А. 1990. Античные и раннесредневековые монеты музея Истории Народов Узбекистана [Ancient and early Mediaeval coins of the Museum of History of the Peoples of Uzbekistan]. in Э.В. Ртвеладзе (ред.) Нумизматика Узбекистана: 18–31. Ташкент: Fan.

Naymark 1987 = Наймарк. А.И. 1987. Древние монеты из Кум-Совтана [Ancient coins from Kum-Sovtan]. *Вторая Всесоюзная Нумизматическая Конференция*: 50–51. Москва.

Naymark 1995 = Наймарк, А.И. 1995. О начале медной чеканки в Бухарском Согде [On the beginning of copper coinage in Bukharan Soghd]. *Нумизматика Центральной Азии I*: 29–50. Ташкент.

Naymark, A. 2001 *Sogdiana, its Christians and Byzantium: A Study of Cultural and Artistic Connections in Late Antiquity and Early Middle Ages*. Ph.D. dissertation. Bloomington, Indiana.

Naymark 2008 = Наймарк, А. 2008. О причинах появления подражаний эллинистическим монета в Согдиане [Imitations of Hellenistic coins in Sogdiana: causes for their appearance]. (Translated into Russian by Nataliya Smirnova). Вестник Древней Истории 1: 55–70.

Naymark, A.I. 2016. The Coinage of Nakhshab during the First–Fourth Centuries CE. Towards a New Systematization of Sogdian Coinages and the Political History of Sogd during Antiquity. *Journal of Inner Asian Art and Archaeology* 7: 55–77.

Naymark 2020a = Наймарк, А. 2020a. Самаркандский чекан второй половины III – начала VI веков н.э. [Samarqand coinage of the 3rd to the beginning of the 6th century CE]. Узбекистан и Центральная Азия в системе мировой цивилизации. Материалы международной научной онлайн конференции, посвященной 50-летию Самаркандского института археологии Национального центра археологии Академии наук Республики Узбекистан и 85-летию академика А.А. Аскарова: 180–183. Самарканд.

Naymark 2020b = Наймарк, А.И. 2020b. Монеты нахшебского князя Аштата [Coins of Nakhshab ruler Ashtat]. История и археология Турана # 5: 204–248. Самарканд.

Naymark 2021 = Наймарк, А.И. 2021. Медная монета с "арамейской надписью", воспроизводящая тип халков Евтидема: медный чекан Бухары в I веке н.э.? [Copper coin with 'Aramaic inscription' reproducing the type of Euthydemus's chalkoi: copper coinage of Bukhara in the 1st century AD]. Двадцать первая Всероссийская нумизматическая конференция. Тверь, *24-29 мая 2021*. Москва.

Naymark 2022 = Наймарк, А.И. 2022. "Подражания тетрадрахмам Евтидема с тамгой: аланская династия в Бухаре в I веке н.э.?" [Imitations of the tetradrachms of Euthydemus with tamga: the Alanian dynasty in Bukhara in the 1st century AD?], *Ellinistic sharq: an'ana va inovatsiya*.

Nikitin 1986 = Никитин, А.Б. 1986. Монеты с всадником из Мерва [Coins with a horseman from Marw]. Советская Археология, 1986, no. 3: 243–249.

Olbrycht, M.J. 2014. Dynastic Connection in the Arsacid Empire and the Origins of the House of Sasan, in V. Sarkhosh Curtis, E.J. Pendleton, M. Alram and T. Daryaee (eds), *The Parthian and Early Sasanian Empires: Adaptation and Expansion. Proceedings of a Conference held in Vienna, 14-16 June 2012*: 23–35. Oxford: Oxbow.

Omelchenko 2001 = Омельченко, А.В. 2001. Подражание драхме с типом Александра Македонского в Южном Согде [An imitation of a drachm with a type of Alexander of Macedon in South Soghd]. Нумизматика Центральной Азии, вып. V: 14–16. Ташкент.

Omel'chenko, A.V. 2016. On the Question of Sasanian Presence in Sogdiana. Recent Results of Excavations in Paykand. *Journal of Inner Asian Art and Archaeology* 7: 79–107.

Omelchenko and Gorin 2019 = Омельченко, А.Н. Горин. 2019. Завоевания Сасанидов в Средней Азии: новые свидетельства по материалам раскопок в Пайкенде (Бухарский оазис) [Sasanian conquests in Central Asia: new evidence from the excavations in Paykand (Bukharan oasis)]. История и археология Турана. № 4. Посвященный юбилею Мухамаджана Исамиддинова: 119–136. Самарканд.

Rapson, E.J. 1904. Ancient Silver Coins from Baluchistan. *Numismatic Chronicle*, Fourth Series, Vol. 4: 311–325.

Rosenfield, J.M. 1967. *The Dynastic Arts of the Kushans*. Berkely-Los Angeles: University of California Press.

Rtveladze 1987 = Ртвеладзе, Э.В. 1987. Древние монеты Средней Азии [Ancient coins of Central Asia]. Ташкент: Издательство им. Гафура Гуляма.

Rtveladze, E.V. 1992. The Coinage of Phseigakharis. *Bulletin of the Asia Institute*. New Series/Vol. 6: 151-154 (Russian version, but with different illustrations see in Rtveladze 2002: 173–182).

Rtveladze 1999 = Ртвеладзе, Э.В. 1999. Новый тип монет Фсейгахариса [New type of Phseighacharis coins]. Нумизматика Центральной Азии IV: 82. Ташкент (reprinted in: Rtveladze 2002: 183–184).

Rtveladze 2002 = Ртвеладзе Э.В. 2002. Древние и раннесредневековые монеты историко-культурных областей/*Ancient and Mediaeval Coins of the Historical and Cultural Regions of Uzbekistan*, том I. Ташкент.

Rtveladze 2015 = Ртвеладзе Э.В. 2015. О подражаниях монетам Александра Македонского. Центры чеканки и ареал обращения [About the imitations of the coins of Alexander of Macedon. Centers of minting and zones of circulation]. Нумизматика и Эпиграфика, том XIX: 46-51. Москва.

Rtveladze and Nefedov 1995 = Ртвеладзе, Э. Нефедов, Н. 1995. Уникальная серебряная монета греческого правителя из Ер-Кургана (Южный Согд) [Unique silver coin of a Greek ruler from Yer-Kurgan (South Soghd)]. Нумизматика Центральной Азии. Вып.

I. Ташкент: 6062 (reprinted in: Rtveladze 2002: 114-116).

Schindel, N. 2010. The 3rd Century 'Marw Shah' Bronze Coins Reconsidered, in Henning Börm and Josef Wiesehöfer (eds) *Commutatio et Contentio. Studies in the Late Roman, Sasanian and Early Islamic Middle East*: 23–32. Düsseldorf.

Senior, R.C. 2001. *Indo-Scythian Coins and History*, vols 1–3. Lancaster, PA: Classical Numismatic Group.

Sims-Williams, N. and Cribb, J. 1995/6. A New Bactrian Inscription of Kanishka the Great. *Silk Road Arts and Archaeology*, 4: 75–127.

Smirnova 1981 = Смирнова О.И. 1981. Сводный каталог согдийских монет. Бронза [*Catalogue raisonné of Sogdian coins. Bronze*]. Москва: Наука, ГРВЛ.

Tabari/de Goje 1893 = *Annales quos scripsit Abu Djafar Mohammad ibn Djarir al-Tabari*. M.J. de Goje (ed.). Leiden: E.J. Brill, 1879–1901 (multiple vols)

Tabari/Powers 1989 = *The History of al-Tabari. Vol. XXIV. The Empire in Transition*. Transl. and annotated by D.S. Powers. Albany: State University of New York Press.

Whitehead, R.B. 1914. *Catalogue of Coins in the Panjab Museum, Lahore, vol. I, Indo-Greek Coins*. Oxford: Clarendon Press.

Yakunchikov 1911 = Якунчиков, Б.М. 1911. Неизданные и редкие древнегреческие монеты [Unpublished and rare ancient Greek coins]. Записки Нумизматического отделения Императорского Русского археологического общества, 1909, том I, вып. 2–3, с. 56–57, табл. X: 126–127.

Zeymal 1973 = Зеймаль Е.В. 1973. Раннесогдийские монеты с изображением Геракла и Зевса [Early Sogdian coins with representations of Hercules and Zeus] Сообщения Государственного Эрмитажа XXXVII: 68–73.

Zeymal 1975 = Зеймаль, Е.В. 1975. Монеты Западных Кшатрапов в коллекции Государственного Эрмитажа [Coins of Western Kshatrapas in the collection of the State Hermitage]. Е.И. Лубо-Лесниченко, ред. Культура и Искусство Индии и Стран Дальнего Востока. Сборник Статей. Ленинград: Аврора, 1975: 4–20.

Zeymal 1978 = Зеймаль, Е.В. 1978. Политическая история древней Трансоксианы по нумизматическим данным [The political history of ancient Transoxiana according to numismatic data]. Культура Востока. Древность и раннее средневековье: 192–214. Ленинград: Аврора.

Zeymal 1983a = Зеймаль, Е.В. 1983а. Начальный этап денежного обращения древней Трансоксианы [The initial stage of the monetary circulation in ancient Transoxiana]. Б. А. Литвинский [ред.] *Средняя Азия, Кавказ, и зарубежный Восток в древности*: 161–80. Москва: Наука, ГРВЛ.

Zeymal 1983b = Зеймаль, Е.В. 1983b. Древние монеты Таджикистана [Ancient coins of Tajikistan]. Душанбе: Дониш.

Zeymal, E.V. 1983c. The Political History of Transoxiana. The Cambridge History of Iran. Vol. 3, part 1: The Seleucid, Parthian, and Sasanian Periods: 232–62. Cambridge.

Zeymal 1984 = Зеймаль, Е.В. 1984. Приложение: подражания оболам Евкратида [Appendix: imitations of the obols of Eucratides]. Б. А. Литвинский, А. В. Седов. Культы и ритуалы Кушанской Бактрии.: 177–191. Москва: Наука, ГРВЛ.

Plates I to 5

Drachm denomination

1. British Museum 1860,1220.98, W – 2.4g, D – 15mm, A – XII
2. British Museum 1922,0424.4537, W – 2.38g, D – 16mm, A – XII
3. British Museum IOC.255, W – 2.41g, D – 15mm, A – I
4. Lahore Museum, W – 2.92g, D – 15mm
5. British Museum 1890,0404.24, W – 2.55g, D – 15mm, A – X.
6. Zeno 70347 posted by Vetra W – 2.31g, D – 14.5mm, A – XI, from the shores of Chim-Kurgan reservoir.
7. Tashkent Museum, W – 2.18g, D – 15mm, A – I
8. Zeno 20068 from the site "Coins of Central Asia", W – 1.9g; D – 15mm, A – XII, on the site it is supplied with generic information: 'South Soghd'.
9. Zeno 50226 posted by gazali, W – 2g, D – 15.1mm, A – XII, from the shores of Chim-Kurgan reservoir.
10. Zeno 101229 posted by gazali, W – 1.8g, D – 14.3 x 14.9mm, A – XI, from the shores of Chim-Kurgan reservoir.
11. British Museum 1894,0506.1743, W – 1.76g, D – 14mm. A -XI.
12. Zeno 69712 posted by gazali, W – 1.6g, D – 14.5mm, A -XII, from the shores of Chim-Kurgan reservoir.
13. Hermitage Museum, no metrological data is currently available.
14. Zeno 131349 posted by sherpa, W – 1.15g, D – 13.43 x 13.45mm, A - XII, from the shores of Chim-Kurgan reservoir.
15. Hermitage Museum, 37827, W – 1.15g, D – 14.9mm, A - XII.
16. British Museum 1894,0506.1744, W – 1.52g, D – 15mm, A - XI
17. Ashmolean Museum, W – 1.57g, D – 14mm, A - XII.
18. Zeno 35294 posted by hfrans, W – 1.33g, D – 14.7mm, A - I, from the shores of Chim-Kurgan reservoir.

Obolus denomination

19. Private Collection, W – 0.45g, D - 9mm, A - XII, from the "castle" near Sarykul, 45km S-W-W of Samarqand.
20. Private Collection, W – 0.4g; D – 8.5mm, A - XII, from the "castle" near Sarykul, 45km S-W-W of Samarqand.
21. Zeno 228938 posted by venedw, W – 0.2g, D – 8mm; A - XII, most likely from Sazagan Steppe

Comparative materials included in the plates

22. Hermitage Museum, modern cast copy of a lost Phseigha Charis coin. According to E.V. Zeymal it is one of the three specimens cast in one mold that are kept in the Numismatic Department of the State Hermitage. Yet the mold must have been made of an original coin, which is now lost.
23. Kesh imitation of a drachma with the types of Alexander, Zeno 202952 posted by hfrans, W – 0.95g, D – 15.1mm, A – XII, from the shores of Chim-Kurgan reservoir.
24. Kesh imitation of a drachma with the types of Alexander, Zeno 85905 posted by gazali, W – 1.4g, D – 17.3mm, A - XII, from the shores of Chim-Kurgan reservoir.
25. Kesh coin with the images of Hercules and Zeus, Zeno 83144 posted by hfrans, W – 0.7g, D – 12mm, A - XII.

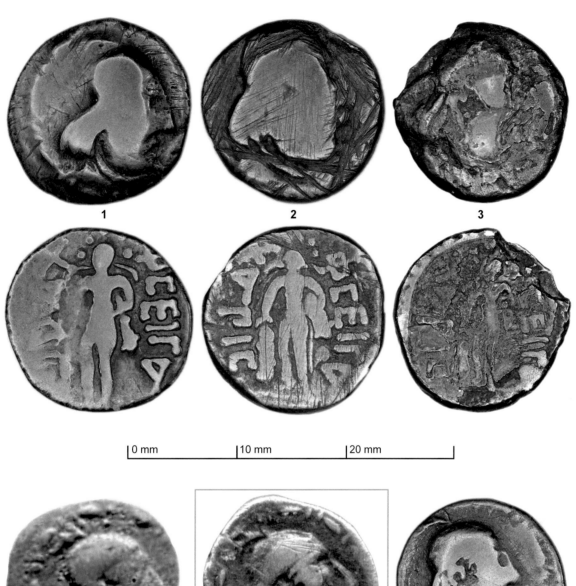

0020   0021

| 0 mm | 10 mm | 20 mm |

6   7   8

15 **16**

0 mm 10 mm 20 mm

17 **18** **0022**

0 mm   10 mm   20 mm

Imperial Ambitions: Coins and Medals of the Two Pahlavi *Shahs* of Iran

Vesta Sarkhosh Curtis

My contribution to Joe's previous *Felicitation* volume was about ancient Persia on Islamic coins and modern banknotes of Iran (Sarkhosh Curtis 2011b). The present paper focuses on the imagery and rhetoric of 20th-century Iranian medals and commemorative coins. The iconography, particularly of the last Shah, Mohammad Reza Pahlavi, is rich and informative for understanding the politics and society of Iran at that time. It is also a valuable source for our understanding of Iran's pre-1979 society which was so very different from the Islamic Republic today. Reza Shah Pahlavi (1926-1944) and his son Mohammad Reza Shah (1944-1979) encouraged the modernizing of the country without taking into account the great divide between rich and poor, and a religious majority which opposed these rapid changes.

This paper does not claim to be a comprehensive survey of the history of the Pahlavi era in modern Iran. It is merely a glimpse at historical and political events of the period 1926-1979 as reflected in the collection of Iranian commemorative coins and medals acquired by the British Museum in recent years. A generous bequest to the Department of Coins and Medals by the late Marion Archibald has made it possible to expand this collection. I hope that Joe Cribb, whose interests are timeless and limitless, will enjoy this light excursion

into modern Iran's imperial iconography under the two Pahlavi *shah*s.

Introduction

A wish to return to the supposed glorious past of ancient Iran had already developed in the previous Qajar period in the 19th – early 20th century. A recent in-depth study of Qajar rock-reliefs, inscriptions and other sources by Hubertus von Gall and Paul Luft (2020) has brought together important information about the creation of a royal iconography, which was closely related to revivalism or 'return', known in Persian as *bāzgasht*. This trend developed during the reign of Fath 'Ali Shah Qajar (1797-1834) when he and many members of the aristocracy became interested in pre-Islamic traditions. The art of ancient Persia, as known from the ruins of Persepolis, and the nearby Sasanian reliefs contributed to the formation of an official royal iconography which was influenced by the ancient past. Equestrian scenes and enthronement scenes inspired by Sasanian rock-reliefs of the 3rd -4th centuries AD became a popular motif on Qajar rock-reliefs, coins and medals, and they were also copied on tiles and architectural reliefs in palaces and public buildings (Lerner 1998; Soucek 2001, Luft 2001; Sarkhosh Curtis 2011 a, b; von Gall & Luft 2020).

Figure 1. Gold medal showing Reza Shah and Mohammad Reza Shah Pahlavi, 40 mm, BM 2018,4065.1 Archibald Bequest.
© Trustees of the British Museum

The notion of revivalism continued from the Qajars under the two Pahlavi *shah*s, and the role that archaeology played here has attracted scholarly attention in recent years (Abdi 2001). A Persepolitan building style as well as the Sasanian palace architecture of Ctesiphon- now in modern Iraq- inspired many public buildings in the 1930s, such as banks, police headquarters and the National Museum of Iran in Tehran (Grigor 2015). Ancient monuments and objects featured prominently on commemorative coins, bank notes and postage stamps (Siebertz 2005; Sarkhosh Curtis 2011a,b; Curtis 2013a,b).

In this essay we shall discuss in brief the rise and fall of the short-lived Pahlavi dynasty, and relate some of the important historical and political events to medals and coins, which served as a popular commemorative tool for royal and political propaganda particularly in the second half of the 20th century until the Islamic Revolution of 1979.

The founder of the Pahlavi dynasty, Reza Khan, came from Mazandaran in the Caspian region of northern Iran. He is described by his son as 'of genuine Persian stock' (Pahlavi 1960: 35). He had served as an officer in the Persian Cossack Brigade (Axeworthy 2007: 225), and after a coup d'état in 1921, which was largely supported by the British Government, the last Qajar ruler Ahmad Shah went into exile in 1923 and was removed from power in 1925. In 1926 Reza Khan was crowned as Reza Shah.

> When my late father was crowned, he became known, in the style of our ancient royal nomenclature, as ShahanShah (King of Kings), Shadow of the Almighty, Vice-Regent of God, and Centre of the Universe (Pahlavi 1960: 36).

Reza Shah adopted the dynastic name Pahlavi, which is the name of the Middle Persian language of pre-Islamic Iran as well as the name of the dynasty of the Parthians who ruled from 248 BC – AD 224.

About the Parthians, Mohammad Reza Shah Pahlavi (1960: 22) wrote as follows:

> About 248 BC, the Parthians, a relatively less civilized Aryan tribe from what is now north-east Iran, ousted the successors of Seleucus... But again our higher culture gradually transformed the newcomers. They adopted Persian manners, worshipped Persian gods...

Both the young Shah and his father were full of admiration for the glories of pre-Islamic Iran. This was also the case with the educated nationalistic middle-class and intelligentsia who were passionately anti-Arab because of the conquest of the Sasanian empire by the Arabs in AD 651.

In 1935 a decree was passed requiring foreign delegations to adopt Iran and not Persia as the official name of the country (Abdy 2001; Milani 2012: 68). In fact, for Iranians Iran had always been the name of their country. As early as around 500 BC Darius the Great (522-486 BC) referred to himself in his monumental rock inscription at Naqsh-e Rustam near Persepolis as 'a Persian, son of a Persian, an Iranian, of Iranian lineage'. Persia or Parsa (modern Fars) is the name of a province in southern Iran and the Achaemenid heartland, and the Greeks adopted the name to refer to the whole country as Persia and the Persians. By the early 20th century, the terms Persia and Persians had acquired negative connotations amongst Iranians (Abdi 2001).

> My father decreed that in all foreign relations, Persia should be known only as Iran. I remember that during the Second World War Winston Churchill told me, grumpily but with a twinkle in his eyes, that he, Churchill, would never be intimidated into speaking of Persia in any way except Persia. (Pahlavi 1960: 43).

Nazi Germany had passed a decree in 1936 whereby Iranians were regarded as pure-blooded Aryans, and Reza Shah misinterpreted the Nazi term 'Aryan' for the term Aryan/Iranian (Milani 2012: 68).

Reza Shah was also an admirer of Kemal Ataturk and his modernization and secularization of his country. He visited Turkey in 1934 and was much impressed by the policy of westernization (Axeworthy 2007: 230). Girls' school were established across Iran, the Persian language was reformed, and many Arabic words were removed. The Islamic hijab or head cover was banned in 1936, so that women were not allowed to wear it in public. This had a mixed reaction amongst the population, as women from a traditional or religious background refused to appear with uncovered heads or with European-style hats. They, therefore, decided not to appear in public at all. Others embraced this bold decision of Reza Shah's and appeared bare headed (Milani 2012:58). Surnames or family names were also introduced in Iran during this time.

Other changes included the introduction of Persian month names. The Persian Jalali solar calendar of the 11th century had already replaced the Islamic Lunar calendar in 1911 under the Qajars, so that the Iranian New Year or Nowruz could begin on the vernal equinox on 20/21 March. But it was not until 1925 that the Arabic month names of the calendar were changed and replaced with ancient Iranian month names after Zoroastrian divine beings or *yazata*s. The starting point

Figure 2. Gold medal showing the coronation of Mohammad Reza Shah Pahlavi and Empress Farah, 38 mm, BM 2007,4210.1.
© Trustees of the British Museum

of the Solar Calendar remained at AD 622, the year Prophet Muhammad fled from Mecca to Medina.

In 1941 the Shah was forced to abdicate by the Allies, in particular Britain and the Soviet Union. The reason behind his removal from power was supposedly his pro-German sentiments during World War II. Reza Shah had to leave Iran. He was first sent via Bombay, where he was not allowed to leave the ship, and then to Mauritius. From there he went into exile in Johannesburg in South Africa where he died in 1944.

Apparently, Reza Shah did not believe in his heir's ability to take over the reins from him in these critical times, and the crown prince himself showed 'reluctance to take the throne' in 1941 (Milani 2012: 86 –88; Pahlavi 1960: 75). The new young Shah realized that he had to keep the Western Allied Forces on his side, and in 1943 all relations with Germany, Italy and Japan were broken off (Pahlavi 1960: 76). From now on Britain and the US kept a close eye on the new Shah and political events in Iran.

After a period of turbulence and insecurity in the 1950s when the popular Prime Minister Dr Mohammad Mossadegh, who had nationalised the Anglo-Iranian Oil Company, was ousted in August 1953 with help of MI6 and CIA, the Shah returned to Tehran from a short temporary exile in Rome. The 1960s were marked by attempts to modernise the country and resistance against the growing influence of the Communist Tudeh party. The Shah began his land reforms in 1960, which came to a temporary halt because of the economy slowing down and pressure by the Kennedy

government to introduce liberalisation. Opposition to the Shah's so-called reforms came also from the religious authorities (Axeworthy 2007: 246 –247). In 1963 Mohammad Reza Shah introduced the 'White Revolution' (*enghelāb-e sefīd*) which included land reforms, privatisation of state factories, a campaign against illiteracy, the formation of a literacy corps (*sepāh-e dānesh*), as well as the introduction of women's rights. These were important points in a bloodless revolution of a socio-political nature with the intention of modernising the country (Ansari 2001: 2). At the same time, the power of the religious authorities was reduced, but not altogether removed. There was strong opposition to the Shah's so-called liberalisation policy from landowners, many politicians and theologians. In addition, the so-called reforms had not gone through Parliament (Axeworthy 2007: 247). Amongst the latter group passionately opposing the Shah was a young cleric in Qom, the future Ayatollah Ruhollah Khomeini.

The Shah's coronation in 1967 and in 1971 the lavish celebrations of the 2500th Anniversary of the Foundation of the Persian Empire by Cyrus the Great (officially scheduled for 1961) undoubtedly contributed to dissatisfaction amongst many elements in Iranian society allowing the clergy to become more powerful and establish a well-structured and efficient network to undermine the regime. The rise in oil prices increased the country's revenues amongst the upper middle classes, and the Shah's grandiose behaviour reflected in the adoption of titles such as 'King of Kings' (*shāhanshāh*), 'Light of the Aryans/Iranians' (*Aryāmehr*) made many Iranians uncomfortable. All these events are reflected in the imagery and inscriptions on Pahlavi

Figure 3. Gold medal of Mohammad Reza Shah Pahlavi showing the Cyrus Cylinder, 38 mm, BM 2007,4161.1.
© Trustees of the British Museum

medals and commemorative coins and bank notes which celebrate the Shah's achievements and those of his late father. The latter received posthumously from the Iranian parliament, the Majlis, the title 'the Great' in 1950 (Figure 1). Medals of the Shah commemorating various anniversaries related to his father refer to Reza Shah as 'His Imperial Majesty the Great King of Kings' (Shahnampoor 2006: 115, no. 92).

In March 1975, four years after the 2500th Anniversary celebrations another unpopular decision was made. Parliament approved the introduction of a new era that was based on the year Cyrus the Great came to the throne of Anshan in Fars in 559 BC. It was actually in 550 BC that Cyrus defeated his Median grandfather Astyages and was crowned King of the Medes and the Persians. On 21 March 1976, the first day of the Iranian New Year or Nowruz, the date of 2535 was introduced in the imperial or *shāhanshāhi* calendar of Iran (Abdollahy 1900: 673). Its appearance created much confusion as well as raising eyebrows. Many coins and medals, as well as some banknotes between 1976 and 1979 bear this impressive date, and official documents in ministries opted for this new date, too. A medal with the profiled busts of the two Pahlavi shahs both wearing military uniforms shows on the reverse the magnificent National Bank in Tehran, and on the obverse the Persian inscription at the bottom refers to the imperial date of 2536 (Figure 1).

This new imperial calendar appeared also on ordinary denominations from 1976 onwards, for example a 20 Rial coin of Mohammad Reza Shah Pahlavi, Light of the Aryans, King of Kings of Iran, has below the profiled

bust of the ruler the date 2536= 1976/1977, and on the reverse a sword-holding lion with the sun on its back and the Pahlavi crown at the top set in the midst of a floral garland (Haghsefat 1389/2010: 245). The lion and the sun motif with the Pahlavi crown towering above the majestic animal carrying a sword in its raised right paw remained the emblem of Imperial Iran and appeared on many commemorative coins and medals of the Shah, a tradition that the father had passed on to his son and heir.

Unlike his father Reza Shah, who was not religious and implemented 'a planned policy of limiting the power and role of the clergy in Iran' after he came to power (Milani 2012: 32), Mohammad Reza Shah Pahlavi was religious and very much under the influence of his superstitious mother and her devotion to Shi'i traditions.

For example, in his *Mission for my Country*, he describes vividly his personal religious experience when he fell seriously ill with typhoid at the age of seven, and 'it was during that acute illness that my religious life begun' (Pahlavi 1960: 54):

> In my dream, Ali had with his two-pronged sword, which is often seen in paintings of him. He was sitting on his heels on the floor, and in his hands, he held a bowl containing a liquid. He told me to drink, which I did.

Another time while still very young he was riding on the horse of a relative, when the horse slipped, and he was thrown onto a rock. He fainted but woke up without

Figure 4. Gold medal of Mohammad Reza Shah Pahlavi praying at the Holy Shrine of Imam Reza in Mashhad, 38 mm,
BM 2007,4210.2. © Trustees of the British Museum

a scratch and told the entourage that he was saved by the hands of 'Abbas.

> My father was not present, but when he later heard the tale of this vision, he scoffed at my story (Pahlavi 1960: 54).

He also describes another vision when he saw a man with a halo, who he thought was the Twelfth Shi'i imam, the Imām Zamān who is believed to be in occultation. Another incident he referred to was his visit to the University of Tehran in 1949 when shots were fired at him but he survived. He regarded these incidents and the failed CIA and MI6-backed-failed Mossadegh coup in August 1953 as signs of divine support:

> I am convinced that I have been able to accomplish things which, unaided by unseen hand, I could never have done. I make no apologies for my religious faith (Pahlavi: 58).

It has also been suggested that the Shah thought he could rely on the support of the clergy in his fight against the increasingly influential Soviet-backed Tudeh party of Iran. He regarded the clergy as 'an indispensable ally against Communism' (Milani 2012: 100).

There are quite a few medals and coins of a religious character from this time, including the birthday of Imam Reza, the eighth Shi'i leader who is buried in the holy city of Mashhad (Figure 4). A gold medal shows the 'King of Kings, Light of the Aryans' praying in front of the Holy Shrine of Imam Reza in SH 1349/1970. On another of these medals the monument itself is shown and the marginal Persian inscriptions refer to

the Imperial (shāhanshāhi) date 2535 and the 'Fiftieth anniversary of the Pahlavi kingdom'. The date on the reverse is in the Hijri Lunar calendar of AH 1396 (=1976) (Shahnampoor 1385/2006: 118, no. 95).

The Shah's consorts also feature on Pahlavi coins and medals. Mohammad Reza Shah's first wife was the young seventeen-year-old Princess Fawzia of Egypt. In 1939 wedding ceremonies were held in both Cairo and Tehran. Medals commemorating this marriage show the profiled busts of the stunning Egyptian princess and the young Crown Prince of Iran. The marriage, which was regarded as a political arrangement to create an entente between Egypt and Iran, did not survive for long, and they divorced in 1947 (Milani 2012: 139). The infant Princess Shahnaz remained in Tehran with her father, while Fawzia returned to Cairo. In 1951 the Shah married again, and this time his bride was the beautiful half-German Soraya Esfandiari. She accompanied the Shah to Rome when they fled Tehran on 16 August 1953 during the premiership of Dr Mosaddeq but returned to Tehran after the brief exile when the popular Prime Minister was ousted. This marriage, which produced no children, also ended in divorce and Soraya left Iran in 1958. A series of medals shows the royal couple commemorating various events, including the Nowruz or New Year's celebrations at the Spring Equinox on 20/21 March (Figure 5).

The Shah married his third and last wife, Farah Diba, in 1959. In 1960 she produced a long-awaited heir, and in March 1961 she was given the Persian title shahbānū to replace the commonly used Arabic title malekeh for queen (Milani 2012: 274, 276). From now on the Shahbanu or Empress Farah featured prominently on

Figure 5. Gold medal of Mohammad Reza Shah Pahlavi and Queen Soraya, 35 mm, BM 2021,4006.1 Archibald Bequest.
© Trustees of the British Museum

Figure 6. Gold medal of Mohammad Reza Shah Pahlavi and Empress Farah, 37 mm, BM 2018,4104.1 Archibald Bequest.
© Trustees of the British Museum

medals and commemorative coins, both with the Shah (Figure 6), as well as on her own. The birth of an heir to the throne seemed to secure the longevity of the Pahlavi dynasty, and politically the Shah was riding high domestically. Grandiose ideas about himself as king of an ancient nation combined with his extreme nationalism, which was fostered by many in his entourage, led to one accolade after another. In 1965 he was given the title 'Aryamehr' meaning Light of the Aryans/ Sun of the Aryans by Parliament (Steele 2020: 30). The coronation followed in 1967. This was the first of two lavish celebrations, the other being the 2500th Anniversary of the foundation of the Persian Empire in 1971. At his coronation, Shāhan Shāh Aryāmehr (King of Kings, Light of the Aryans) first crowned

himself in the fashion of Napoleon, and then placed a crown on the head of Shahbanu Farah. This event was commemorated on medals showing the royal couple on the obverse and the actual coronation ceremony on the reverse (Figure 2).

It is interesting that Mohammad Reza Shah remarked before his coronation that 'it is not a ... pleasure to bear the crown of such a poor people' (Burda n.d.: 49). In fact, it was not possible to have a coronation before there was an heir to the throne.

The pomp and ceremony of the Shah's coronation would only be surpassed in October 1971 by the 2500th anniversary celebration of Cyrus the Great, the founder of the Persian Empire. The Tomb of Cyrus (Figure 7), the Cyrus Cylinder (Figure 3), and the ruins of the Tachara Palace of Darius at Persepolis (Figure 8) were amongst popular themes on coins, medals, bank notes and stamps of the 1970s.

The most iconic object of these celebrations was undoubtedly the Cyrus Cylinder which was found in Babylon in 1879 by Hormuzd Rassam, who was excavating in Mesopotamia on behalf of the British Museum (Curtis 2013a: 32–33; 2013b). It seems that these celebrations were originally planned for 1961 which would have been 2500 years after the conquest of Babylon by Cyrus the Great in 539 BC, but for 'reasons that are now obscure it was postponed twice' (Curtis 2013b: 87).

The Islamic Revolution brought an end to the rule of the Pahlavi dynasty and Iran's image as a modern and westernised country was shattered after 1979. The collection of Iranian coins and medals in the British Museum provides an important source for an understanding of and an insight into a visual world that seems so alien to contemporary Iran.

References

Abdi, K. 2001. Nationalism, Politics and the Development of Archaeology in Iran, *American Journal of Archaeology* 105, No. 1 January: 51–76.

Ansari, A.M. 2001. The Myth of the White Revolution: Mohammad Reza Shah, 'Modernization' and the Consolidation of Power, *Middle Eastern Studies*, Vol. 37, No. 3 (July): 1–24.

Axeworthy, M. 2007. *Empire of the Mind. A History of Iran.* London: Hurst.

Burda, F. n.d. *Coronation in Tehran. The Imperial Couple of Persia*, Special Edition of Bunte Illustrierte, Berlin: Verlag Offenburg.

Curtis, J. 2013a. *The Cyrus Cylinder and Ancient Persia. A New Beginning for the Middle East*, London: British Museum Press.

Curtis, J. 2013b. The Cyrus Cylinder: the Creation of an Icon and its Loan to Tehran, in I. Finkel (ed.), *The Cyrus Cylinder. The King of Persia's Proclamation from Ancient Babylon*: 85-103. London, New York: I.B. Tauris.

Errington, E. and Sarkhosh Curtis, V. 2011. *From Persepolis to the Punjab. Exploring Ancient Iran, Afghanistan and Pakistan.* London: British Museum Press.

Grigor, T. 2015. Kingship Hybrized, Kingship Homogenized: Revivalism under the Qajar and the Pahlavi Dynasties, in S. Babaei and T. Grigor (eds), *Persian Kingship and Architecture. Strategies of Power in Iran from the Achaemenids to the Pahlavis*: 218-254. London and New York: I.B. Tauris.

Haghsefat, A. 1389/2010. *Do rū-ye sekkehhā-ye Pahlavī.* Tehran. [Both sides of Pahlavi coins]

Figure 7. Bronze medal of Mohammad Reza Shah Pahlavi showing the Tomb of Cyrus the Great (550-535 BC) at Pasargadae, 36 mm, BM 2006,0906.1. © Trustees of the British Museum

Figure 8. Commemorative Pahlavi coin showing the ruins of the Palace of Darius the Great (522-486 BC) at Persepolis, 30 mm, BM 2017,4114.5 Archibald Bequest. © Trustees of the British Museum

Lerner, J. 1998. Sasanian and Achaemenid Revivals in Qajar Art., pl. XIX in V. Sarkhosh Curtis, R. Hillenbrand and J.M. Rogers (eds), *The Art and Archaeology of Ancient Persia. New Light on the Parthian and Sasanian Empires*: 162-167. London and New York: I.B. Tauris.

Milani, A. 2012. *The Shah*. New York: St Martin's.

Pahlavi, M.R. Shah. 1960. *Mission for my Country*. London: Hutchison.

Sarkhosh Curtis, V. 2017. The Lion on Coins of Iran, in *Catalogue of the Exhibition Parviz Tanavoli and the Lions of Iran*: 224-233. Museum of Contemporary Art, Tehran.

Sarkhosh Curtis, V. 2011. The British and Archaeology in Nineteenth-Century Persia, in E. Errington and V. Sarkhosh Curtis (eds), *From Persepolis to the Punjab. Exploring Ancient Iran, Afghanistan and Pakistan*: 166-178. London: British Museum Press.

Sarkhosh Curtis, V. 2011b. Fascination with the Past: Ancient Persia on the Coins and Banknotes of Iran, in S. Bahndare and S. Garg (eds.), *Felicitas. Essays in Numismatics, Epigraphy and History in Honour of Joe Cribb*: 81-99. Mumbai: Reesha Books.

Sarkhosh Curtis, V. 2005. The Legacy of Ancient Persia, in J. Curtis and N. Tallis (eds), *Forgotten Empire. The world of ancient Persia*: 250-257. London: British Museum Press.

Shahnampoor, M. 1385/2006. In Persia: *Medāl-hā va yādbūd-hā Qājār va Pahlavi* (*Medals & Monuments Qajar & Pahlavi*). Tabriz.

Siebertz, R. 2005. *Die Briefmarken Irans als Mittel der Politischen Propaganda*. Vienna: OAW.

Soucek, P. 2001. Coinage of the Qajars: a System in Continual Transition, *Iranian Studies*, 2001, Vol. 34, No. 1/4, Qajar Art and Society (2001): 51–87.

Steele, R. 2020. *The Shah's Imperial Celebrations of 1971: Nationalism, Culture and Politics in Late Pahlavi Iran*. London & New York: I.B. Tauris.

von Gall H. and Luft P. 2020. *Die Qājārischen Felsreliefs*. Berlin: Dietrich Reimer.

The Identity of the Rider on Indo-Greek Coins

Simon Glenn[1]

It may seem a regressive step in a volume dedicated to Joe Cribb, who has done so much to move the study of Graeco-Bactrian and Indo-Greek coinage away from the preoccupations of Classical scholars, to focus on the identity of a particular equestrian figure on these coins. This paper, however, takes as its starting point a remark made by Cribb himself. In a broad analysis of coinage in Central Asia from its introduction by the Achaemenids to the appearance of Islamic coinage in the region in the eighth century AD, Cribb traced the influence of Alexander the Great on the coinage of the Indo-Greeks. Having discussed the introduction of the Attic weight standard, the reference to Alexander on the so-called 'pedigree' coins of Agathocles, and the portrait types chosen by the kings, Cribb comes to the image of a figure on horseback found on the reverses of coins of certain Indo-Greek rulers (Cribb 2007: 339–341). A horse is shown, galloping to the right, ridden by a male figure wearing a plumed Boeotian helmet, the ties of the royal diadem fluttering behind him. In addition, Cribb argued that a similar figure, but now dismounted performing a gesture of blessing with his outstretched right hand should be considered to have the same identity. Table 1 lists the series of each ruler on which these images appear.

The reverse of Graeco-Bactrian and Indo-Greek coins is usually reserved for a divinity or divine attribute, the side of the coin on which we find the figure on horseback with only one exception. In the two rare series of Hermaeus the equestrian figure appears on the obverses of the coins while the reverse features Zeus seated on a throne making a blessing gesture with his outstretched hand. This gesture and its use by the standing figure on the coins of Agathocleia and Nicias were taken by Cribb, along with the reverse position of the image as evidence that the figure was divine and therefore a deified Alexander rather than the king on horseback which had been the traditional explanation.[2]

I wish to offer an argument, made on the basis of a particular feature of the horse ridden by the figure to support further Cribb's identification of Alexander the Great.[3] On many (but not all) of these coins the horse

Table 1: Indo-Greek coins with the figure of 'Alexander'

Ruler	Obverse	Reverse	Bopearachchi 1991 reference
Antimachus II	Nike	Figure on horseback	196–197, série 1
Agathocleia	Bust of Agathocleia	Standing figure making blessing gesture	251, séries 1 & 2
Philoxenus	Bust of Philoxenus	Figure on horseback	288–293, séries 1–9
Nicias	Bust of Nicias	Standing figure making blessing gesture	311–312, séries 2 & 3
Nicias	Bust of Nicias	Figure on horseback	312, séries 5 & 6
Menander II	Bust of Menander	Figure on horseback	313, série 3
Hermaeus and Calliope	Jugate bust of Hermaeus and Calliope	Figure on horseback	325, séries 1 & 2
Hermaeus	Figure on horseback	Zeus, seated on throne making blessing gesture and holding sceptre	329, séries 7 & 8
Apollodotus II	Bust of Apollodotus	Figure on horseback	348, série 4
Hippostratus	Bust of Hippostratus	Figure on horseback	356–358, séries 3–7

[1] I am grateful to the editors of this volume for the invitation to contribute and their comments on this paper. I must also thank Rachel Wood for discussion of the image of Alexander in Central Asia on non-numismatic media. Above all I wish to thank Joe Cribb for his support, guidance, and advice since the beginning of my work on the coins of the Graeco-Bactrian kings a decade ago.

[2] 'Roi cavalier' is the phrase used in Bopearachchi (1991) to describe the figure. Mitchiner (1975) refers to an 'armed horseman' on the coins of Antimachus II (76, type 135) and 'king' elsewhere, whether a generic king or the issuer of the coins is unclear.

[3] The identity of the rider as Alexander had, in fact, been suggested very briefly by Jenkins (1958: 71 and 73) and slightly elaborated by Bivar (1965: 79) with regard to the features of the horse's head. Both scholars were aware only of the phenomenon on the coins of Philoxenus.

Figure 1.1. Antimachus II, 2.33 g, 15 mm, Ashmolean
Museum, HCR51627

Figure 1.2. Antimachus II, 2.42 g, 18 mm, Ashmolean
Museum, HCR45265

Figure 1.3. Agathocleia, 2.57 g, 19 mm, ANS, 1947.48.1

seems to have protuberances on its head. Although close to the position of the horse's ears, these features seem intended to represent a different part of the head. These features are not depicted in a consistent manner. On some examples they are positioned parallel to and are not much larger than the horse's ears (figure 1.12). On other coins the depiction of a single horn appearing from the horse's head seems likely (figures 1.4, 1.6, 1.11). There are also clear multiple horn features on other coins, sometimes showing two (figure 1.10) and occasionally three (figure 1.9). On other coins the features are quite elaborate, with horizontal sections at right angles to the horn attached directly to the head (figure 1.7). There are also instances where there appear to be uncertain features on the head of the horse which are distinct from the ears, mane, and other natural parts of the horse's anatomy (figures 1.1, 1.5). Finally, it is very important to note that the horns are not a consistent feature of the depiction of the horse and two coins (figures 1.2, 1.13) are presented here from the beginning and end of the sequence to illustrate this phenomenon.

Although the horse ridden by Alexander is not universally depicted with horns, there is enough evidence to conclude that there was an intention to show these unnatural features. The occasional appearance of such 'horns' might be attributed to die breaks or other flaws, but the feature appears too often to allow such an explanation. Our understanding of the production process of the coins is limited, although it is highly likely that dies were engraved following instruction from mint officials and that, in this case, the engravers chose to depict the horn features in different ways, perhaps not comprehending why a horse should be given horns, leading to the varying depictions, even to the extent of the number of horns for inclusion. If we accept the suggestion that the horse was intended to be depicted with horns on its head, we come to the obvious question: why?

Horns had long had an association with power and divinity, a tradition found in the Old Testament (Süning 1984: 328–333). The so-called Pashupati Seal of the Indus Valley Civilisation famously depicts a figure with a large horned headdress. Closer in time to our coins the deified Alexander had been depicted on coins of Ptolemy I and Lysimachus with the ram's horn of Zeus Ammon emanating from his temple. Seleucus I had also been depicted posthumously with bull's horns on coins of his successors (Kroll 2007: 116–120). Horns on the head of a horse, however, might have a specific meaning.

Alexander's own horse was famous both in his lifetime and, like much of the Alexander legend, for long after. Named Bucephalus ('ox head' in Greek) Alexander first encountered the horse when it was offered for sale to his father, Philip II, as a magnificent, but untameable beast.[4] Alexander, however, was able to mount and ride the horse which became his steed throughout his later campaigns until its death in 326 BC following the Battle of the Hydaspes (Arrian, *Anabasis*, V, 19). Arrian tells us that Alexander founded two cities at this point in his conquests, one called Nicaea to commemorate the victory and the other Bucephala in memory of his horse. The location of the city is not known although it was probably on the west bank of the Jhelum (Hydaspes) river (Cohen 2013: 308–312). Although Narain was sceptical that the city was still in existence at the time of Menander I, later references, notably in the *Periplus of the Erythraean Sea* (47) suggest that it survived well into the first century AD (Narain 1957: 80–81).

The origin of Bucephalus's name is uncertain, although it most likely comes from a bucranium brand on the horse's flank, indicating its Thessalian origin and therefore high quality. The clear meaning of the

---

[4] Plutarch, *Alexander*, 6. The literary accounts of Bucephalus are collected in Anderson (1930).

Figure 1.4. Philoxenus, 16.56 g, 33 mm, ANS, 1995.51.147

Figure 1.5. Philoxenus, 9.04 g, 22 mm, Ashmolean Museum, HCR51937

Figure 1.6. Philoxenus, 2.35 g, 12 mm, Ashmolean Museum, HCR51939

name to any Greek speaker as 'ox head' led to other suggestions, some more extraordinary than others. Bucephalus may have received this name because of a patch of white hair in the shape of an ox's head in the middle of his forehead, a particularly fierce appearance like that of a bull, an especially broad head, a head the same shape as an ox's, or, most interestingly for our purpose, because he had horns on his head like an ox (Anderson 1930: 3–8). This latter explanation only appears relatively late in the tradition and is rejected by Byzantine scholars before reappearing in the *Roman d'Alexandre en Prose* and elsewhere. It should be noted at this point that, although it is apparently possible for

horses to have bony growths on their foreheads they do not, of course, have fully-fledged horns (Miller 1917).

Although this may seem to be a rather tenuous conclusion, other earlier numismatic evidence can support the suggestion. Horses with horns were a type regularly used under the early Seleucids, particularly in the east of their empire (figures 2.1–2; Miller and Walters 2004: 49). There seems to have been a particular focus at the mints of Bactra and Aï Khanum with the type appearing on a wide range of denominations. The horned horse head was also used by the Seleucids as a small symbol subordinate to the main type, appearing presumably to demonstrate some piece of information relating to the coins which was important for mint administration (figure 2.3). Here, however, it has no broader significance, being simply one of a range of such symbols. The larger type of the horned horse head had been thought of as depicting Bucephalus, although this explanation has been rejected and it has been suggested that these Seleucid coins were in fact the basis for the later legend in the literary tradition that Alexander's horse had literal horns (Miller and Walters 2004: 52–53).

Figure 1.7. Philoxenus, 9.29 g, 22 mm, Ashmolean Museum, HCR51945

Figure 1.8. Nicias, 2.49 g, 17 mm, Ashmolean Museum, HCR45355

Figure 1.9. Menander II, 2.35 g, 15 mm, ANS, 1944.100.74813

There is, however, one further Seleucid type of importance to our discussion. In 1999 Arthur Houghton and Andrew Stewart published a previously unknown tetradrachm of Seleucus I (Houghton and Stewart 1999; Houghton and Lorber 2002: 81, no. 203). The obverse features the usual image of the lifetime and posthumous coins in the name of Alexander the Great: a beardless Heracles wearing a lion scalp. On the reverse appears a figure on horseback wearing a helmet adorned with horns and a cloak which bellows behind him while he holds a spear in his right hand. The horse on which he is sitting clearly has horns protruding from its head (figure 3.1). The coin is dated by Houghton and Lorber to c. 295 BC. The type is also known from drachms (figure 3.2) and hemidrachms (Houghton and Lorber 2002: 84, no. 209; 85, no. 213). The series is securely attributed to the mint of Ecbatana.

Although this much is known we find ourselves in the familiar position of being uncertain regarding the identity of the rider on the reverse of the coins. E.T. Newell (1938: 181; Houghton and Lorber 2002: 71–73, nos 173–175) suggested that the rider was Seleucus I himself, linking the horned helmet worn by the horseman to that found on the obverse of Seleucus's Susa victory coinage (figure 3.3). The identity of the male head on these latter issues is also the subject of debate. The figure is clean shaven and shown wearing a helmet adorned with a bull's horn and ear and covered in a panther skin the paws of which are tied at the figure's neck. The clear allusion in this imagery is to Dionysus and by extension to the Graeco-Macedonian conquest of the East. For Newell (1938: 156–157) the head depicts Seleucus, while Hadley (1974) argued that it instead shows Alexander, in either case the figure is shown in the guise of Dionysus.

More recently Hoover (2002) has rejected the identification with Alexander, preferring Seleucus on the grounds that other Diadochi had begun to have themselves depicted on coins by the time of these issues. The fact that, unlike other posthumous representations of Alexander, such as the famous image found on the coins of Lysimachus in which Alexander sports a ram's horn and *anastolē*, this helmeted image is absent from the depictions of Alexander in other media is taken by Hoover as further evidence that the great conqueror is not the one represented on these coins. The lack of a continuing tradition of showing Alexander in this manner is not, however, necessarily a barrier to his identification in the image. The coins were produced at a time of considerable iconographic experimentation and by no means were all depictions widely adopted. For example, the early issues of Ptolemy I showing a deified Alexander with ram's horn at his temple wearing an elephant scalp headdress, *mitra*, and *aegis* were not widely reproduced elsewhere.[5] A direct connection to the obverses of the Indo-Greek kings who, following Demetrius I, were depicted wearing elephant scalp helmets, seems unlikely.

---

[5] For the type see Lorber (2018), 256–270, e.g., no. 40.

Figure 1.10. Hermaeus and Calliope, 9.71 g, 21 mm, Ashmolean Museum, HCR53897

Figure 1.11. Apollodotus II, 9.12 g, 28 mm, Ashmolean Museum, HCR54090

Figure 1.12. Hippostratus, 8.99 g, 29 mm, Ashmolean Museum, HCR45476

Figure 1.13. Hippostratus, 8.69 g, 30 mm, Bibliothèque nationale de France, Bopearachchi 6

Figure 2.1. Seleucus I, Pergamum, 16.75 g, 29 mm, ANS, 1967.152.675

Figure 2.2. Antiochus I, Aï Khanum, 16.7 6g, 27 mm, Bibliothèque nationale de France, L 1598

Figure 2.3. Seleucus I, Susa, 16.95 g, 25 mm, ANS, 1944.100.72213

Hoover also deals with the equestrian figure. The identification of Alexander as the horse rider is rejected on the basis that the figure is shown wearing trousers, a garment Diodorus tells us Alexander refused to adopt (Hoover 2002: 59). On the examples of this type available for study it is far from clear that the figure is indeed wearing trousers. For Hoover the horns of the horse are not conclusive evidence that it is Bucephalus and being ridden by Alexander. The prevalence of horns on horses is to be explained as a general symbol of power rather than as a direct punning reference to Alexander's horse (Hoover 2002: 58). Other, and later, depictions of Bucephalus are not particularly helpful in clarifying whether he was regularly given horns. On the one hand, his appearance on the famous Alexander Mosaic from Pompeii sees him with ears a different colour from the rest of his head, and indeed the other horses in the scene, giving a similar appearance to

Figure 3.1. Seleucus I, Ecbatana, 17.07 g, Nomos 1, 6/5/2009, lot 119

Figure 3.2. Seleucus I, Ecbatana, 3.92 g, 16 mm, Bibliothèque nationale de France, R 2317

Figure 3.3. Seleucus I, Susa, 16.89 g, 26 mm, ANS, 1944.100.74108

horns. (Houghton and Stewart 1999: 31). On the other hand, of the large numbers of coin types produced in the Koinon of Macedonia in the third century AD depicting Alexander riding or taming Bucephalus none clearly show the horse with horns (figure 5).

The image of Alexander was, of course, used in Central Asia in other ways and was clearly important. Imitations of his coins showing Heracles wearing a lion scalp continued to circulate in the region, in various styles, until the second century AD (Abdullaev 2017: 219). These issues may have helped contribute to the conclusion that the image on the obverse was Alexander, a misapprehension which seems to have

been demonstrated by the so-called 'pedigree' coins of Agathocles on which the legend 'of Alexander, son of Philip' appears (Glenn 2020: 135–143). Indeed, it is quite possible that the intention of those responsible for making the image of the equestrian figure on the coins differed from how it was interpreted by those who encountered the coins later. Unlike other forms of visual representation, however, we have all the same information on the coin as users in the ancient world. It is likely, therefore, that the image had a degree of ambiguity even at the time of its production. The image of Heracles (perhaps considered to be Alexander by this time) wearing a lion scalp headdress was clearly a powerful one and is found on an ivory miniature

Figure 4. Ptolemy I, Alexandria, 17.05 g, 28 mm, Bibliothèque nationale de France, Vogüé 580

Figure 5. Koinon of Macedonia, 11.57 g, Bibliothèque nationale de France, Fonds général 223

makhaira handle discovered among the votive offerings at Takht-i Sangin (Litvinskij and Pičikjan 1980: 67).

Alexander's lasting influence on the imagery used by the Graeco-Bactrian and Indo-Greek rulers in the region is, however, beyond doubt and, although we shall never know for certain the intended identification of the figures and horses adorned with horns, it seems likely that the figure on the reverse of these Indo-Greek coins is, given the position on the coins, deified and a king, since he wears the diadem. The horse he rides, which in many cases seems to have been adorned with horns, may have been intended to represent Bucephalus, or perhaps was simply a horse with supernatural power. Given the use of the great conqueror's image and legacy elsewhere in the Graeco-Bactrian and Indo-Greek kingdoms he is surely the only candidate as a deified king and in either case the identity of the rider is Alexander.

References

Abdullaev, K. 2017. The Royal Portrait in Hellenistic Bactria. *Morphomata* 34: 213–254.

Anderson, A.R. 1930. Bucephalas and his Legend. *American Journal of Philology* 51: 1–21.

Bivar, A.D.H. 1965. Indo-Bactrian Problems. *Numismatic Chronicle* (seventh series) 5: 69–108.

Bopearachchi, O. 1991. *Monnaies gréco-bactriennes et indo-grecques: catalogue raisonné.* Paris.

Cohen, G.M. 2013. *The Hellenistic Settlements in the East from Armenia and Mesopotamia to Bactria and India.* Berkeley: University of California Press.

Cribb, J. 2007. Money as a Marker of Cultural Continuity and Change in Central Asia, in J. Cribb and G. Herrmann (eds), *After Alexander: Central Asia before Islam*, Oxford: Oxford University Press: 333–375

Fröhlich, C. 2005. La representation du roi cavalier sur les monnaies indo-scythes et indo-parthes: une approche numismatique. *Revue numismatique* 161: 59–78.

Glenn, S. 2020. *Money and Power in Hellenistic Bactria*, New York: American Numismatic Society.

Hadley, R.A. 1974. Seleucus, Dionysus, or Alexander. *Numismatic Chronicle* (seventh series) 14: 9–13.

Hoover, O.D. 2002. The Identity of the Helmeted Head on the 'Victory' Coinage of Susa. *Schweizerische numismatiche Rundschau* 81: 51–60.

Houghton, A. and Lorber, C. 2002. *Seleucid Coins: A Comprehensive Catalogue. Part 1 Seleucus I through Antiochus III*. Lancaster, P.A., London: American Numismatic Society.

Houghton, A. and Stewart, A. 1999. The Equestrian Portrait of Alexander the Great on a New Tetradrachm of Seleucus I. *Schweizerische numismatische Rundschau* 78: 27–35.

Jenkins, G.K. 1958. Greek and Graeco-Indian coins from the Haughton Collection. *The British Museum Quarterly* 21.3: 70–73.

Kroll, J.H. 2007. The Emergence of Ruler Portraiture on Early Hellenistic Coins: the Importance of Being Divine, in P. Schultz and R. von den Hoff (eds) *Early Hellenistic Portraiture: Image, Style, Context*. Cambridge University Press: 113–122.

Litvinskij, B.A. and Pičikjan, I.R. 1980, Monuments of Art from the Sanctuary of Oxus (North Bactria). *Acta archaeological Academiae scientarum Hungaricae* XXVII: 25–83.

Lorber, C.C. 2018. *Coins of the Ptolemaic Empire. Part 1. Ptolemy I through Ptolemy IV*. New York: American Numismatic Society.

Miller, J.E. 1917. Horned Horses. *Journal of Heredity* 8.7: 303–305.

Miller, R.P. and Walters, K.R. 2004. Seleucid Coinage and the Legend of the Horned Bucephalas. *Schweizerische numismatische Rundschau* 83: 45–54.

Mitchiner, M. 1975. *Indo-Greek and Indo-Scythian Coinage*. London: Hawkins.

Narain, A.K. 1957. *The Indo-Greeks*. Oxford University Press.

Newell E.T. 1938. *The Coinage of the Eastern Seleucid Mints, from Seleucus I to Antiochus III*. New York: American Numismatic Society.

Süring, M.L. 1984. The Horn-motifs of the Bible and the Ancient Near East. *Andrews University Seminary Studies*, 22.3: 327–340.

The Phonology of Greek Names in Kharoṣṭhī Script

Stefan Baums

In his 1920 poem Νομίσματα, the Alexandrian poet C.P. Cavafy expresses his delight in coming across the names of Greek kings on "coins with Indian inscriptions" – those of the Gandhāran rulers Hermaeus, Eucratides, Strato, and Menander – in a "learned book" (Καβάφης 1968: 181). The book in question was probably Whitehead's catalogue of the Lahore Museum collection (Whitehead 1914; cf. Coloru 2009: 118). In this small token of a deep appreciation for Joe Cribb, not only as a master of these coins and their inscriptions, but as a dear colleague, I will take a closer look at what they reveal about the pronunciation of Greek and Gāndhārī, and transcription strategies for Greek names from Aśoka to the end of the Indo-Greek period.

The *Dictionary of Gāndhārī* (Baums & Glass 2002–) currently covers a total of 45 Greek personal names from coins and inscriptions.[1] The complete list, giving first the original name, then its Kharoṣṭhī transcription(s) and source(s), is as follows:[2]

Ἀγαθόκλεια: Agathukria CKC 56
Ἀγαθοκλῆς: Akathukreya CKC 9
Ἀλέξανδρος: Alikasudara Shāh, Mān
Ἀμύντας: Amita CKC 90–92
Ἀντιαλκίδας: Atialikida CKC 42–45
Ἀντιγένης (Ἀντίγονος): Aṃtikini Shāh, Aṃte(*kini) Mān[3]
Ἀντίμαχος: Atimakha CKC 4, 5
Ἀντίοχος: Aṃtiyoka Shāh, Aṃtiyoga Mān
Ἀπολλόδοτος: Apaladata CKC 21–25, 104–111
Ἀπολλοφάνης: Apulaphana CKC 130
Ἀρτεμίδωρος: Artemitora CKC 93–96
Ἀρχέβιος: Arkhebiya CKC 77–80
Δεινοκράτης: Denukrata CKI 1030
Διονυσίδωρος: Di⟨*u⟩nisidora CKI 1000
Διονύσιος: Diunisiya CKC 123–125, 334
Διομήδης: Diyumeta CKC 74–76

Δημήτριος: Dimetriya CKC 1–3, Demetria CKI 564, Demitria CKI 564
Ἔπανδρος: Epadra CKC 52–53
Ἑρμαῖος: Heramaya CKC 97–103, 262–264, 276, H(*e)ramaa CKI 1170, Hirmaa-CKI 328
Εὐκρατίδης: Evukratida CKC 11–17, 19, 329, CKI 917
Εὐχή(?): Avakha- CKI 178
Ζηνόφιλος: Zenuphila- CKI 987
Ἡλιοκλῆς: Heliyakreya CKC 46–48, Heliyakrea CKC 332–333
Ἡλιόφιλος: Heliuphila CKI 328
*Θαΐδωρος(?): Thaïdora CKI 57[4]
Θεοδάμας: Theudama CKI 34, 978
Θεόδοτος: Theuduta CKI 32
Θεόδωρος: Theutara CKC 88–89
Θεόφιλος: Theuphila CKC 83–85
Θεωρός: Thavara CKI 88, 89, 558
Ἱππόστρατος: Hipustrata CKC 122–120
Ἴσανδρος: Isaṃdra- CKI 972
Καλλιόπη: Kaliyapa CKC 97–98
Λυσίας: Lisika CKC 40, Lisia CKC 41[5]
Μάγας: Maka Shāh, Mān
Μένανδρος: Menadra CKC 26–36, Menaṃdra CKI 257, 331, Miṇaṃdra CKI 143, Minedra CKI 176 (Bühler 1894b, 201)[6]
Νικίας: Nikia CKC 86–89
Νίκη: Ṇika CKI 242
Πευκόλαος: Piyukula CKC 81–82
Πολύξενος: Palasina CKC 49–51
Πτολεμαῖος: Turamaya Shāh
Σοφή: Sapha 118
Στράτων: Strata 54–70, 131–137
Τήλεφος: Telipha CKC 121–122
Φιλόξενος: Philasina CKC 71–73

Taking the individual consonants in order, and setting aside for now their clusters, we see that the Greek unvoiced stops π [p], τ [t], and κ [k] are regularly represented by Kharoṣṭhī p, t, and k with the same phonetic values.

The situation is less clear with the voiced stops. While β has the Kharoṣṭhī correspondent b, intervocalic γ is

---

[1] None of the currently known Gāndhārī manuscripts, nor the wooden documents from Central Asia, contain any Greek names.
[2] CKC refers to coin legends in the corpus, Shāh and Mān to Aśoka's inscriptions, CKI to other inscriptions. The Gāndhārī versions of the names are given in the stem form, as the attached Indian endings do not contribute anything to the understanding of Greek-Gāndhārī sound correspondences.
[3] As Bühler 1886, 137, 1894, 200 rightly remarks, the Gāndhārī form cannot correspond to Ἀντίγονος, and Ἀντιγένης is the only common Greek name that does match. Hultzsch 1925, xxxi equally correctly points out that no contemporary Greek king of such name is known. It seems possible that the intended reference is to Antigonus Gonatas of Macedonia, but with some confusion about the correct form of his name.

[4] I find it impossible to reconcile the Kharoṣṭhī spelling of this name with Θεόδωρος (so still in Baums 2018, 36, 38), and tentatively suggest the female (non-divine) name Θαΐς (borne among others by a female companion of Alexander the Great) as its first element.
[5] The /k/ in the first form of this name stands for [j] and is thus equivalent to the unwritten glide in this position in the second form.
[6] This last spelling, in a very early inscription on the Shinkot casket, appears to be based on a folk-etymological interpretation along the lines laid out in Fussman 1993, 72–73.

represented by *k* in Aśoka's edicts, and δ by both *d* and *t* on the coins and later inscriptions. While in the case of Maka we might suspect a non-Macedonian form of the name—Μάχης or Μάκης (see Fraser & Matthews 1987; 2000; Corsten 2010 s.vv.; and cf. Schwyzer 1939: 69)—the names Aṃtikini, Artemitora, Diyumeta and Theutara suggest that Bühler (1894) was on the right track in proposing a Prakrit pronunciation habit. The intervocalic voiced and unvoiced stops had merged in the approximant or fricative pronunciations [ʋ], [ð] and [ɣ], which could then indiscriminately be written *p, b, v; t, d;* or *k, g*.[7] It needs to be noted, however, that the original Greek unvoiced stops are never written *b, d* or *g*, in spite of the non-occurrence of simple unvoiced stops between vowels in Prakrit. This suggests that on the Prakrit phonetic and orthographic background, the attested spellings rather reflect the (Koine) Greek linguistic situation of the time, where the voiced stops had turned into fricatives, but the unvoiced ones had remained unchanged.

The letters φ, θ, and χ are regularly represented as *ph, th,* and *kh*. On the Greek side, the aspirates were in transition to fricatives at the time of our coins and inscriptions (Schwyzer 1939: 204–207). Their Kharoṣṭhī equivalents could correspondingly either be understood as exact phonetic representations or substitutions [pʰ], [tʰ], and [kʰ], or as spellings for [f], [θ], and [χ].[8] This leaves the irregular spellings *k* and *g* in Aṃtiyoka, Aṃtiyoga unexplained, which may be best understood as due to folk-etymological association with Sanskrit and Prakrit *yoga* "connection."

The uncombined nasals μ [m] and ν [n] are regularly spelled with their corresponding Kharoṣṭhī letters *m* and *n*. In the post-Aśokan inscriptions, the latter is joined interchangeably by *ṇ* without phonetic difference. Similarly, the liquids λ and ρ are distinguished as *l* and *r* respectively. The one exception is Aśokan Turamaya with *r* for λ, possibly due to folk-etymological association with Sanskrit and Prakrit *tura* "swift". The uncombined sibilant σ is represented by Kharoṣṭhī *s*, which between vowels can stand for either [s] or [z]. The latter is its normal pronunciation in this position in native Gāndhārī words, but since in the loan pronunciations of Greek names uncombined unvoiced stops and maybe unvoiced fricatives seem to have been admitted, there is no reason to rule out an uncombined voiceless sibilant.

Greek initial [h] ("rough breathing"), not noted in the Greek script, is duly written as *h* (properly [ɦ]) in Herama(y)a / Hirmaa, Heliyakre(y)a, and Heliuphila.

Long consonants (so-called "geminates") are treated in exactly the same way as their short (or "simple") equivalents. Thus λλ is written *l*, and ππ is written *p*, following the general convention of the Kharoṣṭhī script that consonant (and vowel) signs stand for the long as well as the short sound.

We can summarize the discussion so far in the following chart, showing the regular correspondences between Greek and Kharoṣṭhī letters and their likely pronunciation in Greek names in Gandhāra:

π p	τ t	κ k	
[p]	[t]	[k]	
φ ph	θ th	χ kh	
[pʰ]~[f]	[tʰ]~[θ]	[kʰ]~[χ]	
β b	δ d/t	γ g/k	
[ʋ]	[ð]	[ɣ]	
μ m	ν n/ṇ		
[m]	[n]		
λ l	ρ r	σ s	h
[l]	[r]	[s]	[ɦ]

Moving on to consonant clusters, the simplest case is those with ρ as a second member, which are preserved unchanged (κρ = *kr*), even when a σ is added in front (στρ = *str*). The Greek combination κλ is likewise spelled *kr*. This is due to the fact that the Gāndhārī language does not have the cluster [kl], which is therefore not provided for by regular Kharoṣṭhī script (as opposed to its later Central Asian variant). It seems likely that in the Gandhāran pronunciation of such names, [kɾ] was substituted for Greek [kl].

Clusters of nasal plus stop are likewise by all appearances preserved unchanged. The Kharoṣṭhī graphical device for writing such preconsonantal nasals is an optional small hook at the base of the preceding consonant sign, the anusvāra (ṃ). A search of the corpus shows that in Aśoka's edicts, anusvāra is only attached to consonants without a vowel sign, i.e., consonants with an inherent [ə] vowel. This would appear to be a graphical restriction since the Gāndhārī language does know the combination of other vowels with following nasal. The Kharoṣṭhī coin legends do not seem to employ the anusvāra sign at all.[9] In the later inscriptions and

---

[7] The Gāndhārī manuscripts similarly write *p, p, v* for [ʋ], *t, ṭ, d, ḍ* for [ð], and *k, g, k, g* for [ɣ].
[8] The name Zenupila, as read by the editors of the clay token on which it occurs (ur Rahman & Falk 2012: 120), would support the former, but inspection of the published photograph reveals that the correct reading is Zenuphila.

[9] I could neither confirm the claim in Bühler (1894: 195) of *jayaṃtasa*, nor the sighting in Glass (2000: 134–135) of anusvāras in the plates of Gardner 1886 and Smith 1906.

manuscripts, the use or otherwise of anusvara seems entirely up to the individual scribe. We thus find the Greek consonant combination ντ represented both as *ṃt* (in Aśoka) and simply as *t* (elsewhere).

As per the above, the three-letter combination νδρ is regularly represented by *ṃdr* and *dr*. The one exception is Alikasudara in Aśoka's edicts, where once again one suspects folk etymology, in this case with Sanskrit and Prakrit *sundara* "handsome".

Combinations of ρ with following stop or nasal are also usually preserved, thus ρτ = *rt*, ρχ = *rkh*, and ρμ = *rm*, but in the name Heramaya / H(*e)ramaa we find ρμ = *ram*. This shows a certain unease with preconsonantal [r] that is also reflected in the manuscripts, which variously preserve or assimilate such combinations. The combination λκ is split up by an epenthetic vowel into *lik*, and on the general evidence of the manuscripts and inscriptions, preconsonantal [l] was not allowed in Gāndhārī.

The Greek consonant cluster ξ (originally [ks]) occurs as *kas* in Alikasudara. This is possibly intended as another folk etymology with Sanskrit *alīka* "disagreeable" (making this Alexander both disagreeable and handsome), but will simultaneously be due to the fact that [ks] is not a possible sound combination in Gāndhārī. The different treatment of ξ as simple *s* in Philasina may illustrate an alternative solution to this phonotactic problem, or reflect a transition on the Greek side from [ks] to [χs] (cf. Schwyzer 1939: 211).

Finally, in the case of initial πτ (impossible in this position in Sanskrit, and in any position in Prakrit), the first consonant is simply dropped, leaving bare *t* [t] – the solution also adopted in the English pronunciation of the name Ptolemy.

Coming to the simple vowels, leaving aside the cases of folk-etymological reshaping already noted above, the picture is as follows. The low central vowel α (both short and long) is written *a*, i.e., in Indian terms, [ə] or [a:]. Short ε is written either *i*, indicating a closed pronunciation [i], or *e*, which possibly stands for [e], though the regular Indian long pronunciation [e:] may have been substituted for it. Both Greek spellings for long e, η and ει, are represented by *e* as well as *i*, indicating a stage in the history of Greek at which they have merged. Greek ι (both short and long) is spelled *i*, i.e., [i] or [i:], the former of which could evidently be confused with ε. Short o is written *u*, indicating the same kind of closed pronunciation that ε has, or using the phonetic approximation *a* [ə][10]. Greek υ (both short and long) is spelled *i*, probably indicating substitution

of [i] and [i:] for [y] and [y:]. Greek ω is approximated as either *o* or *a*.

The following diagrams illustrate the likely system of short vowels in Greek names in Gandhāran pronunciation:

ι/υ i
[i]

ε e/i   o u/a
[e]   [o]

α a
[ə]

and the system of long vowels:

ι/υ i
[i:]

η/ει e/i   ω o/a
[e:]   [o]

α a
[a:]

Not included here is the Greek long-vowel spelling ου. It is not attested in our sample of names, and we thus lack the transcription information to decide between the pronunciations [o:] and [u:] for it.

Three Greek diphthongs are attested in our sample. Of these, αι is followed by another vowel o, and the whole sequence αιο [ajo] is transcribed precisely in Heramaya/ H(*e)ramaa / Hirmaa as [əjə] with explicit or implicit glide. The other two diphthongs are split up and treated regularly as disyllabic sequences. Of these, ευ is spelled *evu* [eʋu] and *iyu* [iju], with different glides depending on the more open or more close pronunciation of its first element; the spelling *ava* in Avakha suggests a pronunciation [aʋu] and is possibly influenced by the Indian prefix *ava-*. The third diphthong εω is regularly spelled *ava* [aʋa:] in Thavara.

In the preceding I hope to have shown how very regular and phonetically observant the spellings of Greek names are on the Indo-Greek coins, and what they can teach us about the pronunciation of both Greek and Gāndhārī in this time and region. By contrast, the spellings of Greek names in the edicts of Aśoka abound in folk-etymological reshapings, and those in the later, often private inscriptions show an element of improvisation.

At the end of this article, I would like to return to Cavafy's poem and give it in full:

---

[10] The closed pronunciation of o is echoed by its primary value in the Greek script as later used for Bactrian (Sims-Williams 1989: 233).

Νομίσματα μὲ ἰνδικὲς ἐπιγραφές.
Εἶναι κραταιοτάτων μοναρχῶν,
τοῦ Ἐβουκρατιντάζα, τοῦ Στρατάγα,[11]
τοῦ[12] Μεναντράζα, τοῦ Ἐραμαϊάζα.
Ἔτσι μᾶς ἀποδίδει τὸ σοφὸ βιβλίον,
τὴν ἰνδικὴ γραφὴ τῆς μιᾶς μεριᾶς τῶν νομισμάτων.
Μὰ τὸ βιβλίο μᾶς δείχνει καὶ τὴν ἄλλην
ποὺ εἶναι κιόλας κ' ἡ καλὴ μεριὰ
μὲ τὴν μορφὴ τοῦ βασιλέως. Κ' ἐδῶ πῶς σταματᾶ εὐθύς,
πῶς συγκινεῖται ὁ Γραικὸς ἑλληνικὰ διαβάζοντας,
Ἑρμαῖος, Εὐκρατίδης, Στράτων, Μένανδρος.

We are now in a better position to appreciate what Cavafy does. After introducing the names of these four rulers in their alien linguistic garb, he finally and climactically reveals their true identity in the original Greek spelling, sharing with us the joyful epiphany he had when the learned book revealed its secret to him. We may additionally marvel at the further complexity of representing Indian spellings of ancient Greek names in modern Greek orthography. One mystery remains, however: The genitive singular ending -asa of these names was in all likelihood pronounced [a:zə] with voiced [z] (cf. the remarks above and Baums (2009: 124). Cavafy correctly reproduces this as -αζα with ζ instead of σ – but how could he have known? Maybe a reader of the present learned book can solve this puzzle.

Bibliography

Baums, S. 2009. A Gāndhārī Commentary on Early Buddhist Verses: British Library Kharoṣṭhī Fragments 7, 9, 13 and 18. Ph.D. dissertation, University of Washington.

Baums, S. 2018. Greek or Indian? The Questions of Menander and Onomastic Patterns in Early Gandhāra. Pages 33–46, in H. Prabha Ray (ed.) *Buddhism and Gandhara: An Archaeology of Museum Collections. Archaeology and Religion in South Asia.* Abingdon: Routledge.

Baums, S., and Glass, A. 2002. *A Dictionary of Gāndhārī.* Viewed Jan 2022. <https://gandhari.org/dictionary>

Bühler, G. 1886. Beiträge zur Erklärung der Aśoka-Inschriften. *Zeitschrift der Deutschen Morgenländischen Gesellschaft* 40: 127–142.

Bühler G. 1894. The Kharoshṭhî Inscriptions on the Indo-Grecian Coins. *Wiener Zeitschrift für die Kunde des Morgenlandes* 8: 193–207.

Coloru, O. 2009. *Da Alessandro a Menandro: Il regno greco di Battriana.* Studi ellenistici, XXI. Pisa: Fabrizio Serra editore.

Corsten, T. 2010. *Lexicon of Greek Personal Names, Vol. V.A: Coastal Asia Minor: Pontos to Ionia.* Oxford: Oxford University Press.

Fraser, P.M., and Matthews, E. 1987. *Lexicon of Greek Personal Names, Vol. I: Aegean Islands, Cyprus, Cyrenaica.* Oxford: Oxford University Press.

Fraser P.M., and Matthews E. 2000. *Lexicon of Greek Personal Names, Vol. III.B: From the Megarid to Thessaly.* Oxford: Oxford University Press.

Fussman, G. 1993. L'Indo-Grec Ménandre ou Paul Demiéville revisité. *Journal Asiatique* 281: 61–138.

Gardner, P. 1886. *The Coins of the Greek and Scythic Kings of Bactria and India in the British Museum.* London: British Museum.

Glass, A. 2000. *A Preliminary Study of Kharoṣṭhī Manuscript Paleography.* M.A. dissertation, University of Washington.

Hultzsch, E. 1925. *Inscriptions of Asoka. Corpus Inscriptionum Indicarum, Vol. I.* Oxford: Clarendon Press.

Καβάφης, Κ.Π. 1968. Ἀνέκδοτα ποιήματα (1882–1923). Ἀθήνα: Ἴκαρος.

Schwyzer, E. 1939. *Griechische Grammatik auf der Grundlage von Karl Brugmanns griechischer Grammatik*, erster Band: Allgemeiner Teil, Lautlehre, Wortbildung, Flexion. Handbuch der Altertumswissenschaft, zweite Abteilung, erster Teil, erster Band. München: C.H. Beck'sche Verlagsbuchhandlung.

Sims-Williams, N. 1989. Bactrian, in R. Rüdiger Schmitt (ed.) *Compendium linguarum Iranicarum:* 230–235. Wiesbaden: Dr. Ludwig Reichert Verlag.

Smith, V.A. 1906. *Catalogue of the Coins in the Indian Museum Calcutta Including the Cabinet of the Asiatic Society of Bengal, Vol. I, Part I: The Early Foreign Dynasties and the Guptas.* Oxford: Clarendon Press.

Whitehead, R.B. 1914. *Catalogue of Coins in the Panjab Museum, Lahore, Vol. I: Indo-Greek Coins.* Oxford: Clarendon Press.

---

[11] This would appear to be a mistake for Στρατάζα, whether on the part of Cavafy or of his editor.
[12] The edition has τοὺ.

Questions of Identity and Interpretation, or When is a Parrot a Goose?

Elizabeth Errington

In the beginning, there was just Joe in charge of the British Museum's collection of all coins from Afghanistan eastwards to China. But in the 1990s until his retirement as Keeper of Coins and Medals in October 2011 he managed to get substantial funding for diverse projects that employed a growing team of aspiring curators and numismatists worldwide, and taught us all his mantra 'look at the coins'. In retrospect, it was a golden age for Asian numismatics at the British Museum, which is sadly now lost. It is therefore perhaps a bit perverse that this offering in celebration of his 75th birthday has nothing whatsoever to do with coins, but it does mention Kanishka in passing. So hopefully he will accept this little diversion from someone who has benefitted from his friendship, instigation and unstinting support of the Masson Project and open-handed sharing of information over the past 20 years.

The present discussion all began with a series of stair riser reliefs in the British Museum (Errington 2022: figs 18–20), found in situ in 1873 on the flight of 16 steps leading to the main stupa courtyard at Jamalgarhi, a Gandhara Buddhist site in the Peshawar basin. The investigation started as a result of what has proved to be a fruitful sharing of ideas with David Jongeward about his current study of Buddhist *jātakas* (stories of previous lives of the Buddha; forthcoming). It then migrated to the Saxon Academy of Science and Humanities in Leipzig, where Ji Ho Yi is working on 'Buddhist Murals of Kucha on the Northern Silk Road' and she kindly provided all the Chinese texts relating stories, mainly about parrots, but also a few other birds including a goose, a pigeon and an owl.

The riser in question belongs to step 7 of the Jamalgarhi sequence, as recorded by Cunningham's Appendix B and its accompanying contemporary photographs (1875: 197–202; Errington 2022: figs 18–20). It survives as two panels, seemingly its entire original length, but with fragments missing from both the left and right

hand reliefs (Figure 1; BM 1880.35; 1880.38; Zwalf 1996: 239–41, nos 313–14). Its subject matter was identified by Albert Foucher (1917: 271–81, pls II–IV). Reading from right to left, it illustrates the story of a jeweller, a monk and a thieving bird recounted in two Chinese texts, the *Tripiṭaka* (Chavannes 1911: no. 440, 210–11) and the *Sutralamkara*, attributed by some scholars to Aśvaghoṣa, the philosopher at the court of the Kushan king Kanishka I (c. AD 127–50) (Huber 1908: 321–30). The tale does not appear to survive as a *jātaka*, but as an *avadāna* (a moral story about any being deemed worthy, i.e. a Buddhist equivalent of Aesop's *Fables*).

In the *Tripiṭaka* version the miscreant is a parrot, in the *Sutralamkara* a goose, as apparently in the Jamalgarhi version, although equally, it appears in depiction, attributes and actions more like a carrion-eating, omnivorous, raven or perhaps a bird of prey. Reading the relief from right to left, it starts with a scene of the jeweller's shop, and depicts a mendicant monk standing behind the jeweller with the outline of a bird at the foot of the counter. While the jeweller is away finding food for the monk, the bird steals a valuable red jewel, mistaking it for a piece of meat (in goose terms more feasibly a pebble to aid digestion, or in raven terms perhaps simply because it was bright and shiny) (Figure 2 A.1–2). Rather than disclose what he has just witnessed and cause the bird's death, the monk accepts culpability and is led away, stripped and flogged (Figure 2 A.3–4). When the bird attempts to drink the monk's blood during this ordeal, it is inadvertently killed by the blows, whereupon the monk is free to tell the truth. This is confirmed when the bird is cut open and the jewel found inside it (Figure 2 A.7).

After his flogging, the monk is shown again fully clothed, with two other figures, one of whom is identified as Indra who came to intercede on the monk's behalf and finally, with the jeweller kneeling in apology (Figure 2 A.5–6). The last two depictions of the monk show him

Figure 1. Jamalgarhi stair riser no. 7 (BM 1880.35, 1880.38). Photograph courtesy Warburg Institute.

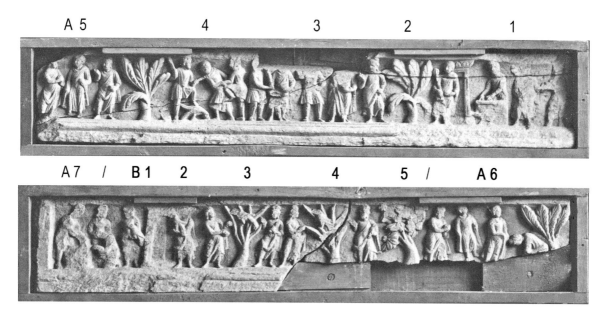

Figure 2. Jamalgarhi riser 7: detail. Photograph courtesy Warburg Institute.

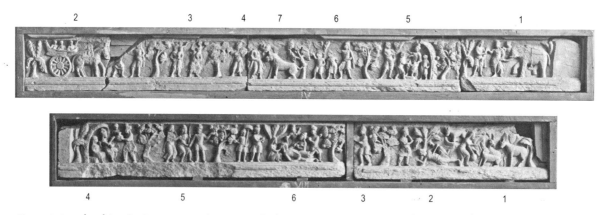

Figure 3. Jamalgarhi stair risers no. 4, *Viśvantara jātaka* (BM 1880.42, 1880.45, 1880.48) and no. 8, *Śyāma jātaka* (BM 1880.54, 1880.55) showing the sequence in which the scenes should be read from left to right, i.e. no. 4: 2, 3, 4 – 7, 6, 5 – 1 and no. 8: 4, 5, 6 – 3, 2, 1. Photograph courtesy Warburg Institute.

slightly elevated above the others perhaps indicating his progress towards ultimate enlightenment by his selfless action.

In a modern version of the story, after the monk is released, he feeds the goose an entire bottle of castor oil, and then waits three hours for the inevitable purge, which enables him to retrieve the jewel, return it to its rightful owner and save the life of the goose, thereby fulfilling two needs with one deed (http://www. buddhism.org/the-jewel-and-the-goose/).

A relief acquired in the 1860s, possibly from Ranigat on the eastern border of the Peshawar basin (Figure 4; Lahore Museum no. 119), illustrates a shorthand version of the same story. It combines the monk tied to the stake with the jeweller and others kneeling to ask his forgiveness and honour him after he had been proved

innocent. There is also a worn shape immediately to the right of the pilaster, but despite attempts to identify it as a bird, it persists in looking more like a stunted tree.

Returning to Jamalgarhi stair riser 7, a tree in full blossom separates the story up to this point from the left hand section of the riser (Figure 2 B.1–5). Still reading from the right, it shows a bird seated twice in the increasingly denuded branches of a tree, flanked by two figures, then the bird being carried indoors where several figures cluster around it. Zwalf identifies the figure pointing to a bird in the tree again as Indra (Figure 2 B.4). But the section appears rather to allude to the *Mahāsuka jātaka* or *Cullasuka jātaka* (the Steadfast Parrot: Cowell 1895–97: vol. III, 291–94, nos 429–30). This tells of a parrot king who lived contentedly in a shady and fruitful fig tree which he vowed never to abandon. Sakka, king of the gods, with his wife Sujā decided to test

Figure 4. Depiction of the monk, still yoked after his flogging, with three supplicants. The figure on the left has one arm raised and holds a round object (Lahore Museum no. 119). Photographic print (BM 1868,0612.1850) courtesy British Museum.

the bird's virtue by slowly killing the tree until it was a withered stump. But the parrot remained resolute and Sakka rewarded his faithfulness by restoring the tree to its former glory, before returning to his heavenly abode.

It is clear from the text that the left half of the relief should depict a parrot, geese not being in the habit of sitting in trees. However, the depictions in riser 7 all show the same non-specific bird. Moreover, by being placed side by side, these two separate stories enable us to understand the narrative in a new way. Like the Jamalgarhi versions of the popular *Viśvantara jātaka* (Figure 4a, riser 4; BM 1880.42; 1880.45; 1880.48)[1] and the *Śyāma jātaka* (Figure 4b, riser 8; BM 1880.54; 1880.55; Errington 2022: figs 18–19),[2] the monk's story starts at one end and reaches its climax with his exoneration in the centre. But in addition, riser 7 depicts two separate tales, both with a bird as the principal protagonist. It is further possible to read the left hand relief in both directions, either right to left with the tree becoming barren, which would result in the inevitable starvation and death of the bird who remained loyal, or what

seems more apt, from left to right culminating in the tree being restored to full bloom and nirvana for the bird. The chamber at the left end (Figure 2 A.7/B.1) can be understood as serving a dual function of determining the fate of both birds – either death and retribution, or rebirth as a higher being – as a result of their own actions.

The species of bird chosen to illustrate the two stories – whether parrot or goose in the texts – appears rather arbitrary as far as the Jamalgarhi sculptor was concerned, especially given its corvid-like actions. But ravens scarcely feature in the *jātakas*. The only reference in Cowell's six volumes occurs in the *Mahānāradakassapa jātaka* (1895–97: vol. VI, 123, no. 544), where the king is warned that as a result of his actions 'thou will see thyself ragged by flocks of ravens and devoured by them as thou livest in hell, and by crows, vultures, and hawks, with thy body torn and dripping blood'.

According to the 5th century Chinese translations of Indian Buddhist texts, even Kanishka I, seeking absolution towards the end of his life after killing more than 300,000 people in his conquests, tried, with help of Aśvaghoṣa (author of the *Buddhacarita*, and perhaps also the *Sutralamkara*), to redress the balance by meritorious acts, but only achieved rebirth as a monstrous fish with a thousand heads (Zürcher 1968: 384–7).

In contrast to these two negative examples, parrots appear mostly in a good light: Ji Ho Yi, in her

---

[1] Viśvantara renounces his life as a prince and gives away his elephant, horses, all material possessions and ultimately his two children to a Brahmin. But Indra, disguised as a lion, warns Viśvantara's wife, who is away collecting food in the forest, and the children are rescued.

[2] Śyāma, while collecting water for his blind parents, is accidently shot by a raja out hunting. Before dying he asks the raja to care for his parents. The raja takes the water to the couple, and then leads them to their dead son, who is miraculously restored to life.

presentation on 'Parrot Stories in Buddhist Texts' (unpublished 06.12.2021), has traced 18 parrot stories so far, several on the theme of loyalty and restoration, and including three in which the parrot is reborn as a Deva or Pratyekabuddha (an individual who has independently achieved enlightenment and who may give moral teachings but does not bring others to enlightenment).

The goose too is favourably represented: elected as king of the birds over a squabbling owl and crow (*Ulūka Jātaka*, Cowell 1895–97: vol. II, 243, no. 270) and above all, as the *haṃsa*, the wild goose symbolising the wandering soul and, in Buddhism, the propagation of the Doctrine to all realms and found in several stories involving preaching the Law (*Cullahaṃsa jātaka* and *Mahāhaṃsa jātaka*, Cowell 1895–97: vol. VI, 183–202, nos 533 – 34). The species is identified as the bar-headed goose (*anser indicus*), known for undertaking the greatest rates of climbing flight ever recorded for a bird, and flying at extreme altitudes (up to c. 6400 m) across the Himalayas during their migration south, inter alia, from Tibet and Kazakhstan to Pakistan and northern India (https://en.wikipedia.org/wiki/Bar-headed_goose). In Gandhara they appear most notably as a frieze encircling the rim of the 'Kanishka' casket from Shah-ji-ki-Dheri, perhaps an indication that some Buddhists at least believed that the king did not suffer rebirth as a thousand-headed monstrous fish (Errington 2002: figs 1–2).

References

Chavannes, É. (tr.) 1911. No. 440 (*Tripiṭaka*, XXXVI, 3 p. 46 v°). *Cinq cents contes et apologues. Extraits du Tripiṭaka chinois et traduits en français*, vol. III, Paris: Librarie Ernest Leroux: 210–211.

Cowell, E.B. (ed.) 1895–1897. *The Jātaka or Stories of the Buddha's Former Births*. 6 vols, Cambridge University Press (repr. New Delhi).

Cunningham, A. 1875. Jamâl-garhi. *Archaeological Survey of India Report for the Year 1872-73*, V, Calcutta: Arachaeological Survey of India: 46–53, 197–202.

Errington, E. 2002. Numismatic Evidence for Dating the 'Kaniṣka' Reliquary, with an Appendix on the Inscription by H. Falk, *Silk Road Art and Archaeology* 8: 101–120.

Errington, E. 2022. Reconstructing Jamālgarhī and Appendix B: the Archaeological Record 1848–1923, in W. Rienjang and P. Stewart (eds) *The Rediscovery and Reception of Gandharan Art*. Gandhara, Connections 4th International Online Workshop 2021: 1-42. Oxford: Archaeopress.

Foucher, A. 1917. 'Interprétation de quelque bas-reliefs du Gandhâra'. *Journal Asiatique* 11ème sér. IX, pp. 257–81.

Huber, É. (tr.) 1908. 63 – Le moine mendiant, le joaillier et l'oie. *Açvaghoṣa, Sûtrâlaṃkâra, traduit en français sur la version chinoise de Kumârajîva*, ch. XI, Paris: Societé asiatique: 321–30.

Jongeward, D., Lenz, T. with Pons, J. forthcoming. *The Buddha's Previous-lives: Gandharan Stories in Birchbark and Stone*.

Zürcher, E. 1968. The Yüeh-chih and Kaniṣka in the Chinese Sources, in A.L. Basham (ed.) *Papers on the Date of Kaniṣka*, Leiden: Brill: 346–90.

Zwalf, W. 1996. *A Catalogue of the Gandhāra Sculpture in the British Museum*, 2 vols, London: British Museum Press.

http://www.buddhism.org/the-jewel-and-the-goose/ (accessed 4/1/2022).

https://en.wikipedia.org/wiki/Bar-headed_goose (accessed 15/1/2022).

First-Century AD Coins in *Stūpa* Deposits and the Beginning of the Buddhist Relic Cult in Afghanistan

Wannaporn Rienjang

My first contact with Joe was fourteen years ago when I sent him an e-mail saying how much I wanted to learn about Buddhism in Gandhāra (present day northwestern Pakistan and eastern Afghanistan). At the time, I didn't have much idea of the key issues in 'Gandhāran studies'. My email to Joe therefore contained naïve enquiries such as how the Indo-Greek king Menander fostered Gandhāran Buddhism and how Gandhāran sculptures were created under his reign. Joe did not reply to those enquiries but instead gave me an opportunity to gain first-hand experience with the coins. In the fourteen years since then I have learned from him, either by listening to his conversations with his co-workers[1] or his communication directed to me both in written or verbal forms, and my focus on the subject has changed. Gandhāran sculptures never stop fascinating me and will continue to do so. However, coins found in Gandhāran sites are engraved with portraits of rulers, deities, legends and 'marks' that are no less expressive than sculptures. They can manifest socio-political histories of the area, as shown in Joe's extensive works, adding important elements for understanding Buddhism in an area often termed the 'Crossroads of Asia' (Cribb 1992; Errington and Cribb 1992; Allchin and Cribb 1992; Cribb and Bopearachchi 1992). Coins found in Gandhāran Buddhist sites also serve as a good tool for a chronological framework of Buddhism in Gandhāra (Errington 1999/2000; Rienjang 2018), which is the topic of my primary concern in this paper.

Unlike in India, coins are relatively common in Gandhāran *stūpas*, monuments conventionally built to house bodily remains of the Buddha. Coins were offered inside Gandhāran *stūpas* with reliquaries and sometimes on their own. Studying how *stūpa* and relic worships were practiced and developed over time in Gandhāra can offer one strand of understanding the Buddhism of this region. My focus has therefore moved towards the inside of Gandhāran *stūpas*. Joe has provided in his work a chronology of the Kushans and a structure for the coinages of associated rulers (e.g. Cribb 2007; 2015b; 2018a; Cribb and Bracey forthcoming), which in turn provides a framework for the study and interpretation of art historical, epigraphic and archaeological finds.

One of Joe's important contributions to the study of the Gandhāran relic cult is his thorough analysis of coins found associated with the famous Bimaran casket which resulted in his identification of these coins as the coins issued by an Indo-Scythian satrap called Mujatria, who ruled in the Jalalabad area in eastern Afghanistan around the late first to early second centuries AD (Cribb 2015a). It is during the latter half of the first century AD – the period of the first Kushan king, Kujula Kadphises, and the Indo-Scythian satraps – that the Buddhist relic cult appears to have begun in Afghanistan, as will be discussed below.

Coins in the *stūpa* deposits of Afghanistan range from the early first century AD to the mid-seventh century AD (Errington 1999/2000; 2012; 2017a-b). The first-century coins have been found with relic assemblages that were buried inside *stūpas* in three areas of eastern Afghanistan: Darunta, the Kabul region and the Jalalabad plain (Figure 1). Although the period of coin circulation is not always limited to the date of their issuers (some coins continued in circulation centuries after being issued), analysis of the coin distribution pattern across Gandhāran *stūpas* suggests that they were originally included in relic deposits when still in circulation (Rienjang 2017). They thus provide important evidence for the chronology of the Gandhāran *stūpa*-relic cult. In Afghanistan, the absence of coins whose issue dates are earlier than the first century AD suggests that the *stūpa*-relic cult in this area started at least during the first century AD, approximately a century later than in Pakistan (Rienjang 2017). Most of the first century coins presented in this paper belong to the Masson Collection at the British Museum (BM). They were excavated by Charles Masson, a nineteenth-century British explorer who explored and excavated *stūpas* in eastern Afghanistan between 1832 and 1835 (Errington 2017a; 2017b).

Gondophares (*c.* AD 32-60)

Finds of coins of an Indo-Parthian ruler Gondophares, in Afghan *stūpas* are rare, being reported from only two *stūpa* deposits: one in Darunta (Bimaran *stūpa* no. 5) and the other in Hadda (Hadda *stūpa* no. 3) (Masson 1841; Errington 2017a; 2017b; Rienjang 2017). Gondophares coins in both *stūpas* occurred with coins of the first Kushan king, Kujula Kadphises (*c.* AD 40-90) and a local satrap ruling in Jalalabad valley, Mujatria (*c.* late first

---

[1] Among whom are Elizabeth Errington, Robert Bracey, Nasim Khan, Gul Rahim Khan, Vesta Curtis, Helen Wang, David Jongeward, Paramdip Khera and John Perkins from whom I also learned about coins.

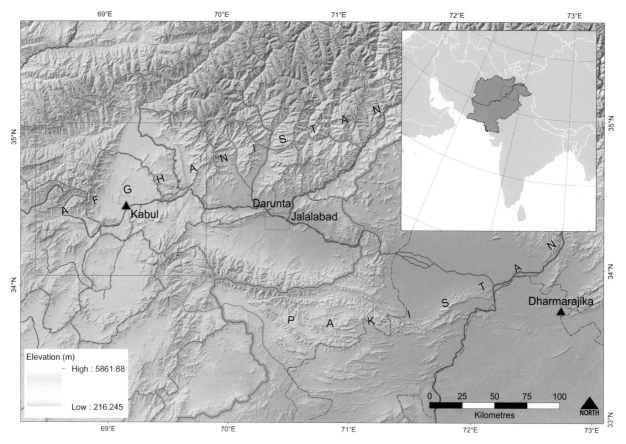

Figure 1. Three areas in Afghanistan where first-century AD coins were found in *stūpa-relic deposits*
(prepared by David Redhouse)

Figure 2. Gondophares coin from Hadda *stūpa* no. 33 (BM 1880.3740.k)
Copper alloy, 8.7g, diameter 22mm. Photo © Trustees of the British
Museum

to early second century AD) (see below) (Cribb 2015a). An example of a Gondophares coin from the Hadda *stūpa* no. 3 survives in the BM (Figure 2). The drawing of the Gondophares coin by Masson, published in *Ariana Antiqua* (Masson: 1841, Pl. V, figs. 12 and 13), and the Hadda example in the BM both belong to a bust of king/ Nike type. This type has a bearded bust of the king to right with a corrupt Greek legend on the obverse ('Basileos Soteros Gondopherrou'), and Nike to right with Kharoṣṭhī legend on the reverse ('Maharajasa

Gudaphanisa Tratarasa'). Senior (2001: 150, type 213) believes this type was minted in the northern Arachosia/Kabul valley, to the west of Darunta.

Kujula Kadphises coins (*c.* AD 40-90)

Coins of Kujula Kadphises occurred in six Afghan *stūpas*: four in Darunta, one in Hadda (Hadda *stūpa* no. 3) and one in the Kabul valley (Tepe Marajan 2) (Masson 1841; Errington 2017a; 2017b; Rienjang 2017; Fussman 2008).

Two types of Kujula Kadphises coins were found in Afghan *stūpas*. The first type is the 'Heraus' issue (Cribb 1993). Only one coin of this type was reported (*stūpa* Kotpur 2 in Darunta). The actual coin, a silver obol, is broken into two fragments (figure 3). The obverse bears a bust of the king facing right, and the reverse is defaced and gilded. While defacing and gilding a coin may have happened as part of the process of deposition, the Kujula Kadphises' Heraus coin type was issued in the northern part of the Kushan empire—in Bactria—and silver coins were not issued in the Gandhara region (Cribb 1993). It is, therefore, possible that the coin had been in circulation for some time before being included in the *stūpa* deposit in the southern part of the Kushan empire.

The remaining Kujula Kadphises coins found in *stūpa* deposits of Afghanistan belong to the second type, 'Kujula/Herakles' (figure 4). This type has a bust of the king to right with a corrupted Greek legend on the obverse, and Herakles standing to front with a club in his right hand and a lion skin on his left with a Kharoṣṭhī legend on the reverse. The Greek legend reads *Kozoulo Kadphizou Koshono* (of Kujula Kadphises Kushan), and the Kharoṣṭhī legend reads *Kuyula kasasa [ku]shana yavugasa dhramathidasa* (of Kujula Kasa Kushan chieftain, steadfast in the law) (Cribb and Bracey forthcoming). The majority of Kujula coins from Darunta *stūpas* now in the BM share the same type of coin legend, symbol and weight (reduced weight: c.3.5–6.5 gr.) with those current in Taxila, rather than Begram (Cribb 2016; Jongeward and Cribb 2015; Khan and Cribb 2012).

Mujatria coins (c. late first to early second century AD)

Coins of Mujatria, a local satrap ruling in Jalalabad, occurred in eight Afghan *stūpa* deposits, seven of which were found inside *stūpas* in Darunta, and one in a Hadda *stūpa* (Hadda *stūpa* no. 3). Some occurred on their own,

while others occurred with coins of Kujula Kadphises (Kujula/Herakles type) and Gondophares (of the above type, bust of king/Nike). Two types of his coins were found in Afghan *stūpas*: the 'Bimaran' type and the square-shaped type.

The 'Bimaran' type

The 'Bimaran' type of Mujatria had earlier been identified as those issued by an Indo-Scythian king, Azes, and therefore been dated to the mid first century BC (Azes I) and the early first century AD (Azes II). However, as mentioned above, Joe's thorough study and analysis of Indo-Scythian coins in relation to those of the first two Kushan kings—Kujula Kadphises and Wima Takhto—results in the new identification of the issuer as Mujatria, an Indo-Scythian satrap ruling in Jalalabad during the late first to early second century AD (Cribb 2015a). This breakthrough and the new identification have pushed almost a century forward for the *deposition* of the relic deposit in which the famous Bimaran casket was associated (Cribb 2015a; 2016; 2018b). Such a late first to early century AD date for the *deposition* of the Bimaran deposit aligns well with the early relic deposits in eastern Afghanistan.

The 'Bimaran' type-coins are copper alloy coins issued in the name of the Indo-Scythian king Azes (Cribb 2018b). Their production period—the late first to early second century AD—overlaps that of the Kushan coins of Kujula Kadphises and Soter Megas (see below), the Indo-Parthian Sasan (c. AD 64-70), and the Apraca ruler, Asparvarma (c. late first century AD) (Cribb 2015a; 2016; 2018b). The obverse shows a horseman to right, with Greek legend *Basileon Basileos Megalos Azou*. The reverse bears the goddess Tyche holding a cornucopia in her left hand, with Kharoṣṭhī legend *Maharajasa mahatasa Dhramikasa Rajatirajasa Ayasa* (Figure 4). There are six Mujatria coins of the Bimaran type from the Darunta *stūpas* in the BM. It is to be noted that Mujatria coins of this type are highly localized, their distribution being

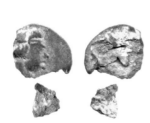

Figure 3. Kujula Kadphises coin from Kotpur *stūpa* no. 2 (BM 1880.3735 a+b) Silver obol, diameter 11mm. Photo © Trustees of the British Museum

Figure 4. Kujula Kadphises coin from Bimaran *stūpa* no. 5 (BM 1880.4135.a) Copper alloy, 5.03g, diameter 21mm. Photo © Trustees of the British Museum

Figure 5. Mujatria coin from a *stūpa* in Darunta (BM 1894,0506.636) Copper alloy, 9.57g, diameter 20mm. Photo © Trustees of the British Museum

Figure 6. Mujatria coin from Deh Rahman *stūpa* no. 1 (BM 1880.3885.p) Copper alloy, 1.9g, 11x10mm. Photo © Trustees of the British Museum

Figure 7. Soter Megas coin from Bimaran *stūpa* no. 4 or Passani Tumulus no. 2 (BM 1880.3740.l) Copper alloy, 1.89g, diameter 14mm. Photo © Trustees of the British Museum

largely restricted to Darunta and the Jalalabad plain (Errington 1999/2000; Cribb 2015a; Cribb 2016; 2018b).

Square-shaped Type

The second type of Mujatria coins, also in copper alloy, has a square shape. They were found in two *stūpa* deposits (*stūpas* Deh Rahman no. 1 and Kutchera) and a mound of Passani 5, all in Darunta. This type has a horseman on the obverse and a lion on a reverse. Four very corroded square copper coins from *stūpa* Deh Rahman no.1 are in the BM (Figure 6). On the basis of their size and shape, these four coins are also identified as Mujatria square copper issue (Cribb *e-mail correspondence; 2015a;* Senior 2001: 125-6).

'Soter Megas' coins

'Soter Megas' coins have not been reported from *stūpa* deposits of other areas in Afghanistan. According to the records, all 'Soter Megas' coins from the Darunta deposits bear a diademed male bust, with rays emanating from his head on the obverse, and a horseman on the reverse with a Greek legend *Basileos Basileon Soter Megas* (Masson 1841: 75, 94, pl. IX, fig. 8; Jacquet 1836, pl. XIII.4; Pigou 1841: annexed plate, coin nos 4 and 5). Since the discovery of the Rabatak inscription, these coins have been attributed to Wima Takto (*c.* AD 90-113). However, Joe has recently argued that their issue began under Kujula Kadphises (Cribb 2014; 2015b).

There are only two positively identifiable coins of Soter Megas from the Darunta deposits in the BM. Both are attributable to Cribb's second phase, with the three-pronged tamgas and square letterforms (Cribb 2014) (Figure 7). The two coins are of a small denomination (weighing 2 g), which is scarce in the greater Gandhāra region except at Begram, likely the mint for those coins (Cribb 2014; Khan 2014). The small denomination (2 g) was part of the reform process of the general issue of the Soter Megas coinage, whereby the Kushan coinage developed from a series of local issues to a uniform copper currency and the Attic standard of didrachm (c. 8.5 g) and hemidrachm (c. 2.1 g) was adopted (Jongeward and Cribb 2015: 43). Bracey (2016) maintains a list of hoards containing Kushan coins. Hoards with Soter Megas coins (as well as Kujula Kadphises coins) with later Kushan types (Wima Kadphises, Kanishka, Huvishka) are rare, although hoards containing coins of those kings are common. This suggests that the Soter Megas coins ceased to circulate shortly after the reform of Wima Kadphises, by the mid-second century AD.

As presented in this paper, coins form an important part in the study of the development of Buddhist relic practices in greater Gandhara. The contributions that Joe has made on the coins of this region have built a strong chronological framework for the study of the Gandharan Buddhist relic cult. I once asked Joe what made him interested in Gandharan studies, and his reply was 'because there are so many questions and problems!' This is the Joe that I know.

References

Allchin, F.R. and Cribb, J. 1992. The Historical Context, in E. Errington and J. Cribb (eds) *The Crossroads of Asia. Transformation in Image and Symbols*: 4-7. Cambridge: Ancient India and Iran Trust.

Bracey, R. 2016. Hoards of Copper Kushan Coins. Available at http://www.kushan.org/sources/coin/copperhoards.htm (Accessed: 19 July 2016).

Cribb, J. 1992. Chronology, in E. Errington and J. Cribb (eds) *The Crossroads of Asia. Transformation in Image and Symbols.*: 17-34. Cambridge: Ancient India and Iran Trust.

Cribb, J. 1993. The 'Heraus' Coins: Their Attribution to the Kushan King Kujula Kadphises, c. AD 30–80, in M. Price, A. Burnett and R. Bland (eds) *Essays in Honour of Robert Carson and Kenneth Jenkins*: 107-34. London: Spink.

Cribb, J. 2007. Rediscovering the Kushans. Pages 179–210 in E. Errington and V. Curtis (eds) *From Persepolis to the Punjab: Exploring Ancient Iran, Afghanistan and Pakistan.* London: The British Museum Press.

Cribb, J. 2014. The Soter Megas Coins of the First and Second Kushan Kings, Kujula Kadphises and Wima Takto. *Gandharan Studies* 8: 77–134.

Cribb, J. 2015a. Dating and Locating Mujatria and the Two Kharahostes. *Journal of the Oriental Numismatic Society* 223: 26–48.

Cribb, J. 2015b. Introduction. Pages 1–20 in D. Jongeward and J. Cribb, *Kushan, Kushano-Sasanian, and Kidarite Coins. A Catalogue of Coins from the American Numismatic Society.* New York: American Numismatic Society.

Cribb, J. 2016. The Bimaran Casket: the Problem of its Date and Significance. *Gandharan Studies* 10: 57–92.

Cribb, J. 2018a. Numismatic Evidence and the Date of Kaniska I, in W. Rienjang and P. Stewart (eds) *Problems of Chronology in Gandhāran Art*: 7–34. Oxford: Archaeopress.

Cribb, J. 2018b. The Bimaran Casket: the Problems of its Date and Significance, in J. Stargardt and M. Willis (eds) *Relics and Relic Worship in Early Buddhism: India, Afghanistan, Sri Lanka and Burma*: 47–65. London: The British Museum.

Cribb, J. and Bopearachchi, O. 1992. Coins and the Reconstruction of History, in E. Errington and J. Cribb (eds) *The Crossroads of Asia. Transformation in image and symbols*: 12-16 .Cambridge: Ancient India and Iran Trust.

Cribb, J. and Bracey, R. Forthcoming. *Catalogue of Kushan Coins in the British Museum.* London: The British Museum Press.

Errington, E. 1999/2000. Numismatic Evidence for Dating the Buddhist Remains in Gandhara. *Silk Road Art and Archaeology* 6: 191–216.

Errington, E. 2012. Reliquaries in the British Museum, in D. Jongeward, E. Errington, R. Salomon and S. Baums. *Gandharan Buddhist Reliquaries*: 111-163. Seattle: University of Washington Press.

Errington, E. 2017a. *Charles Masson and the Buddhist Sites of Afghanistan: Explorations, Excavations, Collections 1833-1835.* London: The British Museum Press.

Errington, E. 2017b. *The Charles Masson Archive: British Library, British Museum and Other Documents Relating to the 1832-1838 Masson Collection from Afghanistan.* London: The British Museum Press.

Errington, E. and Cribb, J. 1992. *The Crossroads of Asia. Transformation in Image and Symbols.* Cambridge: Ancient India and Iran Trust.

Fussman, G. 2008. *Monuments Bouddhiques de la région de Coboul,* vol. 2. Mémoires de la Délégation Archéologique Française en Afghanistan, LXXVI. Paris: Diffusion de Boucard.

Jacquet, E. 1836. Notice sur les découvertes archéologiques faites par Mr. Honigberger dans l'Afghanistan. *Journal Asiatique,* II: 234–277.

Jongeward, D. and Cribb, J. 2015. *Kushan, Kushano-Sasanian and Kidarite Coins.* New York: The American Numismatic Society.

Khan, G. 2014. Soter Megas Coins from Taxila. *Gandharan Studies* 8: 135–159.

Khan, G. and Cribb, J. 2012. Coins of Kujula Kadphises from Taxila. *Gandharan Studies* 6: 81–220.

Marshall, J. 1951. *Taxila: an Illustrated Account of Archaeological Excavations Carried Out at Taxila Under the Orders of the Government of India Between the Years 1913 and 1934.* 3 vols. Cambridge: Cambridge University Press.

Masson, C. 1841. A Memoir of the Buildings called Topes, in H.H. Wilson (ed.) *Ariana Antiqua. A descriptive account of the antiquities and coins of Afghanistan*: 55-118. London.

Pigou, R. 1841. On the Topes of Darounta and the Caves of Bahrabad. *Journal of the Asiatic Society of Bengal* X: 381–386.

Rienjang, W. 2017. *Honouring the Body: Relic Cult Practices in Eastern Afghanistan with Comparison to Dharmarajika Pakistan.* PhD thesis, University of Cambridge.

Rienjang, W. 2018. The Chronology of *Stūpa* Relic Practice in Afghanistan and Dharmarajika, Pakistan, and its Implication for the Rise in Popularity of Image Cult, in W. Rienjang and P. Stewart (eds) *Problems of Chronology in Gandhāran Art*: 93-102. Oxford: Archaeopress Archaeology.

Senior, R.C. 2001. *Indo-Scythian Coins and History.* 3 vols. London: Classical Numismatic Group.

A Hoard of Kushan Gold Coins from Swabi

Pankaj Tandon

In 2013, I had the opportunity to examine a reportedly intact hoard of 120 Kushan gold coins apparently found in or near the town of Swabi in the province of Khyber Pakhtunkhwa, Pakistan. Somehow, I failed to inform Joe of this at the time, but now the opportunity has arisen to not only inform him of it, but to present to him a report on the hoard. I expect and hope that he would find this report to be of the utmost interest.

The town of Swabi is located just off the west bank of the Indus river, approximately 20 miles south-southeast from Mardan and about 40 miles northwest of Islamabad (see map). Taxila is about 30 miles away, Peshawar about 50 miles. The village of Hund in Swabi district was also known as Ohind and was the capital of the Hindu Shahi kingdom in the 10th century. Hund was the place where Alexander the Great crossed the river Indus during his Punjab campaign (Pakistan's M-1 highway crosses at roughly the same place today) and the district was the site of a Buddhist monastery visited by Xuanzang. So it is safe to conclude that the area was an important urban site during Kushan times.

The hoard of coins found there was apparently stored in two small clay pots (see Figure 1). At first glance, it seemed to me that the pots were too small to have

contained such a large number of coins, but a simple test showed that they could well have. The larger, beige-colored pot stands 86 mm high and has a diameter at its widest point of 90mm. By filling it with sand, I was able to measure its volume to the brim at approximately 215ml. The smaller, reddish pot stands 64mm high and measures 74mm at its widest point. Its volume came to approximately 100ml. The total capacity of the two pots was therefore about 315ml. By placing 10 of the coins in water, I estimated their volume at between 15 and 20ml (I did not have precise measuring equipment at hand; I was using a simple kitchen measuring cup). Thus the 120 coins together would occupy some 180 to 240ml of volume. Of course, there would also be air gaps between coins in a pot, but in the end I concluded that there was probably enough room in the pots to fit all the coins in. The information I was given seemed to be plausibly true.

The next question in my mind was: was this truly an intact hoard? When examining a purportedly complete hoard, there is always the possibility that coins found separately could have been agglomerated into a 'hoard' or that certain special coins were hived off for individual sale. There was no difference in patina or other characteristics of the coins to suggest an

Map 1. Map showing location of Swabi and surrounding areas (Map Data © 2022, Google)

Figure 1. Clay pots said to have contained the coins of the hoard (not to scale)

agglomeration from different sources. And the fact that the coins I saw included some extremely rare types, including a double dinar of Vima Kadphises, a unique 'Year One' coin of Kanishka with Nanaia reverse, two rare right-facing dinars of Huvishka with Miiro reverse and a very rare Huvishka dinar featuring Mao and Miiro on the reverse, suggests that no coins were hived off for individual sale and that the hoard was indeed intact. So, once again, it seemed to me that the information I was given was plausibly true.

Let me turn now to describe the hoard itself. It contained 120 gold coins, one of which was a double dinar and the remainder were all dinars. In what follows, I will be using the structure for the coinage developed by Cribb and Bracey in their forthcoming British Museum catalogue (Cribb and Bracey forthcoming), although identifying them by their Göbl (1984) number. The breakdown of coins is listed in Table 1. The coins are illustrated in Table 2, with details of each coin provided below its image.

The double dinar is, of course, of Vima Kadphises, the only king to have issued that denomination. The coin belongs to phase four and the two dinars to phase five of Vima's gold coinage, all of which was produced in the Balkh area. Presumably they were made relatively late in his reign, say c. 120 CE or thereafter.

Coins 4–36 are gold dinars of Kanishka I (c. 127–151 CE). The 33 coins include 31 from all three phases of the Balkh mint, where the vast majority of Kanishka's gold coinage was produced, and 2 coins from the subsidiary mint, opened late in the reign in Gandhara, perhaps Peshawar. Finally, coins 37–120 are coins of Huvishka (c. 151–190 CE). These 84 coins include coins from the first four phases of each mint's coinage, thus covering

Table 1. Composition of the Hoard

King	Total # of coins	Breakdown Mint / Phase	# of Coins
Vima Kadphises	3 (1 2-dinar, 2 dinars)	Balkh Phase 4	1
		Balkh Phase 5	2
Kanishka I	33 (All dinars) Balkh = 31 Gandhara = 2	Balkh Phase 1	1
		Balkh Phase 2	14
		Balkh Phase 3	16
		Gandhara Phase 1	2
Huvishka	84 (All dinars) Balkh = 49 Gandhara = 35	Balkh Phase 1	1
		Balkh Phase 2	11
		Balkh Phase 3	22
		Balkh Phase 4	15
		Gandhara Phase 1	3
		Gandhara Phase 2	27
		Gandhara Phase 3	4
		Gandhara Phase 4	1

approximately the first two-thirds or three-quarters of that king's reign. This suggests that the date at which the hoard was buried was somewhere around the years 175–180 CE.

I wanted to get at least a rough idea of what this hoard of coins was equivalent to in today's money. The total weight of all the coins is 957.07g. At today's spot price of gold,[1] this would be worth $57,568. Of course, the relative price of gold is today much lower than what it must have been in Kushan times, when it was a monetary metal. Unfortunately, we do not have information on wage rates or commodity prices in the Kushan empire. The next best alternative is to look at prices or wages in ancient Rome, which also used gold coinage. Two pieces of data yield a modern-day value in the same range. The average salary of a day laborer in Pompeii

[1] Checked on February 17, 2022; the price was $60.15/g.

was 8 *asses* in 79 CE (Vagi 2000: 21). If we allow for some wage escalation, it was perhaps 10–12 *asses* by the 2nd century. Since 400 *asses* equaled 1 *aureus*, 1 *aureus* could finance about 40 man-days of work. By this time, an *aureus* weighed about 7.3 g; therefore, the Swabi hoard coins were equivalent to about 131 *aureii* and could therefore finance about 5,240 man-days of work. A simple search for the average wage paid to casual farm labor in California today yielded values of around $12 per hour. Assuming a Roman laborer worked 10 hours a day (probably an underestimate), the cost in modern wages would be $120. Thus the hoard is equivalent to around $628,800 (= 5,240 × 120) in modern purchasing power.

We get a similar number by looking at the average pay of soldiers. In Rome, after Domitian's reform, soldiers were paid 300 *denarii* per year, which is equal to 12 *aureii*. So 131 *aureii* could pay for roughly 11 soldiers for one year. Looking at the average pay for US Army soldiers, we find it to be approximately $50,000 to $60,000[2] (including the generous allowances they get; base pay is quite a bit lower). Since the hoard could pay roughly 11 soldiers' annual pay, it becomes equivalent to between $550,000 and $660,000 today.

It is possible that prices and wages in the 2nd century were higher in Rome than in Peshawar or Balkh, but of course it is purchasing power that matters. Either way we look at it, the hoard was worth a considerable sum of money, although less than one might think at first glance.[3]

Given that the earliest coin in the hoard was produced sometime after 120 CE, and the fact that there is then an almost continuous accumulation of coins into the hoard over the next roughly 55 years, we can rule out the possibility of the hoard being the annual funds to pay laborers or soldiers. Instead, we seem to have in the hoard the lifetime savings of an individual or family, perhaps of a wealthy merchant who conducted business in an area that spanned territory both north and south of the Hindu Kush mountains. It is a pity that we do not know the exact circumstances and situation of the discovery. My guess would be that the find was in an urban setting, perhaps concealed behind a domestic wall or beneath the floor of a house. We can imagine an elderly man, having concealed his treasure in a 'safe place' in his house, dying rather suddenly before being able to tell his loved ones about the location of his savings.

Turning to individual coins, coin 4 belongs to the short-lived 'Year One' coinage of Kanishka (phase 1) in which the legends were in Greek. This particular example appears to be unique, as it pairs the Nanaia reverse with the crescented crown (Göbl's krone 1, Cribb and Bracey's crown 2), a combination not seen either in Göbl or Cribb and Bracey. This is perhaps the most interesting individual coin in the hoard. I have already mentioned the double dinar of Vima Kadphises (coin 1), the right-facing dinars of Huvishka (coins 39–40) and the Huvishka dinar featuring Mao and Miiro on the reverse (coin 89). There are other rare types, such as Huvishka dinars with Serapis reverse (coins 74–78) and with Mahasena reverse (coins 86–87). Of course, the most interesting thing about the hoard is the fact that it contains coins in an almost continuous accumulation from the end of Vima Kadphises's reign to about two-thirds into Huvishka's reign.

---

[2] From the US Army recruitment website: https://www.goarmy.com/benefits/total-compensation.html.

[3] A quick estimate I made based on evidence on the price of land in Bengal in the early 6th century yielded a value of $21 million for the hoard. This is probably a gross over-estimate since land prices had probably risen considerably between the 2nd and 6th centuries.

Table 2. Images and Details of Coins in the Hoard

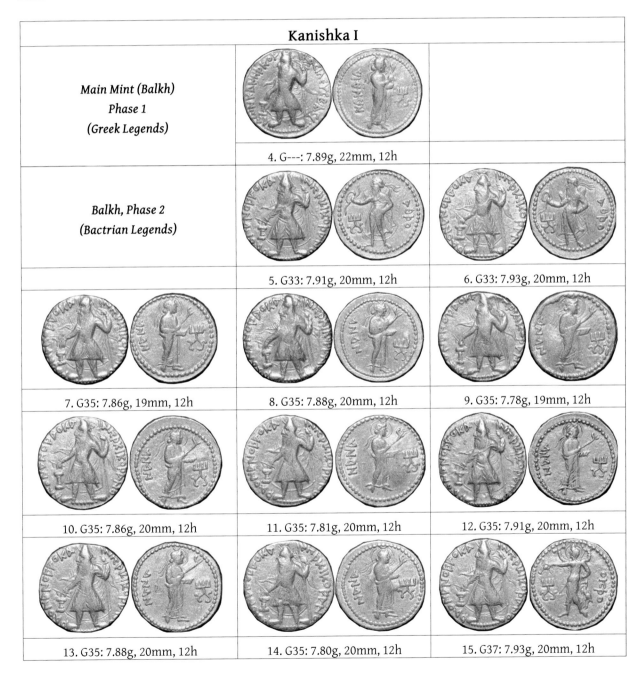

Vima Kadphises		
1. G12: 15.83g, 24mm, 12h	2. G19: 7.81g, 20mm, 12h	3. G19: 7.89g, 21mm, 12h

Kanishka I		
Main Mint (Balkh) **Phase 1** **(Greek Legends)**	4. G---: 7.89g, 22mm, 12h	
Balkh, Phase 2 **(Bactrian Legends)**	5. G33: 7.91g, 20mm, 12h	6. G33: 7.93g, 20mm, 12h
7. G35: 7.86g, 19mm, 12h	8. G35: 7.88g, 20mm, 12h	9. G35: 7.78g, 19mm, 12h
10. G35: 7.86g, 20mm, 12h	11. G35: 7.81g, 20mm, 12h	12. G35: 7.91g, 20mm, 12h
13. G35: 7.88g, 20mm, 12h	14. G35: 7.80g, 20mm, 12h	15. G37: 7.93g, 20mm, 12h

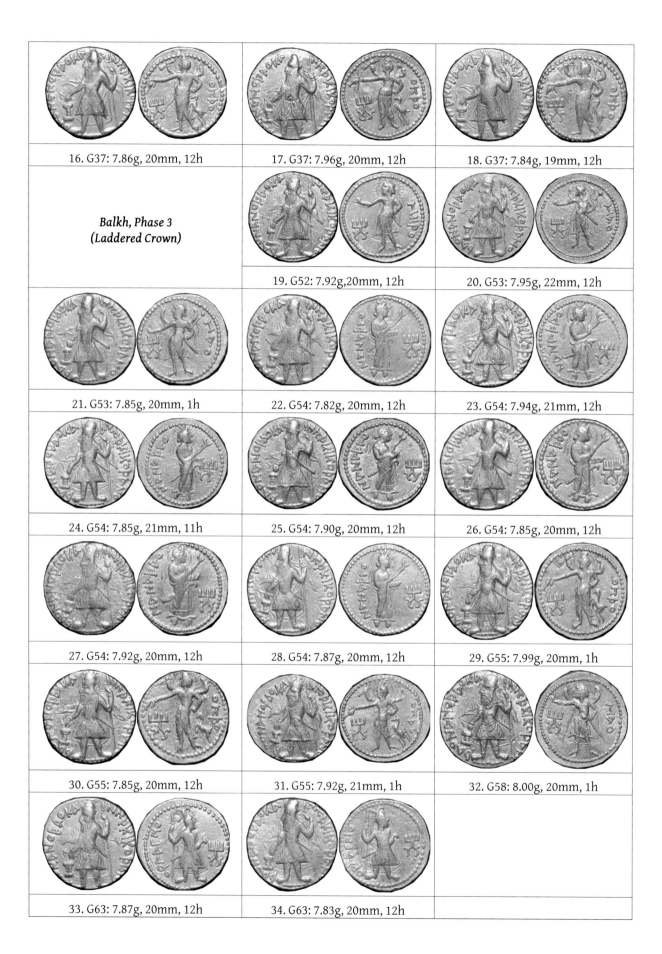

16. G37: 7.86g, 20mm, 12h

17. G37: 7.96g, 20mm, 12h

18. G37: 7.84g, 19mm, 12h

**Balkh, Phase 3
(Laddered Crown)**

19. G52: 7.92g, 20mm, 12h

20. G53: 7.95g, 22mm, 12h

21. G53: 7.85g, 20mm, 1h

22. G54: 7.82g, 20mm, 12h

23. G54: 7.94g, 21mm, 12h

24. G54: 7.85g, 21mm, 11h

25. G54: 7.90g, 20mm, 12h

26. G54: 7.85g, 20mm, 12h

27. G54: 7.92g, 20mm, 12h

28. G54: 7.87g, 20mm, 12h

29. G55: 7.99g, 20mm, 1h

30. G55: 7.85g, 20mm, 12h

31. G55: 7.92g, 21mm, 1h

32. G58: 8.00g, 20mm, 1h

33. G63: 7.87g, 20mm, 12h

34. G63: 7.83g, 20mm, 12h

Subsidiary Mint (Gandhara) Phase 1 (Laddered Crown)	35. G75: 7.99g, 21mm, 12h	36. G75: 7.96g, 20mm, 1h

Huvishka

Main Mint (Balkh) Phase 1 (Kanishka Tamgha)	37. G155: 7.97g, 20mm, 1h	
Main Mint (Balkh) Phase 2 (Huvishka – barred – Tamgha)	38. G136: 7.96g, 20mm, 1h	39. G137: 7.96g, 19mm, 12h
40. G137: 7.95g, 20mm, 12h	41. G138: 7.94g, 19mm, 12h	42. G141: 7.97g, 20mm, 1h
43: G148: 7.93g, 20mm, 1h	44. G154: 7.93g, 19mm, 1h	45. G154: 7.85g, 20mm, 1h
46. G155: 7.93g, 20mm, 1h	47. G155: 7.87g, 20mm, 1h	48. G155: 7.97g, 20mm, 1h
Balkh Phase 3 (Crude Styles)	49. G154: 7.95g, 20mm, 12h	50. G155v: 7.91g, 21mm, 12h

51. G141: 7.93g, 19mm, 12h

52. G148: 7.92g, 20mm, 12h

53. G153: 7.93g, 20mm, 12h

54. G153: 7.81g, 20mm, 12h

55. G154: 7.98g, 19mm, 12h

56. G138: 7.96g, 20mm, 12h

57. G142: 7.94g, 21mm, 12h

58. G143: 7.95g, 20mm, 12h

59. G143: 7.91g, 20mm, 12h

60. G148: 7.94g, 20mm, 12h

61. G148: 7.90g, 20mm, 1h

62. G154: 7.93g, 20mm, 12h

63. G154: 7.90g, 20mm, 12h

64. G154: 7.98g, 20mm, 12h

65. G139: 7.95g, 20mm, 12h

66. G140: 7.95g, 21mm, 1h

67. G144: 7.93g, 21mm, 1h

68. G148: 7.94g, 21mm, 12h

69. G148: 7.50g, 20mm, 12h

70. G148: 7.96g, 21mm, 1h

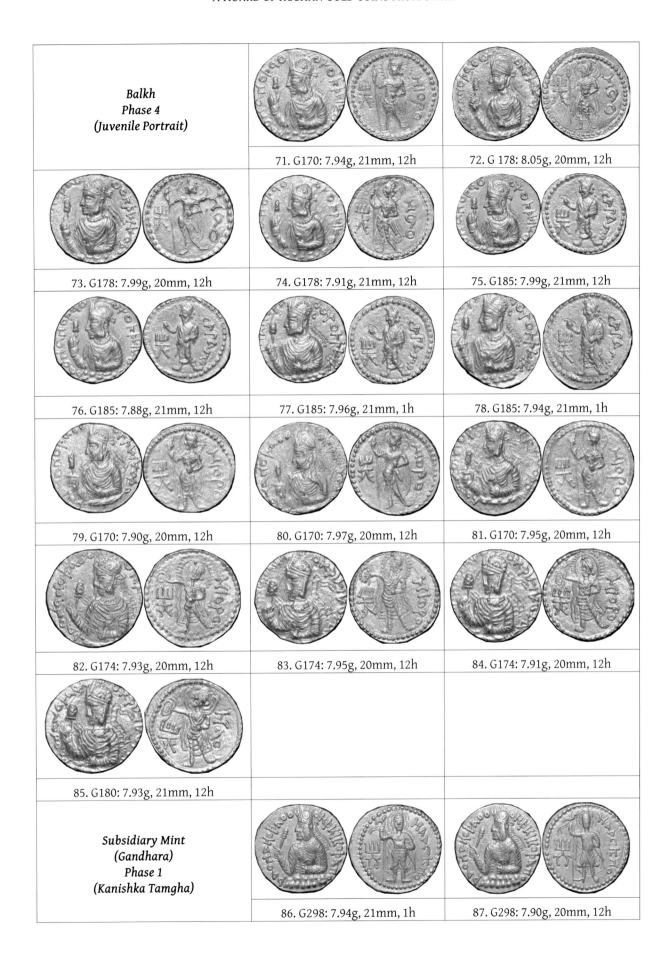

Balkh ***Phase 4*** ***(Juvenile Portrait)***	71. G170: 7.94g, 21mm, 12h	72. G 178: 8.05g, 20mm, 12h
73. G178: 7.99g, 20mm, 12h	74. G178: 7.91g, 21mm, 12h	75. G185: 7.99g, 21mm, 12h
76. G185: 7.88g, 21mm, 12h	77. G185: 7.96g, 21mm, 1h	78. G185: 7.94g, 21mm, 1h
79. G170: 7.90g, 20mm, 12h	80. G170: 7.97g, 20mm, 12h	81. G170: 7.95g, 20mm, 12h
82. G174: 7.93g, 20mm, 12h	83. G174: 7.95g, 20mm, 12h	84. G174: 7.91g, 20mm, 12h
85. G180: 7.93g, 21mm, 12h		
Subsidiary Mint ***(Gandhara)*** ***Phase 1*** ***(Kanishka Tamgha)***	86. G298: 7.94g, 21mm, 1h	87. G298: 7.90g, 20mm, 12h

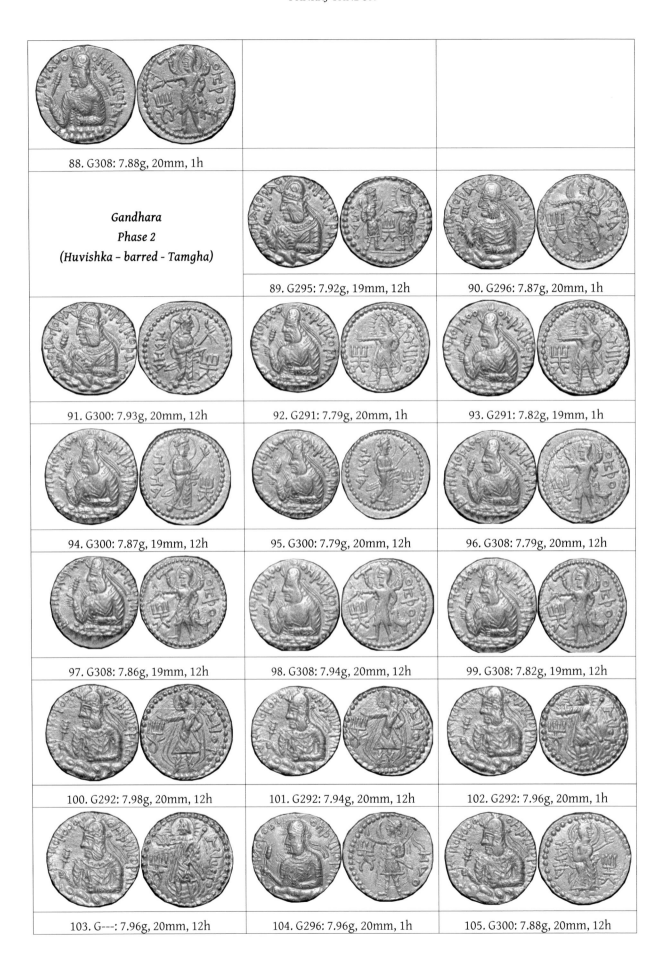

88. G308: 7.88g, 20mm, 1h		
Gandhara *Phase 2* *(Huvishka – barred – Tamgha)*	89. G295: 7.92g, 19mm, 12h	90. G296: 7.87g, 20mm, 1h
91. G300: 7.93g, 20mm, 12h	92. G291: 7.79g, 20mm, 1h	93. G291: 7.82g, 19mm, 1h
94. G300: 7.87g, 19mm, 12h	95. G300: 7.79g, 20mm, 12h	96. G308: 7.79g, 20mm, 12h
97. G308: 7.86g, 19mm, 12h	98. G308: 7.94g, 20mm, 12h	99. G308: 7.82g, 19mm, 12h
100. G292: 7.98g, 20mm, 12h	101. G292: 7.94g, 20mm, 12h	102. G292: 7.96g, 20mm, 1h
103. G---: 7.96g, 20mm, 12h	104. G296: 7.96g, 20mm, 1h	105. G300: 7.88g, 20mm, 12h

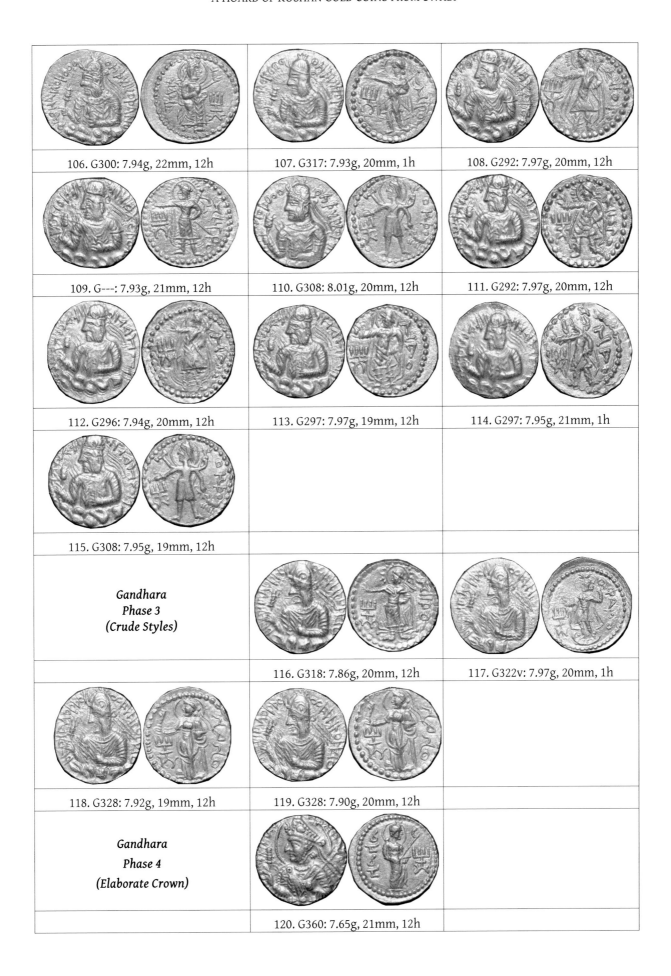

106. G300: 7.94g, 22mm, 12h

107. G317: 7.93g, 20mm, 1h

108. G292: 7.97g, 20mm, 12h

109. G---: 7.93g, 21mm, 12h

110. G308: 8.01g, 20mm, 12h

111. G292: 7.97g, 20mm, 12h

112. G296: 7.94g, 20mm, 12h

113. G297: 7.97g, 19mm, 12h

114. G297: 7.95g, 21mm, 1h

115. G308: 7.95g, 19mm, 12h

Gandhara
Phase 3
(Crude Styles)

116. G318: 7.86g, 20mm, 12h

117. G322v: 7.97g, 20mm, 1h

118. G328: 7.92g, 19mm, 12h

119. G328: 7.90g, 20mm, 12h

Gandhara
Phase 4
(Elaborate Crown)

120. G360: 7.65g, 21mm, 12h

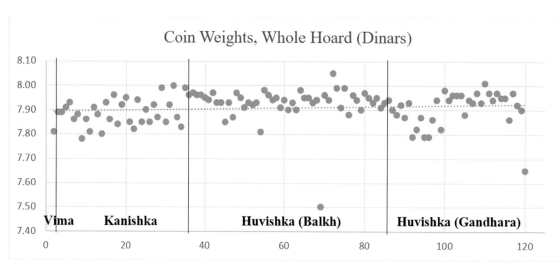

Chart 1. Coin weights of all dinars in the hoard

Analysis of weights

Although I have not attempted a proper die study of the coins, I did order them in an approximation of the order in which they were likely issued and have tried to group together coins that obviously share the same obverse die. Cribb and Bracey have divided Vima Kadphises's coinage into 5 phases; the double dinar comes from phase 4 and the two dinars from phase 5. The coins of Kanishka are divided into three phases for coins from the main mint, probably Balkh, and a single phase for the subsidiary mint, which must have been opened after phase 3 was in full swing at the main mint. Coins from the subsidiary mint are quite scarce. Finally, Huvishka's coins are divided into 6 phases at the main mint and 4 phases at the subsidiary mint, which was undoubtedly in Gandhara, perhaps Peshawar or Taxila. The hoard contained no coins from phases 5 and 6 of Balkh, but did contain 15 coins from phase 4. It also contained a solitary coin from Gandhara's phase 4. We can conclude

that phase 4 at the Gandhara mint probably started at the end of phase 4 or the start of phase 5 at the Balkh mint.

The early coins seemed to me to be distinctly more worn than the late coins and I wondered if this would be discernible in the weights of the coins. Sure enough, if we plot the weights of the coins (dinars only) in a scatter diagram in the order in which they are presented in Table 2, we see a rising trend in the weight (see Chart 1). It could be that the target weight of the coins was rising over time, but a more likely explanation is that the earlier coins, being more worn, have lost a little bit of weight.

Of course, the target weight could also have been changing and it would be more difficult to separate the effects of loss from wear from differences in the target weight if that was the case. To see if this might in fact be the case, I looked at the weights of all the dinars for

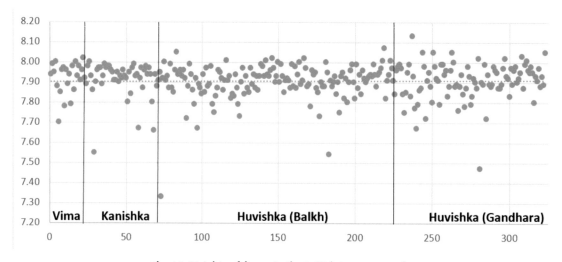

Chart 2. Weights of dinars in the British Museum catalogue

these three kings that are listed in the forthcoming British Museum Catalogue. There are a total of 323 coins for which weights are provided: 21 of Vima, 51 of Kanishka and 251 of Huvishka. Since these coins are not from a single hoard, the number of years for which they circulated are quite random and therefore we should be able to detect whether the weight standard was steady or changing during this period by looking at the weights of these coins. Chart 2 is a scatter diagram showing the weights of all of these coins. We see quite readily that there is no discernible trend in the weights; the trend line is essentially flat. This is confirmed through simple regressions as well. Table 3 shows the average weights of the dinars of the three kings and they are virtually identical; again, statistical tests show that we cannot reject the hypothesis that the actual average weights are the same. Thus it seems entirely reasonable to assume that the target weight of the dinar remained constant through these three reigns and I am going to make this assumption in what follows.

Table 3. Average weights, by king

King	# Coins	Avg Wt	Std Dev
Vima	21	7.9152	0.080475
Kanishka	51	7.9159	0.087136
Huvishka	251	7.9057	0.089316
Total	323	7.9080	0.088273

Returning to the coins of the hoard, the discerning reader would no doubt have noticed that the data in Chart 1 is not strictly chronological. Although the coins are arranged according to the phases of the coinage, there is the possibility that, within a given phase, the coins have not been arranged in chronological order. Since the coins are not dated, there isn't much we can do about that problem. One thing we could do, which I confess I have not done, is to arrange the coins that share dies in an order where the more worn coin is listed earlier in the series than the coin that is less worn. I doubt this would make much of a difference. More important, however, is the fact that the coins of Huvishka from the Gandhara mint are presented at the end of the series, but in fact those coins were produced contemporaneously with the coins from the Balkh mint. In the Appendix (Charts A1-A3), I have presented separate charts for Kanishka's coins, the Huvishka coins from Balkh, and the Huvishka coins from Gandhara. We see that the Huvishka Balkh coins do not exhibit a pronounced rising trend in weights, but the others do.

Putting coins from a hoard in chronological order is essential for estimating the rate at which coins lost weight. This is something that cannot be attempted for a random collection of coins, since we have no idea how long each coin was in circulation before being lost or buried. With a hoard, however, it is reasonable to suppose that all of the coins went out of circulation at around the same time. On the other hand, a hoard that consists of a family's savings, like I suspect this one is, may consist of coins that were taken out of circulation and added to the savings 'piggy bank' at different times, but unfortunately there is nothing we can do about that. So here I will assume that the coins all went out of circulation at the time the hoard was buried and try to measure the rate of weight loss through wear under that assumption.

Kushan coins were not dated, so we do not know when exactly any of these coins was issued. I used a rough and ready approach to try to get a sense of this. I assumed the two Vima dinars were produced in the years 125 and 126, since they were from the final phase of Vima's coinage, and that the Kanishka coins in the hoard were issued uniformly during the years 127–151. I similarly assumed that the Huvishka coins were issued uniformly from each mint during the years 151–180. This gave me a new chart (see Chart 3) in which the weights of the coins are matched to how old the coins were at the time the hoard was buried. Here, the order of coins is reversed from the earlier chart: the Kanishka and Vima Kadphises coins are to the right, since they are older, and the Huvishka coins are to the left. We also see that the Huvishka coins are more densely packed in the chart as compared to the Kanishka coins. This is because the 33 Kanishka coins are spread over 25 years (127–151; 1.32 coins per year), while the 84 Huvishka coins in the hoard are spread over 30 years (151–180; 2.80 coins per year).

We see from the chart that the trend of the weights is downward; as coins get older, they get lighter. A simple linear regression can then be used to estimate a rate at which the coins lost weight.[4] The implicit model is that the coins were all meant to weigh the same amount at the time of production, although there was variability in the weight because of the imprecision of the production process. Over time, as the coins circulated, they lost some weight through wear and tear. The estimated equation, using the whole data set is

$$W_i = 7.9345 - 0.00107 A_i + e_i$$

where W_i is the weight of the ith coin (in grammes), A_i is its age (in years), and e_i is a catch-all "error" term standing for all the other factors affecting the weight, including a deviation of the actual weight from the ideal standard at the time of manufacture and the variation

---

[4] This is essentially the approach taken by Hoyer in his study of weight loss in Roman *sestertii* (Hoyer 2013) except that he uses a multiple linear regression model to allow for a changing initial weight. The actual rate at which a coin loses weight as it circulates is surely much more complex than this model suggests; therefore this should be seen only as a first-order approximation to the actual rate of weight loss.

Relationship of Weight to Age of Coin

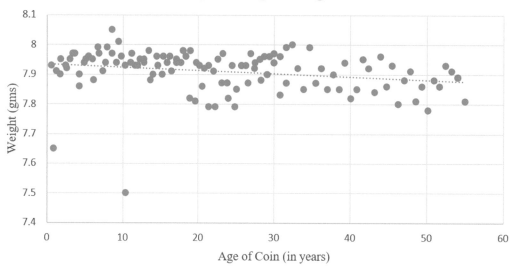

Chart 3. Weights of coins related to how old the coins were when buried

in weight-loss rate for individual coins depending on how frequently they were handled or changed hands during the time they were in circulation. The detailed results are provided in Appendix Table A1.

What the estimated equation says is that, on average, the coins started out weighing 7.9345g and that they then lost, on average, 0.00107 g per year (or 0.0135% of the original weight) as they circulated. This would mean that, on average, a coin would lose 1% of its weight after about 75 years of circulation. Although the fit of this equation appears to be low (the R-squared is 0.05, meaning that age accounts for only about 5% of the variation in the weights), it is highly significant (the P-value on the coefficient is 0.013, well below the accepted threshold level of 0.05). Nevertheless, there are two outlier weights that surely are skewing the results. Coin numbers 69 (7.50g) and 120 (7.65g) have such low weights that they must be pulling down the estimated effect of age. Since these are coins of Huvishka, they were relatively young when buried and so their low weight must surely be an indication of some problems in their manufacture. These problems should not be permitted to skew our estimates of weight loss due to wear.

I therefore ran the regression again with these two observations omitted (see Chart 4 for what the scatter diagram looks like with the two outliers removed). The results were considerably more robust now; details again are in the Appendix (Table A2), but the P-value on the coefficient is now essentially zero (it is equal to 0.00000241), meaning that it is next to impossible that age does *not* lower the weight of the coin (as common sense would tell us as well). The estimated equation is now

$$W_i = 7.9515 - 0.00153A_i + e_i$$

indicating a starting weight of 7.9515g and an annual loss rate of 0.00153 g (or 0.019% of its original weight). At this rate, a coin would lose 1% of its weight after about 52 years.

I should note that I also ran the regression with dummy variables for Kanishka and Huvishka to test whether a change in weight standards could account for the weight differences. If we look at the average weights of coins in the hoard (see Table 3), we see that the coins of Huvishka are, on average, heavier than those of Kanishka, whose coins in turn are heavier than those of Vima Kadphises. Might this reflect a rising weight standard across kings? From the examination of the coin weights from the British Museum Catalogue presented earlier in Chart 3 and Table 2, I had concluded that the target weight for all three kings was the same. But I also wanted to see if the hoard data itself gave us the same result. I tested it by including dummy variables for Kanishka and Huvishka and re-running the regressions and the results unequivocally confirmed the earlier conclusion.[5]

The weight loss rate of 0.00153g (or 0.019%) is, surprisingly, within the range of values estimated by Duncan-Jones for Roman *aurei* (1994: chapter 13). Duncan-Jones had estimated a weight-loss rate of 0.00249 g per year (or 0.034% of the original weight) for his preferred case of a Belgian gold hoard, but he

---

[5] The estimated P-values were far in excess of the threshold value of 0.05. The coefficient on the Kanishka dummy was 0.019, with a standard error of 0.037, leading to a P-value of 0.608, while the corresponding estimates for Huvishka were: coefficient: 0.012, standard error: 0.042, P-value: 0.769.

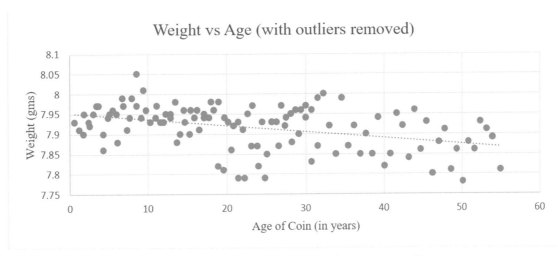

Chart 4. Weights of coins related to age (outliers removed)

Table 3. Average weight of dinars by king and phase

King	Avg Wt	Std Dev	By Phase	Avg Wt	Std Dev
Vima	7.85	0.0566			
Kanishka	7.89	0.0566	Balkh, Phase 1	7.89	*
			Balkh, Phase 2	7.87	0.0529
			Balkh, Phase 3	7.90	0.0555
			Gandhara, Phase 1	7.98	0.0212
Huvishka	7.92	0.0737	Balkh, Phase 1	7.97	*
-- Balkh	7.93	0.0732	Balkh, Phase 2	7.93	0.0393
-- Gandhara	7.90	0.0732	Balkh, Phase 3	7.91	0.0985
			Balkh, Phase 4	7.95	0.0424
			Gandhara, Phase 1	7.91	0.0306
			Gandhara, Phase 2	7.91	0.0642
			Gandhara, Phase 3	7.91	0.0457
			Gandhara, Phase 4	7.65	*

*Standard deviation not meaningful; only one coin in group

found lower loss rates for two other hoards: 0.00158g (or 0.022%) and 0.000816g (or 0.011%) per year. Duncan-Jones's results are not strictly comparable to mine because he ran regressions not on the individual coin data but on median weight for individual kings against the median dates of their reigns. When I ran a similar regression on the Swabi hoard data, I got a weight-loss estimate of 0.00225g per year (or 0.028% of the original weight), which is almost as high as his highest and most preferred estimate. The similarity of results was surprising to me because I had assumed that the velocity of circulation of coins would have been lower in the Kushan realm than in the Roman, which would

have led to a lower weight-loss rate. One factor that might explain this is that the hoards that Duncan-Jones examined were not from Rome or anywhere in Italy for that matter. Rather, his preferred hoard was found in Belgium, and the other two hoards were from Belgium and Britain. It is quite likely that the velocity of money circulation was lower in the provinces than in Rome. So perhaps the estimate of weight loss rate is not as surprising as one might have thought. The present result suggests that the Kushan economy may well have been just as monetized as the provincial Roman economy was, at least at the level of the elites who would have been using gold coins.

XRF analysis of gold content

I recently had the opportunity to perform XRF analysis on the coins of the hoard in order to look at the gold content. The analyzer was a Vanta Element hand-held XRF analyzer made by Olympus and mounted in a rigid stand to ensure uniformity in the testing. I first tested it on a modern (1989) United States $50 gold (Liberty/Eagle) coin and also a modern (2001) US $1 silver coin and found it to be highly accurate. On the gold coin, which is the one most relevant to our analysis, the Vanta measured the gold content to be 91.7938%, as compared to the US Mint stated content of 91.67%,[6] which is well within the 95% confidence interval yielded by the Vanta of (91.6149–91.9727). Indeed, believing the coin to be pure gold when I conducted the test, I was initially taken aback by the result. It was a relief to learn the actual composition according to the mint.

Having satisfied myself of the accuracy of the Vanta tester, I tested each coin in the hoard twice, once on the obverse and once on the reverse, each test with a 10

[6] Viewed online at https://www.usmint.gov/coins/coin-medal-programs/american-eagle/gold-proof.

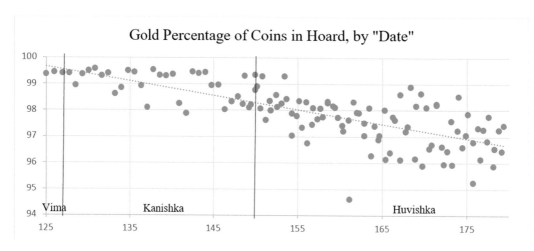

Chart 5. Gold content of coins in the hoard

mm diameter test area and a 30-second exposure.[7] The two readings for each coin were then averaged to get a single measurement for the gold content of the coin. Chart 5 shows the results in a scatter diagram, and the raw numbers are provided in the Appendix (Table A3). The chart shows the gold content of the coins in roughly chronological order; the Huvishka coins are assigned 'dates' in the same way that they were in the weight study. Thus the coins from Gandhara overlap with the coins from Balkh. Note that this data includes the Vima Kadphises double dinar, which had been excluded from the weight study for obvious reasons, but whose gold content obviously does not depend upon its weight.

A glance at the chart shows that the gold percentage seems to be falling over time, consistent with earlier estimates, and also has a tendency to become more variable. Table 4 presents the average gold content by king and by phase and it seems quite clear that the average gold content was falling from one phase to the next. This is not true for the coins of Vima and the transition to Kanishka, but these numbers cannot be taken to be clearly representative as the number of coins is so small: only one coin from Vima's phase 4, two coins from his phase 5 and only one coin from Kanishka's phase 1. We can't come to any statistically robust conclusions based on such sparse data. Similarly, the number for Huvishka's phase 4 in Gandhara is higher than that for phase 3, but, once again, there is a small number problem as there is only one coin from phase 4. Otherwise, we can see that the gold content was declining steadily through Kanishka's and

Table 4. Average gold content by king and phase

King	Avg gold %	Std dev	By phase	Avg gold %	Std dev
Vima	99.3827	0.0522	Balkh, Phase 4	99.3449	*
			Balkh, Phase 5	99.4017	0.0574
Kanishka	98.9660	0.5410	Balkh, Phase 1	99.4058	*
			Balkh, Phase 2	99.1756	0.4302
			Balkh, Phase 3	98.8545	0.5585
			Gandhara, Phase 1	98.1719	0.1058
Huvishka	97.4712	0.9353	Balkh, Phase 1	99.3416	*
-- Balkh	97.6099	0.7382	Balkh, Phase 2	97.8333	0.5300
-- Gandhara	97.2770	1.1399	Balkh, Phase 3	97.8260	0.5796
			Balkh, Phase 4	97.0138	0.6755
			Gandhara, Phase 1	98.8042	0.4674
			Gandhara, Phase 2	97.3011	1.0700
			Gandhara, Phase 3	96.1788	0.6918
			Gandhara, Phase 4	96.4380	*

*Standard deviation not meaningful; only one coin in group

[7] Lengthening the exposure did not seem to systematically change the estimate, but did reduce the estimated standard error of the reading. I decided to use the 30-second exposure because of the limited time I had available to do the testing.

142

Table 5. Average gold content in Three Studies

	Average gold content by king			Excess of Swabi estimate		
	Vima	Kanishka	Huvishka	Vima	Kanishka	Huvishka
Swabi	99.383	98.966	97.471			
Blet-Lemarquand	98.900	98.233	97.320	0.49%	0.75%	0.16%
Maity	98.500	97.656	96.292	0.90%	1.34%	1.22%

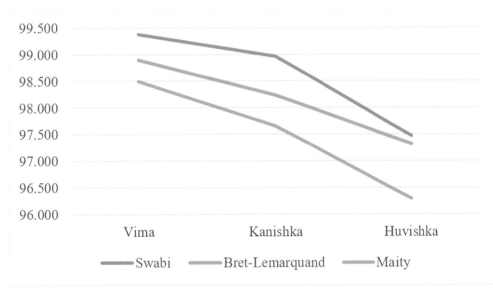

Chart 6. Comparing gold content: three studies

Huvishka's reigns. I believe this is the first time anyone has looked at what was happening to gold content *within* individual reigns.

Note also that the gold content at the Gandhara mint seems to be slightly lower than at Balkh. This is true if we compare Kanishka's phase 1 at Gandhara with his phase 3 at Balkh. It is also true if we compare the gold content overall from the two mints for Huvishka. Finally, if we think of the first four phases at Balkh and Gandhara to be roughly contemporary with one another, the same result holds true. Why this might have been the case is a phenomenon begging for an explanation. Were the mint officials at the Gandhara mint not as capable, or perhaps more dishonest? Or did the Kushan kings think of Gandhara as 'provincial' territory not worthy or needing of the highest quality money? I am sure other explanations may offer themselves.

Finally, it behooves me to compare my results to the earlier results on gold content by others. I looked at the results of Maity (1970), who used specific gravity to estimate gold content, and Blet-Lemarquand (2006), who used proton activation analysis. I used the individual results published by both authors to

calculate their estimated average gold content for the three kings of relevance to this study and report the results in Table 5 and illustrate them in Chart 6. What we find is that the XRF results are higher than those from proton activation analysis, which are in turn higher than Maity's SG results, although the pattern of results is roughly the same in all three cases. The XRF results may be biased upwards, although it is hard to know definitively whether that is true. But it is worth remembering that my test on a modern US gold coin yielded an XRF estimate of 91.78% gold, compared to the known 91.67% true value as reported by the US mint. This is an overestimate of 0.12%, which is a smaller percentage than the amounts by which the XRF estimates here exceed the estimates of Blet-Lemarquand. This dilemma awaits further analysis.

In any case, the trend in gold content is downward over time and, in the present study, we have seen that this is true even within reigns, at least in those of Kanishka and Huvishka, for which we have adequate data. In future, I intend to apply this method to look at the gold content of coins from the entire dynasty to see whether these results extend into the reigns of later kings.

Appendix

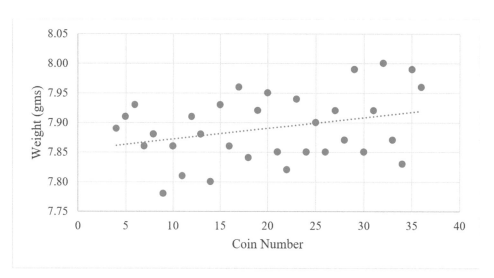

Chart A1. weights of Kanishka dinars

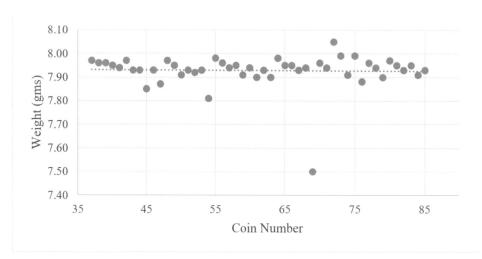

Chart A2. Weights of Huvishka dinars, Balkh mint

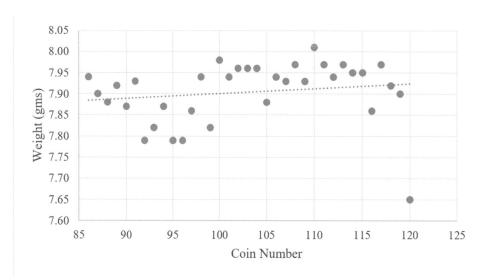

Chart A3. Weights of Huvishka dinars, Gandhara mint

Table A1. Regression results on weight-loss (whole hoard)

	Coefficients	Standard error	t Stat	P-value	Confidence interval
Initial weight	7.934458	0.011697	678.333	3.7E-212	7.9113 – 7.9576
Rate of weight loss	-0.00107	0.000423	-2.52432	0.012932	(-0.0019) – (-0.00023)

Table A2. Regression results on weight-loss (outliers removed)

	Coefficients	Standard error	t Stat	P-value	Confidence Interval
Initial Weight	7.951549	0.008623	922.1605	2.539E-224	7.9345 – 7.9686
Rate of Weight Loss	-0.00153	0.000309	-4.96464	2.4104E-06	(-0.00215) – (-0.00092)

Table A3. Gold content results for whole hoard

Coin #	Au %	Std error	95% confidence interval		Coin #	Au %	Std error	95% confidence interval	
			Lower limit	Upper limit				Lower limit	Upper limit
Vima Kadphises					31	98.5331	0.0375	98.4597	98.6066
1	99.3449	0.0351	99.2762	99.4136	32	99.3115	0.0302	99.2522	99.3707
2	99.3611	0.0352	99.2921	99.4300	33	98.2231	0.0367	98.1512	98.2950
3	99.4423	0.0351	99.3735	99.5110	34	98.9073	0.0325	98.8437	98.9710
Kanishka I					Gandhara – Phase 1				
Balkh – Phase 1					35	98.2467	0.0387	98.1709	98.3225
4	99.4058	0.0373	99.3327	99.4789	36	98.0971	0.0384	98.0219	98.1723
Balkh – Phase 2					Huvishka				
5	99.3985	0.0378	99.3245	99.4725	Balkh – Phase 1				
6	98.9405	0.0293	98.8831	98.9980	37	99.3416	0.0330	99.2769	99.4063
7	99.3646	0.0303	99.3053	99.4240	Balkh – Phase 2				
8	99.5001	0.0275	99.4462	99.5541	38	98.0626	0.0374	97.9892	98.1359
9	99.5705	0.0271	99.5173	99.6236	39	97.6247	0.0397	97.5469	97.7024
10	99.3152	0.0291	99.2582	99.3722	40	97.9911	0.0381	97.9164	98.0657
11	99.4057	0.0280	99.3508	99.4607	41	98.5745	0.0351	98.5057	98.6433
12	98.6200	0.0401	98.5413	98.6986	42	98.2576	0.0386	98.1819	98.3333
13	98.8506	0.0525	98.7477	98.9535	43	98.4261	0.0360	98.3555	98.4967
14	99.4897	0.0277	99.4354	99.5441	44	97.8664	0.0385	97.7909	97.9419
15	99.4449	0.0294	99.3872	99.5026	45	97.7747	0.0380	97.7003	97.8491
16	98.9268	0.0363	98.8557	98.9979	46	97.3394	0.0418	97.2574	97.4214
17	98.0997	0.0419	98.0176	98.1819	47	96.7484	0.0347	96.6804	96.8165
18	99.5312	0.0274	99.4776	99.5849	48	97.4529	0.0401	97.3743	97.5315
Balkh – Phase 3					Balkh – Phase 3				
19	99.3210	0.0327	99.2568	99.3851	49	97.6703	0.0396	97.5926	97.7480
20	99.3122	0.0300	99.2534	99.3711	50	97.7508	0.0389	97.6745	97.8270
21	99.3600	0.0298	99.3016	99.4183	51	98.2690	0.0378	98.1950	98.3430
22	98.2557	0.0370	98.1832	98.3282	52	98.1532	0.0375	98.0798	98.2267
23	97.8741	0.0388	97.7981	97.9501	53	97.7132	0.0409	97.6329	97.7934
24	99.4508	0.0288	99.3943	99.5073	54	97.2148	0.0407	97.1350	97.2945
25	99.4096	0.0290	99.3527	99.4664	55	97.6253	0.0383	97.5503	97.7004
26	99.4341	0.0297	99.3758	99.4923	56	98.3084	0.0382	98.2335	98.3832
27	98.9462	0.0297	98.8879	99.0045	57	97.8945	0.0282	97.8392	97.9499
28	98.9631	0.0284	98.9075	99.0188	58	97.5055	0.0383	97.4304	97.5807
29	98.0326	0.0391	97.9559	98.1093	59	98.0917	0.0381	98.0170	98.1665
30	98.3371	0.0374	98.2638	98.4104	60	97.3887	0.0398	97.3107	97.4667

Coin #	Au %	Std error	95% confidence interval	
			Lower limit	Upper limit
61	97.0336	0.0432	96.9489	97.1182
62	98.0097	0.0392	97.9330	98.0865
63	96.3940	0.0434	96.3089	96.4791
64	97.6324	0.0429	97.5482	97.7165
65	98.5952	0.0357	98.5252	98.6653
66	97.1798	0.0407	97.1001	97.2596
67	98.8831	0.0335	98.8175	98.9487
68	98.1684	0.0379	98.0941	98.2426
69	98.6394	0.0360	98.5688	98.7100
70	98.0986	0.0378	98.0245	98.1727
Balkh – Phase 4				
71	96.6964	0.0435	96.6111	96.7817
72	98.1939	0.0379	98.1196	98.2682
73	96.6083	0.0422	96.5255	96.6911
74	96.4424	0.0427	96.3587	96.5260
75	95.9230	0.0452	95.8345	96.0115
76	97.2182	0.0416	97.1367	97.2997
77	96.5963	0.0428	96.5124	96.6802
78	97.8546	0.0376	97.7809	97.9282
79	96.7876	0.0409	96.7076	96.8677
80	97.3266	0.0406	97.2470	97.4062
81	97.2736	0.0405	97.1942	97.3531
82	97.7516	0.0401	97.6730	97.8302
83	95.8692	0.0461	95.7789	95.9595
84	97.2414	0.0409	97.1612	97.3216
85	97.4240	0.0403	97.3449	97.5030
Gandhara – Phase 1				
86	98.7769	0.0318	98.7146	98.8392
87	99.2846	0.0318	99.2223	99.3469
88	98.3510	0.0378	98.2769	98.4251
Gandhara – Phase 2				
89	98.1273	0.0400	98.0488	98.2057
90	99.2823	0.0297	99.2240	99.3406
91	97.0398	0.0450	96.9515	97.1280
92	98.3530	0.0387	98.2772	98.4289
93	98.3103	0.0381	98.2357	98.3849
94	98.0913	0.0377	98.0174	98.1652
95	98.0701	0.0388	97.9941	98.1460
96	98.3306	0.0383	98.2555	98.4057
97	98.0950	0.0388	98.0189	98.1711
98	97.4156	0.0397	97.3378	97.4933
99	94.6161	0.0507	94.5168	94.7155
100	97.9040	0.0376	97.8304	97.9777
101	97.0340	0.0420	96.9516	97.1163
102	96.2795	0.0438	96.1936	96.3655
103	96.8827	0.0429	96.7987	96.9668

Coin #	Au %	Std error	95% confidence interval	
			Lower limit	Upper limit
104	96.1352	0.0443	96.0483	96.2220
105	97.7428	0.0396	97.6651	97.8205
106	96.1137	0.0430	96.0293	96.1980
107	97.3851	0.0395	97.3077	97.4625
108	96.1606	0.0455	96.0714	96.2499
109	95.8870	0.0465	95.7957	95.9782
110	96.5401	0.0427	96.4565	96.6237
111	98.2330	0.0381	98.1583	98.3077
112	95.9465	0.0464	95.8555	96.0375
113	97.5808	0.0407	97.5010	97.6607
114	98.5219	0.0339	98.4555	98.5883
115	97.0522	0.0419	96.9702	97.1343
Gandhara – Phase 3				
116	95.2323	0.0508	95.1327	95.3318
117	96.1285	0.0450	96.0403	96.2168
118	96.8196	0.0421	96.7372	96.9021
119	96.5346	0.0444	96.4475	96.6217
Gandhara – Phase 4				
120	96.4380	0.0443	96.3511	96.5249

References

Cribb, J., Bracey, R. with Khan, G.R. and Tandon, P. Forthcoming. *Kushan Coins: A Catalogue Based on the Kushan, Kushano-Sasanian and Kidarite Hun Coins in the British Museum, 1st-5th Centuries AD.* London: British Museum.

Göbl, R. 1984. *Münzprägung des Kušānreiches.* Vienna: Verlag der Österreichischen Akademie der Wissenschaften.

Duncan-Jones, R. 1994. *Money and Government in the Roman Empire.* Cambridge: Cambridge University Press.

Hoyer, D. 2013. Calculating the Use-Wear Rates of Roman Coins Using Regression Analysis: A Case Study of Bronze Sestertii from Imperial Gaul. *American Journal of Numismatics* 25: 259-282.

Maity, S.K. 1970. *Early Indian Coins and Currency System.* New Delhi: Munshiram Manoharlal.

Maryse Blet-Lemarquand, M. 2006. Analysis of Kushana Gold Coins: Debasement and Provenance Study, in F. de Romanis (ed.): *Dal Denarius al Dinar: L'Oriente e la Moneta Romana*: 155-171. Rome: Instituto Italiano di Numismatica.

Vagi, D.L. 2000. *Coinage and History of the Roman Empire: c. 82 B.C.-A.D. 480.* Chicago and London: Fitzroy Dearborn.

Gandhāran Jātakas, Avadānas and Pūrvayogas

David Jongeward

I first met Joe Cribb in the early fall of 1985 thanks to a letter of introduction from a coin collector friend in California. Joe transformed my tentative interest in Kushan coins by graciously answering questions and introducing me to books by Robert Göbl and John Rosenfield. I arranged for periodic appointments to the Department of Coins and Medals study room in the British Museum during two years living in London. This was followed by nearly thirty years of annual visits, during which time my interest in Kushan studies included Gandharan sculpture. In 2008, I told Joe about my preliminary survey of Kushan coins in the American Numismatic Society (ANS) collection in New York. "The ANS collection has about 600 Kushan coins," I said, "120 in gold. Would you be interested in co-authoring a book?" Knowing his work load, and expecting a firm negative response, I was greatly surprised when Joe agreed that the project was doable. We published the ANS collection (3,000 coins) seven years later (Jongeward and Cribb 2015). I could not imagine anyone else I would have rather worked with, and it's impossible to properly express my appreciation of Joe's support and friendship during the many years of our association.

I trust that for a volume that celebrates Joe's 75th birthday he will forgive me for submitting a summary of a book in progress that only briefly discusses the Kushan dynasty in the Introduction and concerns previous-birth stories rather than coins (Jongeward, Lenz, Pons [forthcoming]). The book in question is referred to in Elizabeth Errington's contribution to this volume regarding a Jamalgarhi stair-riser relief (*Questions of Identity and Interpretation, or When is a Parrot a Goose?*).

Previous-birth stories of Buddha Śākyamuni have captured the interest of students and scholars alike for as long as our earliest resources allow us to determine. A branch of Buddhist story tradition that has received a prodigious amount of attention is the copious corpus of previous-birth stories referred to as jātakas. A 'classical' jātaka, definitions of which are conceived largely on the basis of the Pali tradition, both in text and commentary, is comprised of three parts: a tale of the present, a tale of the past, and a conclusion. The story of the present records an event or events occurring during the lifetime of the Buddha; the story of the past parallels the story of the present, and is more or less a retelling, although set in a different time and place; the conclusion clarifies the relationship between personages in the story of the present and those in the past. The stories illustrate key Buddhist values of compassion, generosity and self-sacrifice while also emphasizing dedicated practice, morality, and wisdom. Jātaka protagonists, whether human or animal, give characterization and force to specific Buddhist teachings.

Originally drawn from an extensive pool of oral storytelling traditions, the stories migrated along with teachers, monks, pilgrims, merchants and travelers. Texts and image ideas moved along networks of trade routes criss-crossing the Indian subcontinent, working their way into Greater Gandhāra[1] in about the 1st century AD, where some stories were preserved in writing on birchbark scrolls as well as in visual imagery, most often sculpted in stone.

It can be assumed that stories reaching Gandhāra derived from multiple sources and languages, with only limited numbers preserved in written or visual form. The primary purpose of the future volume concerning Gandhāran previous-birth stories is to document what is known so far about literary and visual records of previous-birth stories of the Buddha that circulated in Gandhāra. It is our intention to make scholarship concerning Gandhāran previous-birth stories more accessible by gathering literary and visual depictions together in a single volume and adding new information gleaned from recently discovered birchbark manuscripts written in Kharoṣṭhī script and the Gāndhārī language.

Much has been written about jātakas, especially their Pali representatives. Jātaka notoriety was secured by late nineteenth/early twentieth century translators such as Edward Bayles Cowell (1895–1901). Scholarly interest, however, was not limited to literary productions. Art historians have long documented discoveries of jātakas depicted on the walls, gateways and pillars of ancient Buddhist monuments and stupas: Ajanta, Amaravati, Bharhut, Sanchi and many others (for example, Schlingloff 2013). Jātaka depictions became a focus of interest in studies of Buddhist monuments in Gandhāra by early scholars such as Albert Foucher (1905–51). Foucher identified narrative reliefs on the basis of literary sources available at the time, predominantly

---

[1] See Salomon 1999: 3. Greater Gandhāra includes the Peshawar Valley in the modern-day province of Khyber Pakhtunkhwa in northwestern Pakistan; the Taxila region to the east in the northern Punjab; Bajaur, Swat and Buner districts to the north; the regions of Jalalabad, Kabul and Kapisa. in eastern Afghanistan.

Pali. As the field of Buddhist studies evolved, scholars were able to broaden the lens through which they viewed the objects, basing interpretations on an ever-expanding pool of Buddhist literary resources, written in languages including Sanskrit, Chinese, Tibetan, and Nepalese.

It is now possible to be able to add Gāndhārī, the language of Gandhāra, to the list of languages of Buddhism. A sizable and growing corpus of Gāndhārī manuscript fragments are informing Gandhāran studies in ways that were not possible before these recent discoveries.[2]

The catalogue of previous-birth stories is divided into three parts. Part I is comprised of three chapters. Chapter 1 is introductory. Chapter 2 contains a detailed outline of the Gāndhārī literary tradition as found in recently discovered birchbark manuscript collections, in which previous-birth stories are referred to as avadānas and pūrvayogas. In chapter 3, a theoretical framework is proposed for approaching the special role of the Dīpaṅkara legend as it is portrayed in Gandhāra. Part II contains translations of fifteen stories drawn primarily from Sanskrit sources that help us identify and interpret the depictions of Gandhāran jātakas as found in narrative reliefs and stele. The stories are illustrated with a selection of images drawn from the catalogue and accompanied by analyses and descriptions. Part III constitutes a catalogue of all Gandhāran jātakas found in our comprehensive survey of archives and public and private collections.

Research for this book led to a pair of surprising discoveries, one having to do with visual arts, the other with the relationship between the visual and literary arts. Gandhāran narrative art calls attention to the legend of a student of the Buddhist creed and the path he follows in order to ultimately become a Buddha. The legend concludes with a vow made by a dedicated student, Sumati, who encounters a Buddha of the past, Dīpaṅkara.[3] This vow propels Sumati toward a future birth as the Buddha of the present age, namely, Śākyamuni, and this is highlighted in Gandhāran visual arts by a surprising prominence of depictions illustrating the legend.

In brief, the story as we know it from Sanskrit sources[4] is as follows:

After completing his studies, the ascetic Sumati descended from the Himalayas in search of funds to pay homage to his preceptor. Arriving in town, he noted that it was decked out in festive array, but was unsure why this was the case. Upon learning that the Buddha Dīpaṅkara had arrived in the town, when seeing him, Sumati became filled with faith and decided to honor Dīpaṅkara with lotus flowers that he received from a young woman he met by chance. Sumati threw his lotus flowers as an offering and they remained in the air revolving like a wheel around the Buddha's head. As Dīpaṅkara approached along a muddy road, Sumati spread his hair across the path so that the great sage would not dirty his feet. Sumati vowed that he wished ultimately to become a buddha like Dīpaṅkara. The Buddha set his feet down on Sumati's matted locks and proceeded to walk across his back. Dīpaṅkara then made a prediction that Sumati would be released from the rounds of birth and rebirth, and that once released would become a Buddha in a future age named Śākyamuni. Upon hearing this prediction, Sumati miraculously levitated to the height of seven palm trees. The surrounding crowd saw him standing in the air.

Gandhāra is renowned as a center of arts where representation of the Buddha in human form appeared for the first time in about the first century AD. The Buddha had previously been represented symbolically, ie. in the form of the tree of enlightenment, the dharma wheel, conch shell or other symbolic motifs. Representation of the Buddha in human form opened the possibility of a massive expansion of themes and ideas to be conveyed in narrative reliefs and stele.

The model for living a life faithful to Sumati's vow is the life story of the Buddha himself. Śākyamuni's life history is obviously one to be emulated, hence prominent representations are to be expected. In Gandhāran arts, there appears to be a direct relationship between the prominence of depicting the Dīpaṅkara/Sumati legend and the extreme artistic focus on the life story of Śākyamuni Buddha. Representing the Buddha's life story by including the Dipankara/Sumati legend is a clear Gandhāran priority. If Buddhist narrative art serves to capture the essence of the Buddhist path to be followed by its adherents, Gandhāran depictions of the Dīpaṅkara/Sumati legend seem fundamental to achieving that goal. For example, the Dīpaṅkara panel relief in Figure 1 appears as the first of thirteen reliefs illustrating the life story of Śākyamuni Buddha arranged around the drum of Sikri stupa, now restored and partially reconstructed in the Lahore Museum.

Four episodes of the Dīpaṅkara/Sumati legend in Gandhāran art are beautifully represented in the panel relief from Sikri stupa (Figure 1), a monastery site in the

---

[2] See especially *The Early Buddhist Manuscript Project*, University of Washington, founded in 1996 by Richard Salomon, and the *Early Buddhist Manuscripts from Gandhara* project at Ludwig Maximilian University of Munich, launched in 2012 by a team of researchers led by Jens-Uwe Hartmann and Harry Falk.
[3] The name varies depending on the source--Megha (Nidānakathā), Sumedha (Mahavastu), and Sumati (Divyāvadāna).
[4] Dharmarucyāvadāna excerpt, Divyāvadāna no. 18.

Figure 1. The Dīpaṅkara legend, Sikri stūpa. Lahore Museum G-383-1

Peshawar Valley.[5] In Gandhāran representations, Sumati appears multiple times in a single frame to depict the series of events. The series begins with the scene to the left and shows Sumati holding five lotuses in his right hand, obtained from the young woman facing him. Immediately to her right, Sumati holds a water flask in his left hand, gazing in awe at Dīpaṅkara Buddha who is twice Sumati's height. In the center, Sumati kneels with head bowed nearly to the ground, his hair spread out before Dīpaṅkara's feet. Sumati's thrown lotuses float in the air circling round Dīpaṅkara's head. The fourth depiction concerns what happened after Dīpaṅkara's prediction that Sumati would be reborn in a future age as Śākyamuni Buddha. Sumati is shown levitating, kneeling in mid-air in *añjali*, an expression of reverence and respect. Dīpaṅkara's Buddha-being is emphasized by his stature and centrality as he stands witness to and transcendent over all that unfolds before him.

The list of previous-birth stories that have been securely identified includes fifteen entries. The total number of images that were collected is 177. As shown in Table 1, the Dīpaṅkara legend accounts for 128 of the 177 objects. The 15 previous-birth stories appear in an artistic milieu that includes depictions of nearly 100 episodes from the Buddha's life story.

Table 1. Survey of previous-birth stories in Gandhāra art.

	Story represented	Frequency
1	Dīpaṅkara	128
2	Viśvantara	11 (27 scenes)
3	Śyāma	10 (41 scenes)
4	Ṛṣyaśṛṅga	5
5	Śibi's gift of flesh	4
6	Śibi's gift of his eyes	1
7	Candraprabha	3
8	Vyāghrī	3
9	Maitrakanyaka	3
10	Kiṇṇāra Kinnārī	2
11	Hastī	2
12	Ruru	2
13	Ṣaḍḍanta	1
14	Naḍa	1
15	Śaśa	1

---

[5] The exact location of Sikri monastery is not known, but is believed to have been in the Jamalgarhi area north of present day Mardan, Pakistan.

These numbers differ significantly in comparison to other early Buddhist sites. For example, in Ajanta, 47 cave paintings feature images of the Buddha in previous births, and twelve episodes represent the Buddha's life story (Schlingloff 2013: vol. 1). It's a similar situation at Bharhut, where there are 44 portrayals of the Buddha's previous births, seventeen life-story episodes (See for example, Cunningham 1879). By contrast, at the Great Stūpa of Sanchi, the statistical relationship between previous births and life-story events is reversed. Five jātaka scenes appear together with forty scenes depicting the life of the Buddha (see, for example, Marshall 1918; Huntington 1985). In Central Asia, jātakas inspired a great artistic focus in the caves of Kizil, Xinjiang, (fourth to tenth centuries AD). Well over 100 stories have been identified in cave vaults that are covered with countless paintings of jātakas and avadānas.[6]

Comparisons aside, there is a fundamental difference in regards to research concerning literary and visual mediums of representation. Gandhāran visual arts have been scrutinized prodigiously for nearly 200 years. In contrast, research into Gandhāra's literary tradition has barely begun. Although nearly 25 years of research on newly discovered Gāndhārī manuscripts has yielded novel and interesting insights, there are many more scholarly gems to be mined from the literary corpus currently available and from those that surely will be discovered in the future.

Beginning in 1994, the number of Gāndhārī literary texts available for scholarly study increased exponentially. A collection of 29 birchbark scrolls containing texts written in Gāndhārī Prakrit and Kharoṣṭhī script were acquired by the British Library. Richard Salomon (University of Washington, Seattle, Washington) was commissioned to direct a project dedicated to the study and publication of the texts. This extraordinary discovery launched a new era in the field of Gandhāran studies. Following the British Library collection, the corpus of Gāndhārī literary documents available for study grew exponentially over the next several years as many compilations and fragments came to light that had been preserved in various collections.[7]

The most important documents for purposes of our study include the British Library avadāna and pūrvayoga compilations (Salomon 1999; Lenz 2002.), a narrative compilation from the Split Collection (Falk and Karashima 2012; Falk and Strauch 2014; Falk 2015), an avadāna anthology from Merv, Turkmenistan

(Karashima and Vorobyova-Desyatovskaya 2015), and the *Anavatapta Gāthā* or Songs of Lake Anavatapta (Salomon and Glass 2008).

In addition to findings concerning Dīpaṅkara outlined above, another remarkable discovery is the incongruity between previous-birth narratives found in Gandhāra's literary and visual arts. Only the Vivantara legend is found in both mediums, quite significantly in Gandhāra visual arts, but very abbreviated in its Gāndhārī story form. The name Dīpaṅkara appears twice in Gāndhārī, but not the story. A Gāndhārī text places Dīpaṅkara first in an accounting of the lives of 15 buddhas, 13 who preceded the historical buddha Śākyamuni and the future buddha Maitreya (Salomon 2018: 266–267).

The term jātaka does not appear in Gāndhārī documents. However, the documents contain a treasure trove of fragments of avadānas and pūrvayogas. Avadānas are generally similar to jātakas though not constrained by the necessity of including the Buddha. An avadāna can revolve around the life events of seemingly anyone whose story is deemed worthy for preservation, including monks, nuns, laymen, and laywomen. A characterization of avadānas sounds very much like what we find in jātakas—a story of the present wherein an individual's faith in the teachings of the Buddha are affirmed, strengthened, or newly found; a story of the past detailing past deeds done by characters in the story of the present; and a conclusion wherein the characters in the story of the past are identified with those in the story of the present. That said, Gāndhārī avadānas do not always follow the typical pattern (Salomon 1999).

Unlike a classical jātaka, a Gandhāran pūrvayoga is comprised of one part rather than three, explicitly relating only a tale of the past. Unlike the Pali jātaka tradition with their commentaries, there is no attempt made to pair a Gāndhārī pūrvayoga with a tale of the past or to compare previous and past actions.

An important feature of all Gāndhārī pūrvayogas in the British Library manuscripts is that stories are told as summaries (Figure 2). A monastic reader or compiler presumably knew the stories well enough to be able to recite them in full, and this is made clear by an inclusion in most stories of a concluding statement such as the one translated below: *vistare yasayupamano siyadi vatava*, "Expansion should be according to the model. [23] It should be told."

British Library Fragment 16+25, pūrvayoga 1 (Lenz 2003: 150)[8]

---

[6] A long-term project that commenced in 2016 to document and study the cave paintings of Kizil coordinated by Monika Zin and Eli Franco at the University of Leipzig. See Zin, Konczak 2020.

[7] The collections have been chronicled by Richard Salomon in numerous publications beginning in 1997, and also by Mark Allon beginning in 2007.

[8] Line numbers are in brackets.

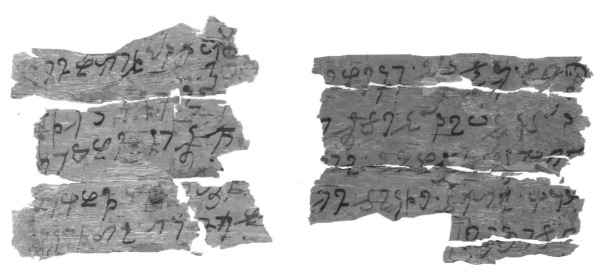

Figure 2. British Library Fragment: Pūrvayoga 1; image courtesy Timothy Lenz

[18] A previous birth (*provayoge*) of the Buddha. Thus it was heard. [19] The Buddha was a merchant, a merchant of the great ocean. Supplies were [20] collected by him. He set out on the great ocean. The ship was destroyed. [21] The merchant met his death on the surface (*of the ocean). It was a favor. . . . The merchant himself [22] was set down here on the shore. He killed himself. Thus the (*pūrva)yoga). Expansion should be according to the model. [23] It should be told.

As our survey of artistic representations of Gandhāran previous-birth stories of the Buddha makes clear, the number of stories that have been identified with a degree of certainty is relatively small and the frequency of occurrence of individual stories is extraordinarily unbalanced. (Table 1). On the literary side, the quantity of literature now available provides avenues for scholarly analysis that previously could hardly have been conceived. Hopefully, the survey of literary and visual materials discussed in our forthcoming book raises questions that generate further investigations. The Dīpaṅkara/Sumati legend and the art it inspired in Gandhāra continued to spread for centuries into the arts of China, Sri Lanka, Burma, Nepal and elsewhere, clearly deserving a book of its own. Back in Gandhāra, there are any number of unidentified narrative reliefs that await interpretation including many that very likely represent jātakas. And furthermore, there are countless Gāndhārī birchbark manuscripts that remain to be deciphered.

References

Allon, M. 2007. Recent Discoveries of Buddhist Manuscripts from Afghanistan and Pakistan: The Heritage of the Greeks in the North-West,1 in H. Prabha Ray and D.T. Potts (eds.) *Memory as History: The Legacy of Alexander in Asia*: 131-141. New Delhi: Aryan Books International.

Cowell, E. (ed.) 1895–1901. *The Jātaka, or Stories of the Buddha's Former Births*. 6 vols. Cambridge: Cambridge University Press.

Cunningham, A. 1879. *The Stûpa of Bharhut: A Buddhist Monument Ornamented With Numerous Sculptures Illustrative of Buddhist Legend and History in the Third Century B.C.* London: W.H. Allen and Co.

Falk, H. 2015. A New Gāndhārī Dharmapada (Texts from the Split Collection 3). *Sōka daigaku kokusai bukkyōgaku kōtō kenkyūjo nenpō* 創価大学国際仏教学高等研究所年報 18: 23–62.

Falk, H. and Karashima, S. 2012. A First-century *Prajñāpāramitā* Manuscript from Gandhāra – *parivarta* 1 (Texts from the Split Collection 1). Annual Report of the International Research Institute for Advanced Buddhology at Soka University 15: 19–61.

Falk, H. and Strauch, I. 2014. The Bajaur and Split Collections of Kharoṣṭhī Manuscripts within the Context of Buddhist Gāndhārī Literature, in P. Harrison and J.-U. Hartmann (eds) *From Birch-Bark to Digital Data: Recent Advances in Buddhist Manuscript Research: Papers Presented at the Conference 'Indic Buddhist Manuscripts: The State of the Field,'* Stanford, June 15-19 2009: 51-78. Österreichische Akademie der Wissenschaften, philosophisch-historische Klasse, Denkschriften, 460. Band / Beiträge zur Kultur- und Geistesgeschichte Asiens, Nr. 80. Wien: Verlag der Österreichischen Akademie der Wissenschaften.

Foucher, A. 1905–1951. *L'art gréco-bouddhique du Gandhâra. Étude sur les origines de l'influence classique dans l'art bouddhique de l'Inde et de l'Extrême-Orient*. 3 vols. Paris: E. Leroux.

Huntington, S. 1985. *The Art of Ancient India*. New York/ Tokyo: Weatherhill.

Jongeward, D. and Cribb, J. 2015. *Kushan, Kushano-Sasanian, and Kidarite Coins: A Catalogue of Coins from the American Numismatic Society.* New York: The American Numismatic Society.

Jongeward, D. 2020. *Kushan Mystique.* London: Spink and Son Ltd. Digital edition, Toronto: Iguana Books.

Jongeward, D., Lenz, T. with Pons, J. [Forthcoming]. *The Buddha's Previous Births: Gandhāran Stories in Birchbark and Stone.*

Karashima Seishi and Vorobyova-Desyatovskaya, M.I. (eds) 2015. The *Avadāna* Anthology from Merv, Turkmenistan, in *The St. Petersburg Sanskrit Fragments.* 2 vols. Buddhist Manuscripts from Central Asia: 145-523. Tokyo: The Institute of Oriental Manuscripts of the Russian Academy of Sciences; The International Research Institute for Advanced Buddhology, Soka University.

Lenz, T. 2003. *A New Version of the Gāndhārī Dharmapada and a Collection of Previous-Birth Stories: British Library Kharoṣṭhī Fragments 16 + 25.* Gandhāran Buddhist Texts, Vol. 3. Seattle: University of Washington Press.

Marshall, J. 1918. *A Guide to Sanchi.* India: Superintendent Government Printing.

Neelis, J. 2019. Making Places for Buddhism in Gandhāra: Stories of Previous Births in Image and Text, in W. Rienjang and P. Stewart, (eds) *The Geography of Gandhāran Art: Proceedings of the Second International Workshop of the Gandhāra Connections Project*: 175-185. Oxford: Archaeopress.

Salomon, R.1999. *Ancient Buddhist Scrolls from Gandhāra: The British Library Kharoṣṭhī Fragments.* Seattle: University of Washington Press.

Salomon, R. 2018. *The Buddhist Literature of Ancient Gandhāra: An Introduction with Selected Translations.* Classics of Indian Buddhism. Somerville: Wisdom Publications.

Salomon, R. and Glass, A. 2008. *Two Gāndhārī Manuscripts of the Songs of Lake Anavatapta (Anavatapta-gāthā)*: British Library Kharoṣṭhī Fragment 1 and Senior Scroll 14. Gandhāran Buddhist Texts, Vol. 5. Seattle: University of Washington Press.

Schlingloff, D. 2013. *Ajanta – Handbook of the Paintings 1.* 3 vols. New Delhi: IGNCA.

Zin, M. and Konczak, I. 2020. *Essays and Studies in the Art of Kucha.* New Delhi: Dev Publishers.

Notes on Indian Imitations of Kushan Coins

Emilia Smagur

Joe's name resonates loudly with anyone who works with Kushan coins, therefore, as a PhD student preparing a thesis on iconography of Kushan deities I visited the British Museum Department of Coins and Medals to meet him. Since that meeting in 2012 he has become a wonderful mentor and friend to me. In this paper, offered in his honour, I would like to discuss some issues that relate to the Indian imitations of Kushan coins that were produced in the territories located outside of the Kushan empire.[1] In numismatics few concepts are as lacking in a generally accepted definition as the term imitation. For the purpose of this paper I apply this term broadly to indicate objects intended to resemble Kushan coins, regardless of the material they are made of, the technology of their production, or their function. However, I am also aware that though we use our own terms which help us to categorise the imitations, in the past they might not have been interpreted in the same way. This is because coinage is a cultural construct and its use and understanding are rooted in cultural norms.

Indian imitations of Kushan coins have been discovered in northern and eastern India. Genuine Kushan issues, some in gold but mostly in copper found in the same region constitute evidence of their penetration as far as Bengal and Odisha (formerly Orissa) (Cribb and Bracey forthcoming; Sharma 2012). Those finds were previously taken as evidence of Kushan direct rule over these territories (e.g. Altekar 1958: 3; Banerji 1951) but, in fact, these regions were never incorporated into the Kushan Empire. However, part of them (Ayodhya and Magadha) remained in its zone of influence (Bracey 2021: 132-133, fig. 13.11). The flow of coinage was not connected with Kushan jurisdiction but with the transregional impact of Kushan copper issues as a medium of exchange as well as with the creation of wider monetary networks that took place in the Early Historic period (see also Morris 2022: 464-465). The major export of Kushan copper coins that took place in the second half of the reign of Huvishka when the official coinage was reduced in weight (Jongeward and Cribb 2015: 243) is reflected in finds of hoards containing coins of the first three Kushan kings, which are common in this territory (Sharma 2012).

Based on surviving evidence Indian imitations of Kushan coins can be divided into two groups according to the function attributed to them during the process of their production. The first group covers coins produced to supplement the official issues of eastern Indian states (Cribb and Bracey: forthcoming; Jongeward and Cribb 2015: 243) while coin-like objects used as ornaments belong to the second category. Kushan imitation coinages are represented by series made in northern and eastern India. When the supply of imported coins was not replenished the worn imported issues started to be replaced by their imitations. Those copper imitations, of Kanishka I coins, were produced by striking (in northern India and Bengal) as well as by casting (in Odisha and Bihar). The identification of their issuers is difficult, however, based on their treatment and style it can be assumed that the struck coins were probably privately made while the Bihar/Odisha series were possibly official in nature. Those imitations started to be produced in the late 2nd century (Bracey 2016; Cribb and Bracey: forthcoming; Jongeward and Cribb 2015: 243-244). In addition, the gold coinage of the kingdom of Samatata in Eastern India issued in the late 5th century is based on Kanishka I types (Bracey 2021: 133; Cribb and Bracey: forthcoming; Mitchiner 2004: 1240-47).

The second group includes coin-like objects used as jewellery. The total number of such finds is unknown. However, even assuming that some unpublished examples reside in private and public collections, it is significantly smaller than the number of imitation coins. That the Kushan coins, and their imitations, were used as ornaments or amulets in northern and eastern India is confirmed by the presence on some of them of attachments or double piercing, to allow suspension. The list, however, is rather short. Gupta (1974: 30-31) mentions four looped gold coins of Wima Kadphises, Huvishka and Vasudeva I reported additional examples from Lohardaga (present Lohardaha Dt., Jharkhand),[2] Belwadaga (Ranchi Dt., Jharkhand)[3] and Sultanganji (Bhagalpur Dt., Bihar).[4] A looped gold coin of Huvishka was found in Bonai (Sundergarh Dt., Odisha) together with a gold ring, gold chain and three coin-like objects imitating Kushan issues. Unfortunately, the photo of only one of those imitations was published and it shows a double pierced bracteate imitating the obverse

[1] This work was supported by The National Science Centre in Poland under Grant SONATINA 1 2017/24/C/HS3/00120.

[2] Looped coins of Wima Kadphises and Vasudeva were deposited as hoard together with a lump of gold.
[3] Three Kushan coins were found: one was issued by Huvishka and had a small gold pin or crown at the top suggesting its use as jewellery; the details of other two are not known.
[4] 'A later Kushan coin with a loop was found in a pot together with looped Samudragupta coin and some ornaments.

Figure 1. Bracteate imitating reverse of Kushan dinara
with Oesho. AV, diameter: 21mm, weight: 0.85g © Classical
Numismatic Group, LLC, www.cngcoins.com

of a Huvishka issue (Behera 1975).[5] Two finds from Bangladesh, a double pierced gold coin of Huvishka (Mainamati region, Comilla Dt.) and a looped coin of Vasudeva I (Godagari, Rajshahi Dt.) were published by Ahmed and Abu Al Hasan (2014: 116, 119-120). A well known, double pierced and looped gold medallion (Lal 1949: 95, 97, pl. XVIII.A) recovered during excavations at Sisupalgarh (Khurda Dt., Odisha) should be excluded from this dataset. According to many scholars (see e.g. Altekar 1949: 100-101; Borell 2014: 28; Lal 1949: 97; Rashke 1978: 752 fn. 465; Suresh 2004: 78) one side of this medallion has an imitation of a Roman emperor portrait, while the other bears the representation of Kushan King Vasudeva I. However, this identification is incorrect. It is actually a crude imitation of a Roman aureus with no Kushan elements in its design (Joe Cribb: personal communication). On its obverse the emperor's portrait is depicted, while the reverse is based on the representation of Mars also found on Roman coins.

In the case of pierced examples two perforations were always placed above or on both sides of the ruler's head ensuring that the depiction was displayed vertically. This diagnostic feature (Darley 2013: 262; Smagur 2018: 68) enables us to identify coins used as ornaments in non-Kushan India even without findspot data since this specific type of piercing is not known among finds from the Kushan territory. Examples include one double pierced gold coin of Kanishka I and two of Huvishka which can be found in the collection of the Allahabad Museum,[6] as well as to the famous Kanishka I coin with Athsho labelled as Hephaistos which was purchased from Alexander Cunningham by the British Museum.[7]

The double piercing of the latter has been refilled with gold blobs constituting evidence of a practice aimed at restoring the coin to its original monetary function and illustrating the next phase in its life-cycle. The remains of the broken loop can also be seen on this piece, suggesting that, at least twice, it was converted into jewellery, before, and probably after refilling the piercing. This practice is also confirmed by finds of Roman coins and their imitations. A pierced aureus of Nerva (Subrahmanyam et al 2008: 6, no. 15132), along with two gold imitations of coins of Tiberius from the Penuganchiprolu hoard (Krishna Dt., Andhra Pradesh; Subrahmanyam et al 2008: 6, nos. 15132, 15136) have perforations refilled with gold. Another aureus, a Claudius issue from the Tirukkoilur hoard (Kallakurichi Dt., Tamil Nadu; Berghaus 2000: 499, fig. 1), has two refilled holes and a tubular loop, just like the Kushan dinara with Athsho. In this case, the loop is most probably a later modification rather than refilling. Another interesting gold-plated and double pierced copper imitation of a Huvishka issue was purchased by the British Museum from Edward Thomas (Bracey 2021: fig 13.14).[8] Double pierced bracteates imitating Kushan coins (Figure 1) appear on the market from time to time.[9] These are often assigned to a group called 'Silk Road bracteates' (see Naymark 2001: 91-169; Pieper 2003; Raspopova 1999; Guo 2020: 342) however, the specific type of perforations are not known among finds from Central Asia and rather point to their Indian origin.

Medallions made of two welded bracteates imitating Kushan issues are particularly interesting. The pendant from Bodh Gaya (Daya Dt., Bihar) was discovered by Cunningham (1892: 20, pl. XXII) in the Mahabodhi temple, in a lump of clay being a relic deposit found below the Enlightenment Throne which contained also coins and other precious objects. It is made of two bracteates

---

[5] Behera (1975: fn. 1) described them as follows: 'Two specimens have two holes at the top. These thin pieces are cast imitations bearing the impression of Kushana coins on one side only, the other being flat (...). One piece, which is somewhat distinct, bears the impression of the bust of Huvishka as found on the obverse of his coins'.

[6] http://museumsofindia.gov.in/repository/record/alh_ald-AM-GC-96-32-8080; http://museumsofindia.gov.in/repository/record/alh_ald-AM-GC-95-09-8075; http://museumsofindia.gov.in/repository/record/alh_ald-AM-GC-47-7863.

[7] BM no. 1888,1208.538; https://www.britishmuseum.org/collection/

object/C_1888-1208-538

[8] BM no. 1850,0305.280; https://www.britishmuseum.org/collection/object/C_1850-0305-280

[9] E.g. CNG, LLC. Electronic Auction 469, lot 200 (3.06.2020)

Figure 2. Medallion made of two bracteates imitating Roman coin. AV, diameter: unknown, weight: 2.24g. © Classical Numismatic Group, LLC, www.cngcoins.com

which are coin impressions taken from an issue of Huvishka joined together and looped. Interestingly, its maker deliberately chose the coin obverse to be imitated instead of its reverse depicting a deity. The inside of those impressions was most probably filled in for functional purposes, or, as recently suggested by Bracey (2021: 131), it might have contained a relic. A technologically similar double pierced coin-like object was found during excavations at Sadargalli in Patna (Patna Dt., Bihar). It bears the depiction of Huvishka on its obverse and Ardochsho on the reverse and was made in the same way as the Bodh Gaya find by joining together two bracteates (Altekar 1958). Another, broken, example was also found in Patna at the site of Kumrahar. It depicts a standing ruler on its obverse and seated Ardochsho on its reverse, and therefore must imitate a coin not earlier than the issue of Vasudeva I (Altekar and Mishra 1959: 131, pl. LIX B 1-2). It is worth noting that the same technique was sometimes used for producing imitations of Roman coins. A gold medallion made of two bracteates welded together and with a loop attached (now missing) appeared on the market in 2004 (Figure 2),[10] however its direct prototype and provenance cannot be established. Another two objects of this type, coming from the same workshop were auctioned together with a third specimen imitating a Roman coin in 2011.[11]

The use of this method for producing coin-like pendants by joining together two bracteates is also seen in a medallion which recently appeared on the market.[12] This piece, made of thin gold sheets hammered against the same prototype, depicts on both sides the ruler's portrait based on representations known from Late Roman issues. However, it differs from the examples mentioned above, since the bracteates are set in an ornate border with an ornate suspension loop. Another

example coming from the same workshop but made of one bracteate is also known (Figure 3).[13]

Looped medallions with similar ornamental frame and made from genuine Roman and Kushan coins along with their imitations have been known since the discovery of the most famous example[14] in the trays of the British Museum Department of Coins and Medals by Robert Göbl in 1963. The British Museum jewellery piece (see Bracey 2021: 134; Errington and Cribb 1992: 146; Gupta 1976; Göbl 1976; 1984: 176, no. 20.1; 1987; 1999) constitutes a hybrid of Roman and Kushan coin designs copied from the coins of Constantine I and of Huvishka. According to Göbl (1976) it was made in north-western Indian at a Kushan mint. This assumption is, however, difficult to sustain (Errington and Cribb 1992: 146). Recently Robert Bracey suggested[15] that those medallions might have been produced in eastern India, somewhere where both Roman and Kushan coins were known but neither was the circulating currency. I believe that this example speaks in favour of the hypothesis of their eastern provenance. In terms of its frame and loop it is a close relative of other known medallions, and the technology used of a central disc produced by joining together two bracteates, is known for the northeast, not northwest India, as indicated by the already mentioned finds from Bodh Gaya and Patna. If we follow Göbl's (1999) theory according to which all of those medallions were made in the same place, the workshop/workshops they were produced in could have been located much farther east than he anticipated.

It is unclear when Kushan coins first reached northern and eastern India, therefore the dating of the production of the coin-like objects is very difficult. In the period between the 3rd and 5th centuries Kushan copper coins supplemented the local currency in the

---

[10] CNG, LLC. Mail Bid Sale 66, lot 1002 (19.05.2004)
[11] Todywalla Auctions, Auction 57, lot 20 (13.11.2011)
[12] CNG, LLC. Electronic Auction 500, lot 588 (22.09.2021)

[13] CNG, LLC. Triton XXII, lot 457
[14] BM no. OR.5200, https://www.britishmuseum.org/collection/object/C_OR-5200
[15] In the discussion during the International Virtual Conference Finds of Foreign Coins from India that took place 17-18 June 2021.

Figure 3. Medallions made of bracteates imitating obverse of Late Roman coin (Constantin I?) set in ornate basels with loops. (left) AV, diameter: 28.5mm, weight: 7.32g., (right) AV, diameter: 33mm, weight: 7.81g. © Classical Numismatic Group, LLC, www.cngcoins.com

Gangetic Valley and the last evidence for them being still in circulation is dated to c. 500 CE (Bracey 2021: 134). The evidence from excavations is not helpful in this regard, as the coins have been used to date the sites rather than the context dating the coins and their deposit. As Bracey (2021: 133) points out, the Bodh Gaya find was dated too early. In Kumrahar the chronology of the site was determined based on finds of Kushan coins among others, not vice versa (see Altekar and Mishra 1959: 18). The Sadargalli pendant has been dated by its excavators to period II (c. 150 BC to c. 500 AD) who also stress that its discovery 'helped much in determining the chronology of the period' (Sinha and Aditya Narain 1970: 12-14). Therefore, they can be only dated very broadly somewhere between the date of the production of their prototypes and the 5th century.

The value of studying Indian imitations of foreign coins is beyond doubt. Kushan coins did not constitute the only type of foreign currency that was imitated in Early Historic India. The most famous and numerous are the above-mentioned imitations of Roman coins (e.g. Berghaus 1991; 1993; 1994; 2006; Darley 2013: 267-273; Smagur 2022; Suresh 2004: 58-66; Turner 1989: 37-41). Another type of foreign currency that was imitated, but rarely, in the subcontinent is Aksumite coinage and an example of a double pierced imitation of an Ousanas coin was found in the Mangalore hoard (Dakshina Kannada Dt., Karnataka) containing Late Roman and Aksumite issues (Hahn 1998). The phenomenon of imitating foreign gold coins in later periods is illustrated by a number of local imitations of Venetian ducats and their derivatives known as putali, which are still being produced and worn as ornaments in many parts of the subcontinent (e.g., Bhandare 2004: 112-114; Smagur 2023). The longevity of imported coins designs constitutes one of the distinguishing features of the Indian coinage tradition (Cribb 2003; 2005).

The preliminary comparison of Indian imitations of Roman and Kushan coins enables us to define certain problems. Firstly, Indian imitations of Kushan issues are

recorded from territories where Roman coins and their imitations are rarely found, perhaps due to the indirect nature of Roman trade with that region, suggested by the absence of amphorae (Tomber 2013). It is, however, equally probable that it was the availability of Kushan coins in that area that might have caused the decreasing interest in the Roman issues. Secondly, the tradition of wearing Roman coins and coin-like ornaments developed from the use of genuine coins. The same is not true for Kushan coins and coin-like jewellery from northern and eastern India. Ornaments made of Kushan coins and their imitations are much less numerous that those made of their Roman counterparts. One might assume that the reason for this lies in the scarcity of Kushan dinars circulating on these territories. It is worth noting that Samatata and Gupta issues, also gold, were seldom transformed into pendants, demonstrating that the metal they were made of was not the decisive factor. Moreover, no Roman imitation coinage has been recorded from the subcontinent so far, and the purpose of the production of many Indian imitations of aurei remains unclear. However, the introduction of high quality gold imitations of weight that was very similar – or even higher – to contemporary aurei, certainly increased the number of functions such items might have had, being ornaments, amulets, prestigious items, and stores of wealth. Therefore, the cultural response to the influx of imported coins to the subcontinent varied according to the region and its social and cultural environment, as well as the identity of the issuer. I believe that further research focused on defining the factors (cross-cultural and culturally specific) that had an impact on the reception of foreign coins in Early Historic India will shed new light on the agency of imported objects.

References

Ahmed, B. and Abu Al Hasan, M. 2014. Kushana Coins from Bangladesh: A Preliminary Study. *Journal of Bengal Art* 19: 113-122.

Altekar, A.S. 1949. A note on the Kushan gold coin (pl. XLVIII A). *Ancient India* 5: 100-101.

Altekar, A.S. 1958. A golden amulet imitating a coin of Huvishka. *Journal of the Numismatic Society of India* 20 (1): 1-3.

Altekar, A.S. and Mishra, V. 1959. *Report on Kumrahar Excavations 1951-1955.* Patna: K. P. Jayaswal Research Institute.

Banerji, A. 1951. Kushanas in Eastern India. *Journal of the Numismatic Society of India* 13: 107-109.

Behera, K.S. 1975. On a Kushana gold coin from Orissa. *Journal of the Numismatic Society of India* 37 (1-2): 76-82.

Berghaus, P. 1991. Roman Coins from India and Their Imitations. Pages 108-121 in A.K. Jha (ed.), *Coinage, Trade and Economy, January 8th-11th, 1991, 3rd International Colloquium*: Bombay: IIRNS.

Berghaus, P. 1993. Indian Imitations of Roman Coins. Pages 305-310 in T. Hackens and G. Moucharte (eds), *Proceedings of the XIth International Numismatic Congress organized for the 150th anniversary of the Societe Royale de Numismatique de Belgique. Brussels, September 8th-13th 1991*, vol. 2. Louvain-la-Neuve: Association Professeur Marcel Hoc.

Berghaus, P. 1994. Two imitations out of the Valuvally Hoard of Roman *Aurei* (Kerala) 1983. *Studies in South Indian Coins* 4: 33-42.

Berghaus, P. 2000. Gestopfte Löcher auf römischen Goldmünzen aus indischen Funden. Pages 499-502 in B. Kluge and B. Weisser (eds), *XII. Internationaler numismatischer Kongress Berlin 1997. Akten – Proceedings – Actes*, vol. I. Berlin: Staatliche Museen zu Berlin.

Berghaus, P. 2006. Strange Mould Links out of the Tirukkoilur Hoard. Pages 11-20 in R. Nagaswamy (ed.), *Sangam: Numismatic and Cultural History-Essays in Honour of Dr. R. Krishnamurthy.* Chennai: New Era Publications.

Bhandare, S. 2004. Foreign Coins in Traditional Jewellery of Deccan. Pages 111-114 in D.W. MacDowall and A. Jha (eds), *Foreign Coins Found in the Indian Sub-Continent:.* Nasik: IIRNS.

Borell, B. 2014. The Power of Images - Coin Portraits of Roman Emperors on Jewellery Pendants in Early Southeast Asia. *Zeitschrift fur Archäologie Aussereuropäischer Kulturen* 6: 7-43.

Bracey, R. 2016. Kushan Dynasty iv. Coinage of the Kushans, *Encyclopædia Iranica*, online edition, available at http://www.iranicaonline.org/articles/kushan-dynasty-04 (viewed 17 December 2021).

Bracey, R. 2021. Numismatic Finds at Bodhgaya. Pages 128-135 in S. van Schaik, D. De Simone, G. Hidas and M. Willis (eds), *Precious Treasures from the Diamond Throne: Finds from the Site of the Buddha's Enlightenment.* London: The British Museum.

Cribb, J. 2003. The Origins of the Indian Coinage Tradition. *South Asian Studies* 19 (1): 1–19.

Cribb, J. 2005. *The Indian Coinage Tradition: Origins, Continuity and Change.* Mumbai: IIRNS.

Cribb, J. and Bracey, R. Forthcoming. *Kushan Coins: a catalogue based on the Kushan, Kushano-Sasanian and Kidarite Hun coins in the British Museum.* London: The British Museum.

Cunningham, A. 1892. *Mahabodhi, or the Great Buddhist Temple under the Bodhi Tree at Buddha-Gaya.* London: W.H. Allen.

Darley, R. 2013. Indo-Byzantine Exchange, 4th to 7th Centuries: a Global History. Unpublished PhD dissertation, University of Birmingham.

Errington, E. and Cribb, J. (eds). 1992. *The Crossroads of Asia: Transformation in Image and Symbol in the Art of Ancient Afghanistan and Pakistan.* Cambridge: The Ancient India and Iran Trust.

Göbl, R. 1976. The Roman-Kushanian Medallion in the British Museum. *Journal of the Numismatic Society of India*: 21-26.

Göbl, R. 1984. *System und Chronologie der Münzprägung des Kušānreiches.* Vienna: Österreichische Akademie der Wissenschaften.

Göbl, R. 1987. Constantin Der Grosse Und Indien: Der Römisch-Kusanische Goldmedaillon Des British Museum in London. *Litterae Numismaticae Vindobonenses* 3: 185-191.

Göbl, R. 1999. The Rabatak Inscription and the Date of Kanishka. Pages 151-205 in M. Alram and D.E. Klimburg-Salter (eds), *Coins, Art, and Chronology: Essays on the pre-Islamic History of the Indo-Iranian Borderlands.* Vienna: Österreichischen Akademie der Wissenschaften.

Guo Yunyan. 2020. Bracteates with Byzantine Coin Patterns Along the Silk Road. Pages 341-356 in F.Gaidetti and K. Meinecke (eds), *A Globalised Visual Culture? Towards a Geography of Late Antique Art.* Oxford: Oxbow Books.

Gupta, P.L. 1974. Kushana-Murunda Rule in Eastern India. *Journal of the Numismatic Society of India* 36: 25-53.

Gupta, P.L. 1976. British Museum Romano-Kushana Medallion: its Nature and Importance. *Journal of the Numismatic Society of India* 38 (2): 73-81.

Hahn, W. (published under the pseudonym of Hanuman and Lakshmi Nawartmal) 1998. Spätantikes Handelsgold in Südindien. *Money Trend* 30: 52-7.

Jongeward, D. and Cribb, J., with Donovan, P. 2015. *Kushan, Kushano-Sasanian, and Kidarite Coins. A Catalogue of Coins from the American Numismatic Society.* New York: American Numismatic Society.

Lal, B.B. 1949. Sisupalgarh 1949: An Early Historical Fort in Eastern India. *Ancient India* 5: 62-105.

Mitchiner, M. 2004. *Ancient Trade and Early Coinage.* London: Hawkins Publications.

Morris, L. 2022. Tools of Economic Activity from the Greek Kingdoms of Central Asia to the Kushan Empire, in S. von Reden (ed.) *Handbook of Ancient*

Afro-Eurasian Economies, Volume 2: Local, Regional and Imperial Economies: 449-490. Berlin/Boston: De Gruyter.

Naymark, A. 2001. Sogdiana, its Christians and Byzantium: A study of Artistic and Cultural Connections in Late Antiquity and Early Middle Ages. Unpublished PhD dissertation, Indiana University.

Pieper, W. 2003. Sogdian Gold Bracteates – Documents of the Cultural Exchange Along the Ancient Silk-Road. *Oriental Numismatic Society Newsletter* 175: 5-8.

Rashke, M.G. 1978. New Studies in Roman Commerce with the East. Pages 604-1361 in H. Temporini (ed.) *Aufstieg und Niedergang der Römischen Welt 9 (2), Geschichte und Kultur Roms in der neueren Forschung, II Principat*. Berlin: De Gruyter.

Raspopova, V. 1999. Gold Coins and Bracteates from Pendjikent in M. Alram and D.E. Klimburg-Salter (eds), *Coins, Art, and Chronology: Essays on the pre-Islamic History of the Indo-Iranian Borderlands*: 453-460. Vienna: Österreichischen Akademie der Wissenschaften.

Sharma, S. 2012. Recent Discovery of Copper Coins Hoard of Kushan Period from Basani, Varanasi, in V. Jayaswal (ed.) *Glory of the Kushans: Recent Discoveries and Interpretations*: 57-76. New Delhi: Aryan Books International.

Sinha, B.P and Narain, L.A. 1970. *Pataliputra Excavation 1955-56*. Patna: The Directorate of Archaeology and Museums, Bihar.

Subrahmanyam, B., Rama Krishna Rao, G.V., and Brahma Chary, P. 2008. *Roman Gold Coins: A Treasure Trove from Penuganchiprolu*. Hyderabad: Department of Archaeology and Museums Government of Andhra Pradesh.

Suresh, S. 2004. *Symbols of Trade: Roman and Pseudo-Roman Objects Found in India*. New Delhi: Manohar.

Tomber, R. 2013. Pots, coins and trinkets in Rome's trade with the East. in P.S. Wells (ed.), *Rome Beyond its Frontiers: Imports, Attitudes and Practices*: 87-104 Portsmouth: Journal of Roman Archaeology Supplement 94.

Turner, P. 1989. *Roman Coins from India*. London: Routledge.

Smagur, E. 2018. From Coin to Bulla: A Cultural Response to the Influx of Roman Denarii into India. *Numismatic Digest* 42: 63-78.

Smagur, E. 2022. Indian Imitations of Roman Aurei Reconsidered. *The Numismatic Chronicle* 182: 153-178.

Smagur, E. 2023. Ethnoarchaeology of foreign coins in India: reinterpreting Venetian ducat design, and implications for archaeonumismatics. *Antiquity* 97(392), E11.

A New Gold Coin of Vasudeva I with Investiture Scene

Gul Rahim Khan and Wasi Ullah

This article deals with a newly discovered gold coin of Vasudeva I, the sixth ruler of the Kushans, who ruled over parts of Central Asia, Afghanistan, Pakistan and the northern part of India. The reign of this king is known from inscriptions from c. 191 to 226 CE after which the Kushan empire began to decline. In the first half of the third century, the Sasanians annexed the north western part of the Kushan empire comprising Central Asia, Bactria, the Kabul valley, and Gandhara and established a vassal kingdom referred to as the 'Kushanshahr' (the coins being known as Kushano-Sasanians) under their suzerainty. After Vasudeva I, his successors, the Late Kushans, retained control of territory to the east and south for over a hundred years.

Recently the co-author showed me some images of a gold coin of Vasudeva I which, unfortunately, has no archaeological context. This specimen is interesting in several respects and appears to be a new type of the gold series of Vasudeva I. It is struck on the Kushan dinar standard, with a weight of 7.98g, diameter of 19.63 mm, and thickness of 2.37 mm. This gold coin looks like other coins of Vasudeva issued from the main mint at the beginning of its third phase production. But the new example portrays a peculiar female flying figure in front of the king, in the left field, instead of a trident. The figure is obviously offering a diadem to the king. A complete description of this coin is as follows:

Obverse. The figure of king standing frontally with head in profile to left, wearing diadem, peaked crown with jewels and forehead device at front and a banner like object behind head. He wears a knee-length chain mail tunic and trousers depicted as rings which are appeared to be tucked into long boots. His right hand is extending over a fire-altar in the left field and is holding a spear in his raised left hand, a sword is hanging from the waist across the shaft of the spear in the right field. Flames emanate from the shoulders of the king and a female flying

figure, perhaps Oanindo (goddess of victory), is shown before the king offering an ornamented diadem. The female figure wears a long robe and holds the diadem with both hands as if about to crown the king. There is a *nandipada* symbol in the right field and the fire altar in the left field is richly ornamented. The obverse is inscribed with Bactrian legend Þ-AONANOÞAO B-A-ZOΔHOKOÞANO clockwise, beginning at 7 o'clock and terminating at 5 o'clock.

Reverse. The figure of Oesho standing facing, wearing a necklace over right shoulder and long dhoti with erect lingum, hair is well-arranged and tied in a topknot and flames emanate from both shoulders. The figure holds a diadem in extended right hand and a trident in raised left hand and behind him bull standing to left. Bactrian legend OHÞO (anti clock-wise) is in the right field and four-pronged tamga in the upper right field.

As an entirely new type in a series that has been well studied it is necessary to consider the authenticity of this coin. Though it has not been possible to physically examine the coin it appears to be of an appropriate weight, and die struck using techniques compatible with Kushan coinage. The design fits appropriately into the sequence of coins at the main mint (discussed below) and there are no egregious errors that might be expected of a modern forger. Nor, despite consultation with colleagues, has it been possible to match the obverse to a known die which might have been modified by a forger, or employed as a prototype (for example the elaboration of detail on the fire altar is in keeping with depictions on Vasudeva coins but it is exceptionally rare for it to be preserved in this detail on any surviving example). All of this suggests its authenticity. However, some negative indicators coexist. It has not been possible to match the reverse to a known die and though all of the details are correct it must be noted that the flames emanating from Oesho's shoulders are stylistically odd, matching the way they are commonly depicted on the king and not how they are usually depicted on Oesho. The field of the obverse lacks the radiating stress marks common on dies of this period, instead having an unusual textured pattern, and though the letters show traces of being engraved into a die face several are engraved slightly oddly (note the N's at 9 o'clock being engraved as three distinct strokes, rather than the normal two, and K at 4 o'clock

Figure 1. Obverse, reverse, and edge of the coin.

Figure 2. 200% enlargement of the obverse and reverse.

depicted with the arms of equal length and connecting to the centre of the vertical stroke, where normally the upper arm is connected to the bottom of the vertical stroke and is of similar length, forming a V shape, and the lower arm connects to the upper arm). Though it is impossible to decide the authenticity without more evidence as it is the first example of its kind known to Vasudeva I.

Gold coins of Vasudeva I are common and their designs and legend are homogeneous. They consistently portray the king wearing chain-mail dress and holding a spear in the left hand standing at altar on the obverse and Oesho wearing necklace and dhoti and holding a diadem and a trident standing before bull on the reverse. The obverse is inscribed with a Bactrian legend giving the name and titles of the king and dynastic name as described above and the reverse names Oesho and uses a four-pronged tamga. However, small changes systematically occurred in which new elements were added in the course of time. Besides this, a few coins, particularly of the first phase were also issued with different reverse designs such as the figure of Nana, four-armed Vasudeva, four-armed dancing Oesho, and Oesho without bull. The limited number and short duration of these varieties are inconspicuous in the presence of mass scale production of the main series bearing standing figure of king at altar on one side and figure of Oesho with bull on the other. The same combination was also carried on by Vasudeva I's successors (Late Kushans) and the Kushan-Sasanian rulers on their coins. During the reign of Vasudeva (I), the gold coins were systematically produced in three phases which are known to have issued from two parallel mints.

The gold coins of Vasudeva I issued in different phases are briefly summarized in the following table.

Kanishka II, the immediate successor of Vasudeva I and the first ruler of the Late Kushans, in the beginning of his reign followed the style of Vasudeva I coins but soon developed his own coinage with a new design. In this

way gold coins of Kanishka II can be divided into two phases.

In view of above classification, the newly discovered coin of Vasudeva can be placed in the transitional phase between phase II and phase III of the main mint. The letter style of the Bactrian inscription has close similarity to the coins of phase II and the addition of the *nandipada* to the obverse is the characteristic feature of coins issued in phase III.

Investiture scenes on Kushan coins

The depiction of a victory figure offering a diadem to the king is unusual on Kushan coins. Silver tetradrachms of the Heraus series, perhaps issued by Kujula Kadphises, the first Kushan king, portray a figure of the goddess of victory (Nike) flying behind the mounted king to crown him. The style of this figure is very similar to those on Greek, Parthian and Indo-Parthian coins. Kujula Kadphises who was a contemporary of the Indo-Parthian rulers obviously borrowed this feature from the coins of that dynasty. After Kujula, the Kushan rulers developed their own coinage on a new pattern and hence the figure of Nike also disappeared from the Kushan coinage. A new victory goddess, a winged figure named Oanindo of Persian origin, was introduced by Huvishka, and was shown standing on the reverse of his gold coins. This figure usually appeared with one obverse type (Göbl 1984: obverse 1, die No. XI.1) which seems to be struck at the late phase of the main mint, producing coins in Afghanistan. The obverse of these coins is uniform but the reverse figure Oanindo is shown in different varieties. However, one example of the reverse variety (D) is also known with a different obverse combination (Göbl 1984: obverse 2, die No. VIII.1). The manifestation of this deity with the obverse combinations of Huvishka is as follows:

Obverse. 1. Bust of king emerging from clouds with head in profile to left, wearing low conical crown, ornamented jacket over embroidered

Table 1. Classification of gold coins of Vasudeva I issued from two mints.

Phase	Mint A (main mint, Bactria)	Mint B (secondary mint, Gandhara)
I	*Obv. IA.* King standing at altar to left, wearing chain-mail dress and pointed crown, holding a spear (or trident) in raised left hand, legend ÞAONANOÞAO BAZOΔHO KOÞANO begins at 7 o'clock *Rev. IAa.* 2-armed Oesho standing before bull, bull facing left with head turned and licking the legs of deity, legend in left field Göbl 1984: 501 *Rev. IAb.* 2-armed and 3-headed Oesho standing before bull, bull facing left, legend in left field Göbl 1984: 502 *Rev. IAc.* 2-armed Oesho standing before bull, bull facing left, legend in left field Göbl 1984: 503	*Obv. IB.* King standing at altar to left, wearing chain-mail dress and pointed crown, flames emanate from right shoulder, holding a spear (or trident) in raised left hand, legend ÞAONANOÞAO BAZΔHO or BAZOΔHO KOÞANO begins at 7 o'clock *Rev. IBa.* 4-armed Vasudeva (Krishna) standing facing, legend in right field Mukherjee 1987: IV.4A-4B *Rev. IBb.* Oesho standing alone, legend in right field Göbl 1984: 515 *Rev. IBc.* Nana standing to right, legend in left field Göbl 1984: 514 *Rev. IBd.* 2-armed Osho standing before bull, bull facing left and licking the legs of deity, legend in left field Göbl 1984: 511 *Rev. IBe.* 2-armed and 3-headed Oesho standing before bull, bull facing left, legend in right field downwards Göbl 1984: 513 *Rev. IBf.* 2-armed Oesho standing before bull, bull facing left, legend in right field downwards Göbl 1984: 512 *Rev. IBg.* 4-armed and 3-headed Oesho standing before bull, bull facing right, legend in left field Göbl 1984: 500 *Rev. IBh.* 2-armed Oesho standing before bull, bull facing left, legend in left field Göbl 1984: 504 *Obv. IBi.* As IA, but king is without flaming shoulder, legend begins at 1 o'clock *Rev. IBia.* Oesho standing alone, legend in right field downwards Göbl 1984: 521-22 *Rev. IBib.* 2-armed Oesho standing before bull, bull facing left, legend in right field Göbl 1984: 519-20
II	*Obv. IIA.* As above but addition of a trident in the left field, legend ÞAONANOÞAO BAZOΔHO KOÞANO begins at 7 o'clock *Rev. IIAa.* 2-armed Oesho standing before bull, bull facing left, legend in left field Göbl 1984: 508 *Rev. IIAb.* 2-armed Oesho standing before bull, bull facing left, legend in right field downwards Göbl 1984: 507 *Rev. IIAc.* 2-armed Oesho standing before bull, bull facing left, legend in right field upwards Göbl 1984: 509 *Rev. IIAd.* 2-armed Oesho standing before bull, bull facing left, Oesho has flaming halo, legend in right field Göbl 1984: 509 (nos. 26-27)	*Obv. IIB.* King at altar wears chain-mail dress as above but a trident is added in the left field and king has long hair, legend ÞAONANOÞAO BAZΔHO KOÞANO begins at 7 o'clock, *Rev. IIBa.* 4-armed and 3-headed Oesho standing before bull, bull facing right, legend in left field Göbl 1984: 506 *Obv. IIBi.* King at altar to left, wears chain-mail coat as IBi, but a trident is added in the left field and legend ÞAONANOÞAO BAZΔHO KOÞANO begins at 1 o'clock *Rev. IIBia.* 4-armed and 3-headed Oesho standing before bull, bull facing left, legend in left field Göbl 1984: 527 *Rev. IIBib.* 4-armed and 3-headed dancing Oesho standing before bull, bull facing right, legend in right field Göbl 1984: 525 *Rev. IIBic.* 4-armed and 3-headed dancing Oesho standing before bull, bull facing right and licking the legs of deity, legend in right field Göbl 1984: 526 *Rev. IIBid.* 2-armed Oesho standing before bull, Oesho has plain halo around head, bull facing left, legend in right field Göbl 1984: 528 (no. 5) *Rev. IIBie.* 2-armed Oesho without halo standing before bull, bull facing left, legend in right field Göbl 1984: 528 *Rev. IIBif.* 2-armed Oesho standing before bull, Oesho has flaming halo round head, bull facing left, legend in right field Göbl 1984: 533 (nos. 1, 3, 5),

Phase	Mint A (main mint, Bactria)	Mint B (secondary mint, Gandhara)
III	*Obv. IIIA.* As IIA, king holds a trident in raised left hand and *nandipada* is added in the right field *Rev. IIIAa.* 2-armed Oesho with flaming halo standing before bull, bull facing left, legend in right field Göbl 1984: 640A	*Obv. IIIB.* As variety IIBi with trident in the left field, king holds a trident in raised left hand and addition of a *nandipada* in the right field *Rev. IIIBa.* 2-armed Oesho with flaming halo standing before bull, bull facing left, legend in right field Göbl 1984: 640 *Obv. IIIBi.* As IIIB, but letter A (or triangle) is added underneath left arm near trident *Rev. IIIBia.* 2-armed Oesho with flaming halo standing before bull, bull facing left, legend in right field Göbl 1984: 532 *Obv. IIIBii.* As IIIBi, but addition of a Brahmi letters like *pa* or *pri* in right field *Rev. IIIBiia.* 2-armed Oesho without halo standing before bull, bull facing left, legend in right field Göbl 1984: 533 *Obv. IIIBiii.* As IIIBi, but a Kharoshthi letter *ha* is added in the right field *Rev. IIIBiiia.* 2-armed Oesho with the bull as IIIBiia, but without flaming halo and Kharoshthi letter *ha* in lower right field, legend in right field Göbl 1984: 536
	Post Vasudeva	
	The coin production of this mint continued under the Kushano-Sasanians. A lot of coins of the same design were imitated by the Kushano-Sasanian kings who added dots and various symbols (like swastika, rosette etc.) in course of time and then wrote their own names along with other changes	Kanishka II, the immediate successor of Vasudeva I struck some early issues on the pattern of last phase of this mint. Both Oesho and bull (Göbl 1984: 547) and Ardoxsho (Göbl 1984: 538) types of Kanishka developed from the coin types (Göbl 1984: 532/533 Göbl: 640A) of Vasudeva I.

tunic. There is a halo around head, flames emanate from both shoulders, holding a club in the right hand and a spear in the left hand over left shoulder. Bactrian legend ÞAO NANOÞAOO – OHÞKE KOÞANO begins at 7 o 'clock (clockwise).

Reverse. A. Winged female figure standing frontally with head turned to left with hair tied in a bun, wearing headdress and long robe tied at waist which reaches upto the ground, holding a garlanded diadem in the right hand and a staff in the left hand over left shoulder. Long ribbons of the diadem are shown one each above and below of the right hand. A barred tamga is in the right field and legend OANI – NAO begins at 7 o 'clock (clockwise, can be read from centre of the coin) and terminates at 11 o 'clock. [Göbl 1984: no. 242]

Reverse. B. Same as 1A, but ribbons of the diadem are curved parallel below the right arm of deity and legend OAN – INAO begins at 11 o 'clock (anticlockwise, can be read from edge of the coin) and terminates at 7 o 'clock. [Göbl 1984: no. 243]

Reverse. C. As 1A, legend OAN – INAO downwards (can be read from edge of the coin) vertically along the standing figure. [Göbl 1984: no. 244]

Reverse. D. As 1A, but ribbons of the diadem are curved parallel above the right arm of deity, holding a cornucopia in crook of left arm instead of staff, and a halo is added around head. The legend OANIN – AO begins at 3 o 'clock (clockwise, can be read from centre of the coin) and terminates at 7 o 'clock and a barred tamga is in the left field underneath right arm. [Göbl 1984: no. 245]

Reverse. E. As 1A, but the deity standing frontally with head in profile to right, halo around head, holding a garlanded diadem in the left hand with curved ribbons parallel below the arm, and a vertical staff in the right hand against her arm. The legend OA – NINAO begins at 1 o 'clock (clockwise, can be read from centre of the coin) and terminates at 5 o 'clock and barred a tamga is in the left field. [Göbl 1984: no. 246]

Obverse. 2. As 1, but wearing low conical crown adorned with pearls and embroidered tunic with jeweled yoke and lozenge-shaped pattern and ornament around upper arms, halo around head, one ribbon falls on the right shoulder and two on the left. The king holds a club in the right hand and a spear in the left hand over left shoulder. Bactrian legend ÞAO NANOÞAOO – OHÞK KOÞANO begins at 7 o 'clock (clockwise).

Reverse. D. Same as 1E. [Khan and Blackburn 2013: 68]

Stein identifies Oanindo with the Persian origin of the Avestan form of Verethraghana in character and appearance. In further explanation, he identifies this deity with the female genius, named Vanaiñti uparatāt̤, "victorious superiority" (Stein 1960: 47).

Besides coins representation, the word 'Oanindo' or victorious associated with the name of Kanishka is attested from a Bactrian inscription unearthed at Surkh Kotal. The Surkh Kotal temple is a dynastic sanctuary known as a bagolaggo. The inscription, written in the Kushana year 31 [Kanishka era] which corresponds to the early part of the reign of Huvishka (Henning 1960: 47-55). It records that the sanctuary was founded by Kanishka and later renovated and enlarged by one *Nokonzoko*, a 'high official' (the lord of the marches) at the time of Huvishka. The Bactrian inscription refers to the site as the 'Kanishko Oanindo bagolaggo' or 'sanctuary of Kanishka the victorious'. (Henning 1960: 47-55; Rosenfield 1967: 154, 158-59; Harmatta et al. 1998: 313).

Vasudeva I, the immediate successor of Huvishka, might have adopted the victory goddess Oanindo, developed from Greek figure Nike, from his predecessor and portrayed it in the investiture form on the coin discussed in this article. A few investiture scenes, although different from the Vasudeva specimen, are exhibited on some rare examples of Huvishka copper. On these coins, the kneeling king with clasped hands is shown venerating a standing deity. In these examples the name of a Karalrang, a high official of Huvishka is inscribed with the name of deity on the reverse. These coins were perhaps issued under the supervision of this official. Two reverse varieties of this design are known to have been produced in combination with four obverse designs of Huvishka. The reverses of the first variety are common compared to the second variety, known only from a single die (and just two specimens). The designs of both coins are slightly different. Altogether, this group of coins were produced from three reverse dies. In view of the reduced weight, style of obverse design, barred tamga on the reverse, legend and reverse combination, such coins of Huvishka were issued in the late phase of a subsidiary mint in Gandhara. An overview of this group of Huvishka coins is as follows.

Obverse. A1. King riding on elephant to right. [Cunningham 1892: XXII.21: Rosenfield 1967: no. 78].

A2. King reclining on a pile of cushions to left, holding a club in raised right hand. It is a rare variety of this design known by only one specimen, which is lost now. [Cunningham 1892: XXII.21: Rosenfield 1967: no. 78]

A3. King seated cross-legged frontally on clouds with head turned to right, holding a staff in raised left hand. [courtesy, Aman ur Rahman]

A4. King reclining on couch to left, wearing knee-length tunic and trousers, right leg bent on the bed and left down on the floor, left elbow resting on pillow, holding something in his right hand in front of him. [courtesy, Aman ur Rahman]

Reverse. i. The king, on proper right, with clasped hand is kneeling before the standing figure of Nana. The king wears round crown, knee-length tunic and trousers, crescent behind shoulders and the sword is hanging from his waist. The deity on proper left, facing left towards the figure, wears long robe, halo around head, holding a lion-protome sceptre in her both hands just above the figure. A barred tamga is in the left field behind deity and Bactrian legend NANA PAΓAN OHOIAΓOΓW PAΓ now deciphered by Joe Cribb as NANA/ OMOIAΓOΓANO KA-PAΛPAΓΓO (clockwise in two lines). [Cunningham 1892: XXII.21-22; 1893: pl. X.3; Rosenfield 1967: no. 78]

Obverse. B1. King riding on elephant to right, holding an elephant's goad in the left hand. [Göbl 1993: 332]

Reverse. ii. As i, but the king on proper left with clasped hands is kneeling before goddess Nana who stands on proper right. The deity wears diadem with crescent on top, long robe with shawl wrapped round arms and hanging down, holds a short sceptre with crescent top in her right hand and perhaps a bowl in the left. Tamga is placed in centre between the two figures and legend NANO (clockwise) in the right field. [Göbl 1993: 332]

Obverse. C1. King seated cross-legged frontally on clouds with head turned to right as A3, holding a staff in raised left hand and right hand resting on lap. [courtesy, Aman ur Rahman]

Reverse. iii. As ii, but the figure of deity is taller than the previous examples and tamga in the left field behind the keeling figure. [Rahman and Falk 2011: fig. 88]

The figure of Nana, moon goddess, is commonly found on the gold and copper coins of Kanishka, and Huvishka and one gold example of Vasudeva I. On such coins the figure of Nana facing left or right, is usually exhibited in the same attitude, holding a short sceptre in the right hand and a bowl in the left. After Vasudeva I, the figure of Nana disappeared from the Kushan coinage.

Investiture scenes on Kushan seals and other materials

Apart from these coins, one similar example is known from an intaglio seal which depicts a kneeling king before an enthroned deity. As described in my previous article this seal obviously belonged to the period of Huvishka (Khan and Zahra: 2015). This seal depicts a four-armed male figure (Manaobago) with crescent behind shoulders, wearing helmet and dhoti (or loose trousers), and enthroned frontally with head in profile to left turned towards the keeling figure. In his four arms, he is offering a diadem with his lower right hand to the kneeling king, and holds a wreath bearing winged figure (victory goddess) in upper right hand, a long staff in the upper left, and an uncertain object in the lower left. The small figure of the king wearing diadem, round crown, tunic and trousers with clasped hands is kneeling before the enthroned deity. An attendant holding a long spear in the right hand across his body is standing behind the kneeling king and looking to the enthroned deity. The winged figure (Oanindo/ Nike, victory goddess) who stands on the right upper hand of Manaobago seems to present a wreath to the attendant as he looks towards her. This indicates that Manaobago is presenting a diadem to the kneeling king and the victory goddess presents the same to the king's attendant (Khan and Zahra 2015; Mukherjee 1966: 61).

Another similar example of an investiture scene on seal depicts a princely figure standing on the proper left, wearing tall rounded crown like Huvishka, both hands clasped standing in a pose of adoration before the tall deity. The four-armed deity seems to be the Indian god Vishnu, standing facing on proper right but slightly turned towards the kneeling figure. He wears crown, dhoti, bracelets and armlets, holding a club in the lower right hand, circlet in upper right, upper left lotus and lower left rests on wheel. Due to the resemblance of headdress, Cunningham attributed this seal to the period of Huvishka (Cunningham 1893: 126-27, pl. X.2).

Other scholars have different opinions, identify the legend with the names of Mihira, Viṣṇu and Śiva, and usually assign it in the late periods like Hephthalites (Drabu 1990: 201).

These seals are similar in many ways, as they have a tall figure of a deity, both deities are shown on the proper right, the small figure of king is shown with clasped hands facing towards deities, the crown and dress of the king in both cases are the same. Looking to the differences, deities are different and standing, and kneeling position of the king are also different. However, style, theme, gesture of the deities and attitude of the king in both examples are quite similar.

Apart from numismatic and seal evidences one investiture scene of the Kushan period, although incomplete and uncertain appeared on a stone panel reported from Surkh Kotal. It portrays a standing figure of king to left, clad in Kushan dress with a sword at waist and holding a wreath in his raised left hand. The other figure perhaps of a deity is missing and undrawn. Other princely figures particularly the statue of Kanishka known from this area usually belonged to the periods of Kanishka and Huvishka (Rosenfield 1967: 156-57, 161, fig. 123).

One more example of the investiture scene of the Kushan king depicted on a terracotta medallion is reported from the Kushan site Khalchayan. The king is seated frontally on a wide throne with feet resting on footstool, wearing peaked headdress and long cloak, holding something in the left hand which rests on his right thigh. The king is slightly turned to a person standing on his right who also wears peaked headdress, and a winged figure perhaps Nike flies behind the king to crown him (Loeschner 2012: no. 14b). The style and peaked crown of the king bears a close resemblance to the images of Kujula depicted on several varieties of his coins such as: (a) bust of king on the obverse of silver coins modelled on Indo-Parthian pattern known from Taxila hoard, (b) king seated on curule chair on the reverse with head of Augustus on the obverse, and (c) king seated cross-legged on the reverse with figure of standing Zeus on the obverse (Mitchiner 1976: nos. 1110, 1053-54; Khan and Cribb 2012: nos. 4.1-2, 6.1-6.2.1; 7.1.1-7.5).

Investiture scenes on Greek coins and medallions

There is a long history of investiture scenes (depicting 'the God-given glory, fortune and splendour') on earlier coins of the Greeks. In these coins the winged Nike usually appeared with gods and goddesses, charioteers and rarely monarchs. On the coins of Leontine, a quadriga is drawn by horses walking to right, winged Nike crowns the horses (Kraay 1966: nos. 13-16). In Catana issues, a river-god is shown in the form of man-faced bull with a kneeling Silenus crowning him (Kraay 1966: nos. 28-30). In other varieties both obverse and reverse, quadriga horses galloping to left and the charioteer is crowning by winged Nike who flies before him (Kraay 1966: nos. 40-43). A group of coins struck at Zancle-Messana in 410-396 BCE depicts a biga of mules driven by a female (Messana) driver, above Nike is crowning the mules (Kraay 1966: no. 54). A similar example of a mule biga depicts winged Nike but she flies to crown the female figure (Messana) instead of the mules (Kraay 1966: nos. 58-60). The coins of Syracuse issued during c. 500-400 BCE show a variety of Nike crowning designs. In some coins, quadriga drawn by horses walking to left or right with male driver; in one variety winged Nike flies to crown the driver, in other winged Nike flies to crown the horses or in one variety crowning one horse (Kraay 1966: nos. 74-76, 78, 83, 85-90, 93). In other similar examples, horses of quadriga are galloping to right or left either on obverse or reverse while a flying Nike is shown to crown (a) female driver, (b) male driver, (c) winged male driver, and (d) horses (Kraay 1966: nos. 97-101, 104, 107-09, 113-24).

On the coins of Nomos (c. 400-360 BCE), the Nymph Terina seated to left with patera in the right hand is crowned by Nike who flies behind her. On the coins of Camarina issued c. 420 BCE, the horse drawn quadriga is driven by a helmeted Athena to right who is crowned by a winged Nike flying in front of her (Kraay 1966: nos. 147-49). Two varieties of horses galloping quadriga with female driver are known from the Gela series (470-20 BCE); (a) Nike crowning horses and (b) Nike crowning the driver (Kraay 1966: nos. 157-62). On the Acragas coins struck during c. 413-11 BCE, depicting quadriga horses to right, Nike crowns the female driver (Kraay 1966: nos. 176-78). On some coins of Eryx (c. 400-390 BCE), the quadriga horses galloping to right and Nike above flies to crown the charioteer. On the same reverse, Aphrodite is seated on stool with flying dove on her right hand, and to left Eros stands with raised right arm towards her. In another similar variety, Aphrodite holds a branch in the left hand and grasps forearms of standing figure with right (Kraay 1966: nos. 192-93). On some coins of Panormus and Rash Melcorth struck during 400-375 BCE, bearing quadriga with horses galloping to right with Nike above crowning the driver (Kraay 1966: nos. 195-96). On Carthage Siculo-Punic issues (c. 390-80 BCE), Nike flies to crown the horse galloping to left (Kraay 1966: no. 205). In one example of Locri (274 BCE), an enthroned Ram holding a sword and a shield is crowned by Pistis who stands before him (Kraay 1966: no. 293). In the issues of Tara (300 BCE), Tara wearing a diadem, rides dolphin over waves, holding two spears and a shield with a Pegasus blazon, flying Nike crowns him. In other specimen, a young rider crowns the horse and Nike flies to crown the rider (Kraay 1966: nos. 313, 319).

An investiture scene is also shown on the reverse of the so-called Alexander's medallion (also known as the 'Porus' Medallion) perhaps issued in the eastern part his empire in the later part of the 4th century BCE. The reverse of this debatable medallion portrays standing figure of Alexander the Great facing to left, wearing Phrygian style helmet, cavalry uniform, a sword hanging from waist, holding a long spear in raised left hand and hurling a thunderbolt with the right. The figure is being crowned by the goddess of victory Nike who flies before him with wreath in both her hands. On the other side of the medallion, Alexander is carrying a lance mounted on a horse to right and is attacking king Porus who is mounted with attendant on elephant moving to right (Mitchiner 1975a: no. 21; Carradice and Price 1988: 111, no. 200). On some examples of the medallions, the flying Nike on the reverse disappears or unclear (Bhandare 2007: fig. 15.2). The style of victory goddess crowning the king from frontal view on Vasudeva I coins is very similar to that depicted on the reverse of the Alexander medallion. On some silver coins of Seleucus Nikator, the successor of Alexander in the east, the victory goddess standing to the right crowns a trophy which is shown like a standing figure (Carradice and Price 1988: 118, no. 225).

Investiture scenes on Parthian coins

The investiture scenes of a king, as mentioned earlier, were commonly depicted on the coins of Parthian rulers (c. 240 BCE-224 CE). Many of these coins were struck parallel to the Kushan rulers like Kujula Kadphises, Vima Taktu, Vima Kadphises, Kanishka I, Huvishka and Vasudeva I. This depiction is also evidenced from rock reliefs, stelae and contemporary accounts. The investiture scenes on Parthian coins became popular after the middle of the first century BCE. On these coins the king is being crowned with diadem or palm-branch presented to him by Hellenistic deities like Nike, Tyche, or Athena and sometimes by bird, perhaps an Eagle (Curtis 2012: 71-75). In the late period, the bird with outstretched wings holding a ring or a wreath in its beak is shown on the reverse of Parthian copper coins of Mithradates II, Vologases IV and Vologases V (Curtis 2012: 72, 76). On such coins a notable investiture scene is known from the period of Phraates III (70-57 BCE). A silver tetradrachm portrays the figure of an enthroned king facing to the left holding an eagle in outstretched right hand and standing behind him the Greek goddess Tyche crowns the king with her right hand (Wroth 1903: pl. XI, no. 1; Curtis 2012: pl. I. no. 7). Earlier, the coins of Phraates II and Artabanus I depicted the seated figure of Apollo and a deity holds a cornucopia and is receiving a diadem from a small figure of Nike (Curtis 2012: 69). Later, the reverse of Orodes II coins (57-38/37 BCE) regularly portrayed investiture scenes which are shown in different forms. In such coins, the bust of the king is crowned by a winged Nike who is standing behind him with a diadem (Wroth 1903: pl. XIV. 2-3), the enthroned king raising the right hand of Tyche who kneels with one leg before him (Wroth 1903: pl. XIV. 10-11), or the enthroned king receiving a palm-branch from Tyche who stands before him (Wroth 1903: pl. XIV. 14). In another variety Nike stands on the right hand of the enthroned king offering a diadem to the king (Wroth 1903: pl. XV. 1-2). On Pacorus I coins, the bust of the king facing left is being crowned by a small winged Nike who is shown behind the king's head with a diadem in her right hand (Wroth 1903: pl. XVIII. 12). On the reverse of one variety of Phraates IV, the enthroned king is being crowned by Tyche who stands before him with a diadem in the right hand (Wroth 1903: pls. XVIII. 15, XIX. 6, 9, XX. 1). In another the enthroned king is receiving a palm-branch from Tyche (Wroth 1903: pls. XVII. 16, XIX. 1, 5, 7-8, XX. 3), and in a third Nike stands on the right hand of the enthroned king offering a wreath to him (Wroth 1903: pls. XVIII. 17, XIX. 3-4) and in a fourth the enthroned king is holding the right hand of Tyche who kneels before him (Wroth 1903: pl. XIX. 2). Besides this, on the obverse of this king's coins an eagle is crowning the king with diadem and sometimes a wreath which it holds in its beak behind the king's head (Wroth 1903: pls. XX. 4-11, XXI. 1-27, XXII. 1-12). In other varieties of the obverse, a winged Nike is crowning the king with wreath while stands behind him (Wroth 1903: XXII. 20-21, XXIII. 1). On the reverse of Tiridates II, the enthroned king is receiving a palm-branch from Tyche who stands before him (Wroth 1903: pl. XXIII. 8-9). Similarly, on the reverse of Phraataces (Phraates V), the standing Tyche is offering a diadem to the enthroned king (Wroth 1903: pl. XXIII. 10). On the obverse of other coins of this king, winged Nike crowning the king with wreath from each side (Wroth 1903: pl. XXIII. 11-17). The same design can be seen on the joint issues of Phraataces and Musa (Wroth 1903: pl. XXIV. 1-4). On some coins of Artabanus III, standing Tyche is offering a palm-branch with her right hand to the enthroned king (Wroth 1903: pl. XXV. 1). In new variety the king is seated on a throne to left, receiving a palm-branch from standing Tyche and a kneeling figure nearby king offering him a diadem (Wroth 1903: pl. XXV. 2). In other varieties, the king is riding a horse to left and receiving a palm-branch from Tyche who stands in front of horse (Wroth 1903: pl. XXV. 5-6). Vardanes, like his predecessors is shown seated on a throne and receiving a palm-branch from Tyche who stands before him (Wroth 1903: pl. XXVI. 1-2). The following king Gotarzes (40/41-51 CE) is similarly shown seated on a throne to right being crowned by Tyche who stands before him with wreath in her right hand (Wroth 1903: pls. XXVI. 12-14, XXVII. 1). On obverses, Vologazes I as above, is seated on a throne to left being crowned by Tyche who stands in from of him with wreath in the right hand (Wroth 1903: pl. XXVIII, 12-14). In another

variety, the enthroned king, on the reverse, is receiving a palm-branch from Tyche who stands before him on left (Wroth 1903: pl. XXIX. 5). Pacorus II like above, is enthroned to left on the reverse receiving a diadem from Tyche who stands before him. In another variety, the king is riding on a horse to left on the reverse and receiving a diadem from Tyche while another figure stands behind Tyche holding an untied diadem (Wroth 1903: pl. XXX. 3, 10).

Artabanus IV issued some investiture coins; the king is shown enthroned on the reverse and perhaps receiving a diadem from Tyche who stands before him on the left (Wroth 1903: pl. XXXI. 5). Vologases II continued the investiture design, seated on a throne to left on the reverse and receiving a diadem from Tyche who stands before him (Wroth 1903: pl. XXXII. 5-10). Vologases III, like his predecessors, enthroned to left on the reverse and receiving diadem from Tyche who stands before him (Wroth 1903: pl. XXXIV. 1-4). Following this pattern, Vologases IV (147-191 CE) is seated on a throne to left and receiving a diadem from Tyche who stands before him on the left (Wroth 1903: pl. XXXV. 7-8). Vologases V (191-208 CE) has the same reverse design, king enthroned to left and receiving a diadem from Tyche who stands before him (Wroth 1903: pls. XXXV. 14-15, XXXVI. 1)[1].

Investiture scenes on Indo-Scythian and Indo-Parthian coins

Investiture scenes are well known from the local coins issued under Zeionises. This king was a satrap of the Indo-Scythian king Azes II and became an independent king after his death. Zeionises retained his rule for a long time and seems to have been contemporary to the early reign of Kujula Kadphises. In one variety of his silver coins, the reverse depicts the king standing frontally with hands resting on swords and being crowned by the winged Nike who stands on his right side with another female figure in the same attitude on the opposite side (Senior 2001: no. 130.1T). In a second variety, the king is standing to right with left hand resting on a sword and looking to a winged Nike who stands in front of him on the right and is crowning the king with a wreath in her right hand while holding a palm-branch in the left hand (Senior 2001: no. 131.1T). A third variety exhibits the king on the reverse standing in the same attitude but Nike is replaced with a city goddess who stands on the right side crowning the king with her right hand

---

[1] In most cases the names and dates of these rulers are arranged according to the catalogue of the British Museum (Wroth 1903) but in newer chronologies, Artabanus I is considered as Artabanus II, Orodes I as Orodes II, Artabanus II as Artabanus III, Artabanus III as Artabanus IV, similarly Tridates I as Tridates II, Tridates II as Tridates III, and Vologases II as Vologases III, Vologases III as Vologases IV Vologases IV as Vologases V and Vologeses V as Vologases VI.

and holding a cornucopia in the left hand. The coins of this variety are common and bear different Kharoshthi letters (Senior 2001: no. 132). Kujula Kadphises imitated one of Zeionises coin designs showing bull on the obverse and Bactrian camel on the reverse. Coins of this type, of both Zeionises and Kujula are said to be issued from the same region.

On the coins of Gondophares I, an Indo-Parthian king, investiture scenes are shown in different series issued from different places. In one variety, silver drachms struck in Seistan, the obverse portrays the king seated on a chair in profile to right where winged Nike flying or standing is shown behind the king, crowning him with a wreath (Mitchiner 1976: nos. 1067-72; Senior 2001: nos. 210.1D-4D). Some coins of the same variety are assigned to another Gondophares named as Orthagnes (Mitchiner 1976: nos. 1073-75). The square coins of the same king, struck in copper, and perhaps issued from Kabul region also exhibits investiture scene. The obverse of these coins depicts a mounted king to left and winged Nike standing before horse offering a wreath to the king (Mitchiner 1976: nos. 1113-14; Senior 2001: no. 215). The silver tetradrachms of Gondophares perhaps issued from Gandhara, represents almost the same design, mounted figure of king to left and winged Nike flying behind to crown the king with right hand (Mitchiner 1976: no. 1112; Senior 2001: no. 216). Like Gondophares I coins issued from Seistan, silver drachms of Gondophares-Sases portrays an investiture scene on the reverse. The king is enthroned to right, a winged Nike standing behind crowning him with right hand (Senior 2001: no. 240).

The rule of Zeionises and Gondophares I is said to have been contemporary with the early part of Kujula Kadphises' reign. As described above, Kujula Kadphises followed some coin designs of these rulers including investiture scenes performed by a winged Nike. Later investiture scenes were revived by Huvishka based on a new pattern accompanied by a new group of gods mostly of Persian origin. Such coins of Huvishka, as highlighted above, are known from many examples. The new gold coin of Vasudeva subject matter of this paper suggests that such iconography was also persisted under Vasudeva I, though this seems to be the last evidence of investiture scenes on Kushan coins. Thereafter it is absolutely absent from the coins of Late Kushans.

References

Bhandare, S. 2007. Not Just a Pretty Face: Interpretations of Alexander's Numismatic Imagery in the Hellenic East, in H.P. Ray and D.T. Potts (eds.), *Memory as History: The Legacy of Alexander in Asia*: 208-256. New Delhi: Aryan Books International.

Carradice, I and Price, M. 1988. *Coinage in the Greek World*. London: B. A. Seaby Ltd.

Cribb, J. 1993. The Heraus Coins: their Attribution to the Kushan King Kujula Kadphises, c. A.D. 30-80, in M. Price (ed.). *Essays in Honour of R. Carson and K. Jenkins*:107-34. London: Spink.

Cunningham, A. 1892. Coins of Kushans, or Great Yu-ti, Class C. *The Numismatic Chronicle*, ser. III, Vol. XII: 40-82, 98-159, pls. IV-VIII, XIX-XXIV.

Cunningham, A. 1893. Later Indo-Scythians, Introduction and Later Kushans. *The Numismatic Chronicle*, Ser. III, Vol. XIII: 93-128.

Curtis, V.S. 2012. Parthian Coins: Kingship and Divine Glory. In: P. Wick and M. Zehnder (eds.), *The Parthian Empire and its Religions*. Band 5: 67-81. Gutenberg: Computus Druck Satz and Verlag.

Drabu, V.N. 1990. Śaivāgamas: A Study in the Socio-economics Ideas and Institutions of Kashmir (*200 BC to AD 700*). New Delhi: Indus Publishing.

Göbl, R. 1984. *System und Chronologie der Munzpragung des Kusanreiches*. Wien: VÖAW.

Göbl, R. 1993. *Donum Burns: Die Kusanmuzen im Munzkabinett Bern und Die Chronologie*. Wien: Fassbaender Verlag.

Harmattan, J., Puri, B.N., Lelekov, L., Umayun, S., and Sircar, D.C. 1998. Religions in the Kushan Empire. *Silk Route Studies*, Vol. II, UNESCO.

Henning, W.B. 1960. The Bactrian Inscription. *Bulletin of the School of Oriental and African Studies*, Vol. 23 (1): 47-55.

Khan, G.R. and Blackburn, M. 2013. Some Selected Coins of the Kushan Period in the Cabinet of the Fitzwilliam Museum, Cambridge, *Gandharan Studies*, Vol. 7: 59-113.

Khan G.R. and Cribb, J. 2012. Coins of Kujula from Taxila. *Gandharan Studies*, Vol. 6: 81-219.

Khan, G.R. and Zahra, N. 2015. An Intaglio Seal from Peshawar Revisited. *Gandharan Studies*, Vol. 9: 115-120

Kraay, C.M. 1966. *Greek Coins*. London: Thames and Hudson.

Loeschner H. 2012. Kanishka in Context with the Historical Buddha and Kushan Chronology, in V. Jayasval (ed.), *Glory of the Kushans – Recent Discoveries and Interpretations*: 137-194, New Delhi: Aryan Books International.

Mitchiner, M. 1975a. *Indo-Greek and Indo-Scythian Coinage (1) – The Early Indo-Greeks and Their Antecedants: Alexander the Great, the Satrap of Egypt, Babylon, Ecbatana, Bactria and Kapisa: the Seleucids: circa 330 to 150 BC*. London: Hawkins Publications.

Mitchiner, M. 1975b. *Indo-Greek and Indo-Scythian Coinage (4) - Contemporaries of the Indo-Greeks: Kings of Sogdiana; Scythians of Merv, Choresmia and Balkh; Yueh Chi and Early Kushans; Indian States of Taxila-Gandhara and the Punjab: Audumbara, Kuninda etc. Indo-Greek*

Mints, Coin Denominations and Forgeries. London: Hawkins Publications.

Mitchiner, M. 1976. *Greek and Indo-Scythian Coinage (8) – The Indo-Parthians – Their Kushan Contemporaries.* London: Hawkins Publications.

Mukherjee, B.N. 1966. An Intaglio Seal from Peshawar. *Journal of the Numismatic Society of India*, Vol. XXVIII, 1: 60-20.

Mukherjee, B.N. 1987. Lord Vasudeva on a Coin of King Vasudeva I. *Journal of the Numismatic Society of India*, Vol. XLIX: 46-47.

Rahman, A.U. and Falk, H. 2011. *Seals, Sealings, and Tokens from Gandhara.* Reichert Verlag Wiesbaden.

Rosenfield, J.M. 1967. *The Dynastic Arts of the Kushans.* Repr. 1993, Delhi.

Senior, R.C. 2001. *Indo-Scythian Coins and History – the Illustrated Catalogue of Indo-Scythian and Indo-Parthian Coins.* Volume II. London: Classical Numismatic Group, Inc.

Stein, M.A. 1960. Zoroastrian Deities on Indo-Scythian Coins. *The Indian Numismatic Chronicle*, Vol. I, parts 1 and 2: 39-60.

Wroth, W. 1903. *A Catalogue of the Greek Coins in the British Museum - Catalogue of the Coins of Parthia.* London: The British Museum.

Speculation is Futile: Reflections on 30 Years of Studies of Roman Coins Found in India

P.J. Turner

In a recent Royal Numismatic Society lecture Andrew Burnett referred to some ancient foreign coins found in India in the late seventeenth century. The author, Sir Thomas Browne, a noted antiquarian, had written of 'Some handsome Engraveries and Medals, of Justinus and Justinianus, found in the custody of a Bannyan in the remote parts of India, conjectured to have been left there by Friers mentioned in Procopius.' I immediately searched on the internet for the work mentioned.[1] It took about two minutes to find a facsimile of the work online.

It piqued my interest because although the coins were Byzantine in date it was nonetheless a very early reference to such a find. Hitherto a hoard of aurei dating from the second century AD found in Nellore in Andhra Pradesh has been quoted as the earliest published mention of ancient Roman coins found in India (Sydenham 1789, with a full account by Davidson 1790). Furthermore, it showed that the interest in Roman and other ancient coins found there continues to be keen and a lively area for debate.

My interest in Roman coins found in India began when, as an undergraduate, I learned about Roman trade. It fascinated me that hoards of Roman coins had reached India as palpable evidence of trade over the Indian Ocean. Objects familiar from British museums had been found over 5,000 miles away on another continent. Research in libraries quickly revealed that the subject had caught the imagination of numerous scholars since the publication of that first hoard from Nellore. The archaeologist Sir Mortimer Wheeler had excavated the site of Arikamedu in south India in the 1940s and published a list of the finds of Roman coins known to date (Wheeler 1946), so I made this my starting point to see what had been found in the 30 or so years since then.

I found a plethora of new finds, including notably another list of coins by the great Indian numismatist P.L. Gupta (1965). I set about collecting as much information as I could from these two lists and eventually published my own work, *Roman Coins from India*, published jointly by the Royal Numismatic Society and the Institute of Archaeology, University of London, in 1989. My aim had been to prepare a full and detailed bibliography of the finds accompanied by an essay discussing the nature of the finds, especially their geographical distribution. I had discovered that reports of finds were often sketchy, and no one seemed to have thought about where the coins had gone after being discovered, so I tried to locate as many as I could in public museums.

It was quite difficult to do work of that kind at the time. Any sources had to be viewed in their repositories, so it was a case of visiting libraries and museums in person. Fortunately, the libraries in London were easily accessible, and staff at the British Museum's Department of Coins and Medals made me very welcome, in particular Andrew Burnett and Joe Cribb, who encouraged me enormously, both to pursue my studies and more importantly to extend them to areas that were new to me. Travel to India was costly, and making arrangements to visit museums had to be done by writing letters, which was time-consuming and frequently unsuccessful. Gaining access to collections to view the coins often proved not to be straightforward and sometimes took more than one visit. It did not prove possible for me to see all the coins that were housed in collections, many of which were not fully published, if at all. But I included as much as I could.

Apart from tracking down artefacts and printed sources, another problem was identifying and locating place names. It was necessary to consult published atlases which rarely included very small villages, and the spelling of names varied widely from publication to publication. The India Office Records, then housed in Blackfriars and now in the British Library at St Pancras, were the main source of help. My aim was to provide as accurate a list as possible, and to provide maps showing the geographical distribution of the finds. Orthography and duplication made this difficult. The Kottayam find, for example, was not found in the town of Kottayam south of Kochi (Cochin) but much further up the coast, near Kannur (Cannanore).[2] Names recorded in the published notes were reported in different forms; Karur was regularly reported by its ancient form Karuvur. It is so easy to check these now on Google Earth!

---

[1] The lecture was to announce the publication of Burnett 2020 and the reference to Thomas Browne's book, *Musaeum Clausum*, can be found at volume 2, p. 754.

[2] Turner 1989: 9, where I noted it as near Cochin and p. 62 where I said not near Cochin but near Cannanore!

The characteristics of Roman coin finds from India are well known and I noted them in summary (Turner 1989: 42–44). My study looked at gold and silver hoards up to the time of Constantine I, because the distribution of the finds showed that finds of Roman or early Byzantine coins fell into distinct groups. These were, broadly, silver hoards of the Julio-Claudian period, and gold hoards which I thought could be divided into an early phase of aurei which resulted from the rejection of silver coins dating after Nero's debasement of the denarius in 64 followed by a gap before aurei of the second century appeared in significant numbers. There then seemed to be a lacuna until in the fourth and fifth centuries substantial numbers of small-denomination copper coins were recorded and gold finds from the period of Constantine I onwards started to appear. Hence the first- and second-century precious-metal coin finds seemed to be a discrete group.

The geographical distribution of these was important. The Julio-Claudian coins were concentrated in what is now Tamil Nadu in south India, while the second-century gold coins had a wider distribution with concentrations near the Krishna river and towards the east coast of India.

The finds had notable features that were not typical of hoards found within the Roman empire. First, the silver and early gold finds were principally of only two types: the Gaius and Lucius Caesares reverse type of Augustus (RIC 1² 206ff) and the PONTIF MAXIM (seated Livia) type of Tiberius (RIC 1² 25ff). Furthermore, coins were often cut across the emperor's portrait on the obverse, and some had punch-marks on them reminiscent of those used on the punch-marked silver coins that were minted in India until about 100 BC. Imitations of Roman coins are not uncommon in Indian finds, and very often coins from India are pierced or mounted to be used as jewellery. Both of these features suggest continued use and re-use of the coins on the subcontinent.

However, the number of coin finds is not really very large, and many of the finds contain only a few coins. My 1989 list had 79 finds for which there were published details, and around 20 more for which details were vague or unpublished. Of the 79, perhaps 46 had 15 coins or fewer, about a dozen had up to 100 coins, about 13 had 'hundreds' and there were two that certainly had more than a thousand coins, though at least two others may also have contained that many. Of the rest, two contained fourth-century coins and five were from the far north of India. This means that it is difficult to generalize and dangerous to speculate on the meaning of the finds and their characteristics. This has not deterred subsequent writers from doing both.

Thirty years after publishing my finds I was minded to muse on what had happened since. Modern methods of study, especially the use of the internet, must surely have advanced the study of Roman coins from India enormously, so I have started to re-assess the situation. This paper is a brief overview of what I have learned so far.

The establishment of the Indian Institute of Research in Numismatic Studies (IIRNS), now the Indian Numismatic, Historical and Cultural Research Foundation (INHCRF) in Nasik, Maharashtra, in 1980 marked a milestone in numismatic studies in India. It was the brainchild of Parmeshwari Lal Gupta, a numismatist who made great contributions to the study of Indian numismatics, and K.K. Maheshwari, a local industrialist with a lifelong interest in numismatics. There, the renowned triumvirate of P.L. Gupta, David MacDowall and Peter Berghaus set out to build a database of Roman finds, mainly coins but also including amphorae and other ceramic artefacts. Berghaus was able to travel extensively in India in the 1980s and 1990s and collected a wealth of anecdotal information, which MacDowall, as the sole survivor of the three, is hoping to publish, and he has generously allowed me to study the preliminary drafts of this work. Both MacDowall and Berghaus published several articles, with new material and some corrections or further details expanding on the finds that I mentioned.[3]

Peter Berghaus visited museums I had not been able to see and found a few examples of unpublished Roman coins, and was also able to see coins I had not been shown in the museums I did visit. There were not, however, many significant new finds in this category. He also noted a lot of finds that he was shown from private collections, mostly from the regions that are known to have yielded Roman finds in the past, especially south India. He also looked for coins dating after Constantine I, which was the cut-off date of my study. In his review of my work, he had noted that my list was deficient in not including coins from the later period although the terminus had been clearly stated (Berghaus 1992: 1). Work on the later period has now been picked up by Rebecca Darley, who lists 189 Byzantine gold coins found in India and about 8,000 copper coins (Darley 2013: 211–212).

A further contribution to the study of these coins, indeed Indian numismatics generally, was made in 1991, when the first volume of *Studies in South Indian Coins*, the journal of the South Indian Numismatic

---

[3] Significant among many contributions include Berghaus 1989 and MacDowall and Jha 2004.

Society, was published under the aegis of the late R. Krishnamurthy, one of the founders of the society. The journal continues to demonstrate the interest in Roman coins found in south India with regular articles about them. The second volume in 1992 carried several papers devoted to Roman coin finds. The study of the later Roman coppers has also been greatly advanced by the work of Krishnamurthy (2007).

In the same year V.V. Krishna Sastry published an important work on the coin finds from Andhra Pradesh, the gold hoards from Pedakodamagundla (three aurei), Nagarvarapupudu (more than 50 aurei) and Dharmavaripalem (26 aurei, some imitations). All finds had coins with cut marks. From his excavations he noted silver coins and imitations from Bavikonda, Peddabankur and Veerapuram (Krishna Sastry 1992: 4–16). A major administrative change in 2014 saw Andhra Pradesh divided into two states, with a new unit, Telengana, in the area to the north-west of the Krishna river. Six of the hoards that Krishna Sastry listed are now in that new division (Nasthullapur, Peddabankur, Nagarvarapupadu, Akenpalle, Yeleswaram and Gothiparti). In 2002 a further gold hoard was found in Andhra Pradesh, at Penuganchiprolu, now known to have been mainly imitations.[4] Recently A. Romanowski has published a new survey of the finds from the Andhra period which concludes with a heartfelt plea that 'It is also beyond all doubt that the research would be very much facilitated by a greater accessibility of the artefacts preserved in the museums of India and the more frequent co-operation with local coin collectors.' Hear, hear!

An imitation aurei was found at Tirukoilur in 1992. (Krishnamurthy 1998; Berghaus 2006). Many of the coins were dispersed on discovery but 193 coins were recovered. This is an area that needs to be researched. Gold imitations seem on anecdotal evidence to be commonly found, but the style and form of the imitations seem to me to be quite varied, and to cover a wide date-range from both the earlier Julio-Claudian period and the second century.[5]

An unusual find of denarii was made in Nedumkundam in Kerala in 1992 (Satyamurthy 1996). More detailed information about this has recently been published by D.W. Macdowall (2018). It is unusual as there were significant numbers of Republican period coins. MacDowall and Berghaus (1998) have both asserted that there are more Republican coins from India than

is usually suggested; certainly there were not many at the time of my list. Berghaus was shown 34 denarii, of which 13 were of Republican date, in 1991 that he thought could have come from the same source as the 'Laccadive hoard' that I had heard rumours of in the 1980s but which never came fully to light. He thought it likely that the hoard comprised around 300 coins and that it was probably found in Thryssa (formerly Trichur) and that stray finds that he had listed represented 'the tip of an iceberg', that is, only a small portion of the coins of this date that had been found in India (Berghaus 1998: 120-1).

He was probably right, and this highlights a particular problem in studying these, and indeed any other, ancient coin finds. Much of the material he saw was in private collections. There has always been a trade the world over in buying and selling ancient artefacts, and market forces have always played a part in making the study of these items difficult. Dealers are often very happy to provide information on provenance but this is equally often accompanied by a concomitant reticence to provide details. Those of an unscrupulous bent will furnish details that they perceive might enhance the value or saleability of objects. Collectors of ancient objects acquire them from many sources, and museum collections often receive donations of material from collectors who have purchased it. Most collectors care about their possessions and keep good records, but on the other hand, how can the provenances be verified? What about the auction catalogues that contain examples from India? It is difficult to know how much credence one can give to the provenances, yet they must be indicative of something. Accession registers in museums contain careful details of how and when coins were acquired, but now there is a heavy burden of proof required for them to make sure artefacts have not been illegally or unethically retrieved. The Archaeological Institute of America has published very clear views on dealing with unprovenanced antiquities and much of the information that has been cited about Roman coins found in India would not meet their criteria for publication.[6] This makes it difficult for objects to get into museum collections where they can be studied by all. The body of evidence 'seen in trade' is thus tantalizing: on the one hand, surely indicative of trends, on the other potentially bogus or at best uncorroborated. This ethical dilemma was only just beginning to be discussed when I was a student.

Material derived from archaeological excavation therefore is of huge importance, and a key contribution to the move towards placing numismatic evidence in a firmly archaeological context was made in *Indo-Roman Trade: From pots to pepper*, a book by Roberta Tomber of the British Museum. This provided an admirable

---

[4] . Subrahmanaym, Rao and Chary 2008. This book is the subject of an excellent review by Smagur and Romanowski 2020, in which the attributions have been changed and several coins newly identified as imitations.

[5] Many of the auction houses over the last decade have advertised coins, usually gold, and often imitations are included and appear to be much sought-after.

[6] https://www.ajaonline.org/submissions/antiquities-policy

summary of the evidence for Indo-Roman trade that went beyond the coin finds. Tomber noted that a new list of them in a recent book by S. Suresh (2004) had increased the number of finds and that Macdowall's list, when published, would 'double the number of entries' (Tomber 2008: 31). But its main impact lay in considering the material relating to the trade as a whole, and as such it, along with work by Himanshu Ray, Vimala Begley and others, has led the way for an archaeological approach.[7]

Suresh's book, published in 2004, promised a new approach, attempting to discuss the coins alongside other types of artefact. Appendix 1 contains a list of 169 finds, which looked very exciting. It appeared that the number of finds had increased substantially from the 79 included in my 1989 list. However, Suresh included as definite some finds which had seemed to me too vague to include in my list, and since his list has no references many of them cannot be verified. Some of the finds in his list simply have no details, which means the record is of almost no use. But he did include a number of finds from excavations and some in museums.

In addition to these works, there has been a plethora of works of a general nature covering the Roman trade with India, importantly advanced with the publication of the texts of P. Vindobonensis G 40822, known as the Muziris papyrus.[8] Many of these works are synthetic studies and, while they discuss possible mechanisms for trade, most do not cite any new information about the coin finds.[9] However, de Romanis also wrote an interesting account of Roman hoards from India. His list included by his calculation 5,728 denarii and 1,243 aurei 'that have been more or less reliably recorded' (de Romanis 2012: 167). This was very much my own aim in 1989. His list has about 25 new hoards, but about two-thirds of these are single finds, several from the article by Berghaus (1998).

In the catalogue of finds that I published in 1989 I too tried to include only finds for which some useful data had been recorded and for which there was some kind of published record, but there is a need to record instances that are anecdotal or incomplete, hence the list of 'possible' finds. As noted, subsequent publications have elevated some of these 'possible' finds to 'actual' ones, and there are many other references to finds for which the provenance details are difficult. These and the other reports that have appeared since need to be collated and untangled.

The picture emerging from my studies so far is that the count of new finds is not as great as Suresh suggested, and many of them are of only one or two coins, but the significant finds, Nedumkandam, Tirukoilur, Nagarvarapupudu, Dharmavaripalem and Penuganchiprolu, are important.

The finds of Roman coins from India are unusual in their composition and much ink has been spilt on the subject of the cut marks that appear on them and the number and different styles of imitations. Speculation has been rife about why these characteristics apply, and what purpose the coins had on the subcontinent. So far there does not seem to be any further hard information that might settle the debates, but the provision of an updated list should at least increase the body of reliable evidence to date in a new single source. The finds since my list are similar in composition to earlier finds, though the number of imitations in hoards, some of which have come to light after renewed study, is obviously an important avenue of research. What is vital is accurate publication of the finds, which has happily occurred in some cases but it looks as though some finds will never come to be 'more or less reliably recorded'.

What is the future of the study, then? A gap of 30 years has provided enough new information to warrant a fully updated list of the finds, and the work is in progress. The internet has made it easier to access published material but there is still no substitute for studying the coins themselves. In addition to the inclusion of the new finds, consideration needs to be given to the scope and extent of the study. The work of Krishnamurthy and Darley noted above has concentrated on the later periods not covered in the original listing. Whether to maintain the break at the Emperor Constantine as I did in 1989 is open to debate, but while scholars are moving in the direction of regarding Indian Ocean trade as a continuum that does not take account of regime change outside the area, it seems to me that the coin finds do nonetheless fall into the phases I originally perceived. Certainly the choice to list finds alphabetically by the toponyms seems to be the easiest to handle, and the creation of Telengana is a good example of why listing them according to modern state boundaries that were irrelevant in the distant past is not helpful. Mapping these places is now substantially easier than it used to be, and one important aim of the revised listing will be the production of more detailed maps, and certainly more reference to the archaeological settings. The number of publications, not just numismatic ones, that has appeared is large. Work on updating the list goes on apace. Watch this space.

---

[7] Good summaries are in Begley and De Puma 1991 and Ray and Salles 1996.
[8] Harrauer and Sijpestein 1985 and more recently in a magisterial work by de Romanis 2020.
[9] Some examples of this are De Romanis and Tchernia 1997; Young 2001; McLaughlin 2010; Cobb 2018. The bibliography on Indian Ocean trade is now very extensive and of mixed worth.

References

Begley, V. and de Puma, R.D. (eds) 1991. *Rome and India: The Ancient Sea Trade.* Madison, Wisconsin: University of Wisconsin Press.

Berghaus, P. 1989. Funde severischer Goldmünzen in Indien. Pages 93–101 in H.J. Drexhage and J. Sünskes (eds), *Migratio et Communatio: Studien zur alten Geschichte und deren Nachleben, Festschrift Thomas Pekáry.* Münster: Scripta Mercatura Verlag.

Berghaus, P. 1992. Zu den römischen Fundmünzen aus Indien. *Schweizerische Numismatische Rundschau* 71: 226–47.

Berghaus, P. 1998. 'Republican and Early Roman Imperial Denarii from India'. Pages 119–127 in A.K. Jha and S. Garg (eds), *Ex Moneta: Essays on numismatics in honour of Dr. David MacDowall,* vol. 1. New Delhi: Harman.

Berghaus, P. 2006. Strange Mould Links out of the Tirukoilur Hoard. Pages 11–20 in R. Nagaswamy (ed.) *Sangam: Numismatics and cultural history: Essays in honour of Dr. R. Krishnamurty.* Chennai: New Era Publications.

Burnett, A. 2020. *The Hidden Treasures of this Happy Island': A History of Numismatics in Britain from the Renaissance to the Enlightenment.* Royal Numismatic Society Special Publication 58. London: Royal Numismatic Society.

Cobb, M.A. 2018. *Rome and the Indian Ocean Trade from Augustus to the Early Third Century CE.* Leiden: Brill.

Darley, R. 2013. Indo-Byzantine Exchange, 4th–7th Centuries: A Global History, unpublished PhD dissertation, University of Birmingham.

Davidson, A. 1790. On Some Roman Coins Found at Nelore. *Asiatick Researches* 2: 331–2.

Gupta, P.L. 1965. *Roman Coins from Andhra Pradesh.* Hyderabad: Government of Andhra Pradesh.

Harrauer, H. and Sijpestein, P.J. 1985. Ein Neues Dokument zu Roms Indienhandel, P. Vindob. G40822 *Anzeiger der philosophisch-historischen Klasse* 122: 124–155.

Krishna Sastry, V.V. 1992. *Roman Gold Coins: Recent Discoveries in Andhra Pradesh*: 4–16. Hyderabad: Government of Andhra Pradesh.

Krishnamurthy, R. 1998. Imitation Gold Coins from Tirukoilur Hoard, Tamilnadu. Pages 145–149, in A.K. Jha and S. Garg, *Ex Moneta: Essays on Numismatics in Honour of Dr. David MacDowall,* vol. 1. New Delhi: Harman.

Krishnamurthy, R. 2007. *Late Roman Copper Coins from South India: Karur, Madurai and Tirukkoilur.* Chennai: Garnet Publishers.

MacDowall D.M. and Jha A. (eds) 2004. *Foreign Coins Found in the Indian Subcontinent: 8-10 January, 1995, 4 International Colloquium,* Mumbai, IINRS.

MacDowall, D.M. 2018. The 1992 Hoard of Roman Silver Denarii from Nedumkandam. *Studies in South Indian Coins* 28: 60–63.

McLaughlin, R. 2010. *Rome and the Distant East: Trade Routes to the Ancient Lands of Arabia, India and China.* London: Continuum.

Ray, H.P. and Salles, J.-F. 1996. *Tradition and Archaeology: Early Maritime Contacts in the Indian Ocean,* New Delhi: Manohar.

RIC 1² = Sutherland, C.H.V. and Carson, R.A.G. (eds). 1984. *The Roman Imperial Coinage,* vol. 1. London: Spink.

de Romanis, F. 2012. Julio-Claudian Denarii and Aurei in Campania and India: *Annali dell'Istituo Italiano di Numismatica* 58: 161–92.

de Romanis, F. 2020. *The Indo-Roman Pepper Trade and the Muziris Papyrus,* Oxford University Press.

de Romanis, F. and Tchernia, A. (eds) 1997 (reprint 2005). *Crossings. Early Mediterranean Contacts with India.* New Delhi: Manohar.

Romanowski, A. 2021. Roman Coins in Andhra in the Early Historical Period, *Wiadomości Numizmatyczne [Numismatic News]* 65: 15–76.

Satyamurthy, T. 1996. Nedumkandam Hord of Roman Dinarii [sic], *Studies in South Indian Coins* 6: 31–42.

Smagur, E. and Romanowski, A. 2020. Review of B. Subrahmanyam, G.V. Rama Krishna Rao and P. Brahma Chary, *Roman Gold Coins: A Treasure Trove from Penuganchiprolu. Numismatic Chronicle* 180: 484–90.

Subrahmanyam, B., Rama Krishna Rao, G.V. and Brahma Chary, P. (eds). 2008. *Roman Gold Coins: A Treasure Trove from Penuganchiprolu.* Hyderabad: Government of Andhra Pradesh.

Suresh, S. 2004. *Symbols of Trade: Roman and Pseudo-Roman Objects Found in India,* New Delhi: Manohar.

Sydenham. 1789. Letter from Colonel Sydenham to Lord Macartney at St. Thomas's Mount, Madras: communicated by Dr. Lort. Dated Oct. 14, 1786, *Archaeologia* 9: 36, 81–83.

Tomber, R. 2008. *Indo-Roman Trade: From Pots to Pepper.* London: Duckworth.

Turner, P.J. 1989. *Roman Coins from India.* London: Royal Numismatic Society.

Wheeler, R.E.M. 1946. Arikamedu: An Indo-Roman trading station on the east coast of India. *Ancient India* 2: 17–124.

Young, G.K. 2001. *Rome's Eastern Trade: International Commerce and Imperial Policy 31 BC-AD 305.* London: Routledge.

Interrogating 'Heraṇika' in the Inscriptions of the Western Deccan (c. 200 BC–300 AD)

Suchandra Ghosh

Introduction

The Deccan, encompassing the present states of Maharashtra, Karnataka, Andhra Pradesh and Telengana of India, was home to many important Buddhist sites in pre-modern times. These sites were repositories of donative records written in Brahmi script and Prakrit language. These records are not prescriptive statements and reveal gifts of paving stones, cross bars, railing pillars, caves and sculptures and things of public utility like *poḍhi* (cistern) together with the names of those who gifted them. Through the practice of *dāna* (gift giving)[1] and in several cases *deyadhamma* (donation for the sake of acquiring merit), the laity and monastics unconditionally supported the monastic establishments. Gifts and endowments involved the mobilization of resources and larger networks. The records often suggest geographical data which help us to trace the movement of donors from both distant lands and nearby territories. Moreover, the donors refer to positions within the kinship structure and occupations, which may imply an attempt to record their identity. A host of occupations/professions and personal names are inscribed in these records, thereby suggesting the participation of many individuals. To quote Vidya Dehejia, "the early Buddhist cave monasteries were constructed through the generosity of the common man, by a process of collective donation that is attested to by masses of inscriptional material" (Dehejia 1992: 35–45). The non-royal donations far outnumbered the royal donations. These non-royal persons were commoners and were obviously resourceful. The act of patronage meant parting with some of the resources at their disposal. The inscriptions also give us an idea of the geographically widespread nature of collective patronage. The occupation of the donor is often mentioned, at least for male lay donors, and includes vadhaki (carpenter), gaṁdhika (perfumer), vāṇijaka (merchant), seṭhi (rich merchant), kamāra (blacksmith), suvarṇakāra (goldsmith), maṇikāra (jeweller), negama (merchant) etc. Among the rarely mentioned occupational groups were vaidyas (physician), mithika (polisher) and heraṇika (treasurer/gold dealer). Heraṇika is often translated as gold smith though we have suvarṇakāra as a separate category of

donor who are goldsmiths. The two terms hiraṇya and suvarṇa were widely used to refer to gold. When they were mentioned in similar contexts as for example with coins, it created confusion. Hiraṇya was also meant a tax paid in cash. Unlike suvarṇakāra who made objects in gold, heranikas were treasurers or dealers of gold. I believe they formed an influential economic group who were deeply associated with Buddhist establishments. In this essay I wish to interrogate this donor category and shall try to understand their network of interactions.

Heranika in select epigraphic records of the western Deccan

Perhaps the first reference to *hiraṇakar* (*hiraṇyakāra*)[2] comes from the site of Pitalkhora, located in the north-west of Aurangabad district, one of the earliest centres of rock-cut architecture in western India. It lies alongside an ancient trade route that connected the Deccan plateau with the port of Bharuch on the west and the ancient city of Ujjain to the north. The inscription dated to the 2nd century BC which is inscribed in two lines on the back of the palm of the right hand of a huge Yaksha figure reads *Kaṇhadāsena hiraṁakarena* (*kata* made by Kaṇhadāsa, a goldsmith) (Deshpande 1959: 81). The sculpture represents a standing corpulent male yaksha with his hands raised upwards to hold a shallow bowl. It is significant that we have the word *katā* (made by) in the inscription, and that the act of donation is inscribed on the palm which indicates that he was actually the donor of the Yaksha image. Was Kaṇhadāsa both the donor and a sculptor adept at working both in hard stone and soft gold? Regardless, there is no doubt that he possessed the necessary resources to donate a monumental image, a donation beyond the means of most. This image is now housed in the National Museum, New Delhi.

Two 2nd century AD inscriptions from Kanheri present a different picture. They mention donations made by two sons of a heraṇika from Chemula (present day Chaul port). The first records the donation of a podhi (water cistern) to the vihāra of Kanhagiri (present day Kanheri (Kanhagiri).[3] The inscription

---

[1] 1The concept of *Dāna* here is different from the dāna and dakṣiṇā in the Brahmanical or Vedic context. For an understanding of gift giving in the Vedic context see Thapar 2000. For a recent study on *Dāna*, see Singh 2017. For a critical understanding of gift giving in South Asia, one could also see Heim 2015.

[2] A hiraṇyakāra is a goldsmith and it is mentioned in the Vājasenayi Samhita XXX,17, cited by Mylius 1978. I am thankful to Dr Dev Kumar Jhanjh for drawing my attention to this.

[3] Kanheri is an important Buddhist cave site in the western Deccan, very near Mumbai. Its Prakrit name Kaṇhagiri derived from Sanskrit

reads: *Chemulakasa heraṇikasa Rohiṇimitasa putasa Sulasadatasa poḍhi, deyadhaṁam* (A water cistern, the meritorious gift of Sulasadatta, son of mint master/gold dealer Rohiṇimitra of Chemula). The second records *Chemulikasa heraṇikasa Rohiṇimitasa putasa Dhamaṇakasa patho, Deyadhamo* (the meritorious gift of a pathway by Dhamaṇakah, the son of mint master/gold dealer Rohinimitra). It is clear from these two records that Sulasadatta and Dhamaṇaka were both sons of Rohiṇimitra. Thus, the sons of this gold dealer came all the way from Chaul to donate at the Buddhist monastic establishment at Kanheri(presently the distance between Chaul to Kanheri by road is 142.8 km). The inscriptions were located in appropriate places: Sulasadatta's inscription above the water tank and Dhamaṇaka's inscription on the back of a low bench along the flight of steps opposite Cave no.7.

Interestingly, from Cave no. 4 we find a donation from Dhamaṇaka's wife. The inscription reads *Siddham heraṇikasa Dhamaṇakasa bhāya Sivapālitanikāya deyadhaṁma therāna bhayato Dhaṁmapālānaṁ thuba* (Success! The Stūpa of the Thera, the reverend Dhammapāla, the meritorious gift of Sivapālitanikā, the wife of the gold dealer or mint master Dhamaṇaka.) This record bears evidence to the fact that the wives of these donors were mobile and perhaps often accompanied their husbands when an act of donation was to be made. It is also significant that the wife records not only the name of the husband Dhamanaka but also his occupation, which demonstrate that in the context of the donation by a wife, the occupational identity of the husband is vital. For his own donation, Dhamanaka does not allude to his own occupation but indicates his father's occupation. These are pointers to the social mores of the given period.

Turning to another rock cut cave site, Junnar (in Pune district, Maharashtra), we find a donative record inscribing the meritorious gift of the construction of a cetiyaghara (outer building protecting a stupa) by the distinguished Sulasadata, son of a heranika from Kalyana (*kaliyanasa heranika putasa sulasadatasa ekapurisasa cetiyogharoniyutodeyadhama*). Sulasadata seems to have been a common name.

Discussion

Scholars have often translated *heranika* as "goldsmith". The Prakrit term *heranika*, Sanskrit *hairaṇyaka*, is obviously related to *hiraṇya* meaning gold. Since the suffix *kāra* which implies action/work is not added, we cannot say with confidence that a heranika is

a goldsmith. Moreover, for goldsmith we have the term *suvarṇakāra* from the corpus of Kanheri records. Translating *suvarnakāra* as goldsmith and *heranika* as treasurer/gold dealer seems to distinguish effectively between the two. For example, in Cave no. 2, it is recorded that a cistern was the meritorious gift of the *suvaṇakāra* Samidata of Kalyan together with the community of ascetics and lay brothers (Gokhale 1991: 47), indicating that Samidata had made the cistern himself. Sircar (1966: 125) suggested that a *heranika* could be a treasurer or gold dealer, or a mint master. The mint master is perhaps too distant a proposition and I would prefer to identify *heranika* with a treasurer or dealer in gold.

There is also a technical sense to the term *hiraṇya*. The Arthaśāstra, a Sanskrit manual on statecraft with a thrust on financial matters believed to have been compiled between the 2nd century BC and the 3rd century AD, refers to the *hiraṇya* as a tax on certain goods payable in cash. Interestingly, the term *hiraṇya* referred to silver and copper coins in spite of the fact that it means gold. The discussion on the production of coins (2.12.24) mentions only silver and copper coins and refers to them as *hiraṇya*. The Arthaśāstra also categorically mentions the *sauvarṇika* as an officer under the superintendent of gold, doing the actual manufacturing work (2.13.2; Olivelle 2013: 536). Thus, the technical sense of *hiranya* also points to the *heranika* being a treasurer or gold dealer (but not a goldsmith).

It is important to note that the *heranikas* came from the port towns of Kalyan and Chaul, both of which were trading centres where wealth could be accumulated in the hands of certain classes of people. Therefore, we have a number of donations from different professional groups of Kalyan and Chaul. During the heydeys of the Śaka Kṣatrapas in the 2nd century AD Kalyan lost its glory as a port (which it regained in the 6th century AD). There were also donors coming from the port sites such as Sopara who made donations at Kanheri: for example, a merchant from Sopara donated a water tank – a donation of public utility. There were several other donors from Sopara too, indicating that Sopara was intimately connected with Kanheri. Sopara was an important port town and the *Suppāraka Jātaka* reflects its maritime activity. The *Suppāraka Jātaka* (no. 463) tells us that the Bodhisattva was a *mahānāvika*, a master mariner who lost his eyesight owing to the wind at sea. A group of 700 merchants prepared a ship for a voyage to *Suvarṇabhūmi* (mainland Southeast Asia), a distant land, but did not have a captain. They asked the Bodhisattva to be their skipper. It is said that the Bodhisattva was born in the family of a master mariner and was named *Suppāraka Kumāra*. He returned safely with the merchants and merchandise to the home port of Bharukaccha (Cowell 1895–97: 86-7).

Kṛṣhṇagiri occurs in the Nasik inscription of the Sātavāhana ruler Vāsishṭhiputra Pulumāvi. The period of Kanheri's occupation as a cave site ranges from 1st century CE to 9th century CE. For inscriptions of this site see Shobhana Gokhale, *Kanheri Inscriptions*, Pune: Deccan College Post Graduate and Research Institute, 1991.

The evidence above suggests an active strong coastal trading network which allowed people from these port towns to reach the Buddhist cave sites which were located inland but along major routes and within a few days' travel. Merchants and different occupational/ professional groups formed the main category of donors. Kanheri's proximity to the ports of the western Deccan (around 41 km from Nalla Sopara and 51 km from Kalyan at present) led to its flourishing state in the early centuries of the common era. As for Junnar (about 100 km inland), the Sātavāhanas made systematic efforts to develop Junnar which was linked with the ports of the west coast. A significant discovery from Junnar was a carved alabaster depicting the birth of Eros in an eggshell. Could this figure of Eros have been in the personal possession of a Roman (or western) merchant who brought it from Alexandria to the site of what is now modern Junnar? Could it have been brought back by an Indian merchant as a souvenir? However it arrived, there were people living in Junnar who had some contact with the Mediterranean world. Naneghat served as an outlet for the products around Junnar – it was an ancient pass on an important trade route which is active even today.

We may now take a close look at the description given by the author of the *Periplus Maris Erythraei* (Casson 1989) about these ports. The *Periplus* (section 52) speaks specifically about the local ports of Dachinabades and mentions Suppara (Sopara) and Kalliena (Kalyan) which was a port of trade during the time of the early Sātavāhanas. And it says that beyond Kalliena there were other local ports of trade including Semylla (Chaul). It is quite evident that Semylla is taken from Chemullya, the way it was pronounced locally. In a similar fashion Barygaza comes from Bharugaccha and not Sanskrit Bhrigukaccha. Semylla/Chaul flourished as an important port from about the 6th century AD. We know that commercial relations connecting the entire Deccan were instituted only after the rise of the Sātavāhana dynasty. Kanheri, Nasik, Junnar and Karle were closely related sites. The presence of *heranika* as donors is seen only in Kanheri and Junnar. The records suggest that these were largely family donations. These families were lay Buddhists and the acquisition of merit through the act of giving was the essential religious act of a lay person. The profession of a *heranika* was not common, but was somehow different from *suvarṇakāra*,

and perhaps in the social ladder they were superior to *suvarṇakāra*. *Heranika* flourished in the port towns where mercantile activities brought enough resources enabling the various occupational groups to donate to śramanic establishments for gaining merit. We can imagine that they travelled along with the merchants in *pravahanas*, (Chakravarti 1998), coastal vessels that plied along the Konkan coast in the quest of merit through donations.

References

Singh, A. (ed.) 2017. *Dāna, Reciprocity and Patronage in Buddhism*. Delhi: Primus Books.

Casson, L. (ed. and tr.) 1989. *The Periplus Maris Erythraei, Text with Introduction, Translation and Commentary*. Princeton: Princeton University Press.

Chakravarti, R. 1998. Coastal Trade and Voyages in Konkan: The Early Medieval Scenario. *Indian Economic and Social History Review* 35: 97–124.

Cowell, E.B. 1895–97, reprint 2001. 'The Supparaka Jātaka(Jātaka no. 463)'. In E.B.Cowell (ed.), *The Jātaka or Stories of The Buddha's Former Births* [repr. Delhi: D.K.Publishers, 2001].

Dehejia, V. 1992. Collective and Popular Bases of early Buddhist Patronage: Sacred Monuments, 100 BC to AD 250. Pages 35–45 in Barbara Stoler Miller (ed.) *Powers of Art, Patronage in Indian culture*. Delhi: Oxford University Press.

Deshpande, M.N. 1959. The Rock Cut Caves of Pitalkhora in the Deccan. *Ancient India* 15: 66–93.

Gokhale, S. 1991. *Kanheri Inscriptions*. Pune: Deccan College Post Graduate and Research Centre.

Heim, M. 2015. *Theories of the Gift in South Asia: Hindu, Buddhist, and Jain Reflections on Dana*. Religion in History, Society and Culture Series. London: Routledge.

Mylius, K. 1978. Sanskrit Index of Young Vedic Names and Things, Part II. *Ethnographic Archaeological Journal* 19: 273–298.

Olivelle, P. 2013. *King, Governance and Law in Ancient India, Kauṭilya's Arthaśāstra*. New York: Oxford University Press.

Sircar, D.C. 1966. *Indian Epigraphical Glossary*. Delhi: Motilal Banarsidass.

Thapar, R. 2000. Dāna and Daksiṇā in Forms of Exchange. Pages 531–536 in *Cultural Pasts: Essays in Early Indian History*. New Delhi: Oxford University Press.

Preliminary Thoughts on the Peck and Shroff Marks of Sixteenth Century North India

Robert Bracey

Introduction

'The need for coins to look like coins is a force stronger than the need for coins to acknowledge their issuer' (Cribb 2009: 515)

Joe is fond of telling prospective numismatists to discard the books and look at the coins. Those who know only his work might find this surprising because it has the ring of an unreformed Rankean historian insisting that we bury ourselves in the primary sources, in this case the numismatic archive. Joe did spend his career in one of the world's largest numismatic archives, the Coins & Medals department of the British Museum. It was there that I first met him, and that he first gave me this advice. But the Joe apparent from his published work is also one of the foremost numismatic theorists of his generation. He has after all dedicated a substantial amount of his published work to the concept of 'numismatic traditions' (Cribb 2003, 2007a; see Bracey 2019 for reflections on this), an attempt to theorise the functionalist response to coins as propaganda model, to epistemological questions related to the sources for early coinage (1983a, 1983b), and he employed his platform as president of the Royal Numismatic Society to lay out a comprehensive numismatic response to the 'linguistic turn' (Cribb 2005, 2006, 2007b, 2009), the most prominent theoretical trend in turn of the century philosophy of history. And, in his time at the British Museum he was the driving force behind the 'money' gallery, marking a theoretical shift from the object itself to the concept it serves.

These two elements I think resolve in Joe's work through a question of priority. Theory is necessary. There are methodological questions which must be asked, and answered, robustly. Without theory you simply cannot offer good answers, but, and I think this is Joe's point, you cannot offer answers at all without data. You need to look at the coins, and looking is a recurrent metaphor in Joe's work precisely because it forms the basis on which all of his contributions to theory have been built.

So, in this article I thought I would look at coins, in particular a very small feature of the coins of north India in the sixteenth century.

Peck marks and shroff marks

The late medieval and early modern silver coinages of north India frequently feature small marks which I will refer to as 'peck' or 'shroff' marks. They are distinct from counter marks, which are also found on some coins in this period, because those usually identify an issuing authority different to that of the original coins, and punch marks which are usually larger symbols impressed into the obverse or reverse. Peck marks, usually found on the obverse or reverse, are round, or very occasionally square, indentations, presumably made by hammering a simple punch into the surface. Shroff marks are typically more complex designs but usually found around the edges of the coin. Though these are symbols, like punches, their use on the edge of coins is distinctive, and almost unique to the rupee, a relatively thick coin introduced into India in the sixteenth century in the brief reign of Sher Shah Suri (1540–1545 CE).

The distinctions I have just made are arbitrary but it is useful to sub-divide the various marks on these coins, as each group has distinct features. And unfortunately there is no standard convention in numismatic literature (see Carrier, Artu, Faucher 2021). For clarity I have summarised the terms I will use on the right with the meaning I intend when using the term in this article. This article will focus primarily on pecks and briefly discuss shroff marks, but all of these types of mark are found on North Indian coins of the mid-sixteenth century, and all would benefit from greater study.

Who made these marks? Why did they make them? What purpose did they serve? With the exception of counter marks the research literature on them is slight (I am grateful to John Deyell for confirming that this is not simply a function of my ignorance of the literature), but in less formal contexts they are often explained either as relating to sicca, a system by which older rupees were discounted, or as a means for detecting forgery. The following remarks were made by Shailendra Bhandare online in a discussion forum (https://www.coinbooks.org/esylum_v19n42a16.html):

Types of marks

counter mark – larger mark on the surface indicating a minting authority.

punch – a symbol impressed on the surface

slash or **gouge** – a deliberate strike or cut into the surface of the coin

edge cut – a cut in the edge made by drawing a blade across it

peck – an indentation made by driving a spike into the surface of the coin

piercing – a hole through a coin

suspension – an attachment, usually with a piercing to convert the coin into jewellery

shroff mark – a small punch, usually a simple symbol, on the edge of the coin

'These are testing marks applied as the coin circulated, to attest whether it was fully of silver, or a forgery made by plating a copper core with silver. This was normal practice in some areas of India during this period. More number of marks will generally be regarded as a downgrading of the coin's condition. The money-changers thought that too—as we have evidence that coins with more test marks were subject to more discount!'

Bhandare's remark is informal and may not reflect his considered opinion, but it is typical of informal assumptions about the marks, and neither of the explanations is a very satisfying answer. That rupees feature a distinctive series of marks and are also known from historical sources to have been managed by a distinctive system of discounting, sicca, in a sophisticated monetary economy suggests the two are related, but does nothing to explain how marking the coin would be necessary or useful when textual evidence suggests discounting was based on the age, clearly recorded in the coins inscription. Likewise, breaking the surface of the coin with a punch would be an effective method of detecting plated or surface enriched silver but the problem of forgery is nearly universal for pre-modern silver coinages, and the peck solution employed here is, if not unique, certainly unusual.

It is also often assumed that in contrast to counter marks, which were frequently an official act, that these various marks were made by private individuals such as traders, money-changers, or bankers. Indeed, 'shroff' is itself an anglicised Indian word for such a class of people. Deyell (2010) in one of the few articles examining this, focusing on the coinage of Bengal, uses 'shroff mark', with some caution as a generic term for all of the marks, subdividing them as follows:

The 'shroff marks' were of three principal kinds or classes, which appear to have had different but related functions:

- test marks, which are shallow circular holes. These were applied by money exchangers and revenue agents to test whether the coin was genuine, by exposing the internal metal.
- identification marks, which are small, light punches bearing Bengali letters, pictorial devices or geometric patterns. These were applied, presumably by the same agents, to attest the bona fides of the coins tested (weight and fineness) by leaving their own private marks of verification.
- cancellation marks, which are large deep chisel gouges. These totally defaced the surface of the coin, obliterating inscriptions. They were obviously intended to demonetise the coins and relegate them to bullion status. Either bankers or revenue officials could be responsible for these, although Abu'l Fazl relates that the former undertook this action aggressively, in order to realise illicit profits from the premature discounting of legitimate coin. (Deyell 2010: 87)

Deyell's 'test' corresponds with my 'peck', 'identification' with 'punch', and 'cancellation' with 'slash'/'gouge'. Deyell is rightly cautious about the use of the term shroff as it implies that we understand who made the marks and why. As I will argue in a moment, even if the peck marks were made by private money changers, the practice of pecking must have originated at a much higher level. Here, I reserve shroff for those marks found on the edges of coins which are most peculiar to this historical context, and whose pattern fits most closely with what might be expected of private actors.

Table 1. Average weight of coins by number of peck marks (zeno.ru and ANS Mantis data)

No. of pecks	1	2	3	4	5	6	7	8	9	10	11	12	13	14	15	18
n	16	12	14	9	17	5	10	6	3	8	2	1	6	1	1	1
mean weight (g)	11.23	11.26	11.27	11.15	11.03	11.25	11.21	11.26	11.18	11.24	11.05	11.11	11.15	11.30	11.16	10.91

Deyell notes that the number of marks is loosely correlated with weight (2010, fig. 4). This is unsurprising and is confirmed by my own examination of sixteenth century Suri coins (see Table 1).

As can be seen from Table 1 as the number of peck marks on a coin increases there is a tendency for the coin's weight to diminish. This is an unsurprising result, as presumably the longer the coin was in circulation the more opportunity it had both to acquire marks and to lose weight due to wear—that is, we would expect a correlation even if there was no causative link between the two.

Though I will present some statistical data in this article I will not be using any statistical tests. Statistical tests primarily measure the null hypothesis, essentially the chance that a result is misleading as a result of random sampling errors. This is by far the least likely cause of distortion in most historical data, which is more likely to be subject to systemic rather than random distortions. And, as will be shown in the next section, there is good reason to believe there are numerous systemic distortions in this data.

Muddy data

For want of a better word the data for the study of peck and shroff marks is 'muddy'. Aside from a series of systemic biases there is a general inconsistency in data gathered from databases, including the possibility of duplication, misattribution, and a great deal of subjectivity in interpreting photographs made with different equipment under a variety of lightings. Take for example Figure 1, a coin from the American Numismatic Society (ANS) database attributed to Sher Shah. How many peck marks have been made on the surface?

I count four on the obverse and seven on the reverse, marked by solid white circles in Figure 1. These are

often quite faint, particularly the two pecks between 3 and 5 o'clock on the obverse. Having examined some coins both in person and through photographs there are marks so faint that they appear to be invisible in the digital images (undoubtedly affected by lighting). It is also possible to overcount: the three features marked by dotted circles share the same general feature of being round depressions but I do not think they are peck marks. Two lack the regularity of shape and may be accidental damage, one, between 10 and 11 o'clock on the reverse, appears to be part of the design.

This 'muddiness' in the data can be compensated for by increasing the size of the dataset. Unfortunately, I have only been able to examine a little over 100 coins (for practical reasons the data on peck marks used here has been drawn from the ANS Mantis database and the online site Zeno.ru.) and it seems a few thousand would be needed for truly robust results. The dataset could also be made more robust through careful re-examination by others, and hopefully this paper will attract attention to a fascinating but under-appreciated subject. Table 4 in the appendix records the coins I have examined and the number of marks I have identified on the 'obverse' (the side on the left of the paired images) and 'reverse' (the side on the right). Since there is little consistency as to which side is treated as the obverse this seemed like a sensible preliminary step. Attributions are those given in the respective databases. Likely there are numerous errors, but hopefully those errors exhibit themselves simply as 'noise' and do not distort the results.

By the way, Joe's dictum does not imply that looking at coins is easy.

Part 1: Peck marks

The question of what I term 'shroff marks' will be deferred to the second half of the paper. In this first half I will examine what I call 'pecks'. These are usually round, and very occasionally square, indentations in

Figure 1. Peck marks on the surface of a Sher Shah Suri rupee (ANS 1917.215.3787, 10.78g, 28mm)

Table 2. Count and average number of marks for Suri coins by year of issue

year	946	947	948	949	950	951	952	953	954	955	956	957	958	959	960	961	962	963	964
n	4	5	7	24	13	11	11	6	8	4	7	2	6	8	4	5	5	3	2
mean pecks	5.8	4.6	7.6	5.9	6.4	5.1	5.8	5.2	5.6	10.0	1.9	5.0	6.3	5.0	6.0	3.6	3.6	10.3	3.5

Table 3. Typical number of marks on dated Bengal Sultanate coins in the Zeno database

year	716	723	727	746	747	749	753	754	761	776	849	893	899	925	926	948	962	966	967	968
no.	1	1	1	1	2	1	1	1	1	1	1	1	2	1	1	1	5	1	2	1
mean pecks	2	2	3	3	4	2	1	2	1	3	2	1	1	1	2	2	4	5	6	4

Figure 2. Modern UK coins showing 'pecks' made by the photographed tool

the faces of the coin, which I presume were made by driving a pointed tool into the surface with a hammer. Figure 2 shows a modern scribing tool and the impact made by it on two modern UK coins. One of these coins is plated (a practice the UK mint adopted in the 1990s) and though this may not be apparent in the photograph a small silverish dot revealing the steel core is apparent in the centre of the pecks.

These pecks were made by applying a series of relatively light taps with a hammer on the scribing tool. The depth of the peck, and its diameter, is a function simply of the number of blows. This is not the only method by which a circular indentation could be made in a coin—for example, Deyell notes the use of a drill on Jaintiapur coins (Deyell 1980)—but it seems the most likely method for the coins under discussion.

How common are pecked rupees?

The first and most obvious question to ask is how common are peck marks on coins? Unfortunately, the answer is not straightforward. Take, for example, the collection of the American Numismatic Society. Of 26 coins examined I was able to discern peck marks on photographs of 17, suggesting that approximately one third of coins were not pecked. However, the coins

in the ANS collection have been subject to a series of selections – first by dealers, then by collectors, subsequently by the ANS which chose both whether to acquire and retain them and also whether to have them photographed for distribution online (only 26 of 62 rupees on the Mantis database have images[1]).

There is good reason to think that at each of these stages there would be a tendency to select against coins with peck marks and in favour of those without marks, potentially greatly exaggerating the number of unmarked coins, and perhaps the number of coins with only a few marks. And a comparison between the ANS data and images collected from the online site zeno.ru confirmed that. Though coins on Zeno would also be subject to selection it is likely to be less pronounced than for the ANS; indeed, unmarked coins are nowhere near as common as one third. Taking just those images on which marks were discernible there were significantly more (an average of 5.8) on Zeno than on the ANS (an average of 4.8).

For this reason, I have chosen to ignore coins with no discernible marks for this paper. Figure 3 shows a histogram of the number of coins recorded with 1 or more mark. A line of best fit has been projected though the data. This would suggest that coins with no marks should constitute about one sixth of the circulating population (half the number suggested by their instance in the ANS data) but even this is likely to be an exaggeration caused by selection. The prevalence of multiple pecks on many coins suggests that unless the practice was limited (geographically, chronologically, or for a particular purpose) most circulating Suri coins would have been marked, and that the surviving unmarked examples were probably removed from circulation early and their prevalence greatly

---

[1] http://numismatics.org/search/results?q=suri%20AND%20material_facet%3A%22Silver%22

Table 4. List of coins examined on Zeno.ru and the ANS Mantis database, with attributions given in those databases

No. (zeno unless specified)	Attributions				Wgt (g)	peck marks		
	Mint	date	issuer	Goron & Goenka		side 1	side 2	total
64690	Sharifabad	946	Sher Shah	D797	11.31	0	1	1
190081	Sharifabad	946	Sher Shah	D797	11.3	3	11	14
122741		946	Sher Shah	D819	11.38	2	1	3
80072		946	Sher Shah	D819	11.3	3	2	5
ANS 1974.26.1608		947	Sher Shah		11.19	0	1	1
64204		947	Sher Shah	D809	11.14	0	3	3
ANS 1974.26.1595		947	Sher Shah		11.3	1	4	5
64703		947	Sher Shah	D809	10.95	5	2	7
ANS 1973.56.382		947	Sher Shah		11.38	4	3	7
64492	Shergarh	948	Sher Shah	D802	10.79	5	8	13
64202		948	Sher Shah	D819	11.3	1	1	2
40229		948	Sher Shah	D818	11.4	1	1	2
64491		948	Sher Shah	D809	11.12	4	3	7
31375		948	Sher Shah	D816	11.3	6	1	7
190115		948	Sher Shah	D816	10.99	6	4	10
160922		948	Sher Shah	D819A	5.22	7	5	12
64702	-	949	Sher Shah	D827	11.23	3	2	5
248655	-	949	Sher Shah	D829	11.11	7	5	12
208224	Agra	949	Sher Shah	D770	11.43	0	1	1
80070	Agra	949	Sher Shah	D770	11.1	5	4	9
161219	Chunar	949	Sher Shah	D776	11.39	3	1	4
ANS 1917.215.3787	Chunar	949	Sher Shah		10.78	4	7	11
251675	Delhi	949	Sher Shah	D806		5	3	8
127395	Gwalior	949	Sher Shah	D781	11?	2	2	4
71300	Gwalior	949	Sher Shah	D781	11.2	1	3	4
ANS 1974 26 1604	Jahanpanah	949	Sher Shah		10.91	6	12	18
134379	Kalpi	949	Sher Shah	D785	11.4	1	2	3
127394	Kalpi	949	Sher Shah	D783	11.3	3	2	5
ANS 1974 26 1598	Kalpi	949	Sher Shah		11.16	3	5	8
248656	Kalpi	949	Sher Shah	D784	11.35	5	5	10
32178	Sharifabad	949	Sher Shah	D798	11?	2	4	6
64206		949	Sher Shah	D827	11.09	0	1	1
184876		949	Sher Shah	D825	11?	0	1	1
64379		949	Sher Shah	D825	11.34	0	1	1
64494		949	Sher Shah	D812	11.34	1	1	2
48670		949	Sher Shah	D813	5.31	1	1	2
ANS 1973.56.381		949	Sher Shah		11.39	1	3	4
32213		949	Sher Shah	D827	11.4	2	3	5
251969		949	Sher Shah	D826	11.35	3	4	7
132687		949	Sher Shah	D827	11?	4	6	10
104809	Agra	950	Sher Shah	D770	11.2	3	2	5
160928	Hisar	950	Sher Shah	D782	11.31	5	6	11
66739	Patna	950	Sher Shah	D795	11.04	6	4	10
211761	Shergarh Bakar	950	Sher Shah	D804	11.28	4	4	8
126959	Shergarh Delhi	950	Sher Shah	D806		5	5	10
64691		950	Sher Shah	D826	10.31	0	1	1
32176		950	Sher Shah	D826	11.3	1	1	2
64708		950	Sher Shah	D827	11.35	2	3	5
97674		950	Sher Shah	D812	10.77	2	3	5

No. (zeno unless specified)	Attributions				Wgt (g)	peck marks		
	Mint	date	issuer	Goron & Goenka		side 1	side 2	total
160929		950	Sher Shah	D813	5.43	3	3	6
231563		950	Sher Shah	D812	11.19	4	2	6
223172		950	Sher Shah	D827	11.26	4	3	7
248657		950	Sher Shah		10.79	3	4	7
202907	Agra	951	Sher Shah	D770	10.9	4	4	8
208233	Gwalior	951	Sher Shah	D781	11.44	0	1	1
2031	Gwalior	951	Sher Shah	D781	11.14	0	2	2
40228	Gwalior	951	Sher Shah	D781	11.4	1	2	3
80071	Gwalior	951	Sher Shah	D781	11.2	0	5	5
10626	Gwalior	951	Sher Shah	D781	11?	5	7	12
64380	Sharifabad	951	Sher Shah	D798	11.28	5	5	10
151541	Shergarh Bakar	951	Sher Shah	D804	11.2	1	1	2
ANS 1917.215.3789		951	Sher Shah		11.09	0	1	1
40230		951	Sher Shah	D827	11.4	0	2	2
120311		951	Sher Shah	D826	11.2	6	4	10
184922	Agra	952	Sher Shah	D770	10.92	1	2	3
160927	Fathabad	952	Islam Shah	D959	11.26	5	5	10
31376	Gwalior	952	Islam Shah	D961	11.3	0	1	1
208474	Gwalior	952	Islam Shah	D961	11.44	2	1	3
64207	Gwalior	952	Islam Shah	D961	11.31	2	1	3
29256	Gwalior	952	Sher Shah	D781	11.5	2	2	4
32271	Gwalior	952	Sher Shah	D781	11.3	5	3	8
208475	Kalpi	952	Islam Shah	D962	11.07	6	3	9
274291	Sharifabad	952	Islam Shah	D790	11.22	5	8	13
127361	Shergarh Bakar	952	Sher Shah	D804	11?	2	3	5
61743		952	Islam Shah	D980	11.23	2	3	5
236633	Biana	953	Islam Shah	D956	11.37	6	3	9
ANS 1974.26.1632	Satganu	953	Islam Shah		10.27	2	3	5
178368	Satgaon	953	Islam Shah	D969	11.2	1	0	1
ANS 1974.26.1633	Sharifabad	953	Islam Shah		11.09	1	0	1
10673		953	Islam Shah	D980	11?	1	1	2
29254		953	Islam Shah	D980	11.1	7	6	13
64712	-	954	Islam Shah		8.86	2	3	5
134498	-	954	Islam Shah	D980	11?	3	6	9
64693	-	954	Islam Shah	D982	11.15	5	8	13
69190	Kalpi	954	Islam Shah	D962	11?	3	2	5
29255	Shergarh Bakar	954	Islam Shah	D975	11.5	2	0	2
ANS 1917.216.3920	Shirgadh urf Shiqq Bakkar	954	Islam Shah		10.65	3	1	4
64716		954	Islam Shah	D980	11.02	2	1	3
ANS 1917.216.3923		954	Islam Shah		11.18	1	3	4
176471	-	955	Islam Shah	D980	11?	1	1	2
64713	-	955	Islam Shah	D980	11.29	1	3	4
223170	-	955	Islam Shah	D980	11.31	8	5	13
127357		955	Islam Shah	D978	11?	11	10	21
64714	-	956	Islam Shah	D983	11.48	0	1	1
132771	-	956	Islam Shah	D980	11.34	0	1	1
70863	-	956	Islam Shah	D980	11.4	1	0	1
115803	-	956	Islam Shah		11?	2	0	2

No. (zeno unless specified)	Attributions				Wgt (g)	peck marks		
	Mint	date	issuer	Goron & Goenka		side 1	side 2	total
160930	-	956	Islam Shah	D984	5.7	1	2	3
144236	Kalpi	956	Islam Shah	D962	11.44	1	1	2
ANS 1917.216.3922		956	Islam Shah		11.4	2	1	3
190361	Gwalior	957	Islam Shah	961A	11.4	2	4	6
112719		957	Islam Shah	D980	11?	0	4	4
145196	-	958	Islam Shah	D980	10.56	2	1	3
64711	-	958	Islam Shah	D980	11.13	3	2	5
64376	-	958	Islam Shah		11.22	1	4	5
96301		958	Islam Shah	D980	11.37	3	4	7
32303		958	Islam Shah	D980	11?	3	5	8
10674		958	Islam Shah	D980	11?	7	3	10
64372	Gwalior	959	Islam Shah	D961	11.38	5	5	10
56425	Shergarh Bakar	959	Islam Shah	D975	11.44	1	2	3
39039		959	Islam Shah	D980	11.2	3	4	7
236670		959	Islam Shah	D975	11.37	3	4	7
226148		959	Islam Shah	D980	11.3	8	5	13
196909	-	960	Islam Shah	961A	11.3	1	4	5
70864	-	960	Islam Shah		11.4	6	4	10
64374	Narnol	960	Islam Shah	D965	11.42	3	5	8
ANS 1938.50.56		960	Islam Shah		11.28	1	0	1
64697	-	961	Adil Shah D1105		11.02	2	0	2
48761	Lahore	961	Sikandar Shah (D1150)	D1150	11.35	2	4	6
64698	Narnol	961	Adil Shah D1100		11.5	1	2	3
64696	Narnol	961	Adil Shah D1100		11.39	2	3	5
ANS 1974.26.1650		961	Adil Shah		11.02	1	1	2
131278	Agra	962	Sikander Shah (D1151)		11?	1	2	3
48675	Delhi	962	Ibrahim Shah		11.49	2	1	3
232401	Lahore	962	Sikander Shah (D1150)	D1150	11.32	1	0	1
ANS 1974.26.1658	Lahore	962	Sikander III		11.077	1	1	2
115804	Lahore	962	Sikander Shah (D1150)	D1150	11?	5	4	9
224543	Gwalior	963	Adil Shah (D1097)	D1097	11.16	6	9	15
115802	Kalpi	963	Adil Shah D1099		11?	6	4	10
160906	Prayag	963	Adil Shah		11.39	3	3	6
160913	Jaunpur	964	Adil Shah D1098A	D1098A	11.35	2	1	3
160926	Jhusi	964	Adil Shah D1098	D1098	11.26	2	2	4
160908	Banaras	962?	Ibrahim Shah		10.51	1	3	4
ANS 1974.26.1600	Delhi		Sher Shah		11.11	4	1	5
112720	Gwalior?		Islam Shah	D961	11?	1	0	1
160916			Sher Shah	D810	5.69	2	0	2
103234			Sher Shah	D812	10.93	4	2	6
77756			Sher Shah	D820	11.5	2	6	8

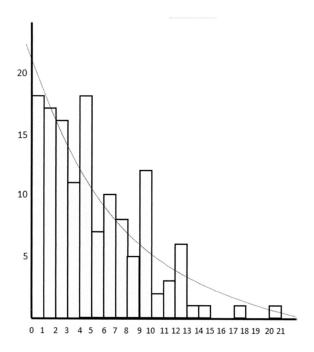

Figure 3. Histogram showing number of examples of Suri silver coins with one or more marks

exaggerated by modern collecting and institutional practice.

Which raises the question of whether the practice of pecking coins was associated with a particular, time, place, of function. Unfortunately, it is hard to identify any geographic distribution. Mint names on the coins, shown in Map 1, are a poor guide to where the coins circulated. In most cases the sample is simply too small to compensate for the effect of any single coin having an unusually large or small number of marks, and it is surprisingly difficult to get accurate mint attributions when the literature disagrees about the location of major mints.

Figure 4 seems to suggest that there is a tendency to find more marks on coins from mints located towards the south-east of Sher Shah's domain. However, there are no mints from which the marks are entirely absent, so while this requires further examination it does not suggest the marks were exclusively made in one province.

Almost all Suri silver coins are dated, usually quite clearly, from AH 946 to AH 964 (roughly 1539–1558 CE), so it is relatively easy to check if the practice changed over time, and as Table 3 indicates it does not seem to have done so.

Typically, coins from each year average 5 to 6 marks per coin, with those years in which an aberrantly high

average (such as AH 955 or AH 963) is seen are those years from which few coins have been examined. The very low number of marks on coins in AH 956 is curious but there are a variety of possibilities, such as an unreported hoard, which might explain it.

Over-all these results indicate that there was no strong geographic or chronological pattern. This in itself is an interesting result, suggesting that the practice of pecking occurred throughout Suri territory and throughout the approximately 20 years of their rule without dramatic change. That requires either that it was already a widespread cultural and economic practice before they assumed power or that it was introduced (or expanded) by an agent with reach and authority, presumably not a shroff or even a small group of shroffs. Such marks are almost entirely absent from the coinage of the Lodis, who preceded the Suris as Sultans of Delhi, which tells against this being a widespread and long-established practice, and suggests it was introduced through a powerful political agent.

Marks on the coins of the Bengal Sultanates

As noted above, quoting Deyell (2020), the coins of the Bengal Sultanates are also well known for featuring a similar range of marks as those just discussed for the Suris. The rupee of the Suris is clearly based on the standard tanka denomination of Bengal, and as Sher Shah Suri was a governor for the Mughals in their eastern provinces it might be reasonable to expect that the peck marks on Suri coins were an adoption of a pre-existing Bengal system.

Zeno.ru curates its entries for the Bengal Sultanates using the catalogue of Goron and Goenka (2001), which makes it a particularly convenient corpus of this coinage. From 329 entries on Zeno.ru I was able to identify 53 coins with a peck mark. Note that Bengal Sultanate coins frequently feature other types of marks, graffiti in the form of small scratches, slashes or gouges into the surface of the coin, and punches with symbolic designs. These are all deserving of study but as round peck marks are the current focus of discussion and graffiti, slashes, and gouges, seem to be rare on Suri coins I have excluded them.

The peck marks on Bengal Sultanate coins fall into distinct chronological groups as indicated in Table 4, though occasional marks are found throughout the series on gold coins. The later group of coins, from the mid-sixteenth century mostly post-date the Suri coins and are undoubtedly either an extension of that system or simply Bengali coins that passed into the circulation zone in which the Suri coins operated. The earlier group, from the early fourteenth century, cannot be a

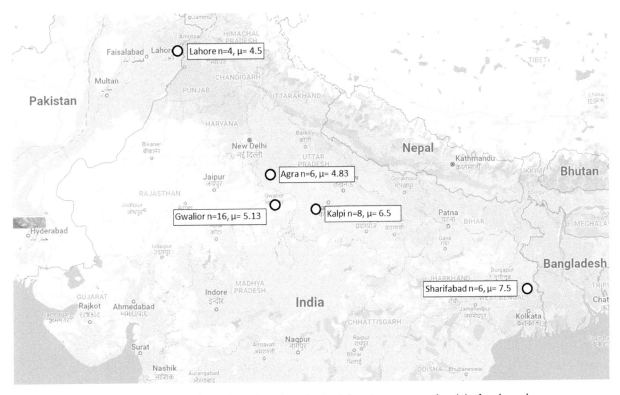

Figure 4. Suri mints with number of attributed coins (n) and average number (μ) of peck marks

precursor to the system used on Suri coins because the practice markedly differs.

Figures 5 and 6 illustrate the difference between the fourteenth century Bengali practice and that found on the Suri coins of the sixteenth. The fourteenth century Bengali marks tend to be fewer in number and tend to be larger. Whether the size of the pecks depends on the tool used or the distance it is driven into the surface is unclear. This could be determined by taking casts of the peck marks and measuring them but is not clear from photographs. The marks on the Bengali coins are also almost exclusively restricted to the same face, while the marks on Suri coins seem to have been distributed relatively evenly between obverse and reverse (whether this was deliberate is unclear).

Though pecks are a very simple marking of a coin, with the apparently simple function of breaking the surface to facilitate checking the core of the coin, they could be deployed within a wide variety of social, economic, and political contexts. And explanations for their use on Suri coins need to encompass why, apparently, virtually all coins were checked, most coins were checked multiple times, and why/how this practice was enforced across the whole of north India, for at least several decades.

A personal anecdote of dubious methodological validity

Although applying modern-day experiences to explain historical phenomena often leads to false conclusions, I will introduce a personal anecdote here, which I believe is helpful to illustrate why such a system might have operated. In 2008 the mint in the United Kingdom introduced new designs for coins and shortly thereafter extended the use of plated steel to the 5p and 10p coins. This necessitated altering the design subtly again, reducing the relief to compensate for the new material. As is normal, such coins did not enter circulation immediately or entirely replace the existing coinage, and in some regions they arrived more slowly than others. My mother, who lives in the north of England, had one of the new coins refused by a market trader on the grounds it was not a UK coin but 'some weird European thing'. It is hard to mistake a coin featuring the Queen of England and the royal arms of the UK as a European coin, but that was not what really happened here.

Joe has discussed this phenomenon under the term 'coinage tradition' (Cribb 2003, 2007a). Coin design serves the monetary function of coins by playing

Figure 5. Silver Tanka of Shams al-Din Ilyas Shah, issued in AH 754 (ANS 1924.26.1660, 10.52 g, 25 mm)

Figure 6. Silver Rupee of Sher Shah Suri (ANS 1974.26.1598, 11.16 g, 27 mm)

on familiarity. Users trust familiarity and suspect novelty. The market trader, presumably unfamiliar with numismatic theory, was expressing this distrust of novelty, explaining his rejection of the coin by attributing it to an imagined foreign/other influence. The explanation was a post-hoc rationalisation for the fear the lack of familiarity created – that he might not be able to pass on the coin again having accepted it. The Suri silver coinage followed a series of monetary changes that were likely to have had a similar impact on confidence.

In 1526 CE Babur defeated Ibrahim Lodi at the battle of Panipat and effectively displaced the Lodi dynasty, establishing the Mughal empire. Babur's coinage has already been subject to a detailed analysis, including a die study (ur Rahman 2005) which I will use here. Babur's silver coinage, the shah rukhi, is a wide thin flanned coin, weighing 4 to 5 g. It replaced the Lodi coinage, a dumpy silver tanka weighing 8 to 10 g, and in turn was largely displaced by Sher Shah's rupees, which are thick but wider than the tanka and weigh 10 to 11 g. Over a period of only 30 years, a single lifetime, the silver coinage, and the authority backing it in northern India changed dramatically several times. This marks a

break in the local coinage tradition even though many of the changes are simply the result of importing coin types known in other regions such as Central Asia and Bengal. The break will have undermined the trust of users in the coins.

Unsurprisingly, although peck marks are largely absent from Lodi coins they do appear on Babur's coinage. There is a common pattern across the coinage but as ur Rahman convincingly argues (2005: 52) the bulk was issued from Kabul and late in his reign (regardless of the mint and date marks), so likely circulated in common. However, the pattern on Babur's coinage is very different to the subsequent pattern on the coinage of the Suris. In some cases ur Rahman uses line drawings, which would not record pecks, and in others he digitally enhances the legend, which can obscure a peck. With these two caveats, of approximately 260 imaged coins in his catalogue, 104 have at least one identifiable peck mark, but only 6 have two marks (29-04, 63-03, 110-01, 110-11, 111-03, 116-01), and just 2 have four marks (50-02, 70-04).

This is precisely the pattern that would be expected if users were genuinely concerned with widespread plating (real or imagined). If concerned with plated forgeries it would make sense to test suspect coins, but only rarely would it be warranted to test a coin which had already been tested, and this is the pattern seen with Babur's coins: the majority are unpecked, and the pecked coins are overwhelmingly pecked only once.

Ur Rahman notes two plated contemporary imitations, one of which (119-08) has a single peck mark which would have revealed its core. The other (119-09) seems not to be pecked. Instead, a similar tool has been used to make two piercings, probably intended to thread the object as part of a piece of jewellery, and likely indicating it was never intended to fool anyone. This is hardly evidence of widespread forgery.

In other words, it is possible that the pecks were a response to an imagined rather than a real problem.

A working hypothesis for sixteenth century pecks

It will be useful to form a working hypothesis on this preliminary data. Such a hypothesis might prove to be unfounded but it is useful to have a scenario to test with future data. My working assumption is that the peck marks found so extensively on the silver coinage of the Suris served primarily as a psychological crutch to encourage a confidence lacking due to the absence of familiarity and the dubious authority the issuers would have enjoyed in a fragmenting and unstable monetary and political situation.

It is likely that the marks began to appear as an already known method for testing if a coin was plated. However, the danger that they were testing for, plated forgeries, was an imagined rather than a real problem, a sort of displacement in which users expressed their lack of comfort caused by novelty and shifts of authority through an abstracted other—a forgery—similar to the market trader's designation of a UK coin as 'European' in my anecdote.

Initially, under Babur, the pecking took on a form suited to the task of testing, but soon the practice of pecking abandoned any pretence of actual testing. Those administering the pecks likely knew this. There can have been little point in testing a coin that had already been checked half a dozen times, and in any case anyone routinely applying the test would know how rarely they encountered an actual forgery. Rather the ritual of pecking and the visual reassurance of the peck marks would have acted as authorities to back the circulation in their own right. Ironically, this is almost exactly the opposite of the assumption that peck marks devalued coins which seems appealing and reasonable when first considering them (see the remark by Bhandare at the beginning of the article)

Who administered this activity? That is a much harder question to answer, but the answer is more likely to be a bureaucratic agent, such as market managers, tax collectors, local officials, rather than a private agent, such as money changers or bankers (the 'shroffs'). It would have been hard for the practice of private agents to spread so widely so quickly and to have remained consistent, but relatively easy for administrators or bureaucrats. Whether it constituted a deliberate act of policy or a pragmatic response to widespread problems is unclear, but it is possible that it had a lasting effect, refocusing the perceived authority which created trust in the coinage away from the state, as personified by the king, and towards more local functionaries, a feature that the British seem to have remarked on when they complained of the power of 'shroffs' in monetary affairs (see Lucassen 2018: 344-5; examples abound in Stevens 2019).

Part 2: The shroff marks

Having argued that shroffs, in the sense of private money changers or bankers, were unlikely to be responsible for the proliferation of peck marks on sixteenth century coins, I intend to reserve the term for a different type of mark, which also seems to appear with the introduction of the rupee, and to persist in use until the British period. These are small punches with distinctive symbols applied to the edges of the coins. They differ from the marks I referred to previously on Bengal Sultanate coinage as 'punch' marks because they are usually smaller and applied to the edge. This application to the edge is itself a curious feature, as it must have posed practical difficulties, and it is not clear why the obverse or reverse, often pecked, were avoided.

Occasionally a mark on the edge will take the form of a cut, presumably made by drawing a blade across it. These edge cuts may have served as tests of some sort, though there is no obvious advantage over a peck mark. However, the shroff marks could not have served as a useful test. They are usually shallow and it is unlikely they would have revealed plating or surface enrichment. See Figure 7 for examples of these marks.

The peck marks on this coin, five in total, are marked with white circles. Images of the shroff marks are arranged at the approximate position they occur around the edge. As can be seen some marks are small enough to be entirely encompassed by the edge while others are only partially visible. Most are relatively simple, but some are more complex. A second example showing a further range of marks is illustrated in Figure 8.

Note that in Figure 8 there are several repetitions of the same punch. The punch consisting of seven dots at 8

Figure 7. Silver Rupee of Sher Shah Suri (BM 1911,0709.2349; 11.12 g; 27 mm; 4h)

Figure 8. Silver Rupee of Sher Shah Suri (BM 1853,0301.754)

and 11 o'clock are probably the same tool, as are the single dot punches at 6 and 11 o'clock. If the design of the punches, rather than the specific tool, identify a person or institution there are several more repetitions.

What were these marks for? Who made them? And why?

Unfortunately, I have not looked at enough coins to offer any answers to these questions or to suggest a hypothesis. Presumably there would be patterns if enough coins were examined, as was apparent with the peck marks. For the moment, I will offer a few preliminary thoughts.

The shroff marks are not as prolific as the peck marks. It is common to encounter a pecked coin with no shroff marks but I have not yet encountered a coin with shroff marks on the edge but no pecks. This suggests either that the practice began at a later time and some pecked coins had left circulation before the shroff marking started, or, and this seems more likely, that the shroff marks were a more restricted practice, perhaps geographically.

Though the marks do not occur on as large a proportion of coins as the pecks they often outnumber the pecks

on the same coin. While we would need a much larger dataset to explore this properly, it implies that the process which necessitated the application of a shroff mark occurred more frequently than that which required a peck mark. It is worth noting that these coins remained in circulation for decades, and so even coins which have accumulated 20 to 30 marks, such as Figure 8, would likely be accumulating marks less frequently than once a year. Clearly, shroff marks were not made at every transaction but on a very limited number of occasions.

Finally, there is the question of identifiability. The shroff marks tend to be evenly distributed around the edge of the coin, and infrequently overlap. The punches seem to have been designed to be small enough to fit onto the edge, or at least mostly fit onto the edge. And there are multiple designs (at least eleven on the two coins illustrated). This all suggests that the marks were intended to be identifiable, that whatever purpose was served it in part worked on an assumption that a future user would be able to examine the marks and glean some useful information from them. It is partly this set of related features which justify, without presupposing who made the marks, the use of the term shroff – it seems likely that the symbols were intended to identify the particular people or institutions responsible for them.

Conclusion

This paper has presented a few reflections on some of the marking systems used on sixteenth century silver coins in northern India. The range of such marks is substantial—counter marks, for example, are common but have not been discussed here. Excluding those counter marks overtly associated with a political authority, it is true to say that punches, pecks, edge cuts, and shroffs marks, have received little attention in the existing literature. This is a pity because they represent one of the most interesting pieces of evidence for the monetary history of early modern India. The rupee was part of a sophisticated system of economic exchange and the marks upon the coins record their interaction with that system. The marks record what happened to the coin between its production, as revealed by conventional numismatic classification, and their deposition, as revealed through hoards and other finds. They deserve closer examination.

I have only been able to sketch out a few ideas in this paper. I need, as Joe would advise, to look at more coins. There are some obvious avenues of research that can be pursued, some of which I plan to take up myself and some I hope others will take up in the future. The simplest is to extend the dataset. This can be done in several ways. First, by extending the data to incorporate hoards which, with their tighter grouping of coins with a similar date of deposition and geographic circulation, might reveal more nuanced patterns in the use of these marks. Second, there is a need to prepare a catalogue of the shroff marks—if the marks can be associated with individuals or institutions this will only be apparent through a catalogue. Third, the same initial examination here could be extended chronologically or geographically. Comparison between Suri coins and those of Akbar would undoubtedly give valuable results. Fourth, there would be substantial value in taking casts of the peck marks. As illustrated in Figure 7, the same tool was sometimes employed to make multiple shroff marks on the same coins (at different times?) but is this true for peck marks? The tools used for pecks are essentially indistinguishable in photographs—it is impossible to tell how wide they were, or how deep they were hammered, though this would be easily discernible with casts. Finally, there is clearly a need for some experimental work. It remains unclear to me how

in practice marks were applied to the edge of the coins, which seems a cumbersome and awkward task.

All of this leaves ample opportunity for looking at coins.

References

Bracey, R. 2019. Propaganda and Function *Historical Perspective 2*, viewed Dec 2021, https://youtu.be/TwfMgeujQt4

Carrier, C., Artru, J. and Faucher, T. 2021. Observing Coins to Learn about Greek Coin Production. *American Numismatic Society*. viewed Dec 2021, https://www.youtube.com/watch?v=wG1ZXoma2p8

Cribb, J. 1983a. Investigating the Introduction of Coinage in India, a Review of Recent Research. *Journal of the Numismatic Society of India* 45: 80-101.

Cribb, J. 1983b. Dating India's Earliest Coins. *South Asian Archaeology 1983*: 535-54.

Cribb, J. 2003. The Origins of the Indian Coinage Tradition. *South Asian Studies* 19, 1: 1-19.

Cribb, J. 2005. Money as Metaphor 1. *Numismatic Chronicle* 165: 417-438.

Cribb, J. 2006. Money as Metaphor 2. *Numismatic Chronicle* 166: 493-517.

Cribb, J. 2007a. Money as a Marker of Cultural Continuity and Change in Central Asia, in J. Cribb and G. Herrmann (eds), *After Alexander: Central Asia before Islam*: 333-75. London: British Academy.

Cribb, J. 2007b Money as Metaphor 3. *Numismatic Chronicle* 167: 361-395.

Cribb, J. 2009. Money as Metaphor 4. *Numismatic Chronicle*, 169: 461-529.

Deyell, J. 1980. Was There a Date Code in Jaintiapur Coinage. *Numismatic Digest*, vol. 4, 2: 45-54.

Deyell, J.S. 2010. Cowries and Coins. *Indian Economic and Social History Review* 47, 1: 63-106.

Goron, S. and Goenka, J.P. 2001. *The Coins of the Indian Sultanates Covering the Areas of Present Day India, Pakistan and Bangladesh*. New Delhi: Munshiram Manoharlal Publishers Pvt. Ltd.

Lucassen, J. 2018. Labour and Deep Monetization in Eurasia, 1000 to 1900, in K. Hofmeester and P. de Zwart (eds), *Colonialism, Institutional Change, and Shifts in Global Labour Relations*: 327-360. Amsterdam: Amsterdam University Press.

ur Rahman, A. 2005. *Zahir-uddin Muhammad Babur: A Numismatic Study*. Azamgarh.

Stevens, P. 2019. *The Coinage of the Bombay Presidency: a Study of the Records of the EIC*, London: Spink & Son.

Henry Ernest Stapleton and the Coin Collection in the Heberden Coin Room, Ashmolean Museum, Oxford: Impact, Importance and Insight

Sutapa Sinha

The collection of coins issued by the Governors and Sultans of Bengal (1205-1576AD) preserved in the Heberden Coin Room of the Ashmolean Museum was first published by the present author in 2010 in a descriptive manner.[1] As we analysed the history of the collection for the above series it became apparent that, unlike the British Museum, whose collection was formed in the 18th and 19th century, the majority of the Ashmolean Museum collection was developed in the 20th century, more specifically after the independence of India in 1947. The new coin cabinet of the Ashmolean Museum was formally opened on 24 October 1922 and was named after Charles Buller Heberden (1849–1921), a classical scholar and Principal of Brasenose College from 1889 until his death. The original coin collection of the Ashmolean Museum, formerly preserved in the Old Bodleian Library, Oxford, was transferred to the newly opened coin room in 1922 (Sinha 2010: 163-64).

In 1888, Stanley Lane-Poole published a catalogue of coins of the Bodleian Library, Oxford[2] which included only 19 coins in the section 'Kings of Bengal'. Of these 19, six were from Mr J.B. Elliot's collection, acquired in 1859, and a single specimen was from the collection of Lady Frere, purchased in 1872. For the remaining twelve coins, no particulars of acquisition are known.[3] After the publication of Lane-Poole's catalogue, two more coins of this series were added to the collection through the gift of Reverend J.C. Murray. In 1911, W.E.M. Campbell donated a single coin of this series to the museum along with coins of other series. Altogether19 coins of Islamic rulers of medieval Bengal were in the custody of the

Bodleian Library in 1922. Along with the coins of many other series, these were transferred to their permanent location at the newly opened Heberden coin room in 1922.

It was to our utter surprise that after opening of the new coin room, not a single specimen of the Bengal Sultan series was acquired by the Museum until 1956 when Dr Henry Ernest Stapleton (1878-1962), a retired officer of the Bengal Education Service, deposited a huge number of coins to the Heberden coin room, intended as a future bequest. At this point, 349 coins of the Governors and Sultans of Bengal, including a few coins of the Delhi Sultans struck at Bengal mints, were added to the Bengal Sultans section of the coin room. After this acquisition, the Heberden coin room bought one coin from Richard Burn in 1962, and one from Lord Minto in 1964. Another 69 coins were purchased from P. Thorburn in 1969. In 1970, Mr R. Friel, Curator of the Shillong cabinet, gifted seven coins to the Museum and in 1989, the most recent addition to the collection of coins of the Bengal Sultans was a bequest of four coins from A.W. Pullan. Further details of the history of the collection of the Bengal Sultan series of coins in the Heberden coin room and its trend of acquisition since the 19th century can be found in the present author's article (Sinha 2010: 164).[4]

In 1998, the present author visited the coin room of the Ashmolean Museum in order to study and document the coin collection as part of her project on the coin hoards and finds of the Bengal Sultans preserved in public collections in India and abroad. When she enquired about accession records for this part of the collection, she was provided with a hand-written inventory prepared by H.E. Stapleton himself before he bequeathed his collection to the museum.[5] In the present article, she intends to analyse Stapleton's inventory, which is full of very useful information about the source and provenance of many of the coins in his collection issued by the early Bengal Governors,

---

[1] See Sinha 2010. This article is an outcome of the author's first visit to the Heberden Coin room of the Ashmolean Museum, Oxford in July 1998 in connection with her project on the study of coin hoards and finds of the Bengal Sultans. Sinha was selected as UK visiting fellow in 1998 and she is much indebted to the Nehru Trust for Indian Collection at the Victoria and Albert Museum, London for sponsoring her entire trip of four months in the UK. She is especially thankful to Dr Luke Treadwell, the then Curator of the Islamic Coins to provide her a slot of one week to study and photo-document the coin collection of the Bengal Governors and Sultans preserved in the coin room.

[2] Lane-Poole (1888: 25) described in short only nineteen coins, no. 573 to 591. In the preface, Lane-Poole mentioned that this Bodleian Library catalogue was intended to be used in connection with the Catalogue of the Department of Coins and Medals of the British Museum, London.

[3] Lane-Poole 1888: xi and xiv, under *Index of Donations and Purchases,* accession details of coin nos. 573- 591 are available. This index was prepared by E.B. Nicholson, Bodley's librarian. The author also noted this accession detail when she visited the Heberden Coin Room in 1998.

[4] The author gathered all this accession-related information of the coin collection of the Heberden Coin in July 1998 during her sojourn in Oxford.

[5] The photocopy of relevant section "Sultans of Bengal' of the said inventory was kindly provided to the author by the then Curator of Islamic Coins of the museum, Dr Luke Treadwell. She remains much indebted and thankful to him, otherwise this research would remain incomplete.

Delhi Sultans, Sultans of Bengal, Mughal Emperors, Suri Sultan and Afghan Sultans of Bengal. Here we need to keep in mind that this collection might have been built up during two phases of his posting in Bengal; first as Inspector of the Bengal Education Service till 1915, and after the war as the Professor of Chemistry and Principal of the Presidency College, Calcutta from 1919 to his retirement in 1933.

This paper has been prepared in honour of Joe Cribb, Keeper of the Department of Coins and Medals, at the British Museum (2003–2009), an erudite scholar and one of the greatest numismatists of the century, who has always inspired the present author to delve deep into the study of the collection history of coins deposited in public collections in the UK that were developed during the colonial and post-colonial period. It is the present author's sincere attempt to pay a befitting tribute to Joe.

H.E. Stapleton's Inventory of the Coins of the Governors and Sultans of Bengal

The section on the 'Sultans of Bengal' starts on the fourth page of Stapleton's inventory and continues for the next 29 legal-size ruled pages until the beginning of the description of coins of the 'Bahamanis of Kulbarga'. The manuscript of the inventory is written in English with coin legends written in Arabic language and *Nashq* script as neatly as in a text-book, with a serial number for each and every entry.[6] Hence, coins under the section 'Sultans of Bengal' start with no. 137 and end with no. 493, including six coins of the Delhi Sultans of the early 13th century which were struck in a Bengal mint in their own names through their deputed Governors in this easterly province.

Of those six coins of Delhi, two are of gold. No. 141 is of Sultan Ala al-din Masud (639-44 AH / 1242-46 AD) and no. 142 is of Sulan Nasir al-din Mahmud (644-64 AH / 1246-66 AD). Stapleton wrote 'Wright 187A (this coin)' and 'Wright 219A (this coin)', respectively, in place of the descriptions of the coins. In the case of no. 140, a silver coin of Jalalat al-din Raziya, Stapleton noted 'Wright 161c' on the extreme right of the entry, referring to no. 161c in H.N. Wright's *Catalogue on the Sultans of Delhi* (1936) as being of a similar type. But in the case of the two gold coins, nos. 141 and 142, Stapleton did not refer to Wright's catalogue for a type reference but made it clear that they were the same coins already published by Wright in his catalogue as nos. 187A and 219A.[7] At the time of publication in 1936, Wright mentioned that

the two coins in question were in the Dacca Museum and gave a reference to their publication in 1910. In the preface, Wright clearly noted that 'the gold and silver coins (58AV -223 AR) were acquired by the Director-General of Archaeology in India for the Delhi Museum.' There is some ambiguity as to how Stapleton got hold of these two gold coins of the Delhi Sultans which had already been catalogued, published and preserved in a public collection. Stapleton also furnished a note below no. 142, a coin of Nasir al-din Mahmud (Wright 219A) which reads as follows:

> E. Thomas, Initial Coinage of Bengal, p. 29, deduces from the fact that this coin bears the name of the Caliph al-Mustansir (640 AH) that it must be an issue of the first prince of this name, governor of Bengal under Iltutmish. This view finds some support from the close similarity of the design to that of the issues of Yuzbak, governor of Bengal, IMC II.

Stapleton tried to record as meticulously as possible the provenance of the specimens that he collected for his own collection or for the collection of the coin cabinet of Eastern Bengal and Assam, which he published in 1911. Herein lies the greatest importance of this detailed inventory, which not only mentioned the typology and other numismatic details but also recorded the source and reference meticulously as and where applicable. We have retrieved at least ten place names, pinpointing the findspots of coin hoards or small finds, mostly found in what was then Eastern Bengal, which tend to match coin hoards and finds of the Sultans and governors of Bengal recovered since 1898, which the present author has studied, compiled and published twice (Sinha 2001; Sinha 2017). Stapleton's inventory can be used as a supplement to the previous research of the coin hoards and finds of the governors and Sultans of Bengal.

No. 139 in the inventory is a silver coin of Rukn al-din Firuz, another Sultan of Delhi (633-34 AH / 1235-36 AD) dated 634 AH and may belong to the Purinda find. Stapleton marks it as such but prefixes it with a question mark. The Purinda find was discovered in 1910 and subsequently found its way to the Provincial Cabinet of Coins in Assam.[8] On a cross check of the details of the Purinda find, we discovered 5 silver coins of Rukn al-din Kaikaus and 19 silver coins of Shams al-din Firuz Shah. The earliest dated coin of Kaikaus is of 693 AH with the mint name Lakhnauti. If we have to take this coin (no. 139) of Stapleton's inventory into account, we have to revise the content analysis of the said coin hoard (Sinha 2017: 183-86) that was based on the *Suppl. Shillong.* We do not have any scope to doubt Stapleton's reading of the name of the Sultan '*Rukn al-din Firuz*', although this

---

[6] For obvious/unavoidable reason, neither reproduction of any page of the inventory nor photograph of any coins mentioned in the text is provided here.

[7] Wright 1936: 46 and 58 respectively. Wright in his catalogue mentioned that both of these coins (nos 187A and 219A) are now in Dacca Museum. See also Stapleton 1910: 149.

[8] This Purinda find was published in catalogue form in Botham and Friel 1919, henceforth referred as *Suppl. Shillong.*

would make the earliest dated coin in the Purinda find one issued by Delhi Sultan Rukn al-din Firuz dated 634 AH. However, as Stapleton himself put a question mark before the words 'Purinda find', a fair doubt remains in this case regarding the provenance of the coin.

The next page of the inventory starts with the coins of Shams al-din Firuz Shah, the Governor of Bengal who consolidated Islamic rule in Bengal in 1300 AD. In addition to Lakhnauti, two new mints came into operation during his reign. Mention of two coins (nos. 144 and 145) found at Mymensingh and one coin from the Enayetpur find (no. 150), are of particular interest. As mentioned earlier, the present author studied and analysed thoroughly all the hoards yielding coins of the Bengal Sultans and allied series unearthed since 1843 from different parts of present political boundary of West Bengal, Bangladesh, Bihar, Jharkhand and Assam, including coins preserved in public collections in India and abroad (Sinha 2017). Therefore, the inclusion of names of a few minor finds or major hoards in Stapleton's inventory, discovered more than a hundred years ago in Bengal and now preserved in the Heberden coin room, Oxford, certainly deserves special mention.

The Enayetpur find contains less than ten coins found in 1909 and was published in 1919.[9] There are two coins of Shams al-din Firuz Shah, one with the mint name Khittah Lakhnauti dated 713 AH written in words (Arabic), not numerals (Suppl. Shillong XIX/12: 136) and the other one without any mint name or date, probably because the margin is cut off the flan. Stapleton's coin no.150 can be counted as the third coin of Firuz Shah from the Enayetpur find. Stapleton read the date as (7)1[...] AH (wrtten in Arabic, not numerals) in the margin but does not give a mint name. He ascribed it to Group 2 with a cross mark (X) above the words Al-Imam of the reverse legend. Typologically, this specimen has been compared to coin no. 10 of IMC by the present author (Sinha 2017: 211).

On the same page of the inventory, there is another silver coin of Ghiyath al-din Bahadur Shah (no. 169), which is similar in type to IMC ii, No.148/14,[10] as classified by Stapleton himself, and which is also a coin from the Enayetpur find. It has the mint name Lakhnauti with epithet 'Shahr' i.e. the city. For the date, only 'sabamayah', that is the hundred unit '7'is extant, the remaining part of the margin being off the flan. In the Suppl. Shillong, four coins of Bahadur Shah found at Enayetpur in the Mymensingh district of Bangladesh are described. Hence, the question may arise how

did these coins, part of the Enayetpur find, enter the collection of Stapleton? When did he collect these coins which were unearthed as a group as treasure trove and deposited in the public collection? From his obituary written by F.H.C. Butler, we came to know that Stapleton's distinguished career was interrupted by the war and in May 1915 he was commissioned in the Indian Army Reserve and in the following September he took a draft to Mesopotamia to join the 24th Punjabis.[11] Butler also mentioned that:

> "At the end of 1919, he resumed his career in India, occupying leading positions in education which included the post of Principal of Presidency College, Calcutta, and also that of Special Officer in connection with the opening of Dacca University. He retired from the Indian Education Service in 1933, re-joining his family in Jersey, but returned to India for a spell two years later, to catalogue and advise on the preservation of manuscripts in the library of Hyderabad University."

H.E. Stapleton had a long association with the Indian Education service, especially with Bengal, which of course explains why the larger amount of his coin collection consists of coins of the Islamic rulers of Bengal. But the question of how he collected coins from the Purinda and Enayetpur finds, unearthed in 1909-1910, and subsequently deposited in, and published as a public collection, namely the Provincial Cabinet of Coin, Assam in 1919, remains unresolved. It is particularly intriguing because Stapleton was usually careful to record the provenance of coins (e.g., Stapleton 1911).

There are two coins of Shams al-din Firuz Shah (nos. 144 and 145), which Stapleton recorded as 'from Mymensingh'. On the next page, there is a single specimen of 'Muhammad ibn Tughlaq of Delhi', which Stapleton noted was struck at the Satgaon mint dated 734 A.H. which he also recorded as from the 'Mymensingh find', putting the provenance in parentheses below the description of that coin. There are six specimens of Muhammad ibn Tughlaq of Delhi in the inventory, issued from three mints: Shahr Lakhnauti, Satganu and Sunargaon were all within the jurisdiction of Bengal in the 14th-15th centuries, the mints at Satganu and Sunargaon only coming into operation after 1300 AD. According to Stapleton, all six coins are of same type, (cf. IMC, 54/328) with dates ranging from 727 to 734 A.H. Out of the four coins issued from Sunargaon mint, Stapleton read Shahr(city) prefixed with Sunargaon on the first three as a mint

[9] Botham, A.W. and Friel, R., Supplement to the Catalogue of Provincial Cabinet of Coins, Assam, Allahabad, 1919. Henceforth to be referred as Suppl. Shillong.

[10] IMC ii refers to H.N. Wright, Catalogue of the Coins in the Indian Museum, Calcutta, Vol. II, Varanasi, 1972 (reprint). Stapleton must have consulted the first edition of the Catalogue.

[11] Obituary of H.E. Stapleton collected from : (https://www.cambridge.org/core/journals/british-journal-for-the-history-of-science/article/henry-ernest-stapleton-18781962/F0753BF5E8190974A3D9ADE6B1392A08)

epithet instead of the more commonly found epithet *Hazrat Jalal* (the holy seat). Sunargaon is located very close to the present capital city of Dhaka, Bangladesh. However, the coin of Muhammad bin Tughlaq from the Mymensingh find is from the Satgaon mint dated 734 A.H. Satgaon was one of the major port towns and headquarters of southern Bengal in the 14th century.

The present author's extensive study of coin hoards and finds revealed that not a single hoard or find recovered since 1843 is known in the literature as 'the Mymensingh find.' There is one hoard of 317 silver coins which was discovered from the village of Jashodal, Station Kishoreganj, district Mymensingh (presently Kishoreganj district of Bangladesh) which was found by Girish Chandra Aich Roy of Jashodal on 27 December 1897. It was first reported in 1898 in the *Proceedings of Asiatic Society of Bengal* (Bloch 1898). The hoard has been critically analysed by the present author (Sinha 2001: 169-72; Sinha 2017: 178-183). The circumstances of its discovery and its content were thoroughly reported by T. Bloch (1898): it starts with a coin of Sikandar bin Ilyas Shah, the second independent Sultan of Bengal with a date 764 AH(?). Therefore, it is extremely unlikely that the two coins of Bengal governor Shams al-din Firuz Shah and one coin of Delhi Sultan Muhammad bin Tughlaq,#found at Mymensingh, according to Stapleton, are from the Jashodal hoard (Mymensingh district).

The Enayetpur find which Stapleton mentions is from the Mymensingh district. As a consequence, it may be assumed that the three coins described as from Mymensingh are either part of a hoard that was dispersed without being reported and published or part of the Enayetpur find but referred to by a different terminology. As Stapleton did not give the date for any of the coins he acquired in this hand-written inventory, we are in dark regarding the year or tentative time of this discovery from Mymensingh in pre-independence India.[12] Although the present author never came across with a published report or published catalogue mentioning a coin hoard or a minor find unearthed directly from the Mymensingh area during the first half of the 20th century, it is true that several treasure troves were found within the territory of Mymensingh district. As Stapleton was very particular about provenance details, the possibility of a separate and small Mymensingh find cannot be ruled out.

Coin no. 156 is of Shihab al-din Bughra Shah, the son of Shams al-din Firuz Shah, who struck silver coins in both Lakhnauti in western Bengal and Sunargaon in eastern Bengal. Stapleton wrote a detailed note on the date, style of inscription and the motif engraved above the word *Al-Imam* on the reverse of this coin. In the last line he wrote in brackets: 'Murshidabad District find, bought fm Calcutta Mint 4.12.06'. This single line renders several pieces of information: first, that this particular silver coin was found in the Murshidabad district; second, that the Calcutta Mint used to sell coins to the coin collectors; and third, that Stapleton bought this coin from that institution on 4 December 1906 for his personal collection.

It is known that around 1905–1906, a hoard of 85 silver coins was discovered in the district of Moorshidabad, without mention of any particular village (Burn 1907). It was mentioned in the report that 'Of the total number, 57 coins were in such poor condition that they were returned by Mr. Nelson Wright as useless. The remaining coins may be classified as follows...' (Burn 1907: 587). As a result, we have a description of the remaining 28 coins, without any mention of their deposition/location. It may be assumed that those coins went into the collection of either the Asiatic Society of Bengal, Calcutta or the coin cabinet of the Indian Museum, Calcutta. There were eleven coins of Shihab al-din Bughda Shah in the Moorshidabad hoard(Sinha 2017: 64-65). This fact leads us to conclude that the coin of Bughda Shah in Stapleton's collection is the twelfth one, which is presently preserved in the Ashmolean Museum's coin cabinet. That Stapleton bought this specimen from the Calcutta mint in December 1906 could easily be explained by the return of 57 of the 85 coins of Moorshidabad hoard—considered as useless because of their poor condition, they must have been sent to the Calcutta mint to be melted down. Earlier, in the case of the Cooch Behar Hoard (unearthed in 1863) and Jashodal Hoard (unearthed in 1898), we know that a significant portion of the total number of coins unearthed were sent to the Calcutta mint, either to pay the long pending revenue of princely states or simply for reuse of the noble metal.[13] In the case of the Moorshidabad find, the first-hand report by Burn (1907) did not mention specifically the disposal of the fifty-seven coins made to the Calcutta mint but study of Stapleton's inventory makes that the likely destination. Nels Wright returned 57 coins which were in poor condition. Wright's purchase from the Mint, and his viewing of this group suggests the rejected 57 coins were sent to the Calcutta mint, partly to sell a few pieces to the collectors and partly to reuse the silver content.

We should point out that Stapleton would not have collected the coin of Bughda Shah if it was in very poor

---

[12] The author would be much indebted to receive any further information regarding discovery or publication reference of this hidden small find from Mymensingh in future.

[13] The practice of sending huge number of coins recovered from hoards to Her Majesty's mint in Calcutta was mentioned by the district authority as a way to pay revenues due from the Princely State of Cooch Behar. Col Haughton mentioned this in his official report on Cooch Behar trove found in 1863 (See Sinha 2017 :47-48).

condition. In fact, the description of the coin in the said inventory showed even the last two units of the date, i.e. (7)17, were legible on the margin though the mint name was off the flan. This feature is very common in most of the silver coins of the Bengal governors and Sultans because they are manufactured by the die striking technique. Nevertheless, on the basis of the above analysis, we wonder whether 57 coins of the Moorshidabad hoard can really be considered as 'useless' or whether sending a large percentage of old silver coins to the Calcutta Royal Mint had merely become government policy in late 19th and early 20th century India to maintain ample silver supply to the mint to strike their current coinage! This needs further research.

In chronological sequence, the next coins are those of Fakhr al-din Mubarak Shah, the first independent sultan of Eastern Bengal who established his capital in Sunargaon, very close to the modern capital city of Dhaka. Five coins of Fakhr al-din Mubarak Shah (nos. 186-190) are 'from Sylhet find (1913)', as Stapleton wrote at the end of the entry for no. 190. All five coins are of the same type and were struck from the same mint of the capital city Sunargaon with a mint epithet *Hazrat Jalal* (the holy seat). All five coins retain the entire reverse marginal legend and each has a different date on it: AH745, 746, 747, 748 and 750, which means all these specimens of the Sylhet find are in good condition with a nicely preserved margin legend.

There are two more coins of the first independent sultan of Bengal, Shams al-din Ilyas Shah, from the same Sylhet find. Stapleton himself put a note 'An unusually fine specimen' below no. 195 in his inventory. It is struck from the mint of *Firuzabad* with the epithet *al-balad* and dated 754 AH. No. 210 is another specimen of the same sultan Ilyas Shah struck at *Shahr-i-Naw* ('the new city') and is actually referring to the newly established capital city of Firuzabad, identified with Pandua situated in the present Maldah district of West Bengal. Stapleton classified these two coins following the British Museum and Indian Museum Catalogues. The Sylhet find was unearthed in 1913 as Stapleton mentioned. Our database of coin hoards and finds of the Islamic rulers of Bengal reveals that in 1913, a hoard of 97 silver coins was discovered from a village called Kastabir Mahalla in the Sadar sub-division of Sylhet district of undivided Bengal and we have named it the Kastabir Mahalla hoard on the basis of the place name or find spot. The present author has mentioned elsewhere that five coins of Fakhr al-din Mubarak Shah from Kastabir Mahalla hoard are preserved in the coin room of the Ashmolean Museum, Oxford. (Sinha 2017: 185 & 189)

The question arises whether these five coins of Mubarak Shah and the two coins of Ilyas Shah are to be included in these 97 coins of the Kastabir Mahalla hoard or not. In all probability, we need to count these 7 coins of 'Sylhet find' (*alias* Kastabir Mahalla hoard) in addition to the 97 coins which were published in the catalogue of the Assam coin cabinet by A.W. Botham and R. Friel (1919). The hoard was unearthed in 1913 and must have been deposited in the nearby Assam coin cabinet no later than 1914. From the obituary written by Butler we know that Stapleton left this country to join the Indian Army service in 1915. We assume that Stapleton collected those seven specimens before this particular hoard was deposited in the museum. According to museum acquisition rules, once an antiquity or any other archaeological artifact has been accessioned in a museum, it cannot be purchased or re-acquired by an individual unless the museum authority takes a decision to distribute or disburse duplicate coins to other museums which involves a long drawn out procedure (see for example, The Treasure Trove Act of 1878 (ACT No. VI of 1878.1) and subsequent amendments). Therefore, it is almost certain that Stapleton collected those seven coins of the Sylhet hoard before the rest of the hoard entered the coin room of the Assam State museum. We know that he started to build up his personal collection of coins as early as in 1906 when he bought one coin of Bughda Shah from the Calcutta mint which belonged to the Moorshidabad find. How did he collect these coins of the Sylhet find or treasure trove? Did Stapleton purchase them from the Government authority before final disposition of the coins of the Sylhet find to the Assam Museum, Shillong? Had he been a decipherer,[14] he could have collected a little percentage of the total number coins found from the hoard. In the case of the Jashodal hoard (discussed above), T. Bloch gave a list of the disbursement of the entire hoard of 317 silver coins at the time of his report presented to the Asiatic Society of Bengal in 1897-1898, where, apart from five museums who received an average of 22 coins each, the decipherer of the hoard received 15 coins and the remaining 188 silver coins were sent to the Calcutta mint. The first catalogue of coins of Eastern Bengal and Assam was prepared and published by H.E. Stapleton in 1911 which suggests the probability that he might have received or collected a number of coins of the Islamic rulers of medieval India by rendering service as a decipherer of the coins unearthed during his tenure in India.

---

[14] In the case of hoard reporting the word 'decipherer' was used by T. Bloch, Edward Thomas, N.K. Bhattasali and others for those who used to decipher the coin legends inscribed in Arabic or Persian (in the case of coins issued by Turko-Afghan rulers and the Mughals), who would submit a first-hand report to the custodian, and the details which would be published mostly in the Proceedings and Journal of the Asiatic Society of Bengal.

There is a single coin of Ilyas Shah (no. 207) dated 755 AH issued at Hadrat Jalal Sunargaon. Stapleton mentions that this coin is from Gaur. Our database reveals that there are two hoards/finds, one called the Gaur hoard discovered in 1892, found at Gaur, PS. English Bazar, Malda district. The other is named the Belbari hoard, found at Mauza Belbari and reported in 1904. Content analysis of these two hoards revealed that not a single coin of Ilyas Shah was found in either of these two hoards found from the Gaur region. In 1957, another hoard of 68 silver coins was recovered from the walled city of medieval Gaur (Khatun 1960; Sinha 2001: 199-200; Sinha 2017: 69-71) but that cannot be taken into consideration. Therefore, this coin of Ilyas Shah was either a stray finds from Gaur and somehow came into the possession of Stapleton or it was a small find that was never formally published or recorded. Hence, we remain indebted to Stapleton for bringing a new coin find into our notice, maybe one hundred years after its discovery.

After this coin of Ilyas Shah from the Gaur find, Stapleton remains silent in his inventory regarding the provenance of the coins in his collection till we come to the section about Rukn al-din Barbak Shah, the second monarch of the later Ilyas Shahi period who ruled almost one hundred years after Shams al-din Ilyas Shah. Stapleton notes that no. 333 is a coin of Barbak Shah from the Bashail find as is no.334, which belongs to Shams al-din Yusuf Shah, third ruler of the dynasty. Bashail is a village under Karimganj subdivision of district Sylhet and the find was unearthed around 1917 and published in *Suppl. Shillong* in 1919. The present author analysed the Bashail hoard first in 2001 and after she visited the Ashmolean Museum, revised her analysis in 2017 (Sinha 2001:184-85; Sinha 2017: 195-97). How did Stapleton collect these two specimens belonging to a find that was discovered when he was far away from Indian territory? In fact, he resumed his duty in Indian Education Service in 1919 as the Principal of the Presidency College, Calcutta. In this case Stapleton cannot be the decipherer of Bashail find as we presumed in the case of the Kastabir Mahalla (*alias* Sylhet) hoard. Was there an organized agency that used to collect coins from the villagers who chanced upon these finds before the administrative authority's intervention? Did they sell those coins to avid collectors? Is it matter of luck that Stapleton took care to record the findspot? Another possibility could be that Stapleton collected these two coins in 1930 when Mr R. Friel, then a member of the Shillong Coin Cabinet, distributed some 168 duplicate coins from the cabinet (Sinha 2017: 196) The coin room of the Fitzwilliam Museum, Cambridge received one coin each of Barbak Shah and Yusuf Shah along with five other silver coins through the initiative of Mr. Friel, documents of which have been published elsewhere by the present author (Sinha 2013: 148-50).

Next in the inventory are two silver coins from the Sonakhira find, one of Ghiyath al-din Mahmud Shah (no. 438) and one coin of Barbak ibn Humayun (no. 452). The Sonakhira find was unearthed in 1909 in Sonakhira, a village in the district of Sylhet in undivided Bengal. Six coins were preserved in the Assam coin cabinet and subsequently published in *Suppl. Shillong*: one is of Nusrat Shah, three are of Mahmud Shah and two are of Barbak al-din Barbak Shah (Sinha 2017: 214-15). All three coins of Mahmud Shah bear the same date, 944 AH, without any mint name. They are of two different varieties. According to Stapleton, the coin of Mahmud Shah here is similar to *IMC Suppl.* 71/221which is probably coin no. XLIX/1 of Botham and Friel's catalogue (*Suppl. Shillong*: 174; Sinha 2017: 215). The other coin from the Sonakhira find is of Barbak ibn Humayun, which Stapleton mentions first in this sub-section:

'The three following coins, bearing the name Barbak b. Humayun, and the date A.H. 949, suggest that Barbak led a revolt against the rule of Sher Shah which from 946 onwards was enforced by Governors and local chiefs.'

Below this note, the description of no. 452 starts and ends with 'Assam Cat. Suppl. (1919) 160/24. from Sonakhira find' which supports our assumption that Stapleton directly collected a number of coins from the collection of the Assam coin cabinet which once served as the repository for finds in Eastern Bengal. So far as the obverse and reverse legend of this particular coin is concerned, Stapleton wrote down the entire legend in Arabic: the obverse reads *Barbak al-dunya wal din/ abu'l Muzaffar Barbak/ Shah al- Sultan bin* while the reverse reads *Humayun Shah Khallada/ Allah mulkahu wa Sultanuhu/ 949*. Identification of Barbak al-din Barbak Shah (as we prefer to ascribe) is still in doubt as he claimed to be the son of Humayun Shah.

There are three coins of the Mughal Emperor Humayun in Stapleton's inventory. No. 446 (which is similar to no. 444) is from the Raipara find. Two coins of Islam Shah dated 952 are also from the Raipara find (nos. 456-57). As part of the present author's coin hoard project, it is known that this find was discovered on 6th March 1928 and reported in the *Journal of the Asiatic Society of Bengal* in 1929 (Stapleton 1929).[15] A detailed description of the findspot is given in that publication along with the circumstances of discovery and has been critically analysed by the present author previously (Sinha 2001: 190-92). Out of the 182 silver coins in the Raipara hoard, 77 coins belong to Husain Shahi Sultans of Bengal, the remaining 105 coins were of Sher Shah and his son Islam Shah – not a single coin of Humayun was included in the report. But in the 1929 report of the hoard, only

---

[15] (*JASB*, NS, vol. XXV, 1929, no. 2, Calcutta.

1/8th of the total coins in the pot could be recovered and therefore it may easily be assumed that there was more than 1400 coins altogether. This truncated find could well have coins of Humayun and of many other rulers which will remain in obscurity forever.

Last but not least are two coins of Islam Shah (nos. 459-460) and one coin of Afghan ruler Ghiyath al-din Bahadur II (no. 461) which were found 'from vicinity of Bairhatta, Dist. Dinajpur' and 'from Mehdiganj, near s. wall of Gaur', respectively. Bairhatta is very close to the famous historic site of Bangarh in present-day south Dinajpur district of West Bengal, whereas Mehdiganj is popularly known as Mahadipur and situated in the Indo-Bangladesh border area just outside the southern city wall of Gaur, district Malda, West Bengal. Importantly, there is no other reference known to the present author of any such coin find recovered from these two places. Maybe they were stray finds, and therefore no formal report was published either on Bairhatta or on Mehdiganj.

On the whole, the detailed inventory prepared by H.E. Stapleton on the coins he collected throughout his service career in India, especially in Bengal, is a rich storehouse of information, not only providing significant information on the collection history of those coins but also projecting an insight on the trend of recovery of coin hoards and minor finds, policy of their deposition in and distribution from the museums and other institutions like the Asiatic Society of Bengal and Her Majesty's mint in Calcutta. A part of Stapleton's personal collection of the coins which have been thoroughly analysed in the present article are directly connected with a number of hoards and small stray finds unearthed in the late 19th and early 20th century in undivided Bengal. This is probably because of his involvement in reading coin legends predominantly written in Arabic, and in the arrangement of the coin cabinets according to their typological classification and publishing museum catalogues as early as in 1911. There were very few scholars at that point of time who could decipher coins of the Bengal Sultans who ruled between the 13th to 16th centuries.

Collecting coins of different series of Indian coinage along with other archaeological artefacts and antiquities became quite typical for many of the British officers and educationists posted in the Indian sub-continent since late 18th century and H.E. Stapleton was no exception. An objective analysis of this partial inventory of 349 coins of the Governors and Sultans of medieval Bengal has brought to light new information on the fluidity of the collection and accession of the coins in early 20th-century British India. From earlier in-depth research on coin hoards, it was known that after a chance discovery of a hoard, mostly by an individual or a group of people,

the local administration used to intervene and seize the entire find and hand it over to the respective institution or museum. In early 20th century, a few hoards were broken up and partially dispersed among the local people before the authorities intervened. We also find a number of examples of official dispersion of hoards after they were deposited in the museums. In cases where acquisition would bring many duplicate coins of the same type into one single repository, the authorities used to prepare a list of duplicate coins and distribute it among the other museums in British India (including Burma) and also to the major museums or repository in Britain as per their requirement. The author came across such a disbursement letter sent to the Director of the Fitzwilliam Museum, Cambridge from the Curator of the Assam Coin cabinet, Shillong, along with a list of duplicate coins. Stapleton's inventory exposed the fact that an individual government official could acquire duplicate coins distributed by the Museum authority. Today, we generally have the notion that after a coin or an antique has been officially acquired for a public collection, it can never move to a private collector. If it moves location it would be either a loan for a limited period or in exchange for other objects.

Stapleton purchased one coin of the Bengal Sultan from the Calcutta Mint in 1906 which was recovered from the Moorshidabad hoard that was partially deposited in the mint. Earlier, in connection with the Cooch Behar treasure, it was reported by the Indologist Rajendra Lala Mitra that he selected around 1000 silver coins for a private collector Colonel C.S. Guthrie who purchased those coins from the Calcutta Mint in 1863/64 and some of those coins were subsequently sold to the British Museum in 1866. Not all coins deposited in the mint were sold or melted down - some specimens were preserved and published in catalogues. At the beginning of the 20th century, the same practice of officially selling good specimens discovered in hoards to British Officers was in vogue in Her Majesty's mint in Calcutta.

A catalogue of the coins in the bequest of Henry E. Stapleton, incorporating the details of its collection history, either in its own right, or as part of a comprehensive catalogue of the Islamic coins in the Heberden Coin Room would be a very welcome publication.

Acknowledgements

The author is sincerely thankful to her then employer Dr Gautam Sengupta (1996-2006) for granting the necessary permission and study leave, and to her colleagues of the Centre for Archaeological Studies and Training, Eastern India, Kolkata for their kind co-operation. She remains ever grateful to her late mentor

Mr Pratip Kumar Mitra for his unstinted guidance and academic suggestions. She remains extremely thankful to Mr Joe Cribb for selecting her as Hirayama Trainee Curator at the Department of Coins and Medals of the British Museum in 1999 which provided her with the opportunity to broaden the spectrum of her numismatic research area and enabled her to make subsequent visits to the Ashmolean Museum and other museums in UK. She is also thankful to other esteemed colleagues of that Department, namely Drs Elizabeth Errington, Vesta Curtis, Venetia Porter, Helen Wang, Robert Bracey and many others who not only provided her with all kinds of academic and official support to complete her tenure as a Trainee Curator but also made her sojourn in London most memorable and enjoyable. At the final stage of completing this article, her sincere thanks go to Mr. Subir Sarkar and Ms. Subhasree Banik of Kolkata.

References

Bloch, T. 1898. Report on 317 Old Silver Coins Forwarded by Collector of Mymensingh. *Proceedings of the Asiatic Society of Bengal,* June 1898, Philological Secretary – Report on Coins, XII: 169-173.

Botham, A.W. and Friel, R. 1919. *Supplement to the Catalogue of Provincial Cabinet of Coins, Assam.* Allahabad: Government Press.

Botham, A.W. 1930.*Catalogue of the Provincial Coin Cabinet, Assam,* 2nd ed. Allahabad, Government Press.

Burn, R. 1907. Pathan and Bengal Coins, *Journal of the Asiatic Society of Bengal, New Series,* 8: 587-588.

Khatun, M. 1960. On Some New Coins of Alaud-din Firuz Shah and Ghiyathud-din Mahmud Shah of Bengal, *Journal of the Numismatic Society of India* XXII-216. Varanasi.

Lane-Poole, S. 1885. *The Coins of the Muhammadan States of India in the British Museum,* Reginald Stuart Poole (ed.), London: British Museum Press.

Lane-Poole, S. 1888. *Catalogue of the Mohammedan Coins Preserved in the Bodleian Library at Oxford,* Oxford: Clarendon Press.

Sinha, S. 2001. Coin Hoards of the Bengal Sultans: An Anatomy of the Hoards. *Pratna Samiksha* (Journal of the Directorate of Archaeology and Museums, West Bengal), 6-8: 36- 242.

Sinha, S. 2010. The Coin Collection of the Bengal Sultans in the Cabinet of Heberden Coin Room, Ashmolean Museum, Oxford, *Pratna Samiksha: A Journal of Archaeology,* New Series, 1:163-175.

Sinha S. 2017.*Coin Hoards of the Bengal Sultans: 1205-1576 AD from West Bengal, Bihar, Jharkhand, Assam and Bangladesh.* Gurgaon: Shubhi Publications.

Sinha, S. 2019. Hitherto Unnoticed Coin Collections of the Bengal Sultans in the Fitzwilliam Museum, Cambridge and National Museum of Scotland, Edinburgh, UK, in S. Basu Majumdar and S.K. Bose (eds) *Money and Money Matters in Pre-Modern South Asia*: 135-160.New Delhi: Manohar.

Stapleton, H.E. 1910. Contributions to the History and Ethnology of North-Eastern India. I, *Journal and Proceedings of the Asiatic Society of Bengal,* vol. VI, no. 4: 141-166, esp. 149.

Stapleton, H.E. 1929. A Find of 182 Silver Coins of the Husaini and Suri Dynasties from Raipara, Thana Dohar, District Dacca, Eastern Bengal, *Journal of the Asiatic Society of Bengal* XXV, Numismatic Supplement XLII: 5-22.

Stapleton, H.E. 1911. *Catalogue of the Provincial Cabinet of Coins, East Bengal and Assam.* Shillong: East Bengal and Assam Government.

Wright, H.N. 1907-1908. *Catalogue of the Coins in the Indian Museum, Calcutta,* Vol. 2. Varanasi, 1972 (Reprint).

Stamford Raffles' Collections: Entangled Objects

Alexandra Green

In autumn 2016, the Singapore High Commission in London enquired as to the possibility of holding an exhibition on Stamford Raffles at the British Museum in 2019, the 200th anniversary of the establishment of Singapore as a British trading port. Over the next year it was determined that I would develop an exhibition based on the British Museum's Raffles collections. It would first be shown at the Asian Civilisations Museum (ACM) in Singapore as part of a larger exhibition addressing Raffles as a collector, and then in its original format in Gallery 91 at the British Museum. The ACM planned to publish a catalogue of the show as presented in Singapore.

I am not a specialist in Enlightenment thought, Stamford Raffles, or Indonesian art, so I immediately embarked upon an intensive reading programme that included Raffles' and his contemporaries' writings, particularly those of people who worked with Raffles. When I started approaching secondary materials, it became clear quite quickly that while aspects of Raffles' collections had been studied, nobody had assessed them as an entity, one that consists of such disparate material as drawings of Hindu and Buddhist sites on Java, Javanese theatrical items, coins and amulets, and miscellaneous other pieces. Moreover, Raffles' objects did not enter museum collections at the same time but arrived in groups over the course of more than a century. This article briefly details some of the methods used in researching Raffles' collections, surveys the ideas behind collecting in the early 19th century, interprets the objects through the lens of Raffles' and his contemporaries' writings and ideas, and finally assesses the way in which the objects were distributed to various institutions. This work entailed travel to Java, archival examinations, visits to museums and historic houses, and discussions with theatrical specialists and practitioners.

There are more than 350 drawings from Hindu and Buddhist sites on Java in the Raffles collection at the British Museum. Fieldwork in Java enabled the identification of some of the unlabelled drawings of buildings and reliefs, as well as some of the current locations of sculptures. For instance, several of the unidentified buildings were from the Gedong Songo group on the mountain Gunung Ungaran, and some sketchily drawn figures were elegant sculptures from Candi Mendut. My intern Indra Djojohadikusumo and I also identified the locations of relief sculptures on Borobudur, and interestingly, all the imagery came from panels close to the staircases, indicating the difficulty

of access to the terraces in the early 19th century. Misidentifications were rectified, including a Candi Sukuh sculpture that had been attributed to Borobudur (Figures 1 & 2).[1] In the UK, further research into the drawings involved comparing them with examples held in the Royal Asiatic Society and the British Library as there are substantial overlaps between the collections. For instance, a sketch in the British Museum could pair with a finished drawing in the RAS or BL, or vice versa.

Another important part of the research involved investigating the provenance of the more than 600 puppets, masks, and musical instruments collected by Raffles, as it has been assumed that they were loot from the sack of the Yogyakarta court that he authorised in 1812. To date, research suggests that the masks originated in central Java, particularly Solo and Yogyakarta, Cirebon on the north coast, and possibly Malang in east Java. The fact that they are unused and the hair on most of them is quite crudely carved suggests

Figure 1. Drawing of Candi Sukuh images labelled incorrectly as Borobudur Sculptures. *c.* 1815. Central Java. Pencil and ink on paper. 23.2 x 18.8 cm. 1939,0311,0.7.112. © Trustees of the British Museum

[1] See British Museum objects 1939,0311,0.5.21; 1939,0311,0.5.20; 1939,0311,0.5.19; 1939,0311,0.7.120; 1939,0311,0.7.119; 1939,0311,0.7.112; 1939,0311,0.7.116; 1939,0311,0.7.114; 1939,0311,0.6.26; and 1939,0311,0.6.25.

Figure 2. Sculptural stone at Candi Sukuh. Central Java. Volcanic rock. Photograph by the author

that they were commissioned by Raffles or were hastily made for him. Stylistically, the puppets appear to have been mostly produced in Cirebon and central Java, possibly Surakarta, rather than Yogyakarta (Figures 3 & 4). Similarly eclectic are the gamelan instruments, many of which stylistically appear to have been made in the northeast of Java, a major production area, although the instruments in Claydon House in Buckinghamshire with their repetitive geometric decoration could have originated in the central region. These investigations were started by Rudi Wiratama and Bima Raharjo of Gajah Mada University in Yogyakarta and Laurie Margot Ross, and the work on the provenance of the theatrical materials remains ongoing.

The Chinese cash coins that Raffles collected have not yet been catalogued in detail, but most appear to be widely circulated types, and other aspects of the collections, such as the few Sumatran objects and the group of items from Nias (Figure 5), also require further research. Henry Noltie published the British Library's natural history drawings in *Raffles' Ark Redrawn: Natural History Drawings from the Collection of Sir Thomas Stamford Raffles*, and the amulets have been extensively discussed by Joe Cribb in his magisterial *Magic Coins of Java, Bali, and the Malay Peninsula* (1999) (Figure 6). Prior work on the Raffles manuscript collection at the Royal Asiatic Society suggests that only two originated with the Yogyakarta court, but further studies are necessary.

Collecting

Collecting is now well-acknowledged as not being a neutral activity, and the role of objects in the consolidation of colonial power has been established and explored in numerous contexts. Collecting as a process, where people engage publicly and privately to construct personal and institutional worlds with material objects, has been deconstructed, and the varying types of collecting defined. While many museum donors collect only a few objects, others present large bodies of material to be accessioned. These groups of objects tell us not only about the culture in which they originated, but also about ideas and norms of the collectors' milieux and about the collectors themselves. Furthermore, they also can tell us about the relationships and interactions between coloniser and colonised: the appropriation, partition, rejection, and manipulation of objects in struggles for power. Although material culture has usually been considered subordinate in Western philosophical traditions with objects as a result of thought and ideas, a means to an end, objects embody the ideas of societies, and therefore also construct those worlds and act as agents in their own right.

There are numerous ways in which people collect, but as the imperial project developed in Britain over the course of the 19th century, it increasingly focused

Figure 3. Shadow puppet of the semi-divine clown Semar. Late 1700s–1816. Cirebon, Java. Hide, horn, hair, gold leaf, cotton. Length 60 cm. Donated by William Raffles Flint. As1859,1228.573. © Trustees of the British Museum

Figure 4. Shadow puppet of the semi-divine clown Semar. Late 1700s–1816. Central Java. Hide, horn, hair, gold leaf, cotton. Length 63 cm. Donated by William Raffles Flint. As1859,1228.784. © Trustees of the British Museum

upon the collection of sets, of systematic bodies of material that encompassed the current state of western knowledge of that subject. The concept of museums as an educational space also became gradually entrenched during this same time, and as a result collections have come to be viewed as offering knowledge of the world in a way that was organised conceptually to facilitate the construction of and reinforce particular hierarchical systems. However, during Raffles' lifetime, these concepts were in their infancy, and he was thus ahead of his time in collecting sets of anthropological objects, in addition to historical ones. There has already been substantial discussion of what Raffles believed, and his collections indicate Enlightenment concepts clearly, including the importance of reason and the scientific method as defined at the end of the 18th and beginning of the 19th centuries, the idea that environment impacts individual and national behaviours, the ranking of societies from savage to civilised, and faith in the potential of humans to become civilised (Harris 2001). He firmly believed in the civilising force of Britain, writing, 'It is the peculiar characteristic of Great Britain, that wherever her influence has been extended,

it has carried civilization and improvement in its train' (Raffles 1830: Appendix 23, 25). He considered himself to be part of this civilising mission, further writing, 'It was at the close of such an administration [his departure from Sumatra in 1824] that I embarked with my family on the *Fame*, carrying with me endless volumes and papers of information on the civil and natural history of nearly every Island within the Malayan Archipelago, collected at great expense and labour, under the most favourable circumstances, during a life of constant and active research, and in an especial manner calculated not only to throw light on the commercial and other resources of these Islands, but to advance the state of natural knowledge and science, and to extend the civilization of mankind' (Raffles 1830: 571–572). Raffles had seen clearly the personal benefits of rendering information and objects to the upper echelons of British society, when he received a knighthood for his publication *The History of Java* in 1817 (Green 2019: 24–39).

The rationales behind Raffles' collations become clearer when viewed through Enlightenment concepts and

Figure 6. Amulet with imagery of a noble on horseback. 1400–1600. Java. Copper alloy. Diameter 7.5 cm. Cribb Series 6, Group 1, no. 143. Donated by Lady Sophia Raffles. CH.663. © Trustees of the British Museum

Figure 5. Ancestral figure (*adu siraha salawa*). Late 1700s–early 1820s. Northern Nias. Wood. Height 70.1 cm, width 11.9 cm. Donated by William Raffles Flint. As1859,1228.168. © Trustees of the British Museum

his consideration of British territorial and mercantile expansion for the 'betterment' of the colonised peoples. Raffles made connections between history, language and literature, and the theatre. He viewed the narratives of the theatre as connected with distant history of the island and noted the different language use in performances. Not only did he consider the Javanese language to be highly sophisticated and felt that 'ignorant' people could learn refined words by watching performances, but he also collected history manuscripts and had the Bratya Yuda poem translated into English, which was then published in his *History of Java*. It was history that prompted the collection of material relating to Java's Hindu-Buddhist past, which by corresponding to European ideals of stone architecture and stone and metal sculpture, emphasised Java's former greatness in his opinion (Green 2019: 24–39). The intersection of language, history, and theatre, in combination with the sophisticated detail of the puppets and instruments, was probably also the impetus for the collection of masks, puppets, and musical instruments. Many of Raffles' theatrical examples are made of high-quality materials, such as buffalo horn, and are carved and painted in detail. In addition, most are substantially covered in gold leaf.

Raffles commented that theatrical performances could be seen constantly across the island, and gamelans could be heard playing at all times (Raffles 1817, 1965 edition: 471). This was a feature not found in other parts of Asia where he resided, and consequently was an unusual characteristic of Java. The focus on the theatre in his collections can thus be viewed as a response to its conspicuousness, and combined with the visually arresting sumptuousness of the objects, which he described as 'painted and gilt with great care and at considerable expense,' conjured the Javanese as a noteworthy colonial possibility (Raffles 1817, 1965 edition: 336; Rousseau and Porter 1990:1–22).

Selections from all his collections – coins, amulets, drawings, metal and stone sculptures, puppets, masks, musical instruments, weapons, and tools – featured in *The History of Java*. Although Raffles formed extensive collections, his responses, or lack thereof, towards the objects individually imply that in and of themselves they were not of particular interest, rather their importance lay in their role as a source of information. In part, this is observable in Raffles' will, in which he only discusses his finances, and there is no mention of how he wanted his collections to be disposed.[2] This suggests that the objects had already served their purpose of providing information for his publication, lectures, and presentations, as well as functioning as gifts to family, friends, and those in power, such as the Prince Regent, Queen Charlotte, and Princess Charlotte. It also marks the extent of his isolation from high

---

[2] National Archives catalogue reference Prob 11/1716.

society at the end of his life after he had lost substantial quantities of invested money, the destruction of all his research and collections from his years on Sumatra and in Singapore with the burning and sinking of the ship returning him to Britain in 1824, and the East India Company's demand for repayment of more than £22,000 for financial losses incurred during his governorships of Java and Bengkulu, Sumatra.

Yet, more direct interventions into the objects also reveals Raffles' view of them as purveyors of information. For instance, many of the theatrical pieces have been identified on the objects themselves. Most of the masks are labelled inside twice – once in Javanese giving the name of the character and once in English giving the name and the position the character held.[3] Some of these labels have been incorrectly applied. For example, the Hanuman monkey mask is labelled as being Rangga Megantara, a minister of Prabu Jaka. Writing on the feet of the shadow puppets identifies them in combinations of Javanese, English, Indonesian, or Dutch. It is the model gamelan orchestra that was reproduced in *The History of Java*, suggesting that models were popular for their ease of use. The two- and three-dimensional puppets (*wayang klitik* and *wayang krucil gilig*) had their central rods removed, possibly for ease of transportation, but also possibly to make them easier to display, since they were no longer to be used in performance.

A similarly cavalier attitude to the information provided by the objects and the firm relocation of the objects into a European context can be seen in the manipulation of imagery in his publication. Despite Raffles' protestations that accuracy was his goal (Raffles 1816: 349–350), most of the reproductions of images of Hindu-Buddhist architecture were in a picturesque style, transforming them into exotic hybrids, rather than accurate sources of information (Tiffin 2016). The images of antiquities in the *History of Java* are presented in a style, popular in Europe at the time, that shows the romance of decaying structures. In part, this relates to the fact that while the pictures were sketched on site, they were often drawn in more detail later, and often much later, as is evident in the complaints about the illustrator Jan Knops who was supposed to produce one hundred images, yet after several months had only rendered ten fully.[4] Additionally, publication required the pictures to be prepared by engravers who had not been to Asia. Anthony Forge has discussed in detail how William Daniell's paintings of Javanese people reproduced in *The History of Java* had been adjusted to appeal and be comprehensible to a European audience (Forge 1994: 109–50). Although Daniell had travelled

extensively and was well-known for his depictions of India, this did not preclude him from utilising a picturesque manner to the detriment of accuracy. His reworking of the imagery is acknowledged by Raffles in his introduction, where he notes that Daniell "devoted his undivided attention in forming a proper conception of his subject..." (Raffles 1817: Vol.1, p. x). Although Raffles did travel around the island viewing ancient sites, it is unclear to what extent he was cognisant of the discrepancies between the images for publication and Javanese actualities.

Some of the drawings for his *History* were collated by Raffles from materials that had already been produced by the Dutch on Java, particularly H.C. Cornelius. He also commissioned and collected further work from Colin Mackenzie, George Baker, J.W.B. Wardenaar, the American naturalist and doctor Thomas Horsfield, and other Dutch and British draughtsmen. Mackenzie spent many months surveying central Java in 1812–1813. Baker started recording sites in 1812, and in 1815, he surveyed central Java, which included a three-week stint on the Dieng Plateau. In 1815, Raffles also instructed Wardenaar to survey Trowulan in east Java, a major Majapahit site during the 14th and 15th centuries (Gomperts *et al.* 2012: 177–196). Yet, the drawings were only working objects, a means of conveying information about Java to Europe, and not all of them were accurate from the outset. In his papers, Mackenzie commented that the imagery of the buildings produced by others could be speculative if drawn as complete and undamaged, because when he visited the sites, the actual states of repair were poor. Contradicting this, however, he surmised that the structures may have been in better repair when the drawings were made, even though most were produced only a short time prior to the British arrival on Java in 1811.[5] George Baker was less forgiving. When, shortly after Raffles' early death in 1826, he assisted Lady Raffles in collating materials for the second edition of the *History of Java* (1830), he annotated a number of drawings with such comments as 'These are all wrong & done from fancy', 'Pure imagination or invention', and amusingly on a topographical map of the Dieng Plateau, 'This is no more like the place than it resembles London'.[6] In keeping with the view that the drawings were working objects, valued for their information, rather than their own status, Baker also annotated, in his distinctive hand, the images to identify them and marked which ones had already been published. All of these examples display a focus on the development of a big picture, rather than on a comprehension of the objects in the collection themselves.

---

[3] While the labels written in English have faded badly, the ink used to write the Javanese ones remains dark and clear.
[4] British Library, Mackenzie Private 36, p. 108.

[5] British Library, Mackenzie Private 36, p. 120.
[6] See British Museum objects 1939,0311,0.6.51; 1939,0311,0.6.51.a; 1939,0311,0.6.54; and 1939,0311,0.6.45.

Javanese theatre

Things made and built by Javanese in the early 19th century did not generally command much admiration among Europeans. In describing the British sack of the Yogyakarta court in 1812, William Thorn wrote that the *kraton* had nothing very magnificent in it (Thorn 1815: 292–293). John Crawfurd, the resident at Yogyakarta went so far as to say that the old Hindu-Buddhist structures excited admiration "though no doubt the effect is heightened by the comparison which we are apt to make between these ruins, and the rude effects of the modern art of the *Javanese* by which we are surrounded" (Crawfurd 1820: 357). Usually, there is very little description of material culture in early writings, and when there is, it primarily focuses upon the elements to which the Europeans could relate. Thus, there are many descriptions of weapons, gold, gems, and evident (to Europeans) marks of status, but often little else.[7] In a rare instance, Colin Mackenzie described a procession during a journey in central Java, writing of baskets, green hoods with white French feathers, Javanese heroes dressed in women's clothing [referring to the sarongs] carrying weapons and kris, and concluding with 'These were among the many grotesque objects which constantly pressed on our notice as we trudged along the tedious way.'[8] These varying attitudes indicate that Europeans not only disapproved of and were disinterested in contemporary Javanese culture, but also raise the question of why Raffles formed large collections of theatrical material – more than 350 shadow puppets, nearly 100 other puppets, more than 140 masks, and over 50 full-size and model gamelan instruments. As mentioned, the theatrical objects represented many themes of civilisation important to Raffles, and these, mingled with the excitement of the exotic, probably made them irresistible, encouraging Raffles to apply contemporary collecting practices and gather together the sizable number of objects known today.

The large numbers of objects suggest that functional sets of puppets, masks, and instruments were acquired, but this was not the case as the sets are not based on Javanese theatrical considerations. None of the full-size gamelan orchestras is complete, nor do the puppets or masks allow for anything more than limited performances. For instance, Prince Panji is a major character in *wayang gedog*, yet there are only a few examples in the collections; nor are there many examples of Arjuna, a main character in *wayang purwa*, who is usually represented by numerous puppets indicating his various moods and stages of life. In the Raffles collections, there are large numbers of monsters and demons, yet few clowns (this also pertains to the masks), which are another important part of performances since they accompany the main characters, are often viewed as disguised deities, and bring local relevance to the performance. Writing about the comic interludes, Raffles does not learn about their roles in performances but views them from a European perspective, stating that "Buffoonery is sometimes introduced, to increase the zest of these entertainments with the multitude, but it does not interfere with the regular course of the performance..." (Raffles 1817, 1965 edition: vol. 1, p. 336). To be fair, however, he does comment that these sections are "...not infrequently ... the most interesting part of the performance" (Raffles 1817, 1965 edition: vol. 1, p. 336). The haphazard nature of the theatrical materials indicates that Raffles acquired them in a piecemeal fashion, rather than as a whole, which is further corroborated by the variety of styles. It also implies that they were not amassed wholesale from the attack on Yogyakarta.

The gamelan instruments have been subjected to greater scrutiny than the other objects for their provenance. Instruments in a variety of styles are in Claydon House, Buckinghamshire and the British Museum. The former were sold to the Verney family after Lady Raffles' death in 1858 and show signs of use and re-tuning, yet Reverend Raffles Flint, Raffles' nephew and executor of Lady Raffles' estate, wrote in a letter to Harry Verney that they were made to order, in which case they would not have been re-tuned as they were new.[9] He also stated that the instruments in the British Museum were of greater antiquity than the Claydon House ones,[10] which, taken with the evidence of the tuning, suggests that he confused the two groups, but given that he was writing more than twenty-five years after Raffles' death, this is not surprising. Amrit Gomperts has described the Claydon gamelan as produced for nobility in the Surabaya-Gresik region between 1775–90.[11] In his writings, Raffles mentioned Gresik as a major centre for the production of gamelan and says that gongs were a valuable export of the city, which corroborates Gomperts' comments for the Claydon gamelan instruments (Raffles 1817, 1965 edition: vol. 1, p. 470).[12] Raffles also wrote that second-hand sets of gamelan instruments were frequently disposed of,[13] which, if accurate, accounts for the mix of instruments in his collection as he likely purchased pieces as they became available. Gomperts further

---

[7] See F. van Boeckholtz "Historical Account of Great Java" in British Library, Mackenzie Private 16; Colonel Adams in Mackenzie Private 86 I, pp. 69–72.

[8] Remarks and observations on the ruins of Prambana in Java in British Library, Mackenzie Private 36, p. 126.

[9] Claydon House archives, letter to Harry Verney from Reverend W. Raffles Flint on 12 September 1861.

[10] Claydon House archives, letter to Harry Verney from Reverend W. Raffles Flint on 12 September 1861.

[11] Claydon House archives, letter to Ralph Verney from Amrit Gomperts on 25 June 1985.

[12] Raffles, *History*, vol. 1, p. 470.

[13] Ibid, p. 471.

noted that the instruments in the British Museum were made in Raffles' honour in 1814.[14] The latter assessment is implausible for the entire museum group as they are carved and painted in several distinctive styles and therefore come from different orchestras.

The variety of styles among Raffles' gamelan instruments ranges from abstract imagery to zoomorphic examples. The Claydon group is decorated with abstract designs. Some pieces at the British Museum also display this type of decoration, so it is not impossible that some examples originated in the Yogyakarta or Surakarta courts, as abstract designs were the standard decorative form there. A smaller grouping, but the largest at the British Museum, is the instruments displaying black, red, and gold animal forms. These likely also come from the northeast coast, where designs were more exuberant than in the central region.[15]

A source of confusion comes from Raffles' writings about a small gamelan set, which he called the most antique in his possession.[16] Which instruments constitute the small set is unknown. The Claydon set is larger in number than any stylistically coherent group in the British Museum and the closest to a complete orchestra. Jeune Scott-Kemball initiated a study of the Raffles gamelan instruments in the 1970s,[17] and she claimed that the small set was the model orchestra, yet why it would be the most antique is not clear. Raffles asked a friend for extra permission to store the small set at her house, but why this would have been necessary given their size further suggests that the small set was not the model orchestra.[18] The zoomorphic set at the British Museum is a small group, but there is some inconclusive evidence that these were the pieces commissioned by Raffles.[19] If this is correct, these too could not be the small set as they would have been new. Such patchy and contradictory information makes it clear that further research into the gamelan instruments is necessary.

Donation of the collections

The fact that Raffles says nothing about how he wanted to dispose of his collections in his will may relate to the state of museum development in the early 19th century (he died in 1826). Indeed, the incremental distribution of Raffles' collections simplistically mirrors museum development over the 19th and early 20th centuries.

Raffles distributed objects prior to his death, notably the gift of weapons to the Prince Regent in 1817, amulets to William Marsden, who was a numismatist and had written on Sumatra (Cribb 1999: 15), and wooden images from Nias to his cousin, the Reverend Thomas Raffles.[20] The whereabouts of other objects is unknown, such as jewellery for a Javanese woman listed on customs forms, but which is not identified in any collection, and the gold ring that Baker found in eastern Java near Banyumas and sent to Raffles. They may have been gifted or sold. The donation of the Raffles collections to museums had to wait until after his death, suggesting that they were not viewed as the type of material relevant to contemporaneous museum collections.

The first tranche to arrive at an institution was the manuscripts, which Lady Raffles gave to the Royal Asiatic Society in 1830. Books and manuscripts were comprehensible to Europeans according to the prioritisation of history and text at the time, and this clarifies at least one of the rationales behind the early donation. The next body of material to be donated only came 25 years later in 1859 after the death of Lady Raffles. Her nephew and executor of her will, Reverend William Raffles Flint, at first offered to sell the coin, amulet, stone and metal sculptures, and theatrical collections to the British Museum for £1,000 in 1858, but the museum declined the objects, and only grudgingly accepted them the following year when they were presented as a gift. Part of the reason for the arrival date relates to the ethnographic nature of much of the materials. While the metal sculptures could be related to European bronze sculpture, in material, if not in form, the puppets and masks were less valued. It was not until the 1830s that ethnographic museums first emerged in Europe, and it was not until the late 19th century that such museums became more prevalent. Although accepted reluctantly in 1859, it was possible conceptually to consider adding the theatrical and other objects to a museum collection. Subsequently, the theatrical material has been exhibited at the Museum of Mankind (the British Museum's Department of Ethnography from 1970 to 1997) and on loans to other institutions. Nigel Barley curated an exhibition called *The Golden Sword: Stamford Raffles and the East* at the British Museum in 1998–99 (Barley 1999), but provenance research and studies of the individual objects have been limited. Despite arriving in 1859, the Chinese coins were only registered in the musem's catalogue in 1908, although, as mentioned, the Southeast Asian amulets have been studied and catalogued in detail.

In 1939, the final batch of objects collected by Raffles arrived at the British Museum. It consisted primarily of the volumes of more than 350 drawings, but also included

---

[14] Claydon House archives, letter to Ralph Verney from Amrit Gomperts on 25 June 1985.
[15] Personal communication, Rudy Wiratama, July 2018.
[16] 1 August 1817 letter from Stamford Raffles to the Duchess of Somerset.
[17] Scott-Kemball's monograph on the gamelan instruments was never published and exists only in manuscript form in the Department of Asia at the British Museum.
[18] Scott-Kemball, *Raffles Gamelan*, ch. 8.
[19] Claydon House archives, letter to Ralph Verney from Amrit Gomperts on 25 June 1985.

[20] Raffles' letter to his cousin, Thomas Raffles on 17 July 1820.

Figure 7. Entrance to the *Sir Stamford Raffles: Collecting in Southeast Asia* exhibition. 19 September 2019–20 January 2020. © Trustees of the British Museum

further metal sculptures, masks, and puppets, as well as model gamelan instruments, model and actual weapons and armour, and items from Sumatra. This was the result of a bit of house-clearing, as Mrs Drake, Raffles' great-grandniece, was downsizing, but the fact that the British Museum accepted the materials without demur indicated quite a substantial shift in attitude towards such collection types. Indeed, even the drawings and watercolours were acceptable, demonstrating that they were now considered as something other than 'working objects', there only to provide information and not of intrinsic interest themselves, as was the case in the early 19th century. Perhaps new ideas about the roles of museums were at work, but it could also be that enough time had passed to increase the historical value of the objects. Now the objects were appreciated for the information they provided about Java, Raffles and his contemporaries, and colonial ideas and attitudes (Tiffin 2016), as well as being viewed as artistic endeavours in themselves.

Conclusion

In summary, it is possible to see the various vicissitudes to which the Raffles collections have been subjected during their more than 200-year history. Moving from acting as records of Java to promote Raffles' schemes for British colonisation and his own advancement, they have become important documents of late 18th- and early 19th-century Javanese art and culture, as well as the history of the British interregnum on Java between 1811–1816, providing insights into Raffles himself, as well as his milieux. There has been revived interest in the collections among scholars and the general public on Java in recent years for the study of Raffles, colonialism, and Javanese art and theatre, but also in relationship to issues of repatriation and nationalist

sentiment. The Raffles collections can demonstrate how the biographies of objects evolve as interpretations and priorities change, producing divergent affects in different people in various times and places. Over time, the collections have become increasingly complex and entangled, requiring continuous examination and exegesis. The exhibitions at the ACM, *Raffles in Southeast Asia: Revisiting the Scholar and Statesman* (Murphy *et al.*, 2019), and the exhibition at the British Museum, *Sir Stamford Raffles: Collecting in Southeast Asia 1811–1824*, both in 2019, re-started this investigation process (Figure 7).

References

Barley, N. 1999. *The Golden Sword. Stamford Raffles and the East*. London: British Museum Press.

Cribb, J. 1999. *Magic Coins of Java, Bali, and the Malay Peninsular*. London: British Museum Press.

Forge, A. 1994. Raffles and Daniell, Making the Image Fit, in A. Gerstle and A. Milner (eds), *Recovering the Orient: Artists, Scholars, Appropriations*: 109-150. Chur: Harwood Academic Publishers.

Gomperts, A., Haag, A., and Carey, P. 2012. Mapping Majapahit: Wardenaar's Archaeological Survey at Trowulan in 1815, *Indonesia* 93: 177–196.

Green, A. 2019. Raffles' Collections from Java: European Evidence of Civilisation, in S. Murphy, N. Wang and A. Green (eds), *Raffles in Southeast Asia: Revisiting the Scholar and Statesman*: 24-39. Singapore: Asian Civilizations Museum.

Harris, M. 2001. 1968 (2001 edition). *The Rise of Anthropological Theory: A History of Theories of Culture*. Oxford: Altamira.

King, J.C.H. 1997. Franks and Ethnography, in M. Caygill and J. Cherry (eds), *A.W. Franks: Nineteenth-Century Collecting and the British Museum*: 136-159. London, British Museum Press.

Murphy, S., Wang, N., and Green, A. (eds). 2019. *Raffles in Southeast Asia: Revisiting the Scholar and Statesman*. Singapore: Asian Civilizations Museum.

Noltie, H.J. 2009. *Raffles' Ark Redrawn: Natural History Drawings from the Collection of Sir Thomas Stamford Raffles*. London and Edinburgh: British Library.

Raffles, T.S. 1816. A discourse delivered to the Literary and Scientific Society at Java, on the 10th of September, 1815 by the Hon. Thomas Stamford Raffles, President, *The Asiatic Journal and Monthly Register for British India and its Dependencies* 1, 4: 349–350.

Raffles, T.S. 1817 (1965 edition). *The History of Java, Vol. 1*. Kuala Lumpur.

Raffles, T.S. 1830. *Memoir of the Life and Public Services of Sir Thomas Stamford Raffles*. London: John Murray.

Rousseau, G.S. and Porter, R. (eds), 1990. *Exoticism in the Enlightenment*. Manchester: Manchester University Press.

Scott-Kemball, J. (n.d.). 'The Raffles Gamelan'. Unpublished manuscript, The British Museum.

Thorn, W. 1815. *Memoir of the conquest of Java with the subsequent operations of the British forces in the Oriental Archipelago to which is subjoined a statistical and historical sketch of Java being the result of observations made in a tour through the country with an account of its dependencies*. London: T. Egerton.

Tiffin, S. 2016. *Southeast Asia in Ruins: Art and Empire in the Early 19th Century*. Singapore: Nus Press.

Key to the Riddle of Hybrids: a Pendant from Khlong Thom

Susmita Basu Majumdar

Introduction

In recent years a remarkable amount of Roman archaeological materials has come to light in Southeast Asia, prompting us to reappraise these finds. It is unlikely that there were any direct links between Southeast Asia and the Mediterranean during the early centuries of the common era but it is increasingly clear that there were trading areas or linked zones between the Mediterranean, India, and mainland Southeast Asia. The creation and distribution of hybrid forms, in particular pendants inspired by coin designs both Roman and Indian, are of great interest. In this essay, I will draw attention to these hybrid forms and the early links between these regions and highlight the significance of two pendants found at the site of Khlong Thom.

Khlong Thom and Southeast Asia as part of a larger trading network

The site of Khlong Thom is located in Krabi province on the western coast of the Thai-Malay Peninsula, located to the south of the Isthmus of Kra (7° 57' 12" N 99° 8' 42" E). It is a significant site that has already yielded evidence of bead manufacturing and tin processing (Borell 2014: 9). Of special importance are the Roman imitation coins, which have tubular loops indicating their use as pendants. A number of Roman intaglios datable between the 1st and 3rd centuries CE have also been found in Khlong Thom, and more have been reported from other sites in the Isthmus region recently.

Khlong Thom is located at a very strategic position. The presence of both Roman finds and early Chinese ceramics help us to understand the character and position of this Khlong Thom in the larger trading nexus, and the interest of the Chinese in using this location as an easy crossover. The Bay of Bengal network also extended up to the Isthmus of Kra, as indicated by the finds of pottery from the eastern coast of India (Borell 2014: 8–10). Trade between the ports of the Red Sea and India resulted in extended access to products/commodities from regions as far as Southeast Asia. Ptolemy's *Geographike Hyphegesis* is of great help in understanding India Extra Gangem, as he mentions places yielding specific products and commodities coveted in the Roman world (Stevenson 1932). China also entered into the trading nexus, responding to the demand for specific goods in the western world and the Indian subcontinent. The participation of Chinese traders thus brings into the frame, the Gulf of Thailand network located beyond the Indian Ocean network. This braided nexus from the Mediterranean to Southeast Asia had multiple connections and offshoots, which were dependent on the exchange of goods either locally produced or relayed within a large network.

Three of the most important sites in Southeast Asia that show evidence of participation in this trading nexus are Khlong Thom (on the west coast of the Thai-Malay Peninsula), U Thong (in Suphanburi province in central Thailand, an inland site north of the Gulf of Thailand), and ÓcEo (in southern Vietnam near the eastern coast of the Gulf of Thailand). They had access to tin and silver, both of which were in high demand in the larger trading nexus. The popularity of bronze objects also increased the demand for tin which was abundantly available in this region. The scarcity of silver resources in the Indian subcontinent led traders to seek silver resources further east in Myanmar. Cassia, cinnamon, camphor and other spices also made Southeast Asia an important region in the larger trade network.

Two important pendants from Khlong Thom

In 2014 Brigitte Borell published two tin pendants discovered at Khlong Thom. Both are similar in shape and size, being round with a tubular loop at the top, which was cast as part of the pendant. Both appear to have been inspired by coins. One is a finished piece, the other is unfinished (cast but not polished).

The unfinished piece has no traces of wear and tear, indicating that it was lost in the process of manufacturing. Compositional elemental analysis indicates that it was made out of almost pure tin (Sn 96–97%, Fe 2%, Pb 1%, Mn traces) (Borell 2014: 21), a metal that is abundantly available in the Thai-Malay peninsula. Borell also showed that Khlong Thom had a tin smelting workshop which is indicated by the discovery of a large amount of metallurgical slag and other tin objects from the site. The unfinished pendant has a head in profile to left within a semi-circular border of dots on the lower half, within a circular raised rim (Figure 1). The upper half of the dotted border could not be completed due to the addition of the tubular loop. The pendant is 18 mm in diameter, weighs 2.31g and the width of the suspension loop is 6 mm. The reverse design bears an indistinct quadruped to the right and a small platform below the hind legs of the animal.

Figure 1. Tin pendant from Khlong Thom Courtesy Brigitte Borell

Figure 2. Tin pendant (Hybrid) from Khlong Thom Courtesy Brigitte Borell

The finished pendant is 21mm in diameter, weighs 5.64g, and the width of the suspension loop is 13mm, and has a dotted border on both sides (Figure 2). On the obverse is a crudely depicted head in profile to right with traces of headgear. Borell (2014: 22) correctly identifies the reverse design as being an imitation of the reverse design of the PONTIF MAXIM type gold and silver coins of the Roman Emperor Tiberius (c. 14–37 CE), though she misidentifies the obverse.[1] The reverse design on the pendant depicts a seated figure of Livia, the priestess of the goddess Pax, holding an olive branch in her left hand in front of her, and a spear in her right hand which is raised. The PONTIF MAXIM type is frequently found in the Indian subcontinent, especially in the Deccan and far south with a concentration in Andhra Pradesh. The finished pendant is corroded, yet on close examination one can see four distinct Brāhmī characters in front of the head reading *taravapa*. Borell misses the legend

completely and fails to notice that while the head does not resemble any of the Roman emperors, it bears close resemblance to the portraits on the coins of the Sātavāhana rulers, such as Vāśiṣṭhīputra Sātakarṇi, Yajña Sātakarṇi (Figure 6), Skanda Sātakarṇi and Vijaya Sātakarṇi. Although it is a crude imitation, one can see that the engraver was trying to depict headgear used by some Sātavāhana rulers and even faint traces of the anchor-shaped earrings depicted on the portraits of these rulers can be noticed. The jeweled head ornament seen on the Sātavāhana issues is, however, missing in the pendant, probably an intentional omission by the die engraver to enable the head to fit within the border of dots. The Brāhmī letters do not make any sense and do not help to identify the ruler whose coin was used as a prototype here. This leads us to the conclusion that this is a pseudo-legend: the characters resemble Brāhmī script but have no meaning. Nonetheless, it is very interesting to see the combination of Sātavāhana obverse and Roman reverse in this pendant.

---

[1] However, she misidentifies the headgear as a stiffly stylized bow and two ribbons.

This begs the question: were the two pendants found at Khlong Thom imported from India or were they made locally? As this pendant was made of tin, it would seem to be of local manufacture bearing Indian influence. It would also seem that the die engraver, not being well conversant with Brāhmī letters, created a pseudo-legend in front of the head on the obverse, at the exact position where the legend occurs on Sātavāhana portrait-type coins. On Sātavāhana coins the legend continues behind the head in circular fashion, but on the pendant this has been replaced by the circular border of dots. This is the first hybrid example in which a portrait from a Sātavāhana coin has been used as a prototype with a Roman reverse design.

This hybrid pendant demands that we examine more closely the tradition of making imitation coins in the Indian subcontinent and Southeast Asia. Some imitations were very close to the original coins. However, a majority of the hybrid pieces reported from the Indian subcontinent are crude imitations with pseudo-legends or illegible gibberish ones in place of a real legend, and some have no legend at all. It is significant to note that such imitations are found mostly in gold, silver, and at times in lead (sometimes covered in gold foil) and tin. The gold, silver and lead pieces were produced locally in India; the tin pieces were produced in Southeast Asia. Often, they are found with two holes at the top so they could be worn around the neck. Some pieces were also made in clay, with a tubular suspension loop, as seen in the pendants from Khlong Thom.

The finished pendant from Khlong Thom is the first hybrid of its kind (combining Sātavāhana obverse and Roman reverse) to be reported. However, it cannot be seen in isolation, and should be studied in comparison with the other coins and pendants from Southeast Asia which have Roman influence. At the time this pendant was made there was probably no direct communication between Southeast Asia and the Mediterranean world – thus, it seems that the Roman design traveled to the Isthmus of Kra due to Indian contact or influence and the pendant was produced locally at Khlong Thom.

The Khlong Thom hybrid pendants compared with other Roman-influenced finds

Gold pendants found in Southeast Asia which copy coin designs often follow the coins of Antoninus Pius (r. 138–161), Commodus (r. 176–192), and Septimius Severus (r. 193–211). Thus, the earliest possible dates for the pendants would be from the mid-2nd to the early 3rd century CE. Some scholars date them as late as the 5th to 6th century CE (Borell 2014: 25). Hybrids, often with pseudo-legends, both cast and struck, have also been reported from sites in Andhra Pradesh and Tamil Nadu in India (Krishnamurthy 2000), and these were

probably produced locally in the Indian subcontinent. Their prototypes are predominantly gold coins of Antoninus Pius and Septimius Severus. There are also Indian imitations of Roman coins in lead and clay. Scholars have reported their widespread distribution: mostly in the Malwa corridor, i.e. from Madhya Pradesh to Maharashtra, and also in the Kaliṅga corridor, i.e. Odisha and Andhra (Ray 1998; Borell 2014: 26).[2]

There is an obvious difference in the manufacturing technique of pendants: some have two holes, and some are cast with looped suspension tubes. Both types have been found at the Kondapur site from the same period, suggesting their parallel usage, and perhaps suggesting that they had different functions. Of course, it may simply be the case that one group of artisans made the holed variety and another group the looped variety. But the wide distribution of pendants, extending from the Indian subcontinent to Southeast Asia, with the dominant type (the looped suspension tube variety) produced locally in Southeast Asia is significant. Borell writes that the manufacture of tin pendants, as well as the mold from Khlong Thom with designs derived from coins of Tiberius, should be seen in close connection with the Indian parallels rather than their original Roman specimens, and suggests that immigrant Indian craftsmen were probably involved in manufacturing these pendants in Southeast Asia. The fact that it was locally produced at Khlong Thom is beyond doubt: the unfinished pendant and the use of tin clearly point to its local manufacture and to the presence of a tin smelting and production site at Khlong Thom.

What makes the Southeast Asian pendants different from their Indian counterparts is the suspension loop. Borell (2014: 28) notes that this was "different from the Indian method of converting coins or coin imitations into pendants." In India, the usual technique was to punch two holes near the upper edge of the obverse so that the piece might be worn using a cord. A hybrid coin imitation of this type was discovered in a foundation deposit in the period III levels in Sisupalgarh, attributed to the mid-3rd century CE. One side imitates a Kuṣāṇa coin and the other side has the obverse of a Roman coin with the head of the emperor to the right and a pseudo-legend (Lal 1949: 95, 97 pl. 48A; Borell 2014: 28). It has the familiar two holes above the head of the emperor, but, crucially, it also has a suspension loop made of a coil of gold wire. Borell (2014: 28) described it as "used as a pendant by perforating at its top two holes through which it was attached to an oblong wire for suspension." This is quite different from the attachment method observed on the Southeast Asian pendants.

---

[2] The present author has argued elsewhere about the presence of three corridors in early India, viz. Malwa, Kaliṅga and forest corridor of Chhattisgarh (Basu Majumdar 2017a).

Figure 3. Hybrid Coin from Sisupalgarh with pendant hole and suspension loop (after Lal 1949)

Does the way in which coin-inspired pendants were worn reflect a different function or meaning? The Sisupalgarh pendant was initially a pendant with two holes at the top, but was subsequently given a suspension loop of coiled wire, with its two ends soldered to the pendant. This conversion indicates a change in function or geographical context. A similar example is known from a coin hoard from Tirukoilur, Tamil Nadu, which consisted of 15 genuine Roman coins and 177 gold imitations (Berghaus 2000; Borell 2014: 28). One imitation is of an aurei of Claudius (41–54 CE) dating from about 41–45 CE (Berghaus 2000: 499; Borell 2014: 28). Like the Sisupalgarh piece (figure 3), it originally had two holes at the top, which were later refilled with metal and the piece was converted into a pendant by attaching a suspension loop made of coiled wire as seen in pendants recorded from Southeast Asia. This particular gold imitation coin of Claudius had a long history of use as a pendant: its reverse is worn down, and the filling of the holes indicates an intentional attempt to hide how it was previously used, before the suspension loop was added.

Stamped emblems – pendants or badges?

The long tradition of making hybrid pendants based on Roman coins commenced with the production of imitation Roman coins and turning them into pendants in various metals—gold, lead, lead coated with gold, silver, potin coated with silver—and also in clay, in huge numbers. Their function was not monetary, but their uniformity and the piercing of two holes at the top makes their purpose intriguing. The present author is of the opinion that these *stamped emblems* (italics mine) probably served the purpose of badges, licensing the wearer to conduct transactions in a trade network, with each variety of hybrid pendant/token carrying its own meaning or limited to members of a specific group of people. This would also explain their discovery together with coins in certain archaeological contexts, as both coins and pendants could have different roles in the same transactional context.

The current author believes that the stamped nature of the pendants is key to understanding their function. As we have seen, the pendants were made in various materials, including a silver-plated lead imitation with two obverse designs from Romans coins recorded from Veerapuram, Andhra Pradesh. But the only piece that was not cast or struck was a repoussé imitation in gold with two holes at the top, found at Nevasa. It bears a head in profile to the right and a pseudo-legend, a distant imitation of a coin design of the period c. 50 BCE – 200 CE (Borell 2014: 29).

These stamped emblems, intentionally created as hybrids, have been found in the Malwa corridor, the Kaliṅga corridor and the Forest corridor (Chhattisgarh), and in Tamil Nadu and part of Karnataka. Parallel pieces have been found in Southeast Asia, which makes it imperative that we consider more than one trading nexus, and pay more attention to the Bay of Bengal Interaction Sphere (Gupta 2005, 2018).

Kuṣāṇa coins and their crude imitations have been found in the ancient Samataṭa region in present day Bangladesh (Basu Majumdar 2014: 585–605, 2018: 233–268), and their presence has been difficult to explain. However, when seen in a broader context, as in this paper, a solution can be found for their crude production, pseudo-legends, degeneration of the original design, departure from their original purpose, and finally, the continuity and combination of Kuṣāṇo-Gupta imitation type. The question then shifts to whether we should regard the gold specimens from Samataṭa as pendants (for adornment) or badges or even monetary tokens? The weight discrepancy of the Samataṭa gold pieces has been overlooked yet could be important. In the early historic phase, Bengal (undivided) lacked a proper state formation, yet we find traces of trade and urban society, both essential for the development of a state society and complex commerce. Owing to its strategic location on the eastern seaboard, the Bay of Bengal Interaction Sphere gradually became very important. Sea-borne trade was vibrant and the evidence of merchants and commodities can be seen as part of an incipient system. Long distance traders probably found the political conditions in the ports of Bengal congenial as there was no regular taxation or śulka for trade as there was in the ports on the west coast of India under the Śakas and the Sātavāhanas. Also, there is no evidence of a royal authority issuing coins in Bengal at this time, hence the hybrid pieces could have functioned like coins, prior to the introduction of a locally issued coinage. The variation in the weight of the gold piece has yet to be addressed, and may prove to be important to our discussion.

Kuṣāṇa hybrid imitations are not restricted to Bengal. A Kuṣāṇa hybrid pendant was recorded from the deposit below the Enlightenment Throne at Bodh Gaya. It was made of two repoussé gold sheets, both being impressed from the obverse of a coin of the Kuṣāṇa king Huviṣka (Cunningham 1892: 20–21, pl. 22, 11; Zwalf 1985: cat. no. 14; Borell 2014: 29).

Clay pendants

Clay pendants are often termed 'bullae' in secondary archaeological literature though this is not a proper term to designate the pendants from various sites in the Indian subcontinent. There are two broad groups of clay pendants: early pieces (predating those copying Roman coins) which bore simple geometric patterns and other designs, and later pieces copying Roman coins. The later pieces (Roman and post-Roman) are more common, particularly those imitating coins of Augustus and Tiberius.[3] While we cannot be sure that the pre-Roman clay pieces had any monetary function, the application of coin designs to the pendant form suggests that they may have had a role in some kind of economic or transactional activity. It is certainly interesting that this form was produced over a long period with remarkable uniformity. Clay pendants, like metal pendants, either had two holes at the top or a suspension loop.

The production and use of clay pendants may date from as early as the c. 4th century BCE or a time bracket of 300 BCE–200 CE (Ray 1986: 135–136). Some clay pendants have been found together with coins, indicating their possible use in economic transactions. For example, at Peddabunkur, Andhra Pradesh, a site where five genuine coins of Augustus and Tiberius have been found, some lead imitations of the PONTIF MAXIM type with two holes at the top were recorded as being from the same layer as Sātavāhana coins (Krishna Sastry 1983: 204–205; Sastri et al. 1984: 86–87; Gupta 2004: 116–117; Borell 2014: 26). At Talkad, Karnataka, a clay mold for making reverse imitations of the PONTIF MAXIM type has been recorded, which may be assigned a date of c. 1st to 2nd century CE (Narasimha Murthy and Devaraj 1995; Devaraj 1997; Borell 2014: 26).

Clay pendants with suspension loops have been found in the eastern part of the Indian subcontinent which suggests that this tradition or practice may have travelled from the east coast to Southeast Asia. Examples include a clay pendant from Sannati, Karnataka, which has been dated as early as the c.1st century CE (Devaraj 1997; Borell 2014: 26); and the nine clay pendants with suspension loops from the site of Sisupalgarh in Odisha. Three of the Sisupalgarh pendants have a human head in profile, and six have humped bull and elephant motifs datable to the 1st century CE. Six others found

together have been assigned a date as early as c. 100 to 200 CE (Borell 2014: 26). Thus, Sisupalgarh may also be considered as a zone of influence, besides Sannati.

Perhaps the most important site for our discussion of clay pendants is Adam, in Maharashtra. This site has yielded original Roman coins, locally made imitations of coins of Augustus in potin with a silver coating, coin molds with bust in profile, and clay pendants. The variety of pendants recorded from this site is of immense significance as the findspots of the clay pendants bearing a Roman portrait do not correspond with the findspots of Roman coins (see Map courtesy Emilia Smagur).

The site of Adam has yielded clay pendants with two holes and clay pendants with suspension loops, as seen at Sisupalgarh. At Sisupalgarh, clay pendants have mainly been recorded from a location outside the city walls: more than 34 clay pendants bearing a human head have been reported from this site (9 in the excavations of 1948, and 25 in recent excavations by Smith and Mohanty (Mohanty and Smith 2008; Smith and Mohanty 2016). Smith suggests that production of the clay pendants was probably a speciality of some pottery craftsmen.

In the present state of knowledge it seems that the influence of making pendants with suspension loop travelled either from Sātavāhana territory (especially Karnataka) or from Odisha. The movement of other types of archaeo-materials has been traced and is instructive here: for example, the motif of *puṣpagrahaṇī* travelled from Deccan to Southeast Asia and was adopted as a motif on their coinage, and the same motif has been found in the sculptural art of the *mahāstūpa* at Sannati (Basu Majumdar 2017b: 448). The evidence from Sisupalgarh appears to indicate large scale production and the use of clay pendants with suspension loops already existing in the 1st century CE. The craftsmen who influenced the production/creation of pendants in Southeast Asia probably had a connection with the eastern coast of India.

Pendants with two holes or suspension loops were intended for display, presumably worn around the neck. Some of the pendants, especially those reported from the forest corridor have huge slash marks or cuts which would have made wearing them difficult (Figures 4 and 5). These pendants have been considered as prestige markers by some scholars. If they were worn merely for prestige, then we would expect them to be more finely made. Perhaps the function was so specific and significant that the roughness and discomfort did not matter to those wearing the pendants. Or perhaps they were only worn for a limited time or not on bare skin. However, the present author believes that considering

---

[3] CL CAESARES of Augustus issued between 27 BC–14 CE and the PONTIF MAXIM type of coins of Tiberius issued between 14-37 CE.

Figure 4. Pierced pendant from Forest Corridor (Chhattisgarh) with cut marks imitating Roman coins

Figure 5. Other side of the Pendant from Forest Corridor

Figure 6. Portrait type coin of Yajña Sātakarṇi

them as mere prestige markers reduces their scope of study.

Some scholars have discussed these clay coin-like pieces in the context of their non-currency functionality, as charms for personal protection (Cribb 1999: 65–66; Brancaccio 2005: n.9; Borell 2014: 30, Smagur 2018). In most cases, clay charms are single-sided. However, the Indian pendants are mostly double-sided, like coins. This further suggests a non-monetary yet associated use for these stamped emblems. The present author believes that the identity passes mentioned in the *Kauṭilīya Arthaśāstra* and used by traders as badges, may offer a useful example. The receivers of duty recorded details of traders arriving in caravans (*sārtha* and *sārthavāha*), itemizing their merchandise and its valuation in writing. After this procedure, an identity pass or stamped impression was made (2.21.2), to confirm the identity of the trader. There are references to *abhijñānamudrā* ('state stamp') in which *mudrā* indicates specifically that something was stamped – in our case, a stamped emblem or badge. At the start of a journey, a caravan trader would be issued with a pass or have some kind of stamping done by *antapāla* (2.34.1–5). Often we find mention of passes, stamped by the controller of shipping (2.28.18), which the bearer had to carry on their person. Such passes were carried not only by traders but also by Brahmins, wandering monks, children, the elderly, the sick, carriers of royal edicts, and pregnant women, and were to be shown at check points when a person was travelling. It seems likely that the clay pendants served as passes of this nature.[4]

Travellers and traders who wished to enter or leave the countryside had to pay a fee in order to receive a stamped pass (*abhijñānamudrā*). The superintendent of passports issued stamped passes for one *māṣaka* (2.34.1), and this association with a payment would explain why clay pendants are sometimes found together with coins. A native of the land travelling without a sealed pass had to pay twelve *paṇas* (2.34.3). The *Kauṭilīya Arthaśāstra* confirms that passes were forged, and that there were different fines for natives and non-natives travelling without a pass.

The finished Khlong Thom pendant raises several basic and vital issues. First, the early clay pendants produced prior to the replication of coin designs are significant, and their provenances and distribution north of the region where the coin finds and clay pendants have been reported is intriguing. Second, the continuity of this practice from non-coin design to coin designs suggests that the function remained the same. The indications are that these stamped emblems (metal or clay) were

---

[4] *Kauṭilīya Arthaśāstra* see 2.21.2 for *mudrā*, 2.6.2 for *mudrādyakṣa* and for *lakṣṇādyakṣa*.

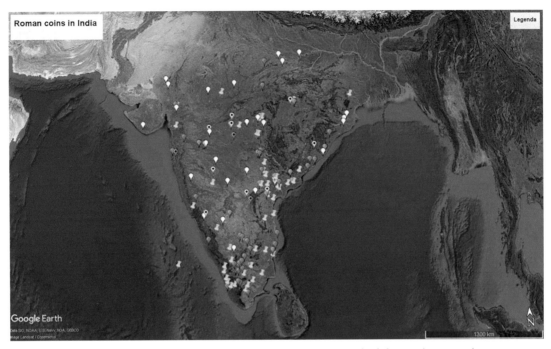

Figure 7. Map Finds of Roman coins and its imitations in India (after Emilia Smagur)

non-monetary, but were associated in some way with monetary transactions, because they are mostly found with coins or coin molds. The molds indicate that they were made on the spot, as and when necessary. The two styles of threading the pendant, through the holes or through the suspension loop, appear to be specific and important. Third, the variety of designs, metals and materials, and the range of hybrids all point to prolonged usage or common functionality. The adoption of foreign designs shows their relevance in the larger trading network between India and the Roman world. Sātavāhana element was adopted in Khlong Thom pendant as it was foreign to Southeast Asia. While the Sātavāhana element would have been foreign in Khlong Thom, the Sātavāhana-Roman hybrid was very popular in South India. Thus, the key to the riddle of the hybrids, lies not only in the two tin pendants from Khlong Thom, but in opening our minds to the bigger picture, in which Southeast Asia was the easternmost limit of a braided trading nexus from the Roman world through the Indian subcontinent.

References

Basu Majumdar, S. 2014. *Monetary History of Bengal: 'Issues and Non Issues'*, in D.N. Jha (ed.), *The Complex Heritage of Early India Essays in Memory of R.S. Sharma*: 585-605. New Delhi: Manohar.

Basu Majumdar, S. 2017a. State formation and Religious Processes in the North-South Corridor of Chhattisgarh (from c. 1st century BC to 8th century AD). *Studies in People's History*, 4, 2: 119-129.

Basu Majumdar, S. 2017b. Metal Money in Mainland Southeast Asia: Exploring the Indian Connection, in A.I. Dallapicola and A. Verghese (eds), *India and Southeast Asia: Cultural Discourses*: 433-458. Mumbai: The K.R. Cama Oriental Institute.

Basu Majumdar, S. 2018. Media of Exchange: Reflections on the Monetary History, in A.M. Choudhury and R. Chakravarti (eds), *The History of Bangladesh, Volume 2*: 233-268. Dhaka: The Asiatic Society of Bangladesh.

Berghaus, P. 2000. Gestopfte Löcher auf römischen Goldmünzen aus indischen Funden. Pages 499–502 in B. Kluge and B. Weisser (eds), *Akten-Proceedings-Actes, XII. Internationaler Numismatischer Kongress, Berlin 1997*.

Borell, B. 2014. The Power of Images – Coin Portraits of Roman Emperors on Jewellery Pendants in Early Southeast Asia. *Zeitschrift für Archäologie Außereuropäischer Kulturen*, 6: 7–44.

Brancaccio, P. 2005. Perceptions of 'Westerners' in Sātavāhana Times: The Archaeological Evidence, in C. Jarrige and V. Lefèvre (eds), *South Asian Archaeology 2001. Proceedings of the Sixteenth International Conference of the European Association of South Asian Archaeologists*: 401-406. Paris: Collège de France.

Cribb, J. 1999. *Magic Coins of Java, Bali and the Malay Peninsula, Thirteenth to Twentieth Centuries*. London: British Museum.

Cunningham, A. 1892. *Mahābodhi or the Great Buddhist Temple under the Bodhi Tree at Buddha Gaya*. London: W.H. Allen.

Devaraj, D.V. 1997. A Roman Terracotta Pendant from Sannati in Karnataka. *Studies in South Indian Coins* 7: 45–48.

Gupta, C. 2004. Foreign Coins and Imitations Used for Ornamentation, in D.W. MacDowall and A. Jha (eds), *Foreign Coins found in the Indian sub-continent. 4th International Colloquium (8-10 January 1995)*: 116-120. Anjaneri: Indian Institute of Research in Numismatic Studies.

Gupta, S. 2005. The Bay of Bengal Interaction Sphere (1000 BC–AD 500), *Indo-Pacific Pre History Association Bulletin* 25, (Taipei Papers Vol. 3): 21–30.

Gupta S. 2018. *The Archaeological Record of Indian Ocean Engagements: Bay of Bengal (5000 BC–500 AD)*. Oxford University Press.

Kangle, R.P. (*tr.*). 2014. *The Kauṭilīya Arthaśāstra*, 3 vols. Delhi: Motilal Banarsidass Publishers Pvt.

Krishna Sastry, V.V. 1983. *The Proto and Early Historical Cultures of Andhra Pradesh*. Hyderabad: Government of Andhra Pradesh.

Krishnamurthy, R. 2000. A Roman Coin Bronze Die from Karur, Tamilnadu, India, in B. Kluge and B. Weisser (eds), *XII. Internationaler Numismatischer Kongress Berlin 1997—Akten-Proceedings-Actes*, vol. I: 552-553, Berlin.

Lal, B.B. 1949. Sisupalgarh 1948: an Early Historical Fort in Eastern India. *Ancient India. Bulletin of the Archaeological Survey of India*, 5: 62–105.

Mohanty, R.K. and Smith, M.L. 2008. *Excavations at Sisupalgarh Orissa*, Special Report No. 2. New Delhi: Indian Archaeological Society.

Narasimha Murthy, A.V. and Devaraja, D.V. 1995. A Roman Coin Mould from Talkad Excavations. *Studies in South Indian Coins* 5: 59–62.

Ray, H.P. 1986. *Monastery and Guild Commerce under the Sātavāhanas*. New Delhi: Oxford University Press.

Ray, H.P. 1998. Ter: An Early Centre on the Trans-Peninsular Route, in A.K. Jha and S. Garg (eds), *Ex Moneta: Essays on Numismatics, History and Archaeology in honour of Dr. David W. MacDowall*, Vol. 2: 501-510. New Delhi: Harman Publishing.

Sastri Tutupalli V.G., Kasturi Bai, M., Rao, J. Vara Prasada. 1984. *Veerapuram, a Type Site for Cultural Study in the Krishna Valley*. Hyderabad: Birla Archaeological & Cultural Research Institute.

Smagur, E. 2018. From Coin to *Bulla*: a Cultural Response to the Influx of Roman Denarii to India, *Numismatic Digest* 42: 63–78.

Smith, M.L. and Mohanty, R.K. 2016. Archaeology at Sisupalgarh: the Chronology of an Early Historic Urban Centre in Eastern India, in V. Lefèvre, A. Didier and B. Mutin (eds), *South Asian Archaeology and Art 2012*, 2: 683-695 Turnhout: Brepols.

Stevenson, E.L. (tr.). 1932. *Geographike Huphegesis of Ptolemy*. New York: New York Public Library.

Zwalf, W. (ed.). 1985. *Buddhism. Art and Faith*. London: British Museum.

Primates of All England

Darwin downed us a peg or two

All children of you know whooo

A short climb from here we are till a

Handy ancestor who's almost a Gorilla

Swinging from a double-helixed ribbon

Humanity's not far from a Gibbon

Each of us this island's Caliban

Kissing cousins of every Orangutan

So part-Bonobo part-Chimpanzee

We fuck or fight everyone we see

Joe Cribb
27 October 2021

My Mate the Poet Joe Cribb

Stephen Sack

I have been friends with Joe ever since I arrived at the British Museum in the fall of 1998 to prepare my exhibition The Metal Mirror. The then Keeper Andrew Burnett said that the images went against everything he believed in, that he had not thought of this possibility, but went ahead and made arrangements for the show. Many curators were concerned about showing art photographs of worthless, worn and corroded coins, but Joe was the first to be 'on board'. His enthusiasm was quickly contagious and was instrumental in the success of the show. We have remained friends ever since.

Joe is a bit of a philosopher and his deep belief is that Money is a social construct, a measure of social relationships. He understands the economy of words and the importance of really 'Looking'. We have spent many delightful hours scrutinising coins, searching for their identities and pondering their hidden meanings and relationships with myths, religions and literature, always laughing without losing sight of the serious nature of our inquiries.

The diversity of Joe's interests is awe inspiring. He is a detective combining multiple disciplines of history, economics, religion, culture and art in his quest to fill the gaps of many lost and forgotten histories... always searching for clues from coins to the chronology of historical events. It is a gargantuan task - sifting through the detritus of archaeological finds, while always watchful for fakes and imitations.

It is his curiosity and above all his desire to LOOK at the coins using all his senses to find an impression of reality (based on the facts), knowing all too well that any unique coin can be surpassed by new finds or hoards. He firmly avows that the logic of history and the logic of historians rarely coincide. History is a metaphor to be created.

He says he is like a rather large dwarf with a wry sense of humour standing on the shoulders of giants, and jests that sometimes they need a kick in the head.

Perhaps most important for Joe was the profound influence of his late brother Steve, an artist, a thinker and a collector of Chinese coins, religious medals and many other things.

Grandfather Joseph was a sculptor and letter cutter and inspired Joe's interest in art as a practice, as a process of production, particularly of making things that are both aesthetically appealing and of utility, with coins being a perfect example.

Grandfather Joseph also collected beetles and Joe's father butterflies and moths, and another brother is a world-leading expert on orchids. They all contributed to Joe's fascination with the interaction of knowledge and the object. Aesthetics is of supreme importance and he surrounds himself with art of all kinds, from South and South East Asia, China and Japan, as well as art medals, sculptures and paintings by his partner Linda Crook and many random finds from local charity shops, stones found on the beach and even works by Stephen Sack.

Always working, he collects ancient Japanese books with woodcuts of Chinese coins, resources for his research and for the articles that he loves to write.

A crucial but hidden part of Joe's life is his love of writing poetry. His poems are an expression of his fascination with metaphor and with the artifice of imagination. None have ever been published. Presented here are a few of his poems with favour given to those that have a relation to his work with coins and medals and a few he wrote for and inspired by Linda, painter, sculptor and art medalist and some springing from my coin photography.

I have dedicated a section on my internet site to Joe's poetry

https://www.stephensack.com/joe-cribb/

The Celestial String

A string of cash to pave your way.
A string of cash to light your night.
A string of cash to make your day,
To flood the night a moon so bright,
Each coin shining in this wonderland,
This blaze of light puts stars to flight.
Across the sky in an ecliptic band
Sun coin and planets follow moon.
A string of colour, cash in hand,
In time with copper compounds strewn,
With cuprous black and cupric red,
With carbonate blue and sulphate green,
As sharp a string of steps to tread,
As sharp as landing on a copperhead.

From where did all these coins spring?
Opening time at the treasure store,
As time will thread them on a string.
Two thousand years roll in your hand,
Royal blessing on the worthy poor.
Each one counted, like stars or sand.
The ancient kings of China's yore
Cast rice bowl filling copper rings
From earth stored green or blue ore,
Drove out poverty through coin that brings
Heaven's round holding earth's square hole,
A cosmic gift fit for buying things,
Rolling treasure stringing the eternal pole
From hand to mouth from dole to bowl.

What words can tell each coin's mould,
Half an ounce from the money spring,
Flowing out hot then broken out cold?
Five grains spreading out beyond its ring,
Five colours spreading across each line,
Across the lines from which meanings spring.
New blue Tang treasures open and shine.
Another opening cuts by string through crust.
Grey-gold red-green, lurking behind, entwine.
Quiet bright and prosperity follows, dust
Of Song fades, blue Ming's noble luck runs away,
Qing to bright heaven's joint control rust.
From here to Nippon, Koryo and old Annam's bay
Where shining fortune makes way for dull decay.

From earth's square, holed in heaven's round,
Mismatched diamonds cross-cutting edge's rim,
Now cog-marked horizons hold the sky as found.
Within and across the sky shadow moons all skim,
Where cruel corrosion attacked the buried string,
Marking coin on coin another edge's rim to trim.
Crescent shapes and crag shapes fire kindling
Planet tones and stardust seen in muddy mire.
Coins cast in puddle mirrors lie cosy cradling
High circling heavenly beings in the cosmic round
Falling falling to slow burial in our earthly fold.
Earth-bound ore cast up to fly then fall to ground
Into earth's square cold, for miners to behold,
Malachite green, azurite blue or chalcopyrite gold.

Round the necks of sinners all,
A knotted rope from which we'll hang,
Hoping for rescue from Adam's fall,
We're bell-less clappers with an empty clang.
Yet here we are, we hang and pray
For those sinners till their final pang.
Old pennies for thoughts, and nothing to pay,
Suspended coins saved for sure salvation,
Each pious penny paid for that rainy day.
But time takes away the first intention,
Time spent hidden next to pious skin,
Sweating away the full dimension
Of these metal metaphors worn within,
With their images worn so thin.

Ecce Homo, look and see, Christ knows who,
Racked on high in right royal pain or glory.
A mother does what mothers do,
Holding in death one she held in memory,
When once a tiny child for all to see,
For everyone to start that story,
A mother's arm and a mother's knee,
A starting place and then he's dead
And wears his crown upon the greening tree
And stains the Virgin's veil blood red.
An evening light, up with the stars on high
Immaculate no more on an angel's pin head.
Crowns for him and crowns for her to try,
Crowns spent out by sinners when they die.

Long lost in churches high and churches low,
The shadow figures who once we knew
Waiting for devotion and now on show,
Worn and wiped out saints peeping through,
The age old crust to provoke some prayers.
Cropped Christopher whose name will no longer do,
Sebastian too, saints familiar, saintly strangers,
Harder to pin down, so smooth and hiding,
Who knows who is bound at the gate and lingers,
Which bishop wears jewels that time's providing
Sprays his fading flock under his fading cross,
And who the others, faces lost, but still abiding.
Will their guardian angels know who to tend?
Can anyone hear the fading bids they send?

As smooth and aged as a step-worn stair,
These pictures holy, preserved in rust,
Fumy, fragrant from incense like nuns' hair,
Bell metal or brass with corrosive crust.
Imagine any god with so sleight a hand
Taking time to do what time surely must.
Rotted and rubbed by pious kisses and
Salivation's lips, bless bathed in holy water,
Tucked in any sinners' sweaty waistband.
Into the devout surfaces man's art fashions
Cuts daily devouring devotion the sin eater,
These images fade as god's salvation reckons.
Corpse plucked from some nun's decaying sister,
Corruption comforts the next corrupted sinner.

Lazarus

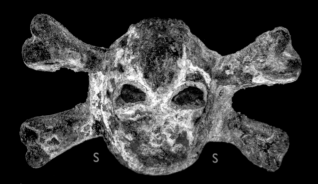

S   S

They said leave him there
Let the dead stay dead
No one asked him that is clear
No one spoke up from death's bed
Life is long enough and who here
needs to go through that again
Why be forced to go on seeing
The mess the rest are making
To see their unlived days in pain
Or relive their failures in such dread

Condemned for ever and again
To eternal bliss in heaven's boredom
Or eternal misery in punishment kingdom
Equally unwelcome when all is said
Stuck in this life he cannot leave
To wait for a second go at death's release
Threatened with another without cease
An eternity of watching others grieve
Death's the way for it all to cease
So let him go and rest in peace

In Alexander's Tracks

Couple of hundred years ago today
We packed our books and packed our pens
We took the path to come what may
To ask ourselves those what happened whens

And as camels do but rarely tell
We cross the deserts in our dreams
With hope to catch the fleeting smell
The lure of historic long lost streams

And scattered starry all along the way
Lay Charon's coins stepping stones to share
Lost kings' fares to keep oblivion at bay
Sure sign posts to who knows where

And Alexander that great king of kings
A light to light us as we tread
The roads he trod to look for things
Eastwards till his ox-head horse fell dead

And seek to flesh out meagre bones
Buried deep in the hourglass sands
Of shadow kings whose broken thrones
Are waiting for our digging hands

Couple of hundred years beyond today
They pick at our books and click their pens
And track our path to come what may
And ask and ask the same what happened whens

© Stephen Sack - *Psyche*

www.stephensack.com

Fish Wife

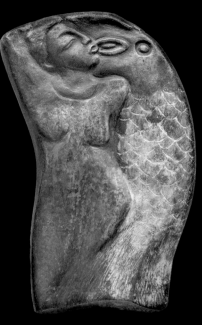

Oh fish wife fish wife gentle knife
Fillet me and take my life
Fillet me with weeds of the sea
Ribbons of kelp to garland me

Fit your fingers to my gills
Hold me up and feel my thrills
Hold me up with iron clasp
I'm out of water make me gasp

Gut me gut me make me squirm
I'll regret the hook-hidden worm
Grill me grill me now I'm yours
Let me be your only course.

Lost and Found:
Dreaming of You

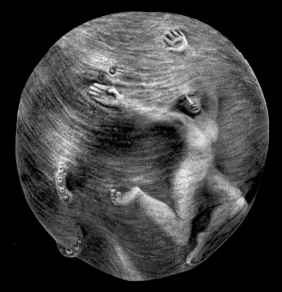

Behind you and beneath you
In the space unseen
Over on the other side
Where the sea unfolds
There lurks a face
A face with arms
A beak to peck and suck
The arms reach through
Towards the side you're on
You push the water down
Do you know its there
Behind you and beneath you
In the space unseen
Where the sea unfolds
There lurks my face
My face with eight arms
My beak to peck and suck
My arms reach through
To breach the side you're on
The water pulls you down
Now you know I'm there
You are lost beneath the wave
I am there to find you
And hold you in my arms
Take you in my close embrace
Behind you and beneath you
In the space unseen
Over on the other side
Where the sea unfolds